TUTTLE

JAPANESE BUSINESS DICTIONARY

Revised Edition

TUTTLE

JAPANESE BUSINESS DICTIONARY

Revised Edition

Boyé Lafayette De Mente

TUTTLE Publishing

Tokyo | Rutland, Vermont | Singapore

ABOUT TUTTLE
"Books to Span the East and West"

Our core mission at Tuttle Publishing is to create books which bring people together one page at a time. Tuttle was founded in 1832 in the small New England town of Rutland, Vermont (USA). Our fundamental values remain as strong today as they were then—to publish best-in-class books informing the English-speaking world about the countries and peoples of Asia. The world has become a smaller place today and Asia's economic, cultural and political influence has expanded, yet the need for meaningful dialogue and information about this diverse region has never been greater. Since 1948, Tuttle has been a leader in publishing books on the cultures, arts, cuisines, languages and literatures of Asia. Our authors and photographers have won numerous awards and Tuttle has published thousands of books on subjects ranging from martial arts to paper crafts. We welcome you to explore the wealth of information available on Asia at **www.tuttlepublishing.com**.

Published by Tuttle Publishing, an imprint of Periplus Editions (HK) Ltd.

www.tuttlepublishing.com

LCC Card No. 2007927799
ISBN 978-0-8048-4581-6
(Previously published under ISBN 978-4-8053-0913-1)

Distributed by:

Japan
Tuttle Publishing
Yaekari Bldg., 3rd Floor,
5-4-12 Osaki,
Shinagawa-ku,
Tokyo 141-0032
Tel: (81) 3 5437-0171
Fax: (81) 3 5437-0755
sales@tuttle.co.jp
www.tuttle.co.jp

North America, Latin America and Europe
Tuttle Publishing
364 Innovation Drive,
North Clarendon,
VT 05759-9436 USA.
Tel: 1 (802) 773-8930
Fax: 1 (802) 773-6993
info@tuttlepublishing.com
www.tuttlepublishing.com

Asia Pacific
Berkeley Books Pte. Ltd.
61 Tai Seng Avenue #02-12
Singapore 534167
Tel: (65) 6280-1330
Fax: (65) 6280-6290
inquiries@periplus.com.sg
www.periplus.com

20 19 18 17   6 5 4 3   1710MP
Printed in Singapore

Contents

How to Use This Dictionary

This book is designed to serve as a quick language reference for business people dealing with the Japanese. It is particularly useful for those who must rely on their opposite party's English-language ability or the ability of their interpreters. There are times when one may wish to verify for oneself that certain crucial points are indeed being understood correctly. The *Japanese Business Dictionary* enables even those with little or no experience with the Japanese language to access specialized vocabulary—vocabulary that will allow them to get to the point immediately.

Of course, being able to pronounce the word or phrase correctly is also of great importance. To help achieve this goal, Japanese words and sentences in this book have been rendered in both standard Hepburn romanization and the author's time-tested phonetic system. One may use either system to attain correct pronunciation.

The Japanese language is based on combinations of only six key sounds, making it a fairly easy language to pronounce. These six sounds are the basis for an "alphabet" of some one hundred syllables that make up all the words in the Japanese language.

While there is only one way to pronounce Japanese properly, there are several ways to write it: using characters imported from China over 1,000 years ago; using one of the two phonetic scripts called *kana* (kah-nah), devised by the Japanese to supplement and sometimes replace the Chinese ideograms; or using more familiar Roman letters called *romaji* (roe-mah-jee) in Japanese.

The most widely used *romanji* system for transcribing Japanese was developed in the late 1880s by an American missionary, Dr. James Hepburn, soon after Japan's opening to the West. There are other Roman letter systems for writing Japanese, but Dr. Hepburn's was designed specifically for English speakers, and is therefore based on English phonetics.

All except one of the approximately one hundred syllables in the Japanese "alphabet" are based on five (romanized) sounds: *a, i, u, e,* and *o*—pronounced ah, ee, uu, eh, oh. The sixth base sound in the Japanese language is represented in English by the letter "n" and is pronounced like "n" in the word "bond." As mentioned above, all Japanese words are made up of syllables consisting of combinations of these six basic sounds. The

Japanese word for book, for example, is made up of two syllables, *ho* and *n* or *hon,* pronounced "hone" (rhyming with "bone"). The present tense of the word for read, *yomimasu,* is made up of four syllables—yo-mi-ma-su—although when said in ordinary speech, the last two syllables are typically run together, sounding like "mahss."

All Japanese syllables, with their English-language phonetic equivalents, are presented here. To pronounce the syllables correctly, just read the phonetics (in parentheses) as if they were ordinary English sounds.

Basic Syllables and Sound Changes

あ **a** *(ah)*	い **i** *(ee)*	う **u** *(uu)*	え **e** *(ay)*	お **o** *(oh)*
か **ka** *(kah)*	き **ki** *(kee)*	く **ku** *(kuu)*	け **ke** *(kay)*	こ **ko** *(koe)*
さ **sa** *(sah)*	し **shi** *(she)*	す **su** *(sue)*	せ **se** *(say)*	そ **so** *(so)*
た **ta** *(tah)*	ち **chi** *(chee)*	つ **tsu** *(t'sue)*	て **te** *(tay)*	と **to** *(toe)*
な **na** *(nah)*	に **ni** *(nee)*	ぬ **nu** *(nuu)*	ね **ne** *(nay)*	の **no** *(no)*
は **ha** *(hah)*	ひ **hi** *(he)*	ふ **fu** *(fuu)*	へ **he** *(hay)*	ほ **ho** *(hoe)*
ま **ma** *(mah)*	み **mi** *(me)*	む **mu** *(muu)*	め **me** *(may)*	も **mo** *(moe)*
や **ya** *(yah)*		ゆ **yu** *(yuu)*		よ **yo** *(yoe)*
ら **ra** *(rah)*	り **ri** *(ree)*	る **ru** *(rue)*	れ **re** *(ray)*	ろ **ro** *(roe)*
わ **wa** *(wah)*				を **wo** *(oh)*
n (as the "n" in "bond")				

が **ga** *(gah)*	ぎ **gi** *(ghee)*	ぐ **gu** *(guu)*	げ **ge** *(gay)*	ご **go** *(goe)*
ざ **za** *(zah)*	じ **ji** *(jee)*	ず **zu** *(zuu)*	ぜ **ze** *(zay)*	ぞ **zo** *(zoe)*
だ **da** *(dah)*	ぢ **ji** *(jee)*	づ **zu** *(zuu)*	で **de** *(day)*	ど **do** *(doe)*
ば **ba** *(bah)*	び **bi** *(bee)*	ぶ **bu** *(buu)*	べ **be** *(bay)*	ぼ **bo** *(boe)*
ぱ **pa** *(pah)*	ぴ **pi** *(pee)*	ぷ **pu** *(puu)*	ぺ **pe** *(pay)*	ぽ **po** *(poe)*

The following thirty-three syllables are combinations of some of those appearing in the two sets above. The first syllable, for example, is a combination of *ki* and *ya*, or *kiya,* phonetically shortened to *kya*. The last syllable, *pyo,* a combination of *pi* and *yo,* is similarly shortened.

きゃ **kya** *(k'yah)*	きゅ **kyu** *(cue)*	きょ **kyo** *(k'yoe)*
しゃ **sha** *(shah)*	しゅ **shu** *(shuu)*	しょ **sho** *(show)*
ちゃ **cha** *(chah)*	ちゅ **chu** *(chuu)*	ちょ **cho** *(choe)*
にゃ **nya** *(n'yah)*	にゅ **nyu** *(n'yuu)*	にょ **nyo** *(n'yoe)*

ひゃ **hya** *(h'yah)*	ひゅ **hyu** *(h'yuu)*	ひょ **hyo** *(h'yoe)*
みゃ **mya** *(m'yah)*	みゅ **myu** *(m'yuu)*	みょ **myo** *(m'yoe)*
りゃ **rya** *(r'yah)*	りゅ **ryu** *(r'yuu)*	りょ **ryo** *(rio)*
ぎゃ **gya** *(g'yah)*	ぎゅ **gyu** *(g'yuu)*	ぎょ **gyo** *(g'yoe)*
じゃ **ja** *(jah)*	じゅ **ju** *(juu)*	じょ **jo** *(joe)*
びゃ **bya** *(b'yah)*	びゅ **byu** *(b'yuu)*	びょ **byo** *(b'yoe)*
ぴゃ **pya** *(p'yah)*	ぴゅ **pyu** *(p'yuu)*	ぴょ **pyo** *(p'yoe)*

While you are becoming familiar with the pronunciation of the various syllables in the Japanese "alphabet" by reading the phonetics aloud, be sure also to familiarize yourself with the Hepburn spelling of each syllable so you can recognize words written in *romaji.*

As you probably noticed, a combination of two or more Japanese syllables often forms the sound of some common English word. For example, the combination of *sa* and *i* (*sai*) is pronounce exactly like the word "sigh." *Hai,* meaning "yes," is pronounced "high." Such words, instead of the phonetic spellings, have frequently been used in this dictionary to facilitate pronunciation.

After you read a word or phrase slowly a few times out loud (always out loud!), practice saying it at ordinary speaking speed to get away from the "textbook sound." In any event, don't be bashful about using the Japanese you learn. Simply by using individual words, you can communicate to a useful and often surprising extent.

Special Language Pointers

There are no definite or indefinite articles in Japanese. There is also usually no differentiation made between the singular and plural form of nouns. 箱 **hako** *(hah-koe)* can be one box or two or more boxes, depending on the context. The number of a noun is usually made clear by context, but there are also special suffixes to express plurals, particularly common with personal pronouns. For example, 達 **tachi** *(tah-chee)* added to the pronouns "I", "he", and "she" gives "we" and "they":

I – 私 **watakushi** *(wah-tock-she)*; We – 私達 **watakushi-tachi** *(wah-tock-she-tah-chee)*
You – あなた **anata** *(ah-nah-tah)*
You (plural) – あなた達 **anata-tachi** *(ah-nah-tah-tah-chee)*; or the polite form あなた方 **anata-gata** *(ah-nah-tah-gah-tah)*
He – 彼 **kare** *(kah-ray)*; あの人 **ano hito** *(ah-noh-shtoe)*; or the polite form あの方 **ano kata** *(ah-noh-kah-tah)*
She – 彼女 **kanojo** *(kah-no-joe)*; or あの人 **ano hito** *(ah-no-shtoe)*
They – あの人達 **ano hito-tachi** *(ah-no-shtoe-tah-chee)*; 彼ら **kare-ra** *(kah-ray-rah)* or 彼女達 **kanojo-tachi** *(kah-no-joe-tah-chee)*; the polite form あの方々 **anokata-gata** *(ah-no-kah-tah-gah-tah)*

The interrogative form is expressed in Japanese by か **ka** *(kah)* at the end of a verb or sentence.

The order of a Japanese sentence is subject/object/verb, as opposed to the English order of subject/verb/object. Because the verb comes last in a Japanese sentence one must wait until the sentence is completed before knowing whether it is affirmative or negative.

An important point to keep in mind is not to be overly concerned with differences in Japanese and English grammar. Especially if you are a beginner, the best idea is to forget about grammar and simply learn Japanese sentences as they are spoken. With repetition, Japanese sentence structure will also sound perfectly natural.

Another point to keep in mind is that the subject is often left out in Japanese sentences, the message expressed with only the verb. For example: the present tense of the verb "to go" 行きます **ikimasu** *(ee-kee-mahss)* means "go" or "going, am going," or "will go." By adding **ka** to it (**ikimasu ka?**), it becomes "are you going?" Japanese often use various verb forms as whole sentences. With just the various tenses of **ikimasu**, for example, you can say the following:

行きます **Ikimasu.** *(ee-kee-mahss)* — I am going.
行きません **Ikimasen.** *(ee-kee-mah-sen)* — I'm not going. / He/She is not going. / They are not going.
行きませんでした **Ikimasen deshita.** *(ee-kee-mah-sen desh-tah)* — I/He/She/They did not go.
行きましょう **Ikimashō.** *(ee-kee-mah-show)* — Let's go.
行きました **Ikimashita.** *(ee-kee-mah-shtah)* — I/He/She/They went.

Three of the primary building blocks of ideas or sentences in Japanese are **désu** *(dess)*, the verb "to be," ある **aru** *(ah-rue)*, which means "have" as well as expressing the idea of "to be"; and いる **iru** *(ee-rue)*, which expresses both existence and "being" as well as an ongoing action when it follows a verb.

です **Désu** *(dess)* expresses the indicative present "is" and, unlike the other "to be/there are" verbs, is never used by itself. The past tense of です **désu** is でした **déshita** *(desh-tah)*. The polite negative is ではありません **de wa arimasen** *(day wah ah-ree-mah-sen)*. In everyday speech this is often abbreviated to ではない **de wa nai** *(day wah nigh)*, and in familiar speech to じゃない **ja nai** *(jah nigh)*.

That is expensive.
それは高いです。
Sore wa takai désu.
(so-ray wah tah-kye dess)

That is not expensive.
それは高くありません。
Sore wa takaku arimasen.
(so-ray wah tah-kah-kuu ah-ree-mah-sen)

それは高くはない。
Sore wa takaku wa nai.
(so-ray wah tah-kah-kuu wa nigh)

それは高くない。
Sore wa takaku nai.
(so-ray wah tah-kah-kuu nigh)

Both ある **aru** *(ah-rue)* and いる **iru** *(ee-rue)* can be used by themselves as well as used in combination with other verbs. **Aru** is used when you want to make a "have" or "there is" statement or ask a "have you" or "is there" question. When used just by itself **aru** conveys the idea of "I have" or "there is." When **iru** is used by itself it generally refers to people or other living things being present at that location or somewhere else.

Another word that will get you a long way in Japanese is **kudasai** *(kuu-dah-sigh)*, which has the meaning of "please do" (something) or "please give" (something) and is used as an ending for verbs and following nouns.

水を下さい。**Mizu wo kudasai.** *(me-zuu oh kuu-dah-sigh)*
Water, please. (Please give me water.)
パンを下さい。**Pan wo kudasai.** *(pahn oh kuu-dah-sigh)*
Bread, please.
食べて下さい。**Tabete kudasai.** *(tah-bay-tay kuu-dah-sigh)*
Please eat.
助けて下さい。**Tasukete kudasai.** *(tah-skate-tay kuu-dah-sigh)*
Please help me.
教えて下さい。**Oshiete kudasai.** *(oh-she-eh-tay kuu-dah-sigh)*
Please show (teach) me.

Again because Japanese grammar is so different from English grammar it is not recommended that anyone begin study or use the language by learning grammatical rules. For many people the grammar-based approach can even be fatal to the learning process.

The easiest approach to the Japanese language, at least at the basic level, is to memorize written and spoken sentences and practice actual conversational dialogue, ignoring grammatical structure. Eventually the structure will become imprinted in your mind and you will automatically use it correctly.

Japanese Business Etiquette

Japan's business etiquette is encapsulated in a number of key terms that I call "cultural code words" because their meanings are impregnated with the values and goals that define and control how the Japanese do business. Here is a selection of some of the most important of these terms with explanations of how they function.

The All-Important Introduction
紹介 Shōkai *(shohh-kie)*

This is the Japanese word for "introduction"—something that is especially important in establishing new relationships in Japan because the Japanese have been culturally conditioned for centuries to avoid dealing with people they do not know. Historically, in their close-knit family and group-oriented society becoming involved with strangers not only complicated their lives, it also represented a possible danger.

The only way to circumvent this cultural-bound limit when business and other considerations required them to develop new relationships was to depend on introductions from friends, classmates, professors or trusted institutions who would take responsibility for the character and behavior of the people being introduced.

The custom of depending on **shōkai** thus became deeply embedded in Japanese culture, and remains today an important tool in both social and business etiquette.

Letter of Introduction
紹介状 Shōkai-jō *(shohh-kie johh)*

A **shōkai-jō** is a written introduction from an individual or from an institution attesting to the character of the bearer, and asking the third party to do whatever they can for him or her. An introduction from a well-known person or institution carries a lot of weight in Japan, and is highly recommended. "Cold calls" and self-introductions are not taboo in Japan, but a **shōkai-jō** will get you much further and faster because it gives you instant "face."

The Indispensable Advisor
相談役 Sōdanyaku *(sohh-dahn-yah-kuu)*

Sōdan means consultation, conference, talk and advice. A **sōdanyaku** is the Japanese word for consultant or advisor. **Sōdanyaku** can be extraordinarily valuable to foreign businesspeople who are considering their first foray into Japan on a relatively large scale—or need to make fundamental changes in existing organizations in Japan.

Foreign companies planning on going into Japan should consider retaining **sōdanyaku** well before the date of the initial contact because there are many things they should do in preparing for the venture—things they generally would not know about if they have not done considerable research or already had hands-on experience in Japan. [And doing a few hours of research on Google or Yahoo doesn't count!] The use of **sōdanyaku** is a well-established custom in Japan.

The Indispensable Go-Between
仲介人 Chukaisha *(chuu-kie-shah)*

This term may be literally translated as "middle-meeting-person" and refers, of course, to a "middleman"—a person who serves as an agent of one party to another in presentations and negotiations, particularly when the matter at hand is sensitive. **Chukaisha** have traditionally played a vital role in political and business affairs in Japan because Japanese culture did not support important dialogue between parties who did not already have a connection.

Chukaisha are generally chosen because they know both parties in a situation and are trusted by both sides, or they have a public reputation as a skilled go-between who can be trusted to be impartial and fair to both parties. **Chukaisha** are also retained to initiate and help establish new relationships between companies and other types of organizations. In this case, an experienced **chukaisha** is far superior to a **shōkai-jō**. Again, **chukaisha** play critical roles in situations where there is a major conflict between two parties because the Japanese will always opt for mediation over litigation.

The Indispensable Business Card
名刺 Meishi *(may-she)*

The first use of **meishi**—name cards or business cards—was apparently in China, when eunuchs serving at the Imperial Court began using them more than 1,000 years ago. Their cards were large in size and came in bright colors… and the original Chinese ideograms used to write **meishi** meant "Famous Gentleman."

Meishi were introduced to the emperor's court in Japan soon thereafter but they did not become common until well after the fall of the Tokugawa shogunate government in 1868. Now, it is commonly said in Japan that you are nobody if you don't have a name or business card. It goes without saying that foreigners doing business in Japan [and in some cases ordinary visitors to

Japan] should have business cards—and they should be bilingual; Japanese on one side and the bearer's native language on the other side.

The manner of presenting business cards in Japan is now much less formal than it used to be [using both hands and bowing slightly], but it pays to be a little formal, and if you are going to be engaging in sit-down discussions after the card exchange, put the ones you received on the table in front of you so you can refer to them during the proceedings. In Japanese, exchanging name cards is 名刺交換 **meishi kokan** *(may-she koh-kahn).*

[A growing number of people in sales positions in Japan now put their photographs on their name cards—a custom this writer originated in the early 1960s.]

The Indispensable Greeting Ritual
挨拶 Aisatsu *(aye-sot-sue)*

The literally meaning of **aisatsu** is "greeting," but its cultural nuances and uses go far beyond the connotations of this English word. **Aisatsu** incorporates the behavior that is a key part of the foundation of the culturally approved interpersonal relationships of the Japanese, including the hierarchical [senior-junior] status of individuals, the obligations that one owes to others, and the process of sustaining and nurturing relationships.

All Japanese are obligated to pay **aisatsu** visits to people who have helped them in the past to express their thanks and appreciation, and particularly when they want to ensure that they continue to benefit from the goodwill and help of the individuals concerned. In the business world, **aisatsu** visits to customers, potential customers, suppliers, etc., are a vital part of keeping the relationships on track.

There are many congratulatory-type occasions when **aisatsu** are called for, from managerial promotions to the introduction of new products. The period between about the 4th and 7th of January each year could be called "**Aisatsu** Season," because that is the period when people as a whole—especially businesspeople—pay their respects to benefactors.

When an **aisatsu** visit involves a middle or senior manager or executive, appointments are advisable because they normally receive many visitors during this New Year's period.

Top Man in a Department
部長 Buchō *(buu-chohh)*

Bu *(buu)* means department or division, and **chō** *(chohh)* means "the chief" or "the head." **Buchō** therefore means department chief or division chief.

[The terms department and division may be interchangeable in smaller companies and organizations, but the larger the group the more likely it may be referred to as a division.]

In any event, the **buchō** in Japanese companies is an important individual, and in larger organizations may be comparable to a vice-president in Western terminology. In military terms, **buchō** are the equivalent of company commanders in smaller organizations and battalion commanders in larger firms. They are the front-line managers in the operation of the company, and it is therefore vital for outsiders wanting to do business with a Japanese company, or already doing business with a firm, to establish and sustain a close relationship with all of the **buchō** in the firm who have anything to do with the product or service involved.

Another reason why it is important for foreign businesspeople to build and nurture close relations with department managers is that some of them will move up in the company hierarchy and become directors. Traditional etiquette calls for people doing business with a company to pay courtesy visits to key **buchō** every other month or so—not to talk business but to show their face.

Key Man in a Section
課長 Kachō*(kah-chohh)*

Departments (and smaller divisions) in Japanese companies are made up of several **ka** *(kah)* or sections, consisting of as few as six or eight individuals to as many as two or three dozen. The head or chief of a section is a **kachō**. Again using military terms, a **kachō** is like a squad leader… and in business in Japan as in war it is the **kachō** who are on the frontlines, who, in fact, oversee virtually all of the administrative work that is done in companies.

The directors, the vice-presidents and the **buchō** in Japanese companies play important roles, but it is the **kachō** who see that the work gets done. It is therefore vital for foreigners who want to do business with or are already doing business with Japanese companies to develop and maintain close relations with all of the **kachō** concerned with the product or service. They can determine if a project succeeds or fails.

Part of the etiquette of developing and nurturing good relations with section chiefs is to invite them and one or two of their top staff out for an evening of drinking and dining. In the natural order of things they will one day become a **buchō** and it pays to have had good relations with them for several years.

"Root Talk" in a Japanese Company

根回し **Nemawashi** *(nay-mah-wah-she)*

The literal meaning of **nemawashi** is "revolving or turning the roots" of a plant being transplanted. As is well-known the roots of a plant in a box or pot become balled up as the plant grows. In the transplanting process the roots must be spread out for the plant to grow properly.

This concept has become a key word in Japan's business vocabulary, referring to the details of a newly proposed project or relationship with another company being spread out among individuals in the company for them to discuss; and to the "lobbying" actions of individuals within companies who are advocating or opposing something. New projects proposed by outsiders invariably go through the **nemawashi** process.

The possibility of a project being accepted can be significantly enhanced by the person who proposed the project doing some **nemawashi** of his or her own with individuals in the company who would be responsible for its implementation—the **buchō** and the **kachō**. The etiquette—or process if you will—of developing a relationship with Japanese companies invariably includes a period of internal **nemawashi** that can take from weeks to months.

The Imperative of Trust

信用 **Shin'yō** *(sheen-yohh)*

In pre-modern Japan there was no body of laws that established or controlled business practices similar to what we are now familiar with. The national laws that did exist were decreed by the shogunate government and were primarily designed to ensure the survival of the government and the feudal system of fiefs and lords.

Fiefs, however, did have a system of laws the pertained to business, but in both essence and practice business relationships in Japan were based on **shin'yō**, or "trust," between the parties concerned.

Since the only thing that the parties could depend upon was unqualified trust, developing the feelings of trust to the point that the parties were bonded was a lengthy and detailed process.

Still today Japanese businesspeople are more concerned with **shin'yō** than with laws, and establishing an acceptable level of trust is their first goal in considering new business relationships. To succeed in Japan foreign businesspeople must give the same high priority to developing and maintaining **shin'yō**-based relationships with their suppliers and customers.

Whether or not one follows proper etiquette in dealing with a Japanese company is taken as a sign of his or her trustworthiness.

When "Difficult" Means "No"

難しい **Muzukashii** *(muu-zuu-kah-she-e)*

The very common word **muzukashii** means hard, difficult and troublesome... and it is also a "cultural code word" that has an altogether different meaning. When Japanese businesspeople are presented with projects in which they don't have the slightest interest—and this happens by the thousands annually—they will almost never say "no, thank you" outright.

They will listen politely enough, often nodding (which doesn't mean acceptance of anything, it just means they are listening), but in the end they will typically say the project would be **muzukashii**… usually with a strained and uncomfortable look on their face. This means "no, it's not going to happen, forget it."

Unless the foreign presenter is aware of this meaning of **muzukashii** he or she will also typically repeat the main points of the presentation, after saying it would be worth it even if it was difficult, and then leave, saying they look forward to hearing from the company. It is deep-seated Japanese etiquette to use such circumlocutions rather than refuse or decline anything directly.

Beware of Hidden Meanings!

善処します **Zensho Shimasu** *(zen-show she-mahss)*

This phrase, which means "I will take proper measures; I will do my best," has caused foreign businesspeople (also diplomats and the heads of foreign governments) who do not know the hidden meaning of the phrase more loss of face and more trouble than can be imagined.

Generally, there is no sense of real commitment or promise in this comment. It is almost always a ploy to avoid saying "no" outright and causing the petitioning party to get upset and/or lose face. Once this comment has been made at the end of presentations, the Japanese side seldom if ever takes any action. Again, this is an example of Japanese etiquette that is designed to avoid upsetting anyone in face-to-face confrontations.

The Power of Cultural Intuition

直感 **Chokkan** *(choke-kahn)*

One of the first lessons that foreign businesspeople should learn about Japanese culture is the role played by **chokkan**, "intuition, intuitive power," in business and all other relationships. The natural intuitive powers of the Japanese—those common to people everywhere—have been dramatically enhanced by their culture, to the point that often they cannot be separated, and in many cases they take precedence over rational or logical thinking based on facts.

The Japanese have a special word that refers specifically to the use of their combined cultural wisdom and native intuition: 腹芸 **haragei** *(hah-rah-gay-e)*, which translates as "the art of the stomach." In virtually all of the occasions when foreigners cannot understand the rationale of business decisions made by the Japanese the answer lies in their **chokkan**.

Most of Japan's leading tycoons—Idemitsu, Matsushita, Honda, etc.—credit their amazing success to guidance provided by their **chokkan**.

The principle of **haragei** in business in Japan accounts for much of the emotional content of Japanese etiquette.

The Power of Tradition

方 Kata *(kah-tah)*

This is one of the most important words in the Japanese language, and is the key to understanding all of the traditional and most of the modern behavior of the Japanese. **Kata** means "form" and the physical process of doing things.

In Japan's traditional culture there was a specific **kata** for virtually everything the Japanese did: **yari-kata** (way of doing things/working); **tabe-kata** (way of eating); **nomi-kata** (way of drinking); **hanashi-kata** (way of talking); **aruki-kata** (way of walking); **yomi-kata** (way of reading); **kaki-kata** (way of writing), and so on. There was also a specific **kata** for all forms of Japanese etiquette.

The actions of each **kata** were precise, and were taught to children from infancy on. Deviations were not allowed. This homogenization of Japanese behavior had a fundamental impact on their mindset, making everyone extremely conscious of how people behaved, and determining many of the rules of etiquette that developed over the millennia.

The power of the **kata** in present-day Japan is much less than what it was until the 1970s and 80s, but it remains a force in society in general and especially in the work-place, where corporate cultures prescribe acceptable etiquette. There is no way foreigners can fully understand the Japanese without knowledge of the ongoing role of **kata** in the culture. [Read more about **kata** from my book—details on page xxi's footnote.]

Making Things "Fit" for Japan

日本的 Nihon-teki *(nee-hoan-tay-kee)*

Japanese things have a distinctive look that clearly identifies them as "Japanese," and is one of the facets of Japanese culture that is especially attractive—in a very sensual way—to most foreigners, especially Westerners.

This distinguishing element, which derives from the material things are made of and their design, is referred to in Japanese as **Nihon-teki**. **Nihon** means "Japan," and **teki** means "suitable, fit, compatible, conforming to," or "similar to."

The workmanship and the design concepts that make a thing **Nihon-teki** go back some 1,500 years, and are a reflection of Shinto concepts of beauty and Zen concepts of refined simplicity.

The distinctive nature of things Japanese is so deeply embedded in the mindset of the people that they do not have to strive to create it. It comes naturally to them, without them having to think about it. When it is missing, as it is in most non-Japanese products, they recognize its absence instantly.

This is the reason why many foreign products have not been acceptable in Japan until they were "Japanized." Foreign businesses proposing to introduce a new product in Japan should first give it the **Nihon-teki** test, to see if it is suitable, fit, and compatible with Japanese tastes.

All Japanese etiquette must also meet the same test. If it is not instantly recognized as **Nihon-teki** it smacks of something foreign. A few forms of foreign etiquette, like the hand-shake, have been incorporated into Japan's culture, but the traditional お辞儀 **O'jigi** *(oh-jee-ghee)*, or bow, continues to be a vital part of the etiquette of present-day Japanese in many formal situations and when groups or large numbers of people are involved.

The Japanese Do-or-Die Syndrome!
頑張る Gambaru! *(gahn-bah-rue)*

Gambaru is one of the most commonly used words in the Japanese vocabulary—in business, in sports, in any endeavor that is taxing in the least. It refers to what I call the "Japanese never-give-up never-say-die" syndrome. It means "stand fast, stand firm, hold out, never give up," and is the term that the Japanese use when encouraging people to do their absolute best in whatever it is they are engaged in or are going to undertake.

The number of daily situations in which **gambatte** *(gahn-bahn-tah)* is used as a rallying cry are virtually uncountable. It is called out to people engaged in sports, when a business colleague departs for an overseas assignment, when someone starts a test of any kind, when anybody undertakes anything new, when a baby tries to stand up the first time, and on and on.

The cultural implications of **gambatte** are deep and abiding, and reflect the built-in drive that the Japanese have to succeed in whatever they set out to do and to do things better than anyone else can. Foreigners should make use of this word whenever an occasion arises because it indicates an intimate knowledge of Japanese culture.

Use of the term is such a spontaneous response that it has become an integral part of the national etiquette.

Japan's Fabled Night-Time Trades
水商売 **Mizu shōbai** *(mee-zoo shoh-bye)*

Mizu shōbai is an old term that refers in particular to Japan's huge and important night-time entertainment trades made up of hundreds of thousands of bars, cabarets and nightclubs and an impressive number of surviving **geisha** inns.

Alcoholic drinks have played a vital role in Japanese culture since the dawn of civilization—first used in Shinto rituals aimed at pleasing the various gods. Shrines often had their own fields for growing the rice to be turned into 酒 **sake** *(sah-kay)* mash, and as time passed into liquid **sake**.

From this stage drinking came to be used as a lubricant when socializing and especially to mark special occasions, including new business deals, and to develop and sustain relationships. Drinking then became an integral part of after-hours business (and political) negotiations because the only time it was possible to break the strict formal patterns of behavior that controlled their normal daytime behavior was when they were drinking.

Virtually all foreigners who do business in Japan are entertained in the **mizu shōbai**, and all should be familiar with its role in business and use it as the Japanese do. It is a vital part of the etiquette of doing business in Japan—and those foreigners who shy away from it because they don't drink and/or don't want to spend time in the evenings in bars or other clubs are foregoing one of the main elements in developing and nurturing relationships in Japan.

The role of the **mizu shōbai** in Japan is not likely to diminish significantly in the foreseeable future. It has thrived since the age of gods (among whom there were a number of famous party-goers!).

Keeping Your "Flattery Filter" Online
胡麻擂り **Gomasuri** *(go-mah-suu-ree)*

Japan's social etiquette has traditionally been based on an extraordinary degree of formality and ritualistic ceremony that permeated the culture from top to bottom, making it essential that individuals spend a great deal of time learning and following the protocol that applied to virtually every aspect of their daily lives, and particularly so in all of their interactions with people of rank and in the need for maintaining harmonious relations with everyone.

This led to the profuse use of what came to be known as **gomasuri**, which literally means "grinding sesame seeds," but in its present-day colloquial usage it means "flattery."

In the old days sesame seeds were ground in earthenware mortars that would cause stray seeds to fly in all directions, clinging to the sides of the bowl "in a cringing way," reminding the Japanese of the ingratiating behavior they had to assume to stay on the good side of the upper class, particularly arrogant samurai.

The use of flattery became so deeply embedded in the culture that it continues today to be a defining characteristic of the Japanese, especially where foreigners are concerned. They have found Westerners to be especially vulnerable to **gomasuri** and make great use of it to manipulate them in many ways—some that turn out to be fun and others that turn out to be seriously disadvantageous.

Westerners dealing with the Japanese should therefore have their flattery filter engaged at all times, and not lower their standards, expectations or requirements as a result of being smothered with **gomasuri**.

For a more detailed discourse on these terms, plus over 200 other key Japanese words, read the author's book *Japan's Cultural Code Words—233 Key Terms that Explain the Attitudes and Behavior of the Japanese* [Tuttle Publishing]. Also, read his book, *Kata—The Key to Understanding & Dealing with the Japanese* [Tuttle Publishing.]

Common Expressions

Greetings

Good morning
おはようございます
Ohayō gozaimasu
(oh-hah-yoh go-zie-mahss)

Good afternoon
こんにちは
Konnichi wa
(kone-nee-chee wah)

Good evening
こんばんは
Komban wa
(kome-bahn wah)

Good night
おやすみなさい
Oyasumi nasai
(oh-yah-suu-me nah-sie)

See you later
またあとで
Mata ato de
(mah-tah ah-toh-day)

See you tomorrow
またあした
Mata ashita
(mah-tah ah-ssh-tah)

Goodbye
さようなら
Sayōnara
(Sah-yoh-nah-rah)

Take care / stay well!
お元気でね
O'genki de, ne!
(oh-gane-kee day, nay!)

How are you?
お元気ですか。
O'genki désu ka?
(oh-gane-kee dess kah?)

I'm fine.
元気です。
Genki désu.
(gane-kee dess.)

Nice weather, isn't it!
いいお天気ですね。
Ii o'tenki désu, ne!
(ee-oh-tane-kee, dess nay!)

It's cold today, isn't it!
今日は寒いですね。
Kyō wa samui désu, ne!
(k'yoe wah sah-mooey dess, nay!)

It's hot, isn't it!
暑いですね。
Atsui désu, ne!
(aht-suuey dess, nay!)

It's muggy hot, isn't it!
蒸し暑いですね。
Mushi atsui désu, ne!
(muu-she aht-suuey dess, nay!)

I think it is going to rain tomorrow.
明日は雨が降ると思います。
Ashita wa ame ga furu to omoimasu.
(ah-ssh-tah wah ah-may gah fuu-ruu toh oh-moy-mahss.)

Do you have an umbrella?
傘を持っていますか。
Kasa wo motte imasu ka?
(kah-sah oh mote-tay ee-mahss kah?)

May I borrow your umbrella?
傘を借りてもいいですか。
Kasa wo karite mo ii désu ka?
(kah-sah oh kah-ree-tay moh ee dess kah?)

Does it snow in Tokyo?
東京で雪が降りますか。
Tokyo de yuki ga furimasu ka?
(tokyo day yuu-kee gah fuu-ree-mahss kah?)

Where is the closest subway station?
一番近い地下鉄の駅はどこですか。
Ichiban chikai chikatetsu no eki wa doko désu ka?
(ee-chee-bahn chee-kie chee-kah-tate-sue no eh-kee wah doh-koh dess kah?)

Is the train station closer?
電車の駅はもっと近いですか。
Densha no eki wa motto chikai désu ka?
(dane-shah no eh-kee wah mote-toh chee-kie dess kah?)

I'm hungry.
お腹が空いています。
Onaka ga suite imasu.
(oh-nah-kah gah sue-ee-tay ee-mahss.)

What time is it now?
いま何時ですか。
Ima nanji désu ka?
(ee-mah nahn-jeee dess kah?)

Let's get something to eat!
何か食べましょう!
Nanika tabemasho!
(nah-nee-kah tah-bay-mah-show!)

What do you want to eat?
何が食べたいですか。
Nani ga tabetai désu ka?
(nah-nee gah tah-bay-tie dess kah?)

How about the famous breaded pork cutlets?
その有名なとんかつはどうですか。
Sono yūmei na tonkatsu wa dō désu ka?
(soh-no yuuu-may-e nah tone-kot-sue wah dohhh dess kah?)

Here is a ritualized expression said before starting to eat or drink, especially when someone else is the host:

いただきます
Itadakimasu
(ee-tah-dah-kee-mahss)

The literal meaning of **itadakimasu** is "I will accept" or I will take." In this case it is a humble, formal and polite way of announcing that you are going to start eating.

Here is a ritualized expression that is said to the host after the meal is finished and everyone starts leaving (if there is no host, it is a common and polite gesture for diners to address the expression to the cook, to the waiter or waitress, and even to the cashier):

ごちそうさまでした
Gochisōsama deshita
(go-chee-sohh-sah-mah desh-tah)

Gochisō literally means a "treat" or "entertainment," but when used in this expression it means "Thank you very much for the delicious meal," as well as "I enjoyed the meal very much. Thank you."

I'm thirsty.
のどが乾いています。
Nodo ga kawaite imasu.
(no-doh gah kah-wie-tay ee-mahss.)

How about a beer?
ビールはどうですか。
Biiru wa dō désu ka?
(bee-rue wah dohhh dess kah?)

I prefer regular green tea.
日本茶のほうがいいです。
Nihoncha no hō ga ii désu.
(Nee-hone-cha no hohhh gah ee dess.)

Don't you drink beer?
ビールを飲みませんか。
Biiru wo nomimasen ka?
(bee-rue oh no-me-mah-sin kah?)

Yes, I drink it but not before breakfast!
飲むけど朝ご飯の前は飲みません。
Nomu kedo asa-gohan no mae wa nomimasen!
(no-muu, kay-doh ah-sah-go-hahn no my-nee wah no-me-mah-sin!)

The food was delicious!
食事はおいしかったです。
Shokuji wa oishikatta désu.
(show-kuu-jee wah oh-ee-shee-kaht-tah dess.)

Getting Acquainted

What is your name?
お名前はなんですか。
O'namae wa nan désu ka?
(oh-nah-my wah nahn dess kah?)

My name is _________.
私の名前は _____ です。
Watakushi no namae wa _________ désu.
(wah-tock-she no nah-my wah _________ dess.)

Where do you live / Where is your home?
お住まいはどちらですか。
O'sumai wa dochira désu ka?
(oh-suu-my wah doh-chee-rah dess kah?)

Where were you born?
どこで生まれましたか。
Doko de umaremashita ka?
(doe-koe day uu-mah-ray-mahssh-tah kah?)

Do you have children?
お子さんはいますか。
Okosan wa imasu ka?
(oh-koe-sahn wah ee-mahss kah?)

Have you been to the United States?
アメリカに行ったことがありますか。
Amerika ni itta koto ga arimasu ka?
(ah-may-ree-kah nee eet-tah koe-toe gah ah-ree-mahss kah?)

How about Europe?
ヨーロッパは。
Yōroppá wa?
(yohh-rope-pahh wah?)

I didn't sleep at all last night!
ゆうべ全然寝ませんでした。
Yūbe zenzen nemasen déshita!
(yuu-bay zen-zen nay-mah-sen deh-sshtah!)

I'm going to take a short rest.
しばらく休みます。
Shibáraku yasumimasu.
(she-bah-rah-kuu yah-sue-me-mahss.)

Making a Business Appointment

I would like to make an appointment for 10 a.m. tomorrow.
明日午前の十時に約束をしたいです。
Ashita gozen no jūji ni yakusoku wo shitai désu.
(ah-ssh-tah go-zane no juu-jee ne yack-so-kuu oh she-tie dess.)

I am staying at the Tokyo Miyako Hotel.
東京都ホテルに泊まっています。
Tokyo Miyako hoteru ni tomatte imasu.
(tokyo me-yah-ko hoh-tay-rue nee toe-mot-tay ee-mahss.)

My room number is 1178.
ルームナンバーは1178です。
Rūmu nanbā wa ichi-ichi-nana-hachi désu.
(rue-muu nahm-bah wah e-chee e-chee nah-nah hah-chee dess.)

My telephone number is 4567-6622.
電話番号は4567-6622です。
Denwa bangō wa yon-go-roku-nana-roku-roku-ni-ni désu.
(dane-wah bahn-go wah yon go roe-kuu nah-nah roe-kuu roe-kuu nee nee dess.)

Please telephone me in the morning at 7 o'clock.
明日の朝、七時に電話を下さい。
Ashita no asa, shichi-ji ni denwa wo kudasai.
(ahssh-tah no ah-sah no she-chee-jee nee dane-wah oh kuu-dah-sie.)

I will meet you in the lobby at 8 o'clock.
ロビーで八時に会います。
Robii ni hachi-ji ni aimasu.
(rohh-bee nee hah-chee-jee nee aye-mahss.)

Where is your office?
オフィスはどこですか。
Ofisu wa doko désu ka?
(oh-fee-suu wah doh-koh dess kah?)

How far is it from the hotel to your office?
ホテルからあなたのオフィスまでどのくらいありますか。
Hoteru kara anata no ofisu made dono kurai arimasu ka?
(hoh-tay-rue kah-rah ah-nah-tah no oh-fee-suu mah-day doe-no koo-rye ah-ree-mahss kah?)

How long will it take to get there?
そこまでどのくらいかかりますか。
Soko made dono kurai kakarimasu ka?
(soe-koe mah-day doe-no koo-rye kah-kah-ree-mahss kah?)

What floor is your office on?
オフィスは何階ですか。
Ofisu wa nankai désu ka?
(oh-fee-suu wah nahn kie dess kah?)

What year was your company founded?
会社は何年に設立しましたか。
Kaisha wa nan nen ni setsuritsu shimashita ka?
(kie-shah wah nahn nane nee sate-sue-reet-sue she-mahssh-tah kah?)

How many employees do you/does it have?
大体どのくらい従業員がいますか。
Daitai dono kurai jūgyōin ga imasu ka?
(die-tie doe-no koo-rye juu-g'yoe-een gah ee-mahss kah?)

What kind of work do you do?
どんな仕事をしていますか。
Donna shigotó wo shiteimasu ka?
(doan-nah she-go-tohh oh she-tay ee-mahss-kah?)

What are your business hours?
営業時間は。
Eigyō jikan wa?
(egg-y'yohh jee-kahn wah?)

Do you have a branch office in Osaka?
大阪に支店がありますか。
Ōsaka ni shiten ga arimasu ka?
(ohh-sah-kah nee she-tane gah ah-ree-mahss kah?)

How long does it take to go to Osaka?
大阪までどのくらいかかりますか。
Ōsaka made dono kurai kakarimasu ka?
(oh-sah-kah mah-day doe-no koo-rye kah-kah-ree-mahss kah?)

I would like to go by Bullet Train.
新幹線で行きたいです。
Shinkansen de ikitai désu.
(sheen-kahn-sin day ee-kee-tie dess.)

Where can I buy a ticket?
切符をどこで買う事ができますか。
Kippu wo doko de kau koto ga dekimasu ka?
(kee-puu oh doe-koe day kow koe-toe gah day-kee-mahss kah?)

Let's go out drinking tonight.
今晩飲みに行きましょう。
Komban nomi ni ikimashō.
(kome-bahn no-me nee ee-kee-mah-show.)

Shall we go to the Ginza?
銀座に行きましょうか。
Ginza ni ikimashō ka?
(gheen-zah nee ee-kee-mah-show kah?)

Ginza is too expensive!
銀座は高すぎます。
Ginza wa takasugimasu!
(gheen-zah wah tah-kah-suu-ghee-mahss!)

I'd like to meet a hostess. Let's go to a cabaret.
ホステスに会いたいです。キャバレーに行きましょう。
Hosutesu ni aitai desu. Kyabarē ni ikimashō.
(hohss-tay-suu nee aye-tie dess. k'yah-bah-ray nee ee-kee-mah-show.)

Shopping

I would like to go shopping.
買い物に行きたいです。
Kaimono ni ikitai désu.
(kie-moe-no nee ee-kee-tie dess.)

I need a new cell phone.
新しい携帯電話が必要です。
Atarashii keitai denwa ga hitsuyō désu.
(ah-tah-rah-shee no kay-tie dane-wah gah heet-sue-yohh dess.)

Where can I buy one?
どこで買う事ができますか。
Doko de kau koto ga dekimasu ka?
(doe-koe day kow koe-toe gah day-kee-mahss kah?)

I would like to go to the famous Akihabara Shopping District.
有名な秋葉原商店街に行きたいです。
Yūmei na Akihabara shōtengai ni ikitai désu.
(yuu-may nah ah-kee-hah-bah-rah shohh-tane-guy nee ee-kee-tie dess.)

Is it far?
遠いですか。
Tōi désu ka?
(tohh-ee dess kah?)

Sightseeing

I would like to go sightseeing this weekend.
今週の週末は観光に行きたいです。
Konshū no shūmatsu wa kankō ni ikitai désu.
(kone-shuu no shuu-mah-t'sue wah kahn-koe nee ee-kee-tie dess.)

Can you recommend a good place?
いい所をおすすめできますか。
Ii tokoró wo osusume dekimasu ka?
(ee toe-koe-rohh oh oh-sue-sue-may day-kee-mahss kah?)

I have heard that the scenery in Hakoné is especially beautiful.
箱根の景色が特に美しいそうです。
Hakoné no késhiki ga toku ni utsukushii sō désu.
(hah-koe-nay no kay-she-kee gah toe-kuu nee uut-sue-kuu-shee sohh dess.)

Are all of the train seats reserved?
列車の席は全部指定ですか。
Resshá no séki wa zembu shitei désu ka?
(ray-shahh no say-kee wah zim-boo she-tay dess kah?)

I would also like to go to a hot spring spa.
温泉にも行きたいです。
Onsen ni mo ikitai désu.
(own-sen nee mohh ee-kee-tie dess.)

For very helpful Japanese language guides read the author's *Instant Japanese and Survival Japanese* (Tuttle Publishing).

A

abacus そろばん **soroban** *(soe-roe-bahn)*
▪ Do you know how to use an abacus? そろばんの使い方を知っていますか。**Soroban no tsukaikata wo shitte-imasu ka?** *(soe-roe-bahn no t'sue-kai-kah-tah oh ssh-tay-ee-mahss kah?)*

abandon 諦める **akirameru** *(ah-kee-may-ruu)*; give up 止める **yameru** *(yah-may-ruu)*
▪ We must abandon this project. この事業を止めなければなりません。**Kono jigyō wo yamenakereba narimasen.** *(koh-no jeeg-yoh oh yah-may-nah-kay-ray-bah nah-ree-mah-sin.)*

abatement 割り戻し **warimodoshi** *(wah-ree-moe-doe-she)*; リベート **ribēto** *(ree-bay-toe)*

abbreviate 省略する **shōryaku suru** *(show-r'yah-kuu sue-rue)*
▪ How do you abbreviate this word? この言葉をどのように省略しますか。**Kono kotoba wo dono yō ni shōryaku shimasu ka?** *(koe-no koe-toe-bah oh doh-no yohh nee shohh-ree-yah-kuu-she-mahss kah?)*

abbreviation 省略 **shōryaku** *(show-r'yah-kuu)*
▪ Is that an abbreviation? それは省略ですか。**Sore wa shōryaku désu ka?** *(soe-ray wah shohh-ree-yah-kuu dess kah?)*

aberration 逸脱 **itsudatsu** *(eet-suu-dot-suu)*
▪ The world has been experiencing climatic aberrations. 世界各地で異常気象が発生しています。**Sekai kakuchi de ijō kishō ga hassei shite imasu.** *(say-kie kah-kuu-chee day ee-joh kee-show hahs-say-ee shtay-mahss.)*

ability 能力 **nōryoku** *(no-rio-kuu)*
▪ I am searching for a person with extraordinary ability. 特別な能力のある人を探しています。**Tokubetsu na nōryoku no aru hito wo sagashite imasu.** *(toh-kuu-bate-sue nah no-rio-kuu no ah-rue ssh-toe oh sah-gah-shtay-mahss.)*

ability to compete 競争能力 **kyōsō nōryoku** *(k'yoh-soh no-rio-kuu)*

ability-to-pay concept 支払能力概念 **shiharai nōryoku gainen** *(she-hah-rye no-rio-kuu guy-nen)*

abnormal 異常 **ijō (na)** *(ee-joh)*
▪ For him, that reaction was abnormal. あの人にとって、その反応は異常でした。**Anohito ni totte sono hannō wa ijō déshita.** *(ah-no-ssh-toe nee toe-tay so-no hahn-no wah ee-johh desh-tah.)*

abolish 廃止 **haishi** *(high-she)*
▪ That law should be abolished. その法律は廃止するべきです。**Sono hōritsu wa haishi surubeki désu.** *(so-no hoe-ree-t'sue wah high-she sue-rue bay-kee dess.)*

about だいたい **daitai** *(dye-tie)*; ごろ **goro** *(go-roe)*; およそ oyoso *(oh-yoe-so)*; ほぼ hobo *(hoe-boe)*
▪ It's about one o'clock. だいたい1時頃です。**Daitai ichi-ji goro désu.** *(dye-tie ee-chee-jee go-roe dess)*
▪ About what time will Mr. Suzuki be back? 鈴木さんは何時頃戻りますか。**Suzuki-san wa nanji goro modorimasu ka?** *(sue-zuu-kee-sahn wah nahn-jee go-roe moe-doe-ree-mahss kah?)*
▪ About how many are there? いくつぐらいありますか。**Ikutsu gurai arimasu ka?** *(ee-kuu-t'sue guu-rye ah-ree-mahss kah?)*
▪ About how much is it? どのぐらい

しますか。**Dono gurai shimasu ka?** *(doe-no guu-rye she-mahss kah?)*

above par value 額面以上で **gakumen ijō de** *(gah-kuu men ee-joe day)*

abroad; foreign country 外国 **gaikoku** *(guy-koe-kuu)*
▪ Next year I am going abroad. 来年、外国に行きます。**Rainen gaikoku ni ikimasu.** *(rie-nane guy-koh-kuu nee ee-kee-mahss.)*

absent (from office, home) 留守 **rusu** *(ruu-suu)*; 欠勤 **kekkin** *(cake-keen)*; 休み **yasumu** *(yah-sue-me)*
▪ I will be absent from the office for a week. 一週間会社を休みます。**Isshūkan kaisha wo yasumimasu.** *(ees-shuu-kahn jim-show oh yah-sue-me-mahss.)*

absenteeism 無断欠勤 **mudan kekkin** *(muu-dann cake-keen)*

absentee ownership 不在所有権 **fuzai shoyūken** *(fuu-zahee show-h'yuu ken)*

absorb the loss 損失を吸収する。**sonshitsu wo kyūshū suru** *(soan sheet-sue oh cue-shuu sue-rue)*

absorption; acquisition 吸収合併 **kyūshū gappei** *(cue-shuu gahp-pay)*

abstract of title 権利要約書 **kenri yōyaku sho** *(ken-ree yoe-yah-kuu show)*

accelerate 加速する **kasoku suru** *(kah-so-kuu suu-ruu)*
▪ Sales are now accelerating. いま売上げは、急成長しています。**Ima uriage wa kyū-seichō shite imasu.** *(eem-mah uu-ree-ah-gay cue-say-choe shtay-mahss.)*

accelerated depreciation 加速減価償却 **kasoku genka shōkyaku** *(kah-so-kuu gen-kah show-k'yack-kuu)*

accent なまり **namari** *(nah-mah-ree)*; アクセント **akusento** *(ah-kuu-sen-toe)*
▪ Your accent is like that of a native. あなたのアクセントはネイティブのようです。**Anata no akusento wa netibu no yō désu.** *(an-nah-tah no ah-kuu-sen-toh wah nay-tee-buu no yoh dess.)*

accept (consent to something) 承諾する **shōdaku suru** *(show-dah-kuu sue-rue)*; 同意する **dōi suru** *(doe-ee sue-rue)*; receive something 引き受ける **hikiukeru** *(he-kee-uu-kay-toe-ree-rue)*
▪ I accept your proposal. あなたの申し出を承諾します。**Anata no mōshide wo shōdaku shimasu.** *(ah-nah-tah no moe-she-day oh show-dah-kuu she-mahss.)*

accept 受ける **ukéru** *(uu-kay-rue)*
▪ Please accept this gift. どうぞ、このお土産をお受け取りください。**Dōzo, kono omiyage wo o-uketori kudasai.** *(doe-zoe koe-no oh-me-yah-gay oh oh-uu-kay-toe-ree kuu-dah-sigh.)*

acceptable 受け入れられる **ukeire-rareru** *(uu-kay-ee-ray-rah-ray-rue)*; 結構(な) **kekkō (na)** *(keck-kohh nah)*; 満足できる **manzoku dekiru** *(man-zoe-kuu day-kee-rue)*
▪ Your offer is acceptable. あなたの申し出をお引き受けします。**Anata no mōshide wo o-hikiuke shimasu.** *(ah-nah-tah no mohh-she-day wo oh he-kee-uu-kay she-mahss.)*

acceptable quality level 合格品質水準 **gōkaku hinshitsu suijun** *(go-kah-kuu heen-sheet-sue sue-ee-june)*

acceptance 引き受け **hikiuke** *(he-kee-uu-kay)*; 承諾 **shōdaku** (*show-dah-kuu)*

acceptance agreement 引受承諾書 **hikiuke shōdaku sho** *(he-kee-uu-kay show-dah-kuu show)*

acceptance bill 引受手形 **hikiuke tegata** *(he-kee-uu-kay tay-gah-tah)*

acceptance sampling 抜き取り検査 **nukitori kensa** *(nuu-kee-toe-ree ken-sah)*

acceptance test 受入検査 **ukeire kensa** *(uu-kay-ee-ray ken-sah)*

access 参入 **sannyū** *(sahn-n'yuu)*; 参加 **sanka** *(sahn-kah)*; 接続 **setsuzoku** *(say-t'sue-zoe-kuu)*

accessory アクセサリー **akusesarii** *(ah-kuu-say-sah-ree)*, 付属品 **fuzoku hin** *(fuu-zoe-kuu heen)*
▪ What floor are accessories on? アクセサリー売り場は何階ですか。**Akusesarii uriba wa nankai désu ka?** *(ah-kuu-say-sah-ree uu-ree-bah wah nahn-kie dess kah?)*

accident 事故 **jiko** *(jee-koe)*; 偶然 **gūzen** *(guu-zen)*
▪ There has been a serious accident at the factory. 工場で重大事故がありました。**Kōjō de jūdai jiko ga arimashita.** *(koe-joe day juu-dye jee-koe gah ah-ree-mahsh-tah.)*
▪ He was killed in a car accident. あの人は自動車事故で亡くなりました。**Ano hito wa jidōsha jiko de nakunarimashita.** *(ah-no he-toe wah jee-doe-shah jee-koe day nah-kuu-nah-ree-mahsh-tah.)*
▪ I met her by accident yesterday. 昨日、彼女に偶然会いました。**Kinō kanojo ni gūzen aimashita.** *(kee-no kah-no-joe nee guu-zen eye-mahsh-tah.)*

accidental damage 偶発的損害 **gūhatsu teki songai** *(guu-hot-sue tay-kee soan-guy)*

accident insurance 損害保険 **songai hoken** *(soan-guy hoe-ken)*
▪ What kind of accident insurance do you have? どんな損害保険がありますか。**Donna songai hoken ga arimasu ka?** *(doan-nah soan-guy hoe-ken gah ah-ree-mahss kah?)*

acclimate 慣れる **nareru** *(nah-ray-rue)*
▪ Have you become acclimated to life in Japan? 日本の生活に慣れましたか。**Nihon no seikatsu ni naremashita ka?** *(nee-hone no say-kaht-sue nee nah-ree-mah-ssh-tah kah?)*

accommodate 便宜を図る **bengi wo hakaru** *(bane-ghee oh hah-kah-rue)*

accompany (go with) 一緒に行く **issho ni iku** *(ee-show nee ee-kuu)*; see off 見送る **miokuru** *(me-oh-kuu-rue)*
▪ I will accompany you. 一緒に行きます。**Issho ni ikimasu.** *(ee-show-nee ee-kee-mahss.)*
▪ I will accompany you to the airport. 空港までお見送りします。**Kūkō made o-miokuri shimasu.** *(kuu-koe mah-day oh-me-oh-kuu-ree she-mahss.)*
▪ Please accompany me. 私と一緒に来てください。**Watakushi to issho ni kite kudasai.** *(wah-tak-she toe ee-show-nee kee-tay kuu-dah-sigh.)*

accomplice 共犯者 **kyōhansha** *(k'yohh-hahn-shah)*

account (statement of money) 勘定 **kanjō** *(kahn-joe)*; calculation 計算 **keisan** *(kay-sahn)*
▪ I would like to pay my account now. 今、自分のお勘定を払いたいです。**Ima jibun no okanjō wo haraitai désu.** *(ee-mah, jee-boon no kahn-joh oh hah-rye-tie dess.)*

account (bank) 預金口座 **yokin kōza** *(yoe-keen koe-zah)*

accountable 責任がある **sekinin ga aru** *(say-kee-neen gah ah-rue)*
▪ He is accountable for the accident. その事故の責任は彼にある。**Sono jiko no sekinin wa kare ni aru.** *(so-no*

jee-koh no say-kee-neen wah kah-ray nee ah-rue.)

accountability (management) 経営責任 **keiei sekinin** *(kay-ee say-kee-neen)*

accountant 会計士 **kaikei shi** *(kye-kay she)*

accountant, chief (chief accountant) 会計主任 **kaikei shunin** *(kye-kay shuu-neen)*

account balance 取引勘定残高 **torihiki kanjō zandaka** *(toe-ree-he-kee kahn-joe zahn-dah-kah)*

account books 決算書 **kessansho** *(case-sahn-show)*

account, current (current account) 当座勘定 **tōza kanjō** *(toe-zah kahn-joe)*

account executive (advertising) 営業担当者 **eigyō tantō-sha** *(eh-ee-g'yoe than-toe shah)*

account executive (securities) 証券会社営業部員 **shōken gaisha eigyō buin** *(show-ken guy-shah eh-ee-g'yoe buu-een)*

account, open (open account) 当座預金 **tōza yokin** *(toe-zah yoe-keen)*

accounting, consolidated (consolidated accounting) 連結決算 **renketsu kessan** *(rane-kay-t'suu case-sahn)*

accounting, cost (cost accounting) 原価会計 **genka kaikei** *(gane-kah kye-kay)*

accounting department 会計係 **kaikei gakari** *(kye-kay gah-kah-ree)*; 経理部 **keiri bu** *(kay-ee-ree buu)*

accounting management 会計管理 **kaikei kanri** *(kie-kay-ee kahn-ree)*

accounting method 会計方法 **kaikei hōhō** *(kye-kay hoe-hoe)*

accounting period 会計期間 **kaikei kikan** *(kye-kay kee-kahn)*; 会計年度 **kaikei nendo** *(kye-kay nen-doe)*
▪ When does your (company) accounting period start? 会社の会計期間はいつからですか。**Kaisha no kaikei kikan wa itsu kara désu ka?** *(kye-shah no kye-kay kee-kahn wah eat-sue ee-t'sue kah-rah dess kah?)*

account number 口座番号 **kōza bangō** *(koe-zah bahn-go)*
▪ Please write your account number here. ここに口座番号を記入してください。**Koko ni kōza bangō wo kinyūshite kudasai.** *(koe-koe nee koe-zah bahn-go oh kee-h'yuu-shtay kuu-dah-sigh.)*
▪ What is your account number? 口座番号は何番ですか。**Kōza bangō wa nanban désu ka?** *(koe-zah bahn-go wah nahn-bahn dess ka?)*

accounts payable 支払勘定 **shiharai kanjō** *(she-hah-rye kahn-joe)*

accounts receivable 受取勘定 **uketori kanjō** *(uu-kay-toe-ree kahn-joe)*

accounts secured 担保付き勘定 **tanpo tsuki kanjō** *(tahn-poe ski kahn-joe)*

accrual 経過利息 **keika risoku** *(kay-kah ree-soe-kuu)*

accrual method 発生主義方式 **hassei shugi hōshiki** *(hah-say shuu-ghee hohh-she-kee)*

accrued assets 見越し資産 **mikoshi shisan** *(me-koe-she she-sahn)*

accrued expenses 未払費用 **miharai hiyō** *(me-hah-rie he-yohh)*

accrued interest 経過利息 **keika risoku** *(kay-kah ree-soe-kuu)*

accrued revenue 未収収益 **mishū shūeki** *(me-shuu shuu-eh-kee)*

accrued taxes 未払税金 **miharai zeikin** *(me-hah-rie zay-ee-keen)*

accumulated depreciation 減価償却累計額 **genka shōkyaku ruikei gaku** *(gen-kah show-kyah-kuu rue-ee-kay-gah-kuu)*

accuracy 正確さ **seikakusa** *(say-e-kah-kuu-sah)*
▪ Can you confirm the accuracy of these figures? この数字が正確か確認できますか。**Kono sūji ga seikaku ka kakunin dekimasu ka?** *(koe-no suu-jee gah say-kah-kuu kah kah-kuu-neen day-kee-mahss kah?)*

accurate 正確（な） **seikaku (na)** *(say-e-kah-ku nah)*
▪ These figures are accurate. この数字は正確です。**Kono sūji wa seikaku désu.** *(koe-no suu-jee wa say-kah-kuu dess.)*

accustom 慣らす **narasu** *(nah-rah-sue)*

accustomed to に慣れる **ni nareru** *(nee nah-ray-rue)*

acknowledge 認める **mitomeru** *(me-toe-may-rue)*
▪ I acknowledge your wish (feelings). あなたの希望を認めます。**Anata no kibō wo mitomemasu.** *(ah-nah-tah no kee-boe oh me-toe-may-mahss.)*

acknowledge receipt of 受け取りを知らせる **uketori o shiraseru** *(uu-kay-toe-ree oh she-rah-say-rue)*

acquaintance 知り合い **shiriai** *(she-ree-aye)*
▪ He is an old acquaintance. あの人は古い知り合いです。**Anohito wa furui shiriai désu.** *(ah-no-ssh-toe wah fuu-rue-ee shi-ree-aye dess.)*

acquire 獲得する **kakutoku suru** *(kah-kuu-toe-kuu sue-ruu)*; 買収する **baishū suru** *(by-shuu sue-ruu)*

acquired rights 既得権 **kitoku ken** *(kee-toe-kuu ken)*

acquisition 取得 **shutoku** *(shuu-toe-kuu)*; 買収 **baishū** *(by-shuu)*
▪ This is a recent acquisition. これは最近取得したものです。**Kore wa saikin shutokushita mono désu.** *(koe-ray wah sie-keen shuu-toe-kuu ssh-tah moe-no dess.)*

acquisition cost 取得原価 **shutoku genka** *(shuu-toe-kuu gen-kah)*

acquit 免じる **menjiru** *(mane-jee-rue)*

acquittal 債務免除 **saimu menjo** *(sie-muu mane-joe)*

acronym 頭文字語 **kashira moji-go** *(kah-she-rah moe-jee-go)*

across-the-board settlement 全面的決着 **zenmen teki ketchaku** *(zen-men tay-kee kay-chah-kuu)*; 全面的な和解 **zenmen teki na wakai** *(zen-men tay-kee nah wah-kei)*

action plan 実行計画 **jikkō keikaku** *(jeek-koe kay-kah-kuu)*; 行動計画 **kōdō keikaku** *(kohh-dohh kay-kah-kuu)*

activate 動かす **ugokasu** *(uu-go-kah-sue)*
▪ When will you activate the factory? 工場をいつ稼働させますか。**Kōjō wo itsu kadōsasemasu ka?** *(koh-joh oh eet-sue kah-doe-sah-say-mahss kah?)*

active account 活動勘定 **katsudō kanjō** *(kah-t'sue-doe kahn-joe)*

active assets 生産資産 **seisan shisan** *(say-ee-sahn she-sahn)*

active debt 活動負債 **katsudō fusai** *(kah-t'sue-doe fuu-sigh)*; 利付き貸し付け **ritsuki kashitsuke** *(ree-t'sue-kee kah-she-t'sue-kay)*

active trust 積極信託 **sekkyoku shintaku** *(sake-k'yoe-kuu sheen-tah-kuu)*

activity chart 活動調査票 **katsudō chōsa hyō** *(kah-t'sue-doe choe-sah h'yoe)*

act of God 不可抗力 **fuka kōryoku** *(fuu-kah koe-rio-kuu)*

actual; real 現実(の) **genjitsu (no)** *(gane-jeet-sue noh)*

actual cash value 時価 **jika** *(jee-kah)*

actual cost 実際原価 **jissai genka** *(jeece-sigh gen-kah)*; 実費 **jippi** *(jee-pee)*

actual income 実収入 **jisshūnyū** *(jeesh-shune-yuu)*

actual liability 実質債務 **jisshitsu saimu** *(jees-sheet-sue sie-muu)*

actual market volume 実質市場取引高 **jissshitsu shijō torihiki daka** *(jees-sheet-sue she-johh toe-ree-he-kee dah-kah)*

actual total loss 現実全損 **genjitsu zenson** *(gane-jeet-sue zen-soan)*

adapt 適応させる **tekiō saseru** *(tay-kee-ohh sah-say-rue)*

adaptable 順応できる **jun'nō dekiru** *(june-nohh day-kee-rue)*

adaptation 適応 **tekiō** *(tay-kee-ohh)*

added cost コスト増 **kosuto zō** *(koe-stow zoe)*; 付加コスト **fuka cosuto** *(fuu-kah koe-stow)*

additional taxation 追徴課税 **tsuichō kazei** *(t'sue-ee-choe kah-zay)*

additives 添加物 **tenkabutsu** *(tane-kah-buut-sue)*
▪ Are there any additives in this? この中に添加物が入っていますか。**Kono naka ni tenkabutsu ga haitteimasu ka?** *(koe-no nah-kah nee tane-kah-buut-sue gah height-tay ee-mahss kah?)*

add-on sales 割賦販売 **kappu hanbai** *(kahp-puu hahn-buy)*

address 住所 **jūsho** *(juu-show)*

addressee 名宛人 **na-ate-nin** *(nah-ah-tay-neen)*; 受取人 **uketori nin** *(uu-kay-toe-ree-neen)*
▪ Are you the addressee? あなたは受取人ですか。**Anata wa uketori nin désu ka?** *(ah-nah-tah wah uu-kay-toe-ree-neen dess kah?)*

adequate 十分(な) **jūbun (na)** *(juu-boon nah)*
▪ Is that adequate? それは十分ですか。**Sore wa jūbun désu ka?** *(soe-ray way juu-boon dess kah?)*

adjusted CIF price 調整済運賃保険料込み値段 **chōsei zumi unchin hoken ryō komi nedan** *(choe-say zuu-me uun-cheen hoe-ken rio koe-me nay-dahn)*

adjusted earned income 調整済勤労所得 **chōsei zumi kinrō shotoku** *(choe-say zuu-me keen-roe show-toe-kuu)*

adjusted rate 調整率 **chōsei ritsu** *(chohh-say-ee reet-sue)*

adjustment 調節 **chōsetsu** *(chohh-sate-sue)*
▪ Let's make a small adjustment. 微調整しましょう。**Bi-chōsei shimashō.** *(bee chohh-say she-mah-show.)*

administer 管理する **kanri suru** *(kahn-ree sue-rue)*

administration 経営管理 **keiei kanri** *(kay-ee kahn-ree)*; 経営陣 **keiei jin** *(kay-ee jeen)*

administrative 管理上の **kanri jō no** *(kahn-ree joe no)*

administrative control 管理統制 **kanri tōsei** *(kahn-ree toe-say)*

administrative cost 管理費 **kanri hi** *(kahn-ree hee)*

administrative expense 一般管理費 **ippan kanri hi** *(eep-pahn kahn-ree he)*

administrative guidance 行政指導 **gyōsei shidō*** *(g'yoe-say she-doe)* *This term refers to guidelines and suggestions made by various government agencies and ministries to Japan's business world.

administrator 経営者 **keiei sha** *(kay-ee shah)*; 管理職 **kanrishoku** *(kahn-ree- show-kuu)*
▪ He is a skillful administrator. あの人は有能な管理職です。**Anohito wa yūnō na kanrishoku désu.** *(ah-no ssh-toe wah yuu-no nah kahn-ree-show-kuu dess.)*

admission 入場許可 **nyūjōkyoka** *(n'yuu-johh-k'yoe-kah)*; admission charge 入場料 **nyūjōryō** *(n'yuu-johh-rio)*

admit 受け入れる **ukeireru** *(uu-kay-ray-rue)*; confess 認める **mitomeru** *(me-toh-may-rue)*

admittance 入場 **nyūjō** *(nyuu-johh)*

admonish 注意する **chūi suru** *(chuu-ee sue-rue)*

advance 進歩する **shinpo suru** *(sheen-poh sue-rue)*; 前払い(金) **maebarai (kin)** *(my bah-rye (keen))*
▪ You must pay in advance. 前金で払わなければなりません。**Maekin de harawanakereba narimasen.** *(my-keen day hah-rah-wah-nah-kay-ray-bah nah-ree-mah-sen.)*
▪ I will pay in advance. 前金で払います。**Maekin de haraimasu.** *(my-keen day hah-rye-mahss.)*

advanced 進んだ **susunda** *(suu-suun-dah)*

advanced; forefront; leading edge 先端 **sentan** *(sane-tahn)*; 最近の **saikin no** *(sie-keen no)*

advanced country 先進国 **senshin koku** *(sen-sheen koe-kuu)*

advanced technology 先進技術 **senshin gijutsu** *(sen-sheen ghee-jute-sue)*; 先端技術 **sentan gijutsu** *(sen-tahn ghee-jute-sue)*

advance freight payment 前払運賃 **mae barai unchin** *(my-bah-rye uun-cheen)*

advancement 進歩 **shinpo** *(sheen-poh)*

advance notice 事前通知 **jizen tsūchi** *(jee-zay-n t'sue-chee)*; 予告 **yokoku** *(yoe-koe-kuu)*
▪ Please give two weeks' advance notice. 2週間前に予告してください。**Nishūkan mae ni yokoku shite kudasai.** *(nee-shuu-kahn my nee yoe-koe-kuu shtay kuu-dah-sigh.)*

advance payment 前金 **maekin** *(my-keen)*; 前払い金 **maebarai (kin)** *(my bah-rye keen)*; 先払い **saki barai** *(sah-kee bah-rye)*

advantage 利益 **rieki** *(ree-eh-kee)*; 有利 **yūri** *(yuu-ree)*; take advantage of 利用する **riyō suru** *(ree-yohh sue-rue)*
▪ This contract is definitely to your advantage. この契約はきっとあなたの利益になります。**Kono keiyaku wa kitto anata no rieki ni narimasu.** *(koe-no kay-yah-kuu wah kitoe ah-nah-tah no ree-eh-kee nee nah-ree-mahss.)*
▪ Let's take advantage of this occasion. この機会を利用しましょう。**Kono kikai wo riyō shimashō.** *(koe-no kee-kye oh ree-yohh she-mah-show.)*

advantageous 都合がいい **tsugō ga ii** *(t'sue-gohh gah eee)*

adversary; rival 競争相手 **kyōsōaite** *(k'yohh-sohh-aye-tay)*; ライバル **raibaru** *(rah-ee-bah-rue)*
▪ That company is a strong rival. その会社は手強い競争相手です。**Sono kaisha wa tegowai kyōsōaite désu.** *(soe-no kie-shah wah tay-go-wah-ee k'yohh-sohh-aye-tay dess.)*

adverse; against 反対(の) **hantai (no)** *(hahn-tie)*
▪ I am against that idea. 私はその考えには反対です。**Watakushi wa sono kangae ni wa hantai désu.** *(wah-tak-she wah soe-no kahn-guy ni wah hahn-tie dess.)*

adverse import balance 輸入超過 **yunyū chōka** *(yuun-yuu choe-kah)*

adversity 逆境 **gyakkyō** *(g'yahk-k'yohh)*

advertise 広告(を)する **kōkoku (wo) suru** *(koe-koe-kuu oh sue-rue)*; place an ad 広告を出す **kōkoku wo dasu** *(koe-koe-kuu oh dah-sue)*

advertisement (request) for bid 入札広告 **nyūsatsu kōkoku** *(nyuu-sah-t'sue koe-koe-kuu)*

advertising; advertisement 広告 **kōkoku** *(koe-koe-kuu)*
▪ Please put this ad in the Sunday paper. この広告を日曜日の新聞に出してください。**Kono kōkoku wo nichiyōbi no shinbun ni dashite kudasai.** *(koe-no koe-koe-kuu oh nee-chee-yoe-bee no sheem-boon nee dah-shtay kuu-dah-sigh.)*
▪ How much will the advertisement cost? 広告はいくらしますか。**Kōkoku wa ikura shimasu ka?** *(koe-koe-kuu wah ee-kuu-rah she-mahss kah?)*

advertising agency 広告代理店 **kōkoku dairiten** *(koe-koe-kuu dye-ree-ten)*

advertising budget 広告予算 **kōkoku hi yosan** *(koe-koe-kuu he yoe-sahn)*

advertising campaign 広告キャンペーン **kōkoku kyanpēn** *(koe-koe-kuu k'yah-n-pay-ee-n)*

advertising drive 宣伝売込 **senden urikomi** *(sen-den uu-ree-koe-me)*

advertising expenses 広告宣伝費 **kōkoku senden hi** *(koe-koe-kuu sayn-dayn he)*

advertising manager 広告部長 **kōkoku buchō** *(koe-koe-kuu buu-choe)*; 宣伝部長 **senden buchō** (*sayn-dayn buu-choe)*

advertising media 広告媒体 **kōkoku baitai** *(koe-koe-kuu by-tie)*; 広告メディア **kōkoku media** *(koe-koe-kuu may-dee-ah)*

advertising rate 広告料 **kōkoku ryō** *(koe-koe-kuu rio)*
▪ What is the advertising rate for one page? 1ページの広告料はいくらですか。**Ichi pēji no kōkoku ryō wa ikura désu ka?** *(ee-chee pay-jee no koe-koe-kuu rio wah ee-kuu-rah dess kah?)*

advertising research 広告調査 **kōkoku chōsa** *(koe-koe-kuu choe-sah)*

advisable 望ましい **nozomashii** *(noh-zoh-mah-she-ee)*

advise アドバイス **adobaisu** *(ah-doh-by-suu)*
▪ Thank you very much for the advice. アドバイスをどうもありがとうございます。**Adobaisu wo dōmo arigato gozaimasu.** *(ah-doh-by-suu oh dohh-moe ah-ree-gah-toe go-zie-mahss.)*

adviser; advisor カウンセラー **kaunserā** *(coun-say-rahh)*

adviser; advisor (consultant) 相談相手 **sōdan-aite** *(so-dahn-eye-tay)*; coun-

selor 相談役 **sōdan-yaku** *(so-dahn-yah-kuu)*; legal advisor 法律顧問 **hōritsu komon** *(hoe-ree-t'sue koe-moan)*; アドバイザー **adobaizā** *(ad-by-zah)*
▪ I will introduce you to our company adviser. 当社の相談役をご紹介します。**Tōsha no sōdan-yaku wo go-shōkai shimasu.** *(toe-shah no so-dahn-yah-kuu oh go-show-kye she-mahss.)*

advisory committee 諮問委員会 **shimon iinkai** *(she-moan ee-een kye)*
▪ The advisory committee is meeting tomorrow at ten. 諮問委員会は、明日十時からです。**Shimon iinkai wa asu jū ji kara désu.** *(she-moan ee-een kye wah ah-sue juu jee kah-rah dess.)*

advisory council 諮問機関 **shimon kikan** *(she-moan kee-kahn)*; 審議会 **shingi kai** *(sheen-ghee kye)*

advocate 支持者 **shijisha** *(she-jee-shah)*

aerial; antenna アンテナ **antena** *(ahn-tay-nah)*

aesthetics 美学 **bigaku** *(bee-gah-kuu)*
▪ Aesthetics is very important in Japanese culture. 美学は日本の文化にとって大変重要なものです。**Bigaku wa Nihon no bunka ni totte taihen jūyō na mono désu.** *(bee-gah-kuu wah nee-hone no boon-kah nee toe-tay tie-hane juu-yoe nah moe-no dess.)*

affect; influence 影響する **eikyō suru** *(eh-ee-k'yohh sue-rue)*
▪ That will have no affect. それは影響しません。**Sore wa eikyō shimasen.** *(soe-ray wah eh-ee-k'yohh she-mah-sin.)*

affidavit 宣誓供述書 **sensei kyōjutsu sho** *(sen-say k'yoe-jute-sue show)*

affiliate 系列会社 **keiretsu gaisha** *(kay-rate-sue guy-shah)*; 関連会社 **kanren gaisha** *(kahn-rayn guy-shah)*

affiliated company 系列会社 **keiretsu gaisha** *(kay-rate-sue guy-shah)*
▪ Do you have any affiliated companies in the U.S.? アメリカに系列会社がありますか。**Amerika ni keiretsu gaisha ga arimasu ka?** *(ah-may-ree-kah nee kay-rate-sue guy-shah gah ah-ree-mahss kah?)*

affiliation 提携 **teikei** *(tay-kay)*; 関係 **kankei** *(kahn-kay)*

affirm; confirm 確立する **kakuritsu suru** *(kah-kuu-ree-t'sue sue-rue)*; 確認する **kakunin suru** *(kah-kuu-neen sue-rue)*

affluent; wealthy 裕福な **yūfuku na** *(yuuu-fuu-kuu nah)*

afford お金がある **okane ga aru** *(oh-kah-nay gah ah-rue)*; 余裕がある **yoyū ga aru** *(yoe-yuu gah ah-rue)*

after-hours trading 時間外取引 **jikan gai torihiki** *(jee-kahn guy toe-ree-he-kee)*

after-sale service アフターサービス **afutā sābisu** *(ah-fuu-tah sah-be-sue)*
▪ After-sale service is very important to customers. お客さんへのアフターサービスは大切です。**O-kyakusan e no afutā sābisu wa taisetsu désu.** *(o-kyack-sahn eh no ahf-tah sah-bee-sue wah tie-say-t'sue dess.)*

after-tax income 税引後所得 **zeibiki go shotoku** *(zay-bee-kee go show-toe-kuu)*

after-tax loss 税引後損失 **zeibiki go sonshitsu** *(zay-bee-kee go soan-sheet-sue)*

after-tax profit 税引後利益 **zeibiki go rieki** *(zay-bee-kee go ree-eh-kee)*

after-tax real rate of return 税引後利益率 **zeibiki go rieki ritsu** *(zay-bee-kee go ree-ay-kee ree-t'sue)*; 実質収益

率 **jisshitsu shūeki ritsu** *(jeesh-sheet-sue shuu-ay-kee ree-t'sue)*

against 反対する **hantai suru** *(hahn-tie)*; 反 **han** *(hahn)*
▪ I am against it. 反対です。**Hantai désu.** *(hahn-tie dess.)*

against all risks (insurance) 全危険担保で **zen kiken tanpo de** *(zen kee-ken tahn-poe day)*

agency (government) (行政)機関 **(gyosei) kikan** *((g'yoe-say) kee-kahn)*

agency fee 代理店手数料 **dairi ten tesūryō** *(dye-ree-ten tay-sue-rio)*

agenda 協議事項 **kyōgi jikō** *(k'yoe-ghee jee-koe)*

agent; agency (company) 代理店 **dairiten** *(dye-ree-ten)*

agent (person) 代理人 **dairinin** *(dye-ree-neen)*

aging population 高齢化 **kōrei ka** *(koe-ray kah)*
▪ The aging population is a serious problem for any developed country. 先進国では、高齢化が深刻な問題です。**Senshin koku de wa kōrei-ka ga shinkoku na mondai désu.** *(sane-sheen koh-kuu day wah kohh-ray-e kah gah sheen-koh-kuu na mone-die dess.)*

aging society and declining birth-rate 少子高齢化(問題) **shoshi kōrei-ka (mondai)** *(show-she koe-ray kah moan-dye)*

agree 賛成する **sansei suru** *(sahn-say sue-rue)*; 同意する **dōi suru** *(doe-ee sue-rue)*
▪ I cannot agree to that. それには賛成できません。**Sore ni wa sansei dekimasen.** *(so-ray nee wah sahn-say day-kee-mah-sen.)*

agreement; treaty 協定 **kyōtei** *(k'yoe-tay)*; commercial agreement 商業協定 **shōgyō kyōtei** *(show-g'yoe k'yoe-tay)*; contract 契約(書) **keiyaku (sho)** *(kay-yah-kuu show)*
▪ I have reached an agreement with Shinwa Bōeki. 進和貿易との契約が成立しました。**Shinwa Bōeki to no keiyaku ga seiritsu shimashita.** *(sheen-wah boe-eh-kee toe kay-yah-kuu gah say-ree-t'sue she-mahsh-tah.)*

agricultural land 農地 **nōchi** *(no-chee)*
▪ Agricultural land in Japan is rapidly decreasing. 日本の農地は急速に減少しています。**Nihon no nōchi wa kyūsoku ni genshōshite imasu.** *(nee-hone no no-chee wah cue-so-kuu nee gayn-show-shtay-mahss.)*

agricultural products 農産物 **nōsanbutsu** *(no-sahn-boot-sue)*

agriculture 農業 **nōgyō** *(no-g'yoe)*
▪ Agriculture is an important industry in Japan. 農業は日本で重要な産業です。**Nōgyō wa Nihon de jūyō na sangyō désu.** *(no-g'yoh wah Nee-hone day juu-yoh nah sahn-g'yoh dess.)*

agriculture and forestry 農林 **nōrin** *(no-reen)*

aid; assistance 援助 **enjo** *(en-joe)*; 世話 **sewa** *(say-wah)*; to aid 援助する **enjo suru** *(en-joe sue-rue)*

aim; purpose; goal 目的 **mokuteki** *(moh-kuu-tay-kee)*
▪ Please explain your aim. 意図を説明してください。**Ito wo setsumei shite kudasai.** *(ee-toe oh sate-sue-may-ee kuu-dah-sie.)*

air 空気 **kūki** *(kuuu-kee)*; in the open air 外で/に **soto de/ni** *(soh-toh day/nee)*
▪ The air in here smells bad. ここの空

気はひどいにおいがする。**Koko no kūki wa hidoi nioi ga suru.** *(koe-koe no kuu-kee wah he-doe-ee nee-oh-ee ga sue-rue.)*

airbase 空軍基地 **kūgunkichi** *(kuuu-goon-kee-chee)*

air-conditioned 冷暖房付 **reidanbō tsuki** *(ray-e-dahn-bohh ski)*

air-conditioner エアコン **eakon** *(eh-ah-kone)*
▪ Please turn on the air-conditioner. エアコンをつけてください。**Eakon wo tsukete kudasai.** *(eh-ah-kone oh skate-tay kuu-dah-sie.)*

air conditioner for auto カーエアコン **kā eakon** *(kah ay-ah-cone)*

aircraft 飛行機 **hikōki** *(hee-kohh-kee)*

aircraft carrier 航空母艦 **kōkūbokan** *(kohh-kuu-boh-kahn)*

air express 航空速達便 **kōkū sokutatsu bin** *(koe-kuu so-kuu-tah-t'sue bean)*

airforce 空軍 **kūgun** *(kuu-goon)*

air freight 航空貨物輸送 **kōkū kamotsu yusō** *(koe-kuu kah-moe-t'sue yuu-so)*

airline(s) 航空 **kōkū** *(kohh-kuuu)*

airline company 航空会社 **kōkū gaisha** *(kohh-kuuu guy-shah)*

airmail エアメール **ea mēru** *(a-ah may-rue)*; 航空便 **kōkū bin** *(koe-kuu bean)*
▪ Please send it by airmail. エアメールで送ってください。**Ea mēru de okutte kudasai.** *(ay-ah may-rue day oh-coot-tay kuu-dah-sigh.)*

airport 空港 **kūkō** *(kuu-koe)*

air shipment 空輸 **kūyu** *(kuu-yuu)*

a la carte 一品料理 **ippin ryōri** *(eep-peen rio-ree)*; full course フルコース **furu kōsu** *(fuu-rue koe-sue)*
▪ I will order a la carte. アラカルトを注文します。**Arakaruto wo chūmon shimasu.** *(ah-rah-kah-rue-toh oh chuu-moan she-mahss.)*
▪ I'll take the full course. フルコースにします。**Furu kōsu ni shimasu.** *(fuu-rue koe-sue nee she-mahss.)*

alcohol アルコール **arukōru** *(ah-ruu-kohh-rue)*

alien (person); **foreigner** 外国人 **gaikokujin** *(guy-koh-kuu-jeen)*

align; alignment 並べる **naraberu** *(nah-rah-bay-rue)*

alike 似た **nita** *(nee-tah)*; 似ている **niteiru** *(nee-tay-ee-rue)*
▪ These two products really look alike. この二つの品物はよく似ています。**Kono futatsu no shinamono wa yoku nite-imasu.** *(koe-no fu-tot-sue no she-nah-moe-no wah yoh-kuu nee-tay ee-mahss.)*

all; entire 全部 **zenbu**; すべて **subete** *(zem-buu)*
▪ Is this all? これで全部ですか?**Kore de zenbu désu ka?** *(koe-ray day zem-buu dess kah?)*

allegation 断言 **dangen** *(dahn-gane)*

allege 断言する **dangen suru** *(dahn-gane sue-rue)*

allegiance; loyalty 忠誠 **chūsei** *(chuu-say-e)*

allergic アレルギーがある **arerugii ga aru** *(ah-ray-rue-ghee gah ah-rue)*
▪ I am allergic to shrimp. エビにアレルギーがあります。**Ebi ni arerugii ga arimasu.** *(eh-bee nee ah-ray-rue-ghee gah ah-ree-mahss.)*

alliance 同盟 **dōmei** *(dohh-may-e)*; 提携 **teikei** *(tay-kay)*

alliance; affiliation; participation 加盟 **kamei** *(kah-may-e)*

all in cost 総費用 **sō hiyō** *(sohh he-yohh)*

allocate 割り当てる **wariateru** *(wah-ree-ah-tay-rue)*

allocation of responsibilities 責任分担 **sekinin buntan** *(say-kee-neen boon-tahn)*

allot; distribute 分配する **bunpai suru** *(boon-pie sue-rue)*; 配給する **haikyū suru** *(hie-cue sue-rue)*

allotment; quota 割り当て **wariate** *(wah-ree-ah-tay)*
▪ I have already used up my allotment. 割り当てをもう使ってしまいした。**Wariate wo mō tsukatte shimaimashita.** *(wah-ree-ah-tay oh moe scot-tay she-my-mahsh-tah.)*

allowance (finance) 引当金 **hikiate kin** *(he-kee-ah-tay keen)*

allowance; discount (sales) 割引 **waribiki** *(wah-ree-bee-kee)*

allowance (money) 費用 **hiyō** *(he-yohh)*

allowances (additional pay) 手当 **teate** *(tay-ah-tay)*; allowance for dependent 扶養手当 **fuyō teate** *(fuu-yoe tay-ah-tay)*; cost-of-living allowance 生活費手当 **seikatsu hi teate** *(say-kah-t'sue hee tay-ah-tay)*; transportation allowance 交通費 **kōtsū hi** *(koe-t'sue-he)*; retirement allowance 退職手当 **taishoku teate** *(tie-show-kuu tay-ah-tay)*; end-of-year allowance 年末手当 **nenmatsu teate** *(nane-mot-sue tay-ah-tay)*; supervisory position allowance 管理職手当 **kanri shoku teate** *(kahn-ree show-kuu tay-ah-tay)*

alloy 合金 **gōkin** *(gohh-keen)*

ally (nation) 同盟国 **dōmeikoku** *(dohh-may-e-koh-kuu)*

alteration; change 変更 **henkō** *(hen-koe)*

alternate 交互の **kōgo (no)** *(kohh-go (no))*

alternating current; AC 交流 **kōryū** *(koe-r'yuu)*

alternative; another one 代わり(の) **kawari (no)** *(kah-wah-ree (no))*

altitude 高度 **kōdo** *(koh-doe)*; 高さ **takasa** *(tah-kah-sah)*

aluminum アルミ **arumi** *(ah-rue-me)*

alumna (female) 女子卒業生 **joshi-sotsugyōsei** *(joh-she-soat-sue-g'yohh-say-ee)*

alumni 卒業生 **sotsugyōsei** *(soat-sue-g'yohh-say-ee)*

alumnus (male) 男子卒業生 **danshi-sotsugyōsei** *(dahn-she-soat-sue-g'yohh-say-ee)*

a.m. 午前 **gozen** *(go-zane)*
▪ Please come at 10 a.m. 午前十時に来てください。**Gozen jūji ni kite kudasai.** *(go-zane no juu-jee nee kee-tay kuu-dah-sie.)*

amateur アマチュア **amachua** *(ah-mah-chu-ah)*; 素人 **shirōto** *(she-roh-toe)*

amazing 驚くべき **odoroku beki** *(oh-doh-roh-kuu bay-kee)*

ambassador 大使 **taishi** *(tie-she)*

ambiguous 曖昧(な) **aimai (na)** *(aye-my (nah))*
▪ His conversation is always ambiguous. あの人の会話はいつも曖昧です。**Anohito no kaiwa wa itsumo aimai désu.** *(ah-no-ssh-toe no kie-wah wah eet-sue-moe aye-my dess.)*

ambition 野心 **yashin** *(yah-sheen)*
▪ We are looking for people who have ambition. 私達はやる気がある人

を捜しています。**Watakushi-tachi wa yaruki ga aru hito wo sagashite-imasu.** *(wah-tak-she-tah-chee wah yah-rue-kee gah ah-rue ssh-toe oh sah-gah-shtay-mahss.)*

ambitious 野心的(な) **yashin-teki (na)** *(yah-sheen-tay-kee (na))*

ambulance 救急車 **kyūkyūsha** *(que-que-shah)*
▪ Hurry! Please call an ambulance! 早く! 救急車を呼んでください! **Hayaku! Kyūkyūsha wo yonde kudasai!** *(hah-yah-kuu! que-que-shah oh yoan-day kuu-dah-sie!)*

amend; alter 変更する **henkō suru** *(hen-koe sue-rue)*; 改正する **kaisei suru** *(kie-say sue-rue)*
▪ I would like to amend this agreement. この協定を改正したいです。**Kono kyōtei wo kaisei shitai désu.** *(koe-no k'yoe-tay oh kie-say she-tie dess.)*

amendment; revision 修正 **shūsei** *(shuu-say)*; 改正 **kaisei** *(kie-say)*
▪ I would like to have an amendment added to the agreement. 協定に修正を付け加えていただきたいです。**Kyōtei ni shūsei wo tsukekuwaete itadakitai désu.** *(k'yoe-tay nee shuu-say oh t'sue-kay-kuu-why-tay ee-tah-dah-kee-tie dess.)*

America アメリカ **Amerika** *(ah-may-ree-kah)*

American アメリカ人 **Amerikajin** *(ah-may-ree-kah-jeen)*

American Club アメリカンクラブ **Amerikan Kurabu** *(ah-may-ree-kahn kuu-rah-buu)*

American Embassy アメリカ大使館 **Amerika Taishikan** *(ah-may-ree-kah tie-she-kahn)*

amortization; depreciation 割賦償却 **kappu shōkyaku** *(kah-puu show-kahn)*; 償却 **shōkyaku** *(shohh-k'yah-kuu)*

amount 総額 **sōgaku** *(so-gah-kuu)*

amount due 満期支払高 **manki shiharai daka** *(mahn-kee she-hah-rye dah-kah)*

amplifier 増幅器 **zōfuku ki** *(zoe-fuu-kuu kee)*; アンプ **anpu** *(ahn-puu)*

analysis 分析 **bunseki** *(boon-say-kee)*
▪ I would like to hear the sales analysis at our next conference. 次の会議で売上分析を聞きたいと思います。**Tsugi no kaigi de uriage no bunseki wo kikitai to omoimasu.** *(t'sue-ghee no kie-ghee day uu-ree-ah-gay no boon-say-kee oh kee-kee-tie toh oh-moy-mahss.)*

analysis (of a competitor) 競合者分析 **kyōgō sha bunseki** *(k'yoe-go shah boon-say-kee)*

analysis, cost (cost analysis) 原価分析 **genka bunseki** *(gen-kah boon-say-kee)*

analysis, financial (financial analysis) 財務分析 **zaimu bunseki** *(zye-muu boon-say-kee)*

analysis, product (product analysis) 製品分析 **seihin bunseki** *(say-heen boon-say-kee)*

analysis, sales (sales analysis) 販売分析 **hanbai bunseki** *(hahn-by boon-say-kee)*

analysis, system (system analysis) システム分析 **shisutemu bunseki** *(she-stay-muu boon-say-kee)*

analyst 分析専門家 **bunseki senmon-ka** *(boon-say-kee sem-moan-kah)*; 解説者 **kaisetsu-sha** *(kye-sate-sue-shah)*

analytical 分析的 **bunseki-teki** *(boon-say-kee-tay-kee)*

analyze 分析する **bunseki suru** *(boon-say-kee sue-rue)*

animated 生き生きした **iki-iki shita** *(ee-kee-ee-kee ssh-tah)*

animation アニメーション **animēshon** *(ah-nee-may-shone)*; アニメ **anime** *(ah-nee-may)*
▪ Yesterday I (we) went to an animation studio. 昨日、アニメスタジオに行きました。**Kinō anime sutajio ni ikimashita.** *(kee-nohh ah-nee-may suu-tah-jee-oh nee ee-kee-mah-ssh-tah.)*

annex (building) アネックス **anekkusu** *(ah-neck-sue)*; 別館 **bekkan** *(bake-kahn)*

anniversary 記念日 **kinenbi** *(kee-nane-bee)*
▪ Today is our company anniversary. 今日は、当社の創立記念日です。**Kyō wa tōsha no sōritsu kinenbi désu.** *(k'yohh wah toe-shah no so-ree-t'sue kee-nane-bee dess.)*

announce 公表する **kōhyō suru** *(koh-h'yoh sue-rue)*; 発表する **happyō suru** (*hop-p'yoe sue-rue)*

announcement (communique) 発表 **happyō** *(hop-p'yoe)*; statement 声明 **seimei** *(say-may)*; notice 通告 **tsūkoku** *(t'sue-koe-kuu)*
▪ I will make an announcement tomorrow. 明日、発表をします。**Ashita happyō wo shimasu.** *(ah-shtah hop-p'yoe oh she-mahss.)*

annual (per year) 年1回の **nen ikkai no** *(nen-ee-kye no)*; 年刊 **nenkan** *(nen-kahn)*

annual accounts 年次決算報告 **nenji kessan hōkoku** *(nen-jee case-sahn hoe-koe-kuu)*

annual audit 年次会計監査 **nenji kaikei kansa** *(nen-jee kye-kay kan-sah)*

annual expenditures 年次歳出 **nenji saishutsu** *(nen-jee sigh-shoot-sue)*

annual income 年収 **nenshū** *(nen shuu)*

annually 年1回 **nen ikkai** *(nen-ee-kye)*; 毎年 **maitoshi** *(my-toe-she)*
▪ The association publishes the results annually. 協会は、毎年結果を出版します。**Kyōkai wa maitoshi kekka wo shuppan shimasu.** *(k'yoe-kye wah my-toe-she kay-kah oh shuu-pahn she-mahss.)*

annual report 年次報告書 **nenji hōkokusho** *(nen-jee hoe-koe-kuu-show)*

annuity 年金 **nenkin** *(nen-keen)*

antenna アンテナ **antena** *(ahn-tay-nah)*

anti-; against 反 **han-** *(hahn)*

anti-depression cartel 不況防止カルテル **fukyō bōshi karuteru** *(fuu-k'yoe boe-she kah-rue-tay-rue)*

antitrust laws 独占禁止法 **dokusen kinshi hō** *(doke-sen keen-she hoe)*

apartment アパート **apāto** *(ah-pah-toe)*

apartment complex (building for ordinary workers) 団地 **danchi** *(dahn-chee)*

apartment in deluxe condo style マンション **manshon** *(mahn-shone)*

apologize 謝る **ayamaru** *(ah-yah-mah-rue)*; 詫びる **wabiru** *(wah-bee-rue)*; 許す **yurusu** *(yuu-rue-sue)*
▪ I apologize (I have no excuse). 申し訳ありません。**Mōshiwake arimasen.** *(moe-she-wah-kay ah-ree-mah-sen.)*
▪ I must apologize to you. 私はあなたに謝らなければなりません。**Watashi wa anata ni ayamaranakereba narimasen.** *(wah-tah-she wah ah-nah-tah nee ah-yah-mah-rah-nah-kay-ray-bah nah-ree-mah-sen.)*

apology 申し訳 **mōshiwake** *(moe-she-wah-kay)*; お詫び **o-wabi** *(oh-wah-bee)*
▪ I owe you an apology. あなたにお詫びをしなければなりません。**Anata ni o-wabi wo shinakereba narimasen.** *(ah-nah-tah nee oh-wah-bee oh she-nah-kay-ray-bah nah-ree-mah-sen.)*
▪ Please accept my apologies. どうぞお許しください。**Dōzo, o-yurushi kudasai.** *(doe-zoe oh-yuu-rue-she kuu-dah-sigh.)*

apparel 服 **fuku** *(fuu-kuu)*

appeal 訴え **uttae** *(uut-tie)*

applause 喝采 **kassai** *(kahss-sigh)*; 拍手 **hakushu** (hah-kuu-shuu)

applicant 志願者 **shigansha** *(she-gahn-shah)*
▪ Have all of the applicants arrived? 志願者は全員到着しましたか。**Shigan-sha wa zenin tōchaku shimashita ka?** *(she-gahn-shah wa zen-een tohh-chah-kuu she-mahsh-tah kah?)*

application form 申込書 **mōshikomi sho** *(moe-she-koe-me show)*; 申請書 **shinsei sho** *(sheen-say show)*

apply for; application 申し込む **mōshikomu** *(moe-she-koe-muu)*
▪ Please apply at that office. あの事務所へ申し込んでください。**Ano jimusho e mōshikonde kudasai.** *(ah-no jeem-show eh moe-she-kone-day kuu-dah-sigh.)*

appointment 約束 **yakusoku** *(yah-kuu-so-kuu)*

appraisal 評価 **hyōka** *(h'yoe-kah)*

appraise 評価する **hyōka suru** *(h'yohh-kah sue-rue)*

appreciation (rise in value) 騰貴 **tōki** *(toe-kee)*; 高騰 **kōtō** *(koe-toe)*

apprentice 見習い **minarai** *(me-nah-rye)*; 弟子 **deshi** *(day-she)*

approval 認可 **ninka** *(neen-kah)*; 許可 **kyoka** *(k'yoe-kah)*

approve 賛成する **sansei suru** *(sahn-say sue-rue)*
▪ I approve. 賛成します。**Sansei shimasu.** *(sahn-say she-mahss.)*
▪ Do you approve? 賛成しますか。**Sansei shimasu ka?** (*sahn-say-ee she-mahss kah?)*

approved delivery facility 承認済引渡し施設 **shōnin zumi hikiwatashi shisetsu** *(show-neen zuu-me he-kee-wah-tah-she she-say-t'sue)*

approximate だいたい **daitai** *(die-tie)*

aptitude 傾向 **keikō** *(kay-ee-kohh)*

arbiter 仲裁者 **chūsaisha** *(chuu-sie-shah)*

arbitrate 調停する **chōtei suru** *(chohh-tay-ee sue-rue)*; 仲裁する **chūsai suru** *(chew-sigh sue-rue)*
▪ Please arbitrate in this dispute. この紛争を仲裁してください。**Kono funsō wo chūsai shite kudasai.** (*koh-no fuun-sohh oh chuu-sie ssh-tay kuu-dah-sie.)*

arbitration (mediation) 調停 **chōtei** *(choe-tay)*

arbitration agreement 仲裁協定 **chūsai kyōtei** *(chew-sigh k'yoe-tay)*; 調停同意書 **chōtei dōi sho** *(doe-ee show)*

arbitrator 仲裁者 **chūsai-sha** *(chew-sign-shah)*; 調停人 **chōteinin** *(chohh-tay-ee-neen)*

arcade (shopping) アーケード **ākēdo** *(ahh-kay-doe)*; 商店街 **shōtengai** *(show-ten-guy)*
▪ Does the hotel have an arcade? ホテルにアーケードがありますか。**Hotéru ni ākēdo ga arimasu ka?** *(hoh-tay-rue*

nee ahh-kay-doh gah ah-ree-mahss kah?)

architect 建築家 **kenchikuka** *(kane-chee-kuu-kah)*

architecture 建築学 **kenchikugaku** *(kane-chee-kuu-gah-kuu)*

archives 記録 **kiroku** *(kee-roe-kuu)*

Arctic 北極 **Hokkyoku** *(hoke-yoh-kuu)*

area; region; zone 地域 **chiiki** *(chee-ee-kee)*
▪ Are there any factories in that area? その地域に工場がありますか。**Sono chiiki ni kōjō ga arimasu ka?** *(so-no chee-ee-kee nee koe-joh gah ah-ree-mahss kah?)*

area code 市外局番 **shigai kyokuban** *(she-guy-k'yoh-kuu-bahn)*
▪ What is your area code? あなたの市外局番は何番ですか。**Anato no shigai kyokuban wa nanban désu ka?** *(ah-nah-tah no she-guy-k'yoh-kuu-bahn wa nahn-bahn dess kah?)*

area manager 地域担当責任者 **chiiki tantō sekininsha** *(chee-ee-kee tahn-toe say-kee-neen shah)*

argue 言い争う **ii-arasou** *(ee-ah-rah-so)*
▪ I do not want to argue about the price. 価格の事でもめるのは避けたいです。**Kakaku no koto de momeru no wa saketai désu.** *(kah-kah-kuu no koe-toe day moe-may-rue no wah sah-kay-tie dess.)*

argument 議論 **giron** *(ghee-roan)*
▪ An argument started. 議論が始まりました。**Giron ga hajimarimashita.** *(ghee-roan gah hah-jee-mah-ree-mahsh-tah.)*

arid 乾いた **kawaita** *(kah-wie-tah)*

armed forces 軍(隊) **gun(tai)** *(goon-tie)*

arm's length 対等な **taito na** *(tie-toe nah)*; 距離を置いた **kyori wo oita** *(k'yoe-ree oh oh-ee-tah)*

arrange 手配する **tehai suru** *(tay-high sue-rue)*
▪ I'll arrange it. 手配します。**Tehai shimasu.** *(tay-high she-mahss)*
▪ Can you arrange for a car? 車を手配できますか。**Kuruma wo tehai dekimasu ka?** *(kuu-rue-mah oh tay-high day-kee-mahss kah?)*

arrangement 手配 **tehai** *(tay-high)*; 準備 **junbi** *(juum-bee)*
▪ Arrangements have been completed. 手配は完了しています。**Tehai wa kanryō shiteimasu.** *(tah-high wah kahn-rio shtay-mahss.)*
▪ Have you finished the arrangements? 手配は終わりましたか。**Tehai wa owarimashita ka?** *(tay-high wah oh-wah-ree-mahsh-tah kah?)*

arrears 滞納金 **tainō kin** *(tie-noh keen)*

arrest 逮捕する **taiho suru** *(tie-hoh sue-rue)*

arrival (at airport or station) 到着 **tōchaku** *(tohh-chah-kuu)*
▪ My arrival time is 2 p.m. 到着時刻は午後2時です。**Tōchaku jikoku wa gogo niji désu.** *(tohh-chah-kuu jee-koe-kuu wa go-go nee-jee dess.)*

arrival gate 到着口 **tōchaku guchi** *(toe-chah-kuu guu-chee)*
▪ What is the number of his arrival gate? 到着口は何番ですか。**Tōchaku guchi wa nanban désu ka?** *(kah-ray no toe-chah-kuu guu-chee wah nahn-bahn dess kah?)*

arrive 着く **tsuku** *(t'sue-kuu)*
▪ What time will you arrive? 何時に着きますか。**Nanji ni tsukimasu ka?** *(nah-jee nee t'sue-kee-mahss kah?)*

arrive safely (goods) 安着する **anchaku suru** *(ahn-chah-kuu sue-rue)*
▪ The goods arrived safely. 品物は安着しました。**Shinamono wa anchaku shimashita.** *(she-nah-moe-no wah ahn-chah-kuu she-mahsh-tah.)*

arriving passengers 到着客 **tōchaku kyaku** *(toe-chah-kuu k'yah-kuu)*

article (newspaper) 記事 **kiji** *(kee-jee)*

articles of the association (for formation of a company) 定款 **teikan** *(tay-kahn)*

artificial (man-made) 人工(の) **jinkō (no)** *(jeen-kohh (no))*; 偽物 **nisemono** *(nee-say-moe-no)*

artist アーチスト **āchisuto** *(ahh-chees-toe)*; 芸術家 **geijutsuka** *(gay-e-juut-sue-kah)*

artistic 芸術的 **geijutsu-teki** *(gay-e-juut-sue-tay-kee)*

asking price 言い値 **iine** *(ee-nay)*

aspect 面 **men** *(mane)*; 側面 **sokumen** *(soh-kuu-mane)*
▪ There are several aspects to the case. 事件にはいろいろな側面がありま す。**Jiken ni wa iro iro na sokumen ga arimasu.** *(jee-kane nee wah ee-roh ee-roh no soh-kuu-mane gah ah-ree-mahss.)*

assay 分析 **bunseki** *(boon-say-kee)*

assemble (a product) 組み立てる **kumitateru** *(kuu-me-tah-tay-rue)*
▪ Please assemble this radio. このラジオを組み立ててください。**Kono rajio wo kumitatete kudasai.** *(koe-noe rah-jee-oh oh kuu-me-tay-tay kuu-dah-sigh.)*

assembly factory 組立工場 **kumitate kōjō** *(kuu-me-tah-tay koe-joe)*

assembly line 流れ作業 **nagare sagyō** *(nah-gah-ray sah-g'yoe)*; 組み立てライン **kumitate rain** *(kuu-me-tah-tay rine)*

assembly operation 組立作業 **kumitate sagyō** *(kuu-me-tah-tay sah-g'yoe)*

assessment 評価 **hyōka** *(h'yoe-kah)*; 査定 **satei** *(sah-tay)*

asset 資産 **shisan** *(she-sahn)*; 財産 **zaisan** *(zye-sahn)*

asset management 資産管理 **shisan kanri** *(she-sahn kahn-ree)*; 資産運用 **shisan unyō** *(she-sahn uun-yoe)*

assets, fixed (fixed assets) 固定資産 **kotei shisan** *(koe-tay she-sahn)*

assets, intangible (intangible assets) 無形資産 **mukei shisan** *(muu-kay she-sahn)*

assets, liquid (liquid assets) 流動資産 **ryūdō shisan** *(ree-yuu-doe she-sahn)*

assets, net (net assets) 純資産 **jun shisan** *(june she-sahn)*

assets, tangible (tangible assets) 有形資産 **yūkei shisan** *(yuu-kay she-sahn)*

assign 割り当てる **wariateru** *(wah-ree-ah-tay-rue)*

assignment (job) 任務 **ninmu** *(neen-muu)*; 職務 **shokumu** *(show-kuu muu)*

assimilate とけ込む **tokekomu** *(toe-kay-koe-muu)*

assist; help 助ける **tasukeru** *(tahss-kay-rue)*; 援助する **enjo suru** *(en-joe sue-rue)*
▪ Can you assist the developing country? 発展途上国に援助することができますか。**Hatten tojo koku ni enjo suru koto ga dekimasu ka?** *(haht-tane toh-joh koh-kuu nee enn-joh sue-rue koh-toh gah day-kee-mahss kah?)*

assistance; aid 援助 **enjo** *(en-joe)*
▪ I really appreciate your assistance. あなたの援助を本当に感謝します。 **Anata no enjo wo hontō ni kansha shimasu.** *(ah-nah-tah no en-joe oh hone-toe nee kahn-shah she-mahss.)*

assistant 助手 **joshu** *(joe-shuu)*; アシスタント **ashisutanto** *(ah-shees-tahn-toe)*

assistant general manager 副総支配人 **fuku sō shihai-nin** *(fuu-kuu so she-high-neen)*

assistant manager 副支配人 **fuku shihai-nin** *(fuu-kuu she-high-neen)*

assistant section manager 係長 **kakarichō** *(kah-kah-ree-choe)*

associate (buddy; pal) 仲間 **nakama** *(nah-kah-mah)*; 同僚 **dōryō** *(dohh-r'yohh)*
▪ I went out drinking with my associate yesterday. 昨日、同僚と飲みに行きました。 **Kinō dōryō to nomi ni ikimashita.** *(kee-nohh dohh-r'yohh toh no-me nee ee-kee-mahss-tah.)*

associate company 関連会社 **kanren gaisha** *(kahn-ren guy-shah)*

association 協会 **kyōkai** *(k'yoe-kye)*
▪ What is the name of the association? 協会の名前は何と言いますか。 **Kyōkai no namae wa nan to iimasu ka?** *(k'yoe-kye no nah-my wah nahn toe ee-mahss kah?)*

assortment of goods 取り合わせ **toriawase** *(toe-ree-ah-wah-say)*

astronaut 宇宙飛行士 **uchūhikōshi** *(uu-chuu-he-kohh-she)*

astronomical 天文学(の) **tenmongaku (no)** *(tane-moan-gah-kuu)*

astronomy 天文学 **tenmongaku** *(tane-moan-gah-kuu)*

as usual 相変わらず **aikawarazuu** *(eye-kah-wah-rah-zuu)*
▪ I'm fine, as usual. 相変わらず元気です 。**Aikawarazu genki désu.** *(eye-kah-wah-rah-zuu gen-kee dess.)*

Atlantic Ocean 大西洋 **Taiseiyō** *(tie-say-e-yohh)*

ATM 現金自動預け払い機 **genkin jidō azuke barai ki** (*gane-keen jee-doe ah-zuu-kay bah-rye kee*); **ATM** *(A-T-M-muu)*
▪ Is there an ATM near here? この近くにATM がありますか。 **Kono chikaku ni ATM ga arimasu ka?** *(koe-no chee-kah-kuu nee A-T-M-muu gah ah-ree-mahss kah?)*
▪ Where is the nearest ATM? 一番近いATM はどこですか。 **Ichiban chikai ATM wa doko désu ka?** *(ee-chee-bahn chee-kie A-T-M-muu wah doe-koh dess kah?)*

atmosphere (air) 大気 **taiki** *(tie-kee)*; ambiance/mood 雰囲気 **fun'iki** *(foon-ee-kee)*
▪ This café has a wonderful atmosphere. このカフェはすてきな雰囲気があります。 **Kono kafé wa suteki na fun'iki ga arimasu.** *(koh-no kah-fay wa suu-tay-kee-nah foon-ee-kee gah ah-ree-mahss.)*

atom アトム **atomu** *(ah-toe-muu)*; 原子 **genshi** *(gane-she)*

atomic 原子(の) **genshi (no)** *(gane-she)*

atomic age 原子力時代 **genshi-ryoku jidai** *(gane-she rio-kuu jee-dye)*

atomic bomb 原子爆弾 **genshi bakudan** *(gane-she bah-kuu-dahn)*

atomic energy 原子力 **genshi ryoku** *(gane-she rio-kuu)*

at par 平価で **heika de** *(hay-kah day)*

at sight 一覧払いで **ichiran barai de** *(ee-chee-rahn bah-rye day)*

attach 付ける **tsukeru** *(t'sue-kay-rue)*; 添付する **tenpu suru** *(ten-puu sue-rue)*
▪ I will attach it to an email. Eメールに添付します。**Imēru ni tenpu shimasu.** *(ee-may-rue nee ten-puu she-mahss.)*

attachment 付属品 **fuzoku-hin** *(fuu-zoe-kuu heen)*
▪ Do you know where the computer attachments are? コンピュータの付属品はどこにあるか知っていますか。**Konpyūta no fuzoku-hin wa doko ni aru ka shitteimasu ka?** *(kon-pew-tah no fuu-zoe-kuu-heen wah doe-koe nee ah-rue kah shtay-ee-mahss kah?)*

attend 出席する **shusseki suru** *(shuu-say-kee sue-rue)*
▪ How many people will attend? 何人が出席しますか。**Nannin ga shusseki shimasu ka?** *(nahn-neen gah shuus-say-kee she-mahss kah?)*

attendance 出席 **shusseki** *(shuu-say-kee)*

attitude 態度 **taido** *(tie-doe)*
▪ I do not like his attitude. あの人の態度は嫌いです。**Ano hito no taido wa kirai désu.** *(ah-no shtoe no tie-doe wah kee-rie dess.)*

attorney; lawyer 弁護士 **bengoshi** *(bane-go-she)*
▪ I will engage an attorney. 弁護士を雇うつもりです。**Bengoshi wo yatou tsumori désu.** *(bane-go-she oh yah-toh-uu t'sue-moh-ree dess.)*

attorney, power of (power of attorney) 委任権 **ininken** *(ee-neen-ken)*

attrition 人員削減 **jin-in sakugen** *(jeen-een sah kuu-gen)*

auction 競売 **kyōbai** *(k'yoe-by)*; 競り売り **seriuri** *(say-ree-uu-ree)*; オークション **ōkushon** *(awk-shone)*

audience 聴衆 **chōshū** *(chohh-shuu)*

audio component system オーディオコンポ **ōdio konpo** *(oh-dee-oh cone-poe)*

audio response equipment オーディオ装置 **ōdio sōchi** *(oh-dee-oh so-chee)*

audit (to audit) 会計監査する **kaikei kansa suru** *(kye-kay kahn-sah sue-rue)*

auditing balance sheet 監査貸借対照表 **kansa taishaku taishō hyō** *(kahn-sah tie-shah-kuu tie-show h'yoe)*

auditor 会計監査役 **kaikei kansa yaku** *(kye-kay kahn-sah yah-kuu)*

auditorium 講堂 **kōdō** *(kohh-dohh)* **kaikan** *(kie-kahn)*; ホール **hōru** *(hohh-rue)*

Australia オーストラリア **Ōsutoraria** *(ohhss-toe-rah-ree-ah)*

Australian オーストラリア人 **Ōsutorariajin** *(ohhss-toe-rah-ree-ah-jeen)*

Australian Embassy オーストラリア大使館 **Ōsutoraria Taishikan** *(oh-sue-toe-rah-ree-ah tie-she-kahn)*

authentic 本物 **honmono** *(hoan-moe-no)*
▪ Are these pearls authentic? この真珠は本物ですか。**Kono shinju wa honmono désu ka?** *(koe-no sheen-juu wa hoan-moe-no dess kah?)*

author 作者 **sakusha** *(sah-kuu-shah)*; 著者 **chosha** *(choh-shah)*

authority; power 権力 **kenryoku** *(ken-rio-kuu)*
▪ Who is the person with authority? 権力のある人はどなたですか。**Kenryoku no aru hito wa donata**

désu ka? *(ken-rio-kuu no ah-rue shtoe wah doe-nah-tah dess kah?)*

authorize 権限を与える **kengen wo ataeru** *(ken-gen oh ah-tie-rue)*
▪ Who authorized this/that? だれが権限を与えましたか。**Dare ga kengén wo ataemashita ka?** *(dah-ray gah kane-gane oh ah-tie-mah-ssh-tah kah?)*

authorized agent 指定代理店 **shitei dairiten** *(she-tay dye-ree-ten)*; 委任代理人 **inin dairi-nin** *(ee-neen-dye-ree-neen)*

authorized dealer 指定販売業者 **shitei hanbai gyōsha** *(she-tay hahn-by g'yoe-shah)*

authorized shares 認定株 **nintei kabu** *(neen-tay kah-buu)*; 授権株式数 **juken kabushiki sū** *(juu-ken kah-buu-she-kee sue)*

authorized signature 正式署名 **seishiki shomei** *(say-she-kee show-may)*

auto-checker オートチエッカー **ōto-chekkā** *(oh-toe check-kah)*

autograph, sign サイン **sain** *(sign)*
▪ May I have your autograph, please? サインしていただけますか。**Sain shite itadakemasu ka?** *(sign ssh-tay ee-tah-dah-kay-mahss kah?)*

automate オートメーション化する **ōtomēshon ka suru** *(oh-toe-may-shone kah sue-rue)*
▪ Can you automate this step? この段階をオートメーション化できますか。**Kono dankai wo ōtomēshon ka dekimasu ka?** *(koe-no dahn-kye oh oh-toe-may-shone kah day-kee-mahss kah?)*

automatic 自動 **jidō** *(jee-doe)*; 自動的 **jidōteki** *(jee-doe-tay-kee)*
▪ In Japan taxi doors are automatic. 日本ではタクシーのドアは自動です。**Nihon dewa takushii no doa wa jidō désu.** *(nee-hone day-wah tah-kuu-she no doe-ah wah jee-doe dess.)*

automatic gearshift オートクラッチ **ōto kuratchi** *(oh-toe kuu-rah-chee)*

automatic transmission 自動変速装置 **jidō hensoku sōchi** *(jee-doe-shah hen-so-kuu so-chee)*

automation オートメーション **ōtomēshon** *(oh-toe-may-shone)*

automobile 自動車 **jidōsha** *(jee-doe-shah)*; 車 **kuruma** *(kuu-rue-mah)*
▪ Whose automobile is this? これはどなたの車ですか。**Kore wa donata no kuruma désu ka?** *(koh-ray wah doh-nah-tah no kuu-rue-mah dess kah?)*

automobile company 自動車会社 **jidōsha gaisha** *(jee-doe-shah guy-shah)*
▪ I work for an automobile company. 私は自動車会社で働いています。**Watashi wa jidōsha gaisha de hataraite imasu.** *(wah-tah-she wah jee-doe-shah guy-shah day hah-tah-rye-tay ee-mahss.)*

auto parts 自動車部品 **jidōsha buhin** *(jee-doe-shah buu-heen)*

avante-garde 前衛的 **zen'ei-teki** *(zane-a-tay-kee)*

average 平均 **heikin** *(hay-keen)*
▪ What is the average price? 平均価格はいくらですか。**Heikin kakaku wa ikura désu ka?** *(hay-keen kah-kah-kuu wah ee-kuu-rah dess kah?)*

average cost 平均原価 **heikin genka** *(hay-keen gen-kah)*

average life 平均寿命 **heikin jumyō** *(hay-keen juu-m'yoe)*

average price 平均価格 **heikin kakaku** *(hay-keen kah-kah-kuu)*

average unit cost 平均単価 **heikin tanka** *(hay-keen tahn-kah)*

averaging 平均法 **heikin hō** *(hay-keen hoe)*

aviation (method) 飛行術 **hikōjutsu** *(he-kohh-jute-sue)*

avoidable costs 回避可能コスト **kaihi kanō kosuto** *(kye-he kah-no cost)*

award 賞 **shō** *(shohh)*
▪ Your department won the sales award. あなたの部門はセールスの賞を取りました。**Anata no bumon wa sērusu no shō wo torimashita.** *(ah-nah-tah no buu-moan wah say-rue-sue no shohh oh tohh-ree-mah-ssh-tah.)*

B

backdate 前の日付にする **mae no hizuke ni suru** *(my no he-zuu-kay nee sue-rue)*
▪ Can you backdate this? これを前の日付にすることができますか。**Kore wo mae no hizuke ni suru koto ga dekimasu ka?** *(koe-ray oh my no he-zuu-kay nee sue-rue koe-toe gah day-kee-mahss kah?)*

background; background circumstances; backdrop 背景 **haikei** *(hie-kay-ee)*

backing, support 支援 **shien** *(she-enn)*

backlash はね返り **hanekaeri** *(hah-nay-kie-ree)*; 反発 **hanpatsu** *(hahn-pah-t'sue)*

backlog 在庫 **zaiko** *(zye-koe)*

backlog of orders 受注残 **juchū-zan** *(juu-chew zahn)*
▪ We have a large number of backlog orders. 受注残がたくさんあります。**Juchū-zan ga takusan arimasu.** *(juu-chew zahn gah tock-sahn ah-ree-mahss.)*

back order バックオーダー **bakku ōdā** *(bah-kuu oh-dahh)*; 再注文 **sai chūmon** *(sei chew-moan)*

backpack リュック **ryukku** *(r'yuu-koo)*

back taxes 追徴課税 **tsuichō kazei** *(t'sue-ee-choe kah-zay)*

backtrack 引き返す **hikikaesu** *(he-kee-kie-sue)*

backup バックアップ **bakkuappu** *(bahk-ahpp)*

bad business period 不景気 **fukeiki** *(fuu-kay-kee)*
▪ This August was a bad business period. この八月は不景気でした。**Kono Hachigatsu wa fukeiki déshita.** *(koh-no Hah-chee-got-sue wa fuu-kay-ee-kee desh-tah.)*

bad check 不渡り小切手 **fuwatari kogitte** *(fuu-wah-tah-ree koe-gheet-tay)*

bad debt 不良債権 **furyō saiken** *(fuu-rio sigh-ken)*

badge バッジ **bajji** *(bahj-jee)*
▪ Don't forget your badge. バッジを忘れないで。**Bajji wo wasurenai de.** *(bah-jee oh wah-sue-ray-nigh day.)*

baggage; suitcase スーツケース **sūtsukēsu** *(suu-t'sue-kay-sue)*
▪ Is this your baggage/suitcase? これはあなたのスーツケースですか。**Kore wa anata no sūtsukēsu désu ka?** *(koe-ray wah ah-nah-tah no suu-t'sue-kay-sue dess kah?)*

balance バランス **baransu** *(bah-rahn-sue)*; 差額 **sagaku** *(sah-gah-kuu)*; 収支 **shūshi** *(shuu-she)*; 残高 **zandaka** *(zahn-dah-kah)*

balance of payments 国際収支

kokusai shūshi *(coke-sigh shuu-she)*; 支払残高 **shiharai zandaka** *(she-hah-rye zahn-dah-kah)*

balance of trade 貿易収支 **bōeki shūshi** *(boe-eh-kee shuu-she)*

balance sheet 貸借対照表 **taishaku taishō hyō** *(tie-shah-kuu tie-show h'yoe)*

balloon payment 残額期日一括返済 **zangaku kijitsu ikkatsu hensai** *(zahn-gah-kuu kee-jee-t'sue ee-cot-sue hen-sigh)*

ballot 投票用紙 **tōhyōyōshi** *(tohh-h'yohh-yohh-she)*

ban, embargo 禁止 **kinshi** *(keen-she)*

bank 銀行 **ginkō** *(gheen-koe)*
▪ Please cash this at a bank. これを銀行で現金にしてください。**Kore oh ginkō de genkin ni shite kudasai.** *(koe-ray oh gheen-koe day gane-keen nee shtay kuu-dah-sigh.)*

bank acceptance 銀行引受手形 **ginkō hikiuke tegata** *(gheen-koe he-kee-uu-kay tay-gah-tah)*

bank account 銀行預金口座 **ginkō yokin kōza** *(gheen-koe yoe-keen koe-zah)*

bank balance 銀行預金残高 **ginkō yokin zandaka** *(gheen-koe yoe-keen zahn-dah-kah)*

bankbook 通帳 **tsūchō** *(t'sue-choe)*
▪ Please fill in the balance in the bankbook. 残高を通帳に記入してください。**Zandaka wo tsūchō ni kinyu shite kudasai.** *(zahn-dah-kah oh t'sue-choh nee keen-yuu ssh-tay kuu-dah-sie.)*

bank charges 銀行手数料 **ginkō tesūryō** *(gheen-koe tay-sue-rio)*

bank check 銀行小切手 **ginkō kogitte** *(gheen-koe koe-gheet-tay)*

bank clerk 銀行員 **ginkō-in** *(gheen-koe-een)*
▪ Excuse me. Are you a bank clerk? 失礼ですが、あなたは銀行員ですか。**Shitsurei désu ga. Anata wa ginkō-in désu ka?** *(sheet-sue ray dess gah ah-nah-tah wah gheen-koe een dess kah?)*

bank deposit 銀行預金 **ginkō yokin** *(gheen-koe yoe-keen)*

bank draft 銀行手形 **ginkō tegata** *(gheen-koe tay-gah-tah)*; foreign exchange bank draft 外国為替手形 **gaikoku kawase tegata** *(kah-wah-say tay-gah-tah)*

banker 銀行家 **ginkōka** *(gheen-koe-kah)*

bank holiday 銀行休業日 **ginkō kyūgyō bi** *(gheen-koe cue-g'yoe bee)*

bank interest 銀行利子 **ginkō rishi** *(gheen-koe ree-she)*

bank letter of credit 銀行信用状 **ginkō shinyō jō** *(gheen-koe sheen-yoe joe)*

bank loan 銀行融資 **ginkō yūshi** *(gheen-koe you-she)*

bank money order 銀行為替 **ginkō kawase** *(gheen-koe kah-wah-say)*

bank note 紙幣 **shihei** *(she-hay)*

Bank of America バンクオブアメリカ **Banku obu Amerika** *(bahn-kuu oh-buu ah-may-ree-kah)*

Bank of Japan (BOJ) 日本銀行 **Nihon Ginkō** *(nee-hone gheen-koe)*

bank rate, official (official bank rate) 公定歩合 **kōtei buai** *(koe-tay buu-eye)*

bankrupt 破産した **hasan shita** *(hah-sahn shtah)*
▪ I heard he went bankrupt. 彼は破産したと聞きました。**Kare wa hasan shita to kikimashita.** *(kah-ray wah hah-sahn shtah toe kee-kee-mahsh-tah.)*

bankrupt person 破産者 **hasánsha** *(hah-saahn-shah)*

bankruptcy 破産 **hasán** *(hah-saahn)*

bank statement 銀行勘定報告書 **ginkō kanjō hōkoku sho** (gheen-*koe kahn-joe hoe-koe-kuu show)*

bank transfer 銀行振込 **ginkō furikomi** *(gheen-koe fuu-ree-koe-me)*
▪ I would like to make a bank transfer. 銀行振込をしたいです。**Ginkō furikomi wo shitai désu.** *(gheen-koe fuu-ree-koe-me oh she-tie dess.)*

banner (advertisement) バナー(広告) **banā (kōkoku)** *(bah-nah (koe-koe-kuu))*
▪ Banner advertising can result in an increase in sales. バナー広告を活用して売上げが伸びた。**Banner kōkoku wo katsuyōshite uriage ga nobita.** (*bah-nah kohh-koh-kuu oh kot-sue-yohh-shtay uu-ree-ah-gay gah no-bee-tah.*)

banquet style party 宴会 **enkai** *(inn-kie)*
▪ Tonight I am going to a company banquet. 今晩、会社の宴会に行きます。**Komban kaisha no enkai ni ikimasu.** *(kome-bahn kie-shah no inn-kie nee ee-kee-mahss.)*

bar バー **bā** *(baah)*
▪ Do you know any good bars near the station? 駅の近くでいいバーを知っていますか。**Eki no chikaku de ii bā wo shitte imasu ka?** *(eh-kee no chee-kah-kuu day ee baah oh shtay ee-mahss kah?)*

bar chart 棒グラフ **bō gurafu** *(boe guu-rah-fuu)*

bareboat charter 裸用船 **hadaka yōsen** *(hah-dah-kah yoe-sen)*

bargain バーゲン **bāgen** *(bah-gain)*; 特売品 **tokubai hin** *(toe-kuu-by heen)*; 格安品 **kakuyasu hin** *(kah-kuu-yah-sue heen)*

bargaining power 交渉力 **kōshō ryoku** *(koe-show rio-kuu)*

bargaining rights 交渉権 **kōshō ken** *(koe-show ken)*

bargain securities 売買約定 **baibai yakutei** *(by-by yah-kuu-tay)*

barometer バロメーター **barométā** *(bah-roh-may-tah)*; 指標 **shihyō** *(she-h'yoe)*

barter 物々交換 **butsu-butsu kōkan** *(boot-sue-boot-sue koe-kahn)*
▪ China does a lot of bartering. 中国は物々交換をたくさんしています。**Chūgoku wa butsu-butsu kōkan wo takusan shite imasu.** *(chew-go-kuu wah boot-sue-boot-sue koe-kahn oh tock-sahn shtay-mahss.)*

base currency 基準通貨 **kijun tsūka** *(kee-june t'sue-kah)*

base point 基礎ポイント **kijun pointo** *(kee-june point-oh)*; 基点 **kiten** *(kee-ten)*

base price 基準価格 **kijun kakaku** *(kee-june kah-kah-kuu)*; ベース価格 **bēsu kakaku** *(bay-suekah-kah-kuu)*; 基本料金 **kihon ryōkin** *(kee-hoan rio-keen)*

base rate ベースレート **bēsu rēto** *(bay-sue ray-toe)*; 基準金利 **kijun kinri** *(kee-june keen-ree)*

base salary 基本給 **kihon kyū** *(kee-hoan-cue)*
▪ The base salary has not changed from last year. 基本給は、ほぼ昨年とかわらない。**Kihon kyū wa hobo sakunen to kawaranai.** *(kee-hone k'yuu wah hoe-boe sah-kuu-nane te kah-wah-rah-nie.)*

base transportation rate 一般運賃率 **ippan unchin ritsu** *(eep-pahn uun-cheen ree-t'sue)*; 運賃表 **unchin hyō** *(uun-cheen-h'yoe)*

base year 基準年 **kijun nen** *(kee-june nen)*

basically; fundamentally 基本的 **kihon-teki** *(kee-hoan-tay-kee)*

basic pension plan 基礎年金(制度) **kiso nenkin (seido)** *(kee-so nen-keen say-doe)*

basic unit 本体 **hontai** *(hone-tie)*
▪ How much is the basic unit? 本体はいくらですか。**Hontai wa ikura désu ka?** *(hone-tie wa ee-kuu-rah dess kah?)*

basis 方針 **hōshin** *(hoe-sheen)*; 基準 **kijun** *(kee-june)*

batch processing 一括処理 **ikkatsu shori** *(ee-kah-t'sue show-ree)*

batch production 定量生産 **teiryō seisan** *(tay-rio say-sahn)*

battery 電池 **denchi** *(den-chee)*; バッテリー **batterii** *(bah-tay-ree)*
▪ Your batteries are weak. You need new ones. 電池が弱いので、新しいものが必要です。**Denchi ga yowai no de atarashii mono ga hitsuyō désu.** *(den-chee gah yoe-wie no-day ah-tah-rah-she moe-no gah he-t'sue-yoe dess.)*
▪ I need a new battery for my computer. コンピュータの新しいバッテリーが必要です。**Konpyūta no atarashii batterii ga hitsuyō désu.** *(kome-pyuu-tahh no ah-tah-rah-she baht-tay-ree ga he-t'sue-yoe dess.)*

battery (for vehicle) バッテリー **batteri** *(baht-tay-ree)*

baud ボー **bō** *(boe)*

bazaar バザー **bazā** *(bah-zahh)*

bearer 持参人 **jisan nin** *(jee-sahn neen)*

bearer bond 無記名債券 **muki-mei saiken** *(muu-kee-may sigh-ken)*

bearer security 無記名証券 **muki-mei shōken** *(muu-kee-may show-ken)*

bear market 売り相場 **uri sōba** *(uu-ree so-bah)*

beat-around-the-bush 回りくどく **mawari kudoku** *(mah-wah-ree kuu-doe-kuu)*

become clear はっきりする **hakkiri suru** *(hock-kee-ree sue-rue)*
▪ It became clear. はっきりしました。**Hakkiri shimashita.** *(hock-kee-ree she-mahssh-tah.)*

behind the scenes talks/work 根回し **nemawashi** *(nay-mah-wah-she)*

bell-shaped curve 釣鐘曲線 **tsurigane kyokusen** *(t'sue-ree-gah-nay k'yoe-kuu-sen)*

"belly art" 腹芸 **hara gei** *(hah-rah gay)*
▪ "Belly art" (cultural intuition) is important when doing business in Japan. 日本でビジネスをする時は、腹芸が大切です。**Nihon de bijinesu wo suru toki wa hara gei ga taisetsu désu.** *(nee-hoan day be-jee-nay-sue oh sue-rue toki wah hah-rah gay gah tie-sate-sue dess.)*

below par 額面以下で **gakumen ika de** *(gah-kuu-men ee-kah day)*

below-the-line item 下線以下の項目 **kasen ika-no kōmoku** *(kah-sen ee-kah-no koe-moe-kuu)*

belt-tightening policy 緊縮政策 **kinshuku seisaku** *(keen-shuu-kuu say-sah-kuu)*

benefit 手当て **teate** *(tay-ah-tay)*; 給付金 **kyūfu kin** *(cue-fuu keen)*

beneficiary 受取人 **uketori nin** *(uu-kay-toe-ree neen)*

berth terms バース条件 **bāsu jyōken** *(bah-sue joo-kay-n)*

beverage (something to drink) 飲み物 **nomimono** *(no-me-moe-no)*
▪ Would you like something to drink? お飲み物はいかがですか。**O-nomimono wa ikaga désu ka?** *(oh-no-me-moe-no wah ee-kah-gah dess kah?)*

bid; offer 入札 **nyūsatsu** *(n'yuu-sot-sue)*

bidder 入札者 **nyūsatsu sha** *(n'yuu-sah-t'sue shah)*

bid for takeover 株式公開買付け **kabushiki kōkai kaitsuke** *(kah-buu-she-kee koe-kye kite-sue-kay)*

big success 大成功 **dai seikō** *(dye say-koe)*
▪ The project was a big success. プロジェクトは大成功しました。**Purojekuto wa dai seikō shimashita.** *(puu-roe-jeck-toe wah dye say-koe she-mahsh-tah.)*

bilingual 二カ国語 **nikakokugo** *(nee-kah-koe-kuu-go)*

bilk out of; defraud 騙し取る **damashitoru** *(dah-mah-she-toe-rue)*

bill (bank note) 紙幣 **shihei** *(she-hay)*; 札 **satsu** *(sah-t'sue)*

bill (for purchases or sales) 請求書 **seikyū-sho** *(say-cue-show)*

bill (statement of money) 勘定書き **kanjō gaki** *(kahn-joe gah-kee)*, お勘定 **okanjō** *(oh kahn-joe)*
▪ Please bring the bill. お勘定を持って来てください。**O-kanjō wo motte kite kudasai.** *(oh-kahn-joe oh moat-tay kee-tay kuu-dah-sigh.)*
▪ Please add up my bill. お勘定を計算してください。**O-kanjō wo keisan shite kudasai.** *(oh-kahn-joe oh kay-sahn shtay kuu-dah-sigh.)*
▪ Add it to my bill. 私(のお勘定)につけておいてください。**Watakushi (no okanjō) ni tsukete oite kudasai.** *(wah-tock-she (no oh-kahn-joe) nee skay-tay oh-ee-tay kuu-dah-sigh.)*

bill (law) 法案 **hōan** *(hoe-ahn)*; bill (legislative) 案 **an** *(ahn)*
▪ The bill is now in the Diet. 法案は今議会に上程中です。**Hōan wa kon Gikai ni jōtei chū désu.** *(hoe-ahn wah kon ghee-kye nee joe-tay chew dess.)*

billboard 掲示板 **keiji ban** *(kay-jee bahn)*; advertising billboard 広告看板 **kōkoku kanban** *(kohh-koh-kuu kahn-bahn)*

billion 十億 **jū oku** *(juu oh-kuu)*
▪ How much is one billion yen in dollars? 10億円は何ドルですか。**Jū oku en wa nan doru désu ka?** *(juu oh-kuu en wah nahn doe-rue dess kah?)*

bill of exchange 為替手形 **kawase tegata** *(kah-wah-say tay-gah-tah)*
▪ I hope you will pay the bill of exchange. 為替手形でお支払いを願いします。**Kawase tegata de oshiharai negaimasu.** *(kay-wah-say tay-gah-tah day oh-she-hah-rye nay-guy-mahss.)*

bill of lading (B/L) 船荷証券 **funani shōken** *(fuu-nah-nee show-ken)*
▪ Two copies of the bill of lading are necessary. 船荷証券が二部が必要です。**Funani shōken ga nibu ga hitsuyō désu.** *(fuu-nah-nee show-ken gah nee-buu hee-t'sue-yoe dess.)*

bill of sale 売渡証書 **uriwatashi shōsho** *(uu-ree-wah-tah-she-show-show)*

bill of sight 仮陸揚げ申請書 **kari rikuage shinseisyo** *(kah-ree ree-kuu ah-ghee she-n say-ee show)*

bimonthly 2ヶ月に1度 **nikagetsu ni ichi do** *(nee-kah-gate-sue nee ee-*

chee-doe); 隔月 **kakugetsu** *(kah-kuu-gay-t'sue)*

binding (obligation) 義務的 **gimu-teki** *(ghee-muu-tay-kee)*

biochemistry 生化学 **seikagaku** *(say-kah-gah-kuu)*

bio-computer バイオコンピュータ **baio konpyūta** *(bio kome-pyuu-tah)*

biodegradable 自然分解できる **shinzenbunkai dekiru** *(she-zane-boon-kie day-kee-rue)*

biometric recognition system 生体認証システム **seitai ninshō shisutemu** *(say-tie neen-show she-suu-tay-muu)* ▪ Use of the biometric recognition system is increasing because of the need for security. セキュリティーのため生体認証システムの需要は高まっている。**Security no tame seitai ninshō shisutemu no jiyō wa takamatteiru.** *(security no tah-may say-tie neen-shohh shees-tay-muu no juu-yohh wah tah-kah-mot-tay-ee-rue.)*

birthday 誕生日 **tanjōbi** *(tahn-joe-bee)* ▪ When is your birthday? お誕生日はいつですか。**O-tanjōbi wa itsu désu ka?** *(oh-tahn-joe-bee wah eat-sue dess kah?)*

BIT (computer) ビット **bitto** *(beet-toe)*

black 黒字 **kuroji** *(kuu-roe-jee)*

black-and-white TV 白黒テレビ **shiro kuro terebi** *(she-roe kuu-roe tay-ray-bee)*

black figure (showing a profit) 黒字 **kuro ji** *(kuu-roe jee)* ▪ Last month our profits were in the black. 先月、黒字が出ました。**Sengetsu kuro ji ga demashita.** *(sen-gate-sue kuu-roe jee gah day-mahsh-tah)*

black list ブラックリスト **burakku risuto** *(buu-rahk rees-toe)*

blackmail ゆすり **yusuri** *(yuu-sue-ree)*

black market 闇市場 **yami ichiba** *(yah-me ee-chee-bah)*; ブラックマーケット **burakku māketto** *(buu-rahk-kuu mah-kate-toe)*

blanket order 一括注文 **ikkatsu chūmon** *(eek-cot-sue chew-moan)*

blanket order for production 一括製造指図書 **ikkatsu seizō sashizu-sho** *(eek-cot-sue say-zoe sah-she-zuu-show)*

bleed (an advertisement that covers the entire page) 裁ち切り **tachikiri** *(tah-chee-kee-ree)*

blemish; scar 傷 **kizu** *(kee-zuu)*

blend; mix in ブレンド **burendo** *(buu-rin-doe)*

blockade 封鎖 **fūsa** *(fuuu-sah)*

blockage of funds 資金封鎖 **shikin fūsa** *(she-keen fuu-sah)*

blocked currency 封鎖通貨 **fūsa tsūka** *(fuu-sah t'sue-kah)*

blog ブログ **Burogu** *(buu-roh-guu)* ▪ Do you have a blog? ブログがありますか。**Burogu ga arimasu ka?** *(buu-roh-guu gah ah-ree-mahss kah?)*

blonde ブロンド **burondo** *(buu-roan-doe)*; 金髪 **kimpatsu** *(keem-paht-sue)*

blowup (enlarge a photograph or piece of art) 引き伸ばし **hikinobashi** *(hee-kee-no-bah-she)*

blowup; explosion 爆破 **bakuha** *(bah-kuu-hah)*; 爆発 **bakuhatsu** *(bah-kuu-hot-sue)*; emotional outburst かんしゃく **kanshaku** *(kahn-shah-kuu)*

blue-chip stock 優良株 **yūryō kabu** *(yuu-rio kah-buu)*

blue-collar worker 労働者 **rōdōsha**

(roe-doe-shah); ブルーカラー **burū karā** *(buu-rue kah-rah)*

blueprint 青写真 **ao jashin** *(ah-oh jah-sheen)*

boarding house 下宿 **geshuku** *(gay-shuu-kuu)*
▪ Is this a company boarding house? ここは社員寮ですか。**Koko wa shain-ryō désu ka?** *(koe-koe wah shine-rio dess kah?)*

boarding pass 搭乗券 **tōjō-ken** *(tohh-johh-ken)*
▪ Please show me your boarding pass. 搭乗券を拝見します。**Tōjō-ken wo haiken shimasu.** *(tohh-johh-ken oh hi-kane she-mahss.)*

board meeting 取締役会議 **torishimariyaku kaigi** *(toe-ree-she-mah-ree-yah-kuu kye-ghee)*

board of directors 役員会 **yakuin kai** *(yah-kuu-ee-n kah-ee)*
▪ He is attending a meeting of the board of directors. 役員会に出席しております。**Yakuin kai ni shusseki shite orimasu.** *(yah-kuu-een kie nee shuus-say-kee ssh-tay oh-ree-mahss.)*

boardroom 会議室 **kaigi shitsu** *(kye-ghee sheet-sue)*

bodyguard 用心棒 **yōjimbō** *(yohh-jeem-bohh)*

boilerplate contract 契約書に含まれる標準条項 **keiyaku sho ni fukumareru hyōjun jōkō** *(kay-yah-kuu show nee fuu-kuu-mah-ray-rue h'yoe-june joe-koe)*

bomb 爆弾 **bakudan** *(bah-kuu-dahn)*

bond 債券 **saiken** *(sigh-ken)*

bond areas 保税地域 **hozei chiiki** *(hoe-zay chee-ee-kee)*

bonded carrier 保税貨物運搬人 **hozei kamotsu unpan nin** *(hoe-zay kah-moat-sue uun-pahn neen)*

bonded goods 保税貨物 **hozei kamotsu** *(hoe-zay kah-moat-sue)*

bonded warehouse 保税倉庫 **hozei sōko** *(hoe-zay so-koe)*

bond issue 社債発行 **shasai hakkō** *(sha-sigh hock-koh)*

bond price 債券価格 **saiken kakaku** *(sigh-ken kah-kah-kuu)*

bond rating 債券格付け **saiken kakuzuke** *(sigh-ken kah-kuu-zuu-kay)*

bonds 債 **sai** *(sie)*; government bonds 国債 **koku sai** *(koh-kuu-sie)*; corporate bonds 社債 **sha sai** *(shah-sie)*; public bonds 公債 **kō sai** *(kohh-sie)*; foreign bonds 外債 **gai sai** *(guy-sie)*

bonus (premium) 利益配当 **rieki haitō** *(ree-ay-kee high-toe)*; bonuses paid to employees 賞与 **shōyo** *(show-yoe)*; ボーナス **bōnasu** *(boh-nah-sue)*

book 本 **hon** *(hone)*, 帳簿 **chobo** *(choe-boe)*; to book 帳簿につける **chōbo ni tsukeru** *(coe-boe nee t'sue-kay-rue)*; 計上する **keijō suru** *(kay-joe sue-rue)*; 予約する **yoyaku suru** *(yoe-yah-kuu sue-rue)*

bookbinding 製本 **seihon** *(say-ee-hoan)*

booking 会計処理 **kaikei shori** *(kye-kay show-ree)*

book inventory 帳簿棚卸 **chōbo tana-oroshi** *(choe-boe tah-nah-oh-roe-she)*

bookkeeper 帳簿係 **chōbogakari** *(choe-boe-gah-kah-ree)*

bookkeeping 簿記 **boki** *(boe-kee)*

booklet パンフレット **panfuretto** *(pahn-fuu-rate-toe)*

bookmark ブックマーク **bukku māku** *(buu-kuu mah-kuu)*
▪ It is convenient to bookmark the Web site. そのウェブサイトを登録(ブックマーク)しておくと便利です。**Sono webu saito wo bukku maku shite oku to benri désu.** *(so-no weh-buu sie-toh oh buu-kuu mah-kuu ssh-tay oh-kuu to bane-ree dess.)*

book price 帳簿価額 **chōbo kagaku** *(choe-boe kah-gah-kuu)*; 簿価 **boka** *(boe-kah)*

book review 書評 **shohyō** *(show-h'yohh)*

bookstore 本屋 **hon-ya** *(hoan-yah)*
▪ Where is the nearest bookstore? 一番近い本屋はどこですか。**Ichiban chikai hon-ya wa doko désu ka?** *(ee-chee-bahn chee-kie hone-yah wa doe-koe dess kah?)*

book value 帳簿価額 **chōbo kagaku** *(choe-boe kah-gah-kuu)*

book value per share 1株あたりの帳簿価値 **hitokabu atari no chōbo kachi** *(shtoe-kah-buu ah-tah-ree no choe-boe kah-chee)*

boom (business) 好況 **kōkyō** *(koe-k'yoe)*; ブーム **būmu** *(buu-muu)*; にわか景気 **niwaka keiki** *(nee-wah-kah kay-kee)*

booth (compartment) ブース **būsu** *(buu-sue)*

border (between countries) 国境 **kokkyō** *(coke-yoe)*
▪ The factory is right next to the border. 工場は国境のすぐそばです。**Kōjō wa kokkyō no sugu soba désu.** *(koe-joe wah coke-yoe no sue-guu so-bah dess.)*

border-tax adjustment 国境税調整 **kokkyō zei chōsei** *(coke-yoe zay choe-say)*

borrow 借りる **kariru** *(kah-ree-rue)*; take out a loan 借金する **shakkin suru** *(shahk-keen-sue rue)*
▪ May I borrow your tool box? 道具箱を借りてもいいですか。**Dōgu bako wo karite mo ii désu ka?** *(doe-guu bah-koe oh kah-ree-tay moe ee dess kah?)*

boss 上司 **jōshi** *(joe-she)*

bossy, acting stuck up 威張っている **ibatteiru** *(ee-baht-tay-ee-rue)*

bottom price 底値 **soko ne** *(so-koe nay)*
▪ Is that your bottom price? それは底値ですか。**Sore wa soko ne désu ka?** *(soe-ray wah so-koe nay dess kah?)*

boycott ボイコットする **boikotto suru** *(boy-cot-toe sue-rue)*

brainstorm ブレーンストーム **burēn sutōmu** *(buu-ray-een stow-muu)*; ひらめき **hirameki** *(hee-rah-may-kee)*

branch (sub-division) 支部 **shibu** *(she-buu)*; 支店 **shiten** *(she-ten)*

branch manager 支店長 **shiten chō** *(she-ten choe)*
▪ He is the new branch manager. 彼は新しい支店長です。**Kare wa atarashii shiten chō désu.** *(kah-ray wah ah tah-rah-she she-ten choe dess.)*

branch office/store 支店 **shiten** *(she-ten)*
▪ Next year I will move to a branch office. 来年、支店に移ります。**Rainen shiten ni utsurimasu.** *(rye-nen she-ten nee uu-tsue-ree-mahss.)*

brand 銘柄 **meigara** *(may-gah-rah)*; ブランド **burando** *(buu-rahn-doe)*

brand acceptance 銘柄承認 **meigara shōnin** *(may-gah-rah show-neen)*

brand image 銘柄イメージ **meigara imēji** *(may-gah-rah ee-may-jee)*; 商標

イメージ **shōhyō imēji** *(show-h'yoe ee-may-jee)*; ブランドイメージ **burando imēji** *(buu-rahn-doe ee-may-jee)*

brand loyalty 銘柄忠実性 **meigara chūjitsu-sei** *(may-gah-rah chew-jee-t'sue-say)*; ブランド信仰 **burando shinkō** *(buu-rahn-doe sheen-koe)*

brand name ブランド品 **burando hin** *(buu-rahn-doh heen)*; ブランド名 **burando mei** *(buu-rahn-doe may)*
▪ There are many famous foreign brand name shops in Japan. 日本には有名な外国ブランドの店がたくさんあります。**Nihon ni wa yūmei na gaikoku burando no mise ga takusan arimasu.** *(nee-hone nee wa guy-koh-kuu buu-rahn-doh no me-say gah tahk-sahn ah-ree-mahss.)*

brand recognition 銘柄認識 **meigara ninshiki** *(may-gah-rah neen-she-kee)*

breach of contract; violation of law 契約違反 **keiyaku ihan** *(kay-yah-kuu ee-hahn)*; 違法行為 **ihō kōi** *(ee-hoh-koe-ee)*; 違憲 **iken** *(ee-kane)*

break (rest from work) 休憩 **kyūkei** *(cue-kay)*; break period 休憩時間 **kyūkei jikan** *(cue-kay jee-kahn)*
▪ Everyone is on break. みんな休憩しています。**Minna kyūkei shiteimasu.** *(mean-nah cue-kay shtay-mahss.)*

breakdown (operational failure) 故障 **koshō** *(koe-shohh)*

breakdown (analysis) 分析(結果) **bunseki (kekka)** *(buun-say-kee cake-kah)*

break even 損益のない **son'eki no nai** *(soan-ay-kee no nigh)*

break-even analysis 損益分岐点分析 **son'eki bunki-ten bunseki** *(soan-ay-kee boon-kee-ten boon-say-kee)*

break-even point 損益分岐点 **son'eki bunki-ten** *(soan-ay-kee boon-kee-ten)*

breakthrough (discovery) 発見 **hakken** *(hahk-kane)*

break-up (dissolution) 解散 **kaisan** *(kye-sahn)*

bribe 賄賂 **wairo** *(wie-roe)*

bribery 買収 **baishū** *(by-shuu)*

brief report (outline/report) 要旨 **yōshi** *(yohh-she)*; 要約 **yōyaku** *(yohh-yah-kuu)*

briefcase ブリーフケース **buriifu kēsu** *(buu-ree-fuu kay-sue)*; かばん **kaban** *(kah-bahn)*

British Embassy 英国大使館 **Eikoku Taishikan** *(eh-ee-koe-kuu tie-she-kahn)*

broadband ブロードバンド **burōdobando** *(buu-roh-doh-bahn-doh)*
▪ Broadband is the next generation's computer network service. ブロードバンドは、次世代のコンピュータネットワークサービスです。**Burodo bando wa jisedai no konpyuta nettowaku sabisu désu.** *(buu-roh-doh bahn-doh wah jee-say-die no kome-p'yuu-tah net-toh-wah-kuu sah-bee-sue dess.)*

broadcasting 放送 **hōsō** *(hohh-sohh)*

brochure パンフレット **panfuretto** *(pahn-fuu-rate-toe)*
▪ Please let me see the brochure. パンフレットを見せてください。**Panfuretto wo misete kudasai.** *(pahn-fuu-rate-toe oh me-say-tay kuu-dah-sigh.)*

broker 仲介人 **nakagainin** *(nah-kah-guy-neen)*; ブローカー **burōkā** *(buu-roe-kah)*

brokerage 証券会社 **shōkengaisha** *(shohh-kane-guy-shah)*

browser (computer) ブラウザ **burauza** *(buu-rah-oh-zah)*
▪ Internet Explorer monopolizes the share of the web browser. Internet Explorer はウェブ・ブラウザのシェアを独占している。**Internet Explorer wa webu burauza no shea wo dokusen shiteiru.** *(Internet Explorer wah web-buu brow-zah no shay-ah oh doke-sen ssh-tay-ee-rue.)*

borrowing 借入れ **kariire** *(kah-ree-ee-ray)*

bottom line 純損益 **jun son'eki** *(june-soan-ay-kee)*; 純利益 **jun rieki** *(june-ree-ay-kee)*

bourse 証券取引所 **shōken torihiki sho** *(show-ken toe-ree-hee-kee show)*

budget 予算 **yosan** *(yoe-sahn)*

budget appropriation 予算割当 **yosan wariate** *(yoe-sahn wah-ree-ah-tay)*

budget forecast 予算予測 **yosan yosoku** *(yoe-sahn yoe-so-kuu)*

budget year 会計年度 **kaikei nendo** *(kye-kay nen-doe)*

buffer memory バッファメモリー **baffa memorii** *(bah-fah may-moe-ree)*

buffet ビュッフェ **byuffe** *(b'yuu-fay)*

bug (computer) バグ **bagu** *(bah-guu)*
▪ A bug has damaged the condition of (my) computer. バグのせいでパソコンの調子が悪くなった。 **Bagu no sei de pasokon no chō-shi ga warukunatta.** *(bah-guu no say day pah-so-kone no chohh-she gah wah-rue-kuu-not-tah.)*

built-in 作り付け **tsukuritsuke** *(t'sue-kuu-ree-t'sue-kay)*

bulletin 報告 **hōkoku** *(hohh-koh-kuu)*

bull market 買い相場 **kai sōba** *(kye so-bah)*; 上げ相場 **age sōba** *(ah-gay so-bah)*

bureaucracy, bureaucrat 官僚 **kanryō** *(kahn-rio)*

bureaucratic 官僚主義 **kanryō shugi** *(kahn-y'yohh shuu-ghee)*

bureau director 局長 **kyoku chō** *(k'yoe-kuu choe)*

business (occupation) 職業 **shokugyō** *(show-kuu-g'yoe)*

business (as in asking someone why they are visiting an office) 用件 **yōken** *(yoe-ken)*; have business with someone 用事がある **yōji ga aru** *(you-jee gah ah-rue)*
▪ What is your business (may I help you)? ご用件は。**Gō-yoken wa?** *(goe-yoe-ken wah?)*
▪ I have business with Mr. Yamamoto. 山本さんに用事があります。 **Yamamoto-san ni yōji ga arimasu.** *(Yah-mah-moe-toe-sahn nee yoe-jee gah ah-ree-mahss.)*

business (trade) 営業 **eigyō** *(eh-ee-g'yoe)*; 事業 **jigyō** *(jee-g'yoe)*; business results 事業内容 **jigyō naiyō** *(jee-g'yoe nigh-yoe)*
▪ Is this a new business? これは新しい事業ですか。**Kore wa atarashii jigyō désu ka?** *(koe-ray wah ah-tah-rah-she jee-g'yoe dess kah?)*

business activity 景気 **keiki** *(kay-kee)*

business affairs section 業務部 **gyōmu bu** *(g'yoe-muu buu)*

business area 商業地区 **shōgyō chiku** *(show-g'yoe chee-kuu)*

business card 名刺 **meishi** *(may-she)*

business condition 景気 **keiki** *(kay-kee)*

business cycle 景気循環 **keiki junkan** *(kay-kee june-kahn)*

business development mission 事業発展のための任務 **jigyō hatten no tame no ninmu** *(ghee-g'yoe hah-tay-n no tah-may no neen-muu)*

business hours 営業時間 **eigyō jikan** *(eh-ee-g'yoe jee-kahn)*

business improvement order 業務改善命令 **gyōmu kaizen meirei** *(g'yoe-muu kye-zen may-ray)*

business integration (merger) 経営統合 **keiei tōgō** *(kay-ee toe-goh)*

businessman 事業家 **jigyo-ka** *(jee-g'yoe-kah)*; 実業家 **jitsugyo-ka** *(jee-t'sue-g'yoe-kah)*; サラリーマン **sararii man** *(sah-rah-ree man)*
▪ All of the guests are businessmen. お客様はみんな実業家です。**O-kyakusama wa minna jitsugyō-ka désu.** *(oh-k'yack-sah-mah wah mean-nah jee-t'sue-g'yoe-kah dess.)*

business management 経営管理 **keiei kanri** *(kay-ee kahn-ree)*

business meeting 会合 **kaigō** *(kye-go)*

business model 事業モデル **jigyō moderu** *(jee-g'yoe model)*
▪ With a new business model the company has received considerable attention. 新しい事業モデルとしてその企業は、注目されている。**Atarashii jigyō moderu to shite sono kigyō wa chūmoku sareteiru.** *(ah-tah-rah-shee jeeg-yohh moe-day-rue toe ssh-tay so-no keeg-yohh wah chuu-moe-kuu sah-ray-tay-ee-rue.)*

business partner 取引先 **torihiki saki** *(toe-ree-he-kee sah-kee)*
▪ This is my business partner. こちらは私の取引先の方です。**Kochira wa watakushi no torihiki saki no kata désu.** *(koe-chee-rah wah wah-tahk-she no toe-ree-he-kee sah-kee no kah-tah dess.)*

business performance 業績 **gyōseki** *(g'yohh-say-kee)*

business plan 事業計画 **jigyō keikaku** *(jee-g'yoe kay-kah-kuu)*

business policy 経営方針 **keiei hōshin** *(kay-ee hoe-sheen)*

business practices 商習慣 **shōshūkan** *(show-shuu-kahn)*

business report 営業報告書 **eigyō hōkokusho** *(eh-ee-g'yoe hoe-koe-kuu-show)*

business strategy 経営戦略 **keiei senryaku** *(kay-ee sen-rah-kuu)*

business tie-up 業務提携 **gyōmu teiki** *(g'yoe-muu tay-kee)*

business transaction 取引 **torihiki** *(toe-ree-he-kee)*

business trip 出張 **shutchō** *(shuu-choe)*
▪ Mr. Lee is away on a business trip. リーさんは出張しています。**Ree-san wa shutchō shite imasu.** *(ree-sahn wah shuu-choe shtay-mahss.)*

business world 業界 **gyōkai** *(g'yoe-kye)*

buttons (electronic) ボタン **botan** *(boh-tahn)*
▪ Advances in technology are making it possible to do almost everything with one button. 技術の進歩によって、ボタン1つで何でもできるようになります。**Gijutsu no shinpo ni yotte botan hitotsu de nandemo dekiru yō ni narimasu.** *(ghee-jute-sue no sheem-poh ni yote-tay boh-tahn he-tote-sue day nahn-day-moh day-kee-rue yoh nee nah-ree-mahss.)*

buy (purchase) 買う **kau** *(cow)*

- I want to buy this new model car. この新型車を買いたいです。**Kono shingata sha wo kaitai désu.** *(koh-no sheen-gah-tah shah oh kie-tie dess.)*
- Please buy this book for me. この本を買ってください。**Kono hon wo katte kudasai.** *(koe-no hone oh kah-tay kuu-dah-sigh.)*

buyback 買い戻し **kaimodoshi** *(kye-moe-doe-she)*

buyer 買い手 **kaite** *(kye-tay)*

buyer's market 買い手市場 **kaite shijō** *(kye-tay she-joe)*

buyer's option 買い手の選択権 **kaite-no sentaku-ken** *(kye-tay-no sen-tah-kuu-ken)*

buyer's responsibility 買い選択 **kai sentaku** *(kye sen-tah-kuu)*

buy on close 引値買い **hikine gai** *(he-kee-nay guy)*

buy on opening 寄り付きで買う **yoritsuki de kau** *(yoe-ree-t'sue-kee day cow)*

buy-out 買収 **baishū** *(by-shuu)*

bylaws 付随定款 **fuzui teikan** *(fuu-zuu-ee tay-kahn)*

by-product 副産物 **fuku-sanbutsu** *(fuu-kuu-sahn-boot-sue)*

byte バイト **baito** *(bye-toe)*

C

cabaret キャバレー **kyabarē** *(k'yah-bah-ray)**
*Cabaret is the legal designation for Japan's famous hostess clubs.

cable (wire) 電信 **denshin** *(den-sheen)*

cable (for computer) ケーブル **kēburu** *(kay-buu-rue)*

- It is now possible to connect to the Internet without cable. 今は、ケーブルなしでインターネットに接続できます。**Ima wa kēburu nashi de intānetto ni setsuzoku dekimasu.** *(ee-mah wah kay-buu-rue nah-she day een-tah-net-toe nee sate-sue-zoh-kuu day-kee-mahss.)*

cable television ケーブル・テレビ **kēburu terebi** *(kay-buu-ruu tay-ray-bee)*

- Do you have a contract for cable television? ケーブルテレビを契約していますか。**Anata wa kēburu terebi wo keiyaku shite imasu ka?** *(ah-nah-tah wah kay-buu-rue tay-ray-bee oh kay-yah-kuu shtay-mahss kah?)*

cable transfer 電信送金 **denshin sōkin** *(den-sheen so-keen)*

calculator 計算機 **keisanki** *(kay-sahn-kee)*; 電卓 **dentaku** *(dane-tah-kuu)*

calendar カレンダー **karendā** *(kah-rane-dahh)*

call-back (product recall) 回収 **kaishū** *(kye-shuu)*

call in 貸金を回収する **kashi kin wo kaishū suru** *(kah-she keen wo kah-ee-shuu sue-rue)*

call-loan コールローン **kōru rōn** *(koe-rue roan)*

call on; visit 訪ねる **tazuneru** *(tah-zuu-nay-rue)*; 訪問する **hōmon suru** *(hoe-moan sue-rue)*

- I want to call on Mr. Watanabe tomorrow. 明日、渡辺さんをお訪ねしたいです。**Ashita Watanabe-san wo o-tazune shitai désu.** *(ah-shtah wah-tah-nah-bay-sahn oh oh-tah-zuu-nay she-tie dess.)*

call-waiting キャッチホン **catchi fon**

- Do you have call-waiting? キャッチ

ホンはついてますか。**Catchi fon (catch phone) wa tsuitemasu ka?** *(catch phone wah t'sue-ee-tay mahss kah?)*

Canada カナダ **Kanada** *(kah-nah-dah)*

Canadian (person) カナダ人 **Kanadajin** *(kah-nah-dah-jeen)*

Canadian Embassy カナダ大使館 **Kanada Taishikan** *(kah-nah-dah tie-she-kahn)*

cancel 取り消す **torikesu** *(toe-ree-kay-sue)*; 解消する **kaishō suru** *(kye-show sue-rue)*; キャンセル **kyanseru** *(k'yahn-say-rue)*
▪ Please cancel my reservations. 私の予約を取り消してください。**Watashi no yoyaku wo torikeshite kudasai.** *(wah-tock-she no yoe-yah-kuu oh toe-ree-kay-shtay kuu-dah-sigh.)*
▪ That flight has been canceled. その便は欠航になりました。**Sono bin wa kekkō ni nari mashita.** *(so-no bean wah kay-koe nee nah-ree-mahsh-tah.)*

canceled check 支払済小切手 **shiharaizumi kogitte** *(she-hah-rye-zuu-mekoe-gheet-tay)*

cancellation キャンセル **kyanseru** *(k'yahn-say-rue)*

cancellation charge 取消手数料 **torikeshi tesūryō** *(toe-ree-kay-she (tay-sue-rio)*

capacity 能力 **nōryoku** *(no-rio-kuu)*; 収容能力 **shūyōnōryoku** *(shuu-yohh-nohh-rio-kuu)*; 生産能力 **seisan nōryoku** *(say-sahn no-rio-kuu)*

capital (country) 首都 **shuto** *(shuu-toe)*

capital (money) 資本金 **shihon kin** *(she-hone keen)*

capital account 資産勘定 **shisan kanjō** *(she-sahn kahn-joe)*

capital adequacy ratio 自己資本比率 **jiko shihon hiritsu** *(jee-koe she-hone hee-ree-t'sue)*

capital alliance 資本提携 **shihon teikei** *(she-hone tay-kay)*
▪ The management of that company has approved a capital alliance. その会社との資本提携によって経営が強化された。**Sono kaisha to no shihon teikei ni yotte keiei ga kyōka sareta.** *(so-no kie-shah toe no she-hone tay-kay nee yote-tay kay-eh-ee gah k'yoh-kah sah-ray-tah.)*

capital allowance 資本控除 **shihon kōjo** *(she-hone koe-joe)*

capital asset 固定資産 **kotei shisan** *(koe-tay she-sahn)*

capital base 自己資本 **jiko shihon** *(jee-koe she-hone)*

capital expenditure 資本支出 **shihon shishutsu** *(she-hone she-shoot-sue)*

capital exports 資本輸出 **shihon yushutsu** *(she-hone yuu-shoot-sue)*

capital formation 資本形成 **shihon keisei** *(she-hone kay-say)*

capital gain/loss 資本利得/損失 **shihon ritoku/sonshitsu** *(she hone ree-toe-kuu/soan-sheet-sue)*

capital goods 資本財 **shihon zai** *(she-hone zye)*

capital increase 資本増加 **shihon zōka** *(she-hone zoe-kah)*; 増資 **zoshi** *(zoe-she)*

capital intensive 資本集約 **shihon shūyaku** *(she-hone shuu-yah-kuu)*

capital investment 設備投資 **setsubi tōshi** *(say-t'sue-bee toe-she)*

capitalism 資本主義 **shihon shugi** *(she-hone shuu-ghee)*

capitalist 資本主義者 **shihónshugisha** *(she-hoan-shuu-ghee-shah)*

capitalization 資本家 **shihon-ka** *(she-hone-kah)*; 資本構成 **shihon kōsei** *(she-hone koe-say)*

capitalize 資本化する **shihon-ka suru** *(she-hone kah sue-rue)*

capital market 資本市場 **shihon shijō** *(she-hone she-joe)*

capital ownership 出資比率 **shusshi hiritsu** *(shuu-she hee-ree-t'sue)*

capital spending 設備投資 **setsubi tōshi** *(say-t'sue-bee toe-she)*; 資本支出 **shihon shishutsu** *(she-hone she-shoot-sue)*

capital stock 株式資本(金) **kabushiki shihon (kin)** *(kah-buu-she-kee she-hone (keen))*

capital structure 資本構成 **shihon kōsei** *(she-hone koe-say)*; 財務基盤 **zaimu kiban** *(zye-muu kee-bahn)*

capital surplus 資本剰余金 **shihon jōyo kin** *(she-hone joe-yoe keen)*

capsule カプセル **kapuseru** *(kahp-say-rue)*

car 自動車 **jidōsha** *(jee-doe-shah)*; **kuruma** *(kuh-rue-mah)*

carbon dioxide 二酸化炭素 **nisanka tanso** *(nee-sahn-kah tahn-so)*

carbon dioxide emissions 二酸化炭素排出量 **nisanka tanso haishutsu ryō** *(nee-sahn-kah tahn-so high-shuu-t'sue-rio)*
▪ The reduction of carbon dioxide emissions is the high-priority issue in the reduction of global warming. 二酸化炭素排出量の削減は、地球温暖化防止の最重要課題です。**Nisanka tanso haishutsu ryō sakugen wa chikyū ondan ka bōshi no saijuyō kadai désu.** *(nee-sahn-kah tahn-so high-shuu-t'sue-rio no sah-kuu-gane wah chee-k'yuu on-dan-kah boe-she no sigh-juu-yoh kah-die dess.)*

career キャリア **kyaria** *(k'yah-ree-ah)*

caretaker 保護者 **hogosha** *(hoh-go-shah)*

cargo; freight 貨物 **kamotsu** *(kah-moat-sue)*; 積荷 **tsumini** *(t'sue-me-nee)*

carpenter 大工 **daiku** *(die-kuu)*

carrier 運送業者 **unsō gyōsha** *(uun-so g'yoe-shah)*

carrier's risk 運送業者危険負担 **unsō gyōsha kiken futan** *(uun-so g'yoe-shah kee-ken fuu-tahn)*

carry (transport) 運ぶ **hakobu** *(hah-koe-buu)*; carry out, put into practice 実行する **jikkō suru** *(jeek-koe sue-rue)*
▪ The goods have already been transported to the warehouse. 品物はもうそこに運ばれました。**Shinamono wa mō sōko ni hakobaremashita.** *(she-nah-moe-noh wah moh so-koh nee hah-koe-bah-ray-mahsh-tah.)*

carry-back 繰り戻し **kurimodoshi** *(kuu-ree-moe-doe-she)*

carry forward 進める **susumeru** *(sue-sue-may-rue)*

carry forward (accounting) 繰り越し **kurikosu** *(kuu-ree-koe-sue)*

carrying charges 諸掛かり **shogakari** *(show-gah-kah-ree)*

carry-over (accounting) 繰り越し **kurikoshi** *(kuu-ree-koe-she)*

carry-over merchandise 残品 **zanpin** *(zahn-peen)*

cartel 企業連合 **kigyō rengō** *(kee-g'yoe ren-go)*; カルテル **karuteru** *(kah-ruu-tay-rue)*

cash 現金 **genkin** *(gane-keen)*
▪ Please pay in cash. 現金で払ってください。**Genkin de haratte kudasai.** *(gane-keen day hah-rah-tay kuu-dah-sigh.)*

cash-and-carry 現金店頭渡しの **genkin tentō watashi no** *(gane-keen ten-toe wah-tah-she noh)*

cash-and-carry (trade) キャッシュアンドキャリー **kyasshu ando kyarii** *(kyah-sshuu an-doe kyah-ree)*

cash balance 現金残高 **genkin zandaka** *(gane-keen zahn-dah-kah)*

cash basis (accounting) 現金主義 **genkin shugi** *(gane-keen shuu-ghee)*; 現金ベース **genkin bēsu** *(gane-keen bay-sue)*

cash before delivery (CBD) 代金前払い **daikin maebarai** *(dye-keen my-bah-rye)*

cash book 現金出納帳 **genkin suitō-chō** *(gane-keen sue-ee-toe choe)*

cash budget 現金予算 **genkin yosan** *(gane-keen yoe-sahn)*

cash delivery 当日決済取引 **tōjitsu kessai torihiki** *(toe-jee-t'sue case-sigh toe-ree-he-kee)*

cash discount 現金割引 **genkin waribiki** *(gane-keen wah-ree-bee-kee)*

cash dividend 現金配当 **genkin haitō** *(gane-keen high-toe)*; 配当金 **haitō kin** *(high-toe keen)*

cash entry キャッシュエントリー **kasshu entorii** *(kaa-shuu en-toe-ree)*

cash flow 現金収支 **genkin shūshi** *(gane-keen shuu-she)*; 資金繰り **shikin guri** *(she-keen guu-ree)*

cash; spots (stock market) 現物 **genbutsu** *(gane-boot-sue)*

cashier 出納係 **suitō gakari** *(sue-ee-toe gah-kah-ree)*; 現金係 **genkin gakari** *(gane-keen gah-kah-ree)*; cashier in restaurant or store 会計 **kaikei** *(kye-kay)*

cashier's check 支払人小切手 **shiharainin kogitte** *(she-hah-rye-neen koe-gheet-tay)*

cash in advance 前払い金 **mae barai kin** *(my-bah-rye keen)*

cash on delivery (COD) 代金引換払い **genkin hikikae-barai** *(gane-keen he-kee-kye-bah-rye)*; 着払い **chaku-barai** *(chah-kuu bah-rye)*

cash register レジスター **rejisutā** *(ray-jees-tah)*; レジ **reji** *(ray-jee)*

casino カジノ **kajino** *(kah-jee-no)*

cassette カセット **kasetto** *(kah-set-toe)*

casual くだけた **kudaketa** *(kuh-dah-kay-tah*); カジュアルな **kajuaru na** *(kah-juu-ah-rue nah)*
▪ Will casual clothes be all right for tonight's party? 今晩のパーテイは普段着でよろしいですか。**Konban no pātii wa fudangi de yoroshii désu ka?** *(comb-bahn no pah-tee wah fuu-dahn-ghee day yoe-roe-she dess kah?)*

casualty insurance 災害保険 **saigai hoken** *(sigh-guy hoe-ken)*; 損害保険 **songai hoken** *(soan-guy hoe-ken)*

catalog カタログ **katarogu** *(kah-tah-roe-guu)*

catalyst 触媒 **shokubai** *(show-kuu-by)*

category (kinds) 種類 **shurui** *(shuu-rue-ee)*; カテゴリー **kategorii** *(kah-tay-goh-ree)*
▪ We have two categories of imported merchandise. 輸入品は2種類あります。**Yunyūhin wa ni shurui arimasu.** *(yuun-yuu heen wah nee shuu-rue-ee ah-ree-mahss.)*

cause 原因 **gen'in** *(gen-een)*
▪ Do you know the cause of the problem? その問題の原因をご存知ですか。**Sono mondai no gen'in wo gozonji désu ka?** *(so-no moan-dye no gain-een oh go-zone-jee dess kah?)*

cause trouble (inconvenience) 迷惑をかける **meiwaku wo kakeru** *(may-wah-kuu oh kah-kay-rue)*
▪ I do not want to cause anybody any trouble. 誰にも迷惑をかけたくないのです。**Dare ni mo meiwaku wo kaketaku nai no désu.** *(dah-ray nee moe may-wah-kuu oh kah-kay-tah-kuu nigh no dess.)*

CB radio (citizen's band radio) 市民ラジオ **shimin rajio** *(she-mean rah-jee-oh)*

CD CD **Shii-Dii** *(she-dee)*
▪ What floor are your CD's on? CD売り場は何階ですか。**CD uriba wa nankai désu ka?** *(she-dee uu-ree-bah wah nahn-kie dess kah?)*
▪ How much are the CD's? CDはいくらですか。**CD wa ikura désu ka?** *(she-dee wah ee-kuu-rah dess kah?)*

CD-ROM CD-ROM **Shii-Dii Romu** *(she-dee roh-muu)*

ceiling (highest point) 最高限度 **saikō gendo** *(sigh-koe gen-doe)*; 最高価格 **saikō kakaku** *(sigh-koe kah-kah-kuu)*

celebrate 祝う **iwau** *(ee-wow)*
▪ My friend celebrated my finding employment. 友人が就職祝いをしてくれました。**Tomodachi gah shūshoku iwai oh shite kuremashita.** *(toh-moh-dah-chee gah shuu-shoh-kuu ee-wie oh ssh-tay kuu-ray-mah-ssh-tah.)*

celebration お祝い **o-iwai** *(oh-ee-wie)*

celebrity 有名人 **yūmejin** *(yuu-may-jeen)*

cell phone 携帯電話 **keitai denwa** *(kay-ee-tie dane-wah)*
▪ I lost my cell phone. 携帯をなくした。**Keitai wo nakushita.** *(kah-ee-tie oh nah-kuu-ssh-tah.)*

censor 非難する **hinan suru** *(he-nahn sue-rue)*

census 国勢調査 **kokuseichōsa** *(koe-kuu-say-e-chohh-sah)*

centigrade 摂氏 **sesshi** *(say-sshe)*

centimeter センチ(メートル) **senchi (mētoru)** *(sen-chee (may-toe-rue))*

Central Bank 中央銀行 **Chūo Ginkō** *(chew-oh gheen-koe)*

centralization 集中化 **shūchū-ka** *(shuu-chew-kah)*

central rate セントラルレート **sentoraru rēto** *(sen-toe rah-rue ray-toe)*; 中心相場 **chūshin sōba** *(chew-seen so-bah)*

century 世紀 **seiki** *(say-e-kee)*

CEO (Chief Executive Officer) 最高経営責任者 **saikō keiei sekinin-sha** *(sigh-koe kay-ee no say-kee-neen shah)*

ceremony 式 **shiki** *(she-kee)*; ritual 儀式 **gishiki** *(ghee-she-kee)*

certificate 証明書 **shōmei sho** *(show-may show)*
▪ All overseas shipments must have a certificate. すべての海外の積み荷には証明書が必要です。**Subete no kaigai no tsumini ni wa shōmeisho ga hitsuyō désu.** *(sue-bay-tay no kye-guy no t'sue-me-nee nee wah show-may-show ga sheet-sue-yoe dess.)*

certificate (securities) 証券 **shōken** *(show-ken)*

certificate of deposit 預金証書 **yokin shōsho** *(yoe-keen show-show)*

certificate of incorporation 会社設立

許可書 **kaisha setsuritsu kyoka-sho** *(kye-shah say-t'sue-ree-t'sue k'yoe-kah-show)*

certificate of origin 原産地証明書 **gensanchi shōmei sho** *(gen-sahn-chee show-may-show)*

certified check 支払保証小切手 **shiharai hoshō kogitte** *(she-har-rye hoe-show koe-ghee-tay)*

certified public accountant 公認会計士 **kōnin kaikeishi** *(koe-neen kye-kay-she)*

certify 証明する **shōmei suru** *(show-may sue-rue)*

chain of command 指揮系統 **shiki keitō** *(she-kee kay-toe)*

chain store チェーンストア **chēn sutoa** *(chain stow-ah)*

chain store group チェーンストア組織 **chēn sutoa soshiki** *(chain stow-ah so-she-kee)*

chairperson of the board 取締役会長 **torishimariyaku kaichō** *(toe-ree-he-mah-ree-yah-kuu kye-choe)*; 会長 **kaichō** *(kye-choe)*

chairperson of a conference 議長 **gichō** *(ghee-choe)*

challenge 挑戦 **chōsen** *(choe-sen)*; serious challenge 真剣な挑戦 **shinken na chōsen** *(sheen-ken nah choe-sen)*
▪ Your project is a very interesting challenge. あなたのプロジェクトは画期的な試みです。**Anata no purojekuto wa kakki teki na kokoromi désu.** *(ah-nah-tah no puu-roh-jek-toh wa kah-kee tay-kee nah koe-koe-roe me dess.)*

Chamber of Commerce and Industry 商工会議所 **Shō Kō Kaigi Sho** *(show koe kye-ghee show)*

champagne シャンペン **shanpen** *(shahn-pane)*

champion チャンピオン **chanpion** *(chahn-pee-own)*; 優勝者 **yūshōsha** *(yuu-shohh-shah)*

change (amend) 変更 **henkō** *(hen-koe)*
▪ If you will change this contract, I will sign it. この契約を変更すれば、署名します。**Kono keiyaku wo henkō sureba shomei shimasu.** *(koe-no kay-yah-kuu oh hen-koe sue-ray-bah show-may she-mahss.)*

change (money back) おつり **otsuri** *(oh-t'sue-ree)*
▪ I forgot my change. おつりを忘れました。**Otsuri wo wasuremashita.** *(oh-t'sue-ee oh wah-sue-ray-mah-shtah.)*

change (small coins for telephone, etc.) 細かいお金 **komakai okane** *(koe-mah-kye oh-kah-nay)*; to change a bill くずす **kuzusu** *(kuu-suu-sue)*
▪ Please change this bill (into smaller units). このお札をくずしてください。**Kono o-satsu wo kuzushite kudasai.** *(koe-no oh-sah-t'sue oh kuu-zuu-shtay kuu-dah-sigh)*

channel 海峡 **kaikyō** *(kie-k'yohh)*; TV channel チャンネル **channeru** *(chahn-nay-rue)*

channel of distribution 流通経路 **ryūtsū keiro** *(ree-uu-t'sue kay-roe)*

charge; cost 料金 **ryōkin** *(ree-ohh-keen)*
▪ How much is the charge? 料金はいくらですか? **Ryōkin wa ikura désu ka?** *(ree-ohh-keen wa ee-kuu-rah dess kah?)*

charge account 売掛金勘定 **urikake-kin kanjō** *(uu-ree-kah-kay-keen kahn-joe)*; クレジット口座 **kurejitto kōza** *(kuu-ray-jeet-toe kohh-zah)*

chart チャート **chāto** *(chahh-toe)*; 表 **hyō** *(h'yoe)*

charter 特許状 **tokkyojō** *(toke-yoh-johh)*

charter (for shipping) 用船 **yōsen** *(yoe-sen)*; charter (a boat, etc.) 貸し切り **kashikiri** *(kah-she-kee-ree)*

chartered accountant 公認会計士 **kōnin kaikeishi** *(koe-neen kye-kay-she)*

chattel 動産 **dōsan** *(doe-sahn)*

chattel mortgage 動産抵当 **dōsan teitō** *(doe-sahn tay-toe)*

cheap 安い **yasui** *(yah-sue-ee)*; cheaper もっと安い **motto yasui** *(moat-toe yah-sue-ee)*; cheapest 一番安い **ichiban yasui** *(ee-chee-bahn yah-sue-ee)*

check (bank) 小切手 **kogitte** *(koe-gheet-tay)*
▪ I will mail you a check tomorrow. 明日郵便で小切手を送ります。**Ashita yūbin de kogitte wo okurimasu.** *(ah-shtah yuu-bean nee koe-gheet-tay oh oh-kuu-ree-mahss.)*

check (investigate) 調べる **shiraberu** *(she-rah-bay-rue)*

checking account 当座預金口座 **tōza yokin kōza** *(toe-zah yoe-keen koe-zah)*

check in/out チェックイン, チェックアウトする **chekku-in/auto suru** *(check-een/ow-toe sue-rue)*

checklist 照合表 **shōgō hyō** *(show-go h'yoe)*; チェックリスト **chekku risuto** *(check-ku ree-sue-toe)*

checkup 健康診断 **kenkōshindan** *(kane-kohh-sheen-dahn)*; 検査 **kensa** *(ken-sah)*

chemical products 化学製品 **kagaku seihin** *(kah-gah-kuu say-heen)*

chemical(s) 化学 **kagaku** *(kah-gah-kuu)*

chief accountant 会計主任 **kaikei shunin** *(kye-kay shuu-neen)*

chief buyer 購買主任 **kōbai shunin** *(koe-buy shuu-neen)*

chief executive officer (CEO) 最高経営責任者 **saikō keiei sekinin sha** *(sigh-koe kay-ee no say-kee-neen shah)*

China 中国 **Chūgoku** *(chuu-go-kuu)*

Chinese food 中華料理 **chūka ryōri** *(chew-kah rio-ree)*

Chinese person 中国人 **Chūgokujin** *(chuu-go-kuu-jeen)*

chip (computer) チップ **chippu** *(cheap-puu)*

choice; option; selection 選択 **sentaku** *(sane-tah-kuu)*
▪ I had no choice. 選択がありませんでした。**Sentaku ga arimasen déshita.** *(sane-tah-kuu gah ah-ree-mah-sin deh-ssh-tah.)*

chopsticks お箸 **o-hashi** *(oh-hah-she)*; splittable wooden chopsticks joined at one end 割り箸 **waribashi** *(wah-ree-bah-she)*

CIF (cost, insurance and freight) 運賃保険料込み値段 **unchin hoken-ryō komi nedan** *(uun-cheen hoe-ken rio koe-me nay-dahn)*

circuit (electrical) 回路 **kairo** *(kie-roe)*

circuit breaker 回路遮断器 **kairo shadanki** *(kye-roe shah-dahn-kee)*; ブレーカー **burēkā** *(buu-ray-kah)*

circulation (publication) 発行部数 **hakkōbusū** *(hock-koh-buu-suu)*

citation 引用 **in'yō** *(een-yohh)*

citizen 市民 **shimin** *(she-meen)*; ~ of

a city or nation 国民 **kokumin** *(koh-kuu-meen)*

citizenship 市民権 **shiminken** *(she-meen-kane)*

civil engineer 土木技師 **doboku gishi** *(doe-boe-kuu ghee-she)*

civil law 民法 **minpō** *(meen-pohh)*

civilian 民間人 **minkan-jin** *(meen-kahn-jeen)*; 一般人 **ippan-jin** *(eep-pahn jeen)*

civilization 文明 **bunmei** *(boon-may-ee)*

claim (demand) 要求 **yōkyū** *(yohh-k'yuu)*

claim (request) 請求する **seikyū suru** *(say-cue sue-rue)*; クレーム **kūrēmu** *(kuu-ray-muu)*
▪ I would like to make a claim on this shipment. この積荷にクレームをつけたいです。**Kono tsumini ni kūrēmu wo tsuketai désu.** *(koe-no t'sue-me-nee nee kuu-ray-muu oh t'sue-kay-tie dess.)*

claim (for business loss) 損害賠償請求 **songai baishō seikyū** *(soan-guy buy-show say-cue)*

claim (for insurance) 支払請求 **shiharai seikyū** *(she-hah-rye say-cue)*

clarification; explanation 説明 **setsumei** *(say-t'sue-may-ee)*

clarify 明らかにする **akiraka ni suru** *(ah-kee-rah-kah nee sue-rue)*
▪ Please clarify these instructions. この指示を明らかにして下さい。**Kono shiji wo akiraka ni shite kudasai.** *(koe-no she-jee oh ah-kee-rah-kah nee ssh-tay kuu-dah-sie.)*

class action (suit) 集団訴訟 **shūdan soshō** *(shuu-dahn so-show)*

class; rank; caste 階級 **kaikyū** *(kie-k'yuu)*

classification 分類 **bunrui** *(boon-rue-ee)*; 区分 **kubun** *(kuu-boon)*

classified ad 項目別広告 **kōmoku-betsu kōkoku** *(koe-moe-kuu-bait-sue koe-koe-kuu)*; 三行広告 **sangyō kōkoku** *(sahn-g'yoe koe-koe-kuu)*; 新聞広告 **shinbun kōkoku** *(sheem-boon koe-koe-kuu)*

classify 分類する **bunrui suru** *(boon-rue-ee sue-rue)*

classmate 同級生 **dōkyūsei** *(doe-cue-say)*
▪ They are classmates. あの人達は同級生です。**Ano hito-tachi wa dōkyūsei désu.** *(ah-no shtoe-tah-chee wah doe-cue-say dess.)*

clause (of contract, law) 箇条 **kajō** *(kah-johh)*; 条項 **jōkō** *(joe-koe)*
▪ Please explain this clause. この条項を説明してください。**Kono jōkō wo setsumei shite kudasai.** *(koe-no joe-koe oh sate-sue-may-ee ssh-tay kuu-dah-sie.)*

clearinghouse 手形交換所 **tegata kōkan-jo** *(tay-gah-tah koe-khan-show)*

clerk in office 事務員 **jimu in** *(jee-muu een)*; clerk in bank 銀行員 **ginkō in** *(gheen-koe een)*; clerk in shop 店員 **ten in** *(tane een)*

client 依頼人 **irainin** *(ee-rye-neen)*; customer お客さん **o-kyaku-san** *(oh-kyack-sahn)*

climate 気候 **kikō** *(kee-koe)*

close 終値 **owari ne** *(oh-wah-ree nay)*

closed 閉店した **heiten shita** *(hey-ten shtah)*; 閉まっている **shimatteiru** *(she-maht-tay-ee-rue)*

closed account 締め切り済み勘定 **shimekiri zumi kanjō** *(she-may-kee-ree zuu-mee kahn-joe)*

closely-held corporation 非公開会社 **hi-kōkai gaisha** *(he-koe-kye guy-shah)*

closing entry 決算記入 **kessan kinyū** *(case-sahn keen-yuu)*

closing price 引け値 **hikene** *(he-kay nay)*

closing time of door/gate 門限 **mon gen** *(moan gane)*; 閉店時間 **heiten jikan** *(hey-ten jee-kahn)*

coffee break 休憩(時間) **kyūkei (jikan)** *(cue-kay (jee-kahn))*

coalition 連盟 **renmei** *(rane-may-e)*; 同盟 **dōmei** *(dohh-may-e)*

coexist 共存する **kyōzon suru** *(k'yohh-zone sue-rue)*

collaborate (work together) 協力する **kyōryoku suru** *(k'yohh-rio-kuu sue-rue)*

collaboration 共同(製作) **kyodō (seisaku)** *(k'yoh-doh (say-sah-kuu))*; 合作 **gassaku** *(gah-ssah-kuu)*

collapse 経営破綻 **keiei hatan** *(kay-ee hah-tahn)*

collate 順序よく並べる **junjoyoku naraberu** *(june-joe-yoh-kuu nah-rah-bay-rue)*

collateral 担保 **tanpo** *(tahn-poh)*; 見返り担保(物件) **mikaeri tanpo (bukken)** *(mee-kye-ree tahn-poe (buu-ken))*

colleague 同僚 **dōryō** *(doe-rio)*

collect 集める **atsumeru** *(aht-sue-may-rue)*

collect-call 先方払い **senpō barai** *(sem-poe bah-rye)*; コレクトコール **korekuto kōru** *(koe-ray-kuu-toe koe-ruu)*

▪ I want to make a collect call to Chicago. シカゴにコレクトコールをかけたいのです。**Shikago ni korekuto kōru wo kaketai no désu.** *(she-kah-go nee collect-call oh kah-kay-tie no dess.)*

collect information 取材する **shuzai suru** *(shuu-zye sue-rue)*

collection (債券)回収 **(saiken) kaishū** *(sigh-ken kye-shuu)*; 取り立て **toritate** *(toe-ree-tah-tay)*

collection period 取り立て期間 **toritate kikan** *(toe-ree-tah-tay kee-kahn)*; 回収期間 **kaishū kikan** *(kye-shuu kee-kahn)*

collective agreement 団体協約 **dantai kyōyaku** *(dahn-tie k'yoe-yah-kuu)*

collective bargaining 団体交渉 **dantai kōshō** *(dahn-tie koe-show)*

collect on delivery (COD) 代金引換払い **daikin hikikae barai** *(dye-keen he-kee-kye bah-rye)*

color 色 **iro** *(ee-roe)*

▪ The color is wrong. 色が違います。**Iro ga chigaimasu.** *(ee-roe gah chee-guy-mahss.)*

color TV カラーテレビ **karā terebi** *(kah-rah tay-ray-bee)*

commemorate 記念する **kinen suru** *(kee-nane sue-rue)*

▪ Let's commemorate our business tie-up. 我々の事業提携を祝いましょう。**Ware ware no jigyō teikei wo iwai mashō.** *(wah-ray wah-ray no jeeg-yoh tay-kay oh ee-wie mah-show.)*

commerce 通商 **tsūshō** *(t'sue-show)*

commercial advertisement (TV) コマーシャル **komāsharu** *(koe-mah-shah-rue)*

commercial attaché 商務官 **shōmu kan** *(show-muu kahn)*

commercial bank 市中銀行 **shichū ginkō** *(she-chew gheen-koe)*

commercial grade 商業格付け **shōgyō kakuzuke** *(show-g'yoe kah-kuu-zuu-kay)*

commercial invoice 商業送り状 **shōgyō okurijō** *(show-g'yoe oh-kuu-ree-joe)*; コマーシャルインボイス **komāsharu inboisu** *(koe-mah-sha-ruu en-boe-ee-sue)*

commission (fee) 手数料 **tesūryō** *(tay-sue-rio)*

commission agency 取次 **toritsugi** *(toe-ree-t'sue-ghee)*

commitment 約定 **yakutei** *(yah-kuu-tay)*; 約束 **yakusoku** *(yah-kuu-so-kuu)*; 債務 **saimu** *(sigh-muu)*

committee 委員会 **i-in-kai** *(ee-een-kay)*

Committee for Economic Development (an important business organization in Japan) 経済同友会 **Keizai Dōyūkai** *(kay-zye doe-yuu-kye)*

committee meeting 委員会 **i-in-kaigi** *(ee-een-kye-ghee)*

commodity 商品 **shōhin** *(show-heen)*

commodity exchange 商品取引所 **shōhin torihikisho** *(show-heen toe-ree-he-kee-show)*

commodity price 物価 **bukka** *(buu-kah)*
▪ Commodity prices have gone up but wages have not gone up at all. 物価は上場するが、給料はちっともあがらない。**Bukka wa jōshō suru ga kyuryō wa chittomo agaranai.** *(buke-kah wah johh-shohh sue-rue gah k'yuu-rio wah cheet-toe-moe ah-gah-rah-nie.)*

commodity tax 物品税 **buppin zei** *(buu-peen zay)*
▪ Does that include the commodity tax? 物品税も入っていますか。**Buppin zei mo haitte imasu ka?** *(buu-peen zay moe height-tay ee-mahss kah?)*

common carrier 一般輸送業者 **ippan yusō gyōsha** *(eep-pahn yuu-so g'yoe-shah)*

common market 共同市場 **kyōdō shijō** *(k'yoe-doe she-joe)*

common stock 普通株 **futsū kabu** *(fuu-t'sue kah-buu)*

communication (correspondence) 通信 **tsūshin** *(t'sue-sheen)*

communism 共産主義 **kyōsan shugi** *(k'yoe-sahn shuu-ghee)*

community 地域社会 **chiiki shakai** *(chee-kee shah-kye)*

commute (travel) 通う **kayou** *(kah-yoh-uu)*; 通勤(通学)する **tsūkin (tsūgaku) suru** *(t'sue-keen (t'sue-gah-kuu) sue-rue)*

commuting allowance 通勤手当 **tsūkin teate** *(t'sue-keen tay-ah-tay)*
▪ Do you receive a commuting allowance? あなたは通勤手当をもらっていますか。**Anata wa tsūkin teate wo moratteimasu ka?** *(ah-nah-tah wah t'sue-keen tay-ah-tay wo moe-rah-tay-ee-mahss kah?)*

compact disc コンパクトディスク **konpakuto disuku** *(cone-pah-kuu-toe disk-uu)*; CD **Shii-Dii** *(she-dee)*
▪ Did you lose a CD? CDをなくしましたか。**CD wo nakushimashita ka?** *(she-dee oh nah-kuu-she-mahss-tah kah?)*

compact disc player コンパクトディスクプレーヤー **konpakuto disuku purēyā** *(cone-pah-kuu-toe disk-uu puu-ray-

yah); CDプレーヤー **Shii-Dii purēyā** *(she-dee puu-ray-yah)*

company 会社 **kaisha** *(kye-shah)*

company employee 会社員 **kaishain** *(kye-shah-een)*; 企業 **kigyō** *(kee-g'yoe)*

company expense, at 会社持ちで **kaisha mochi de** *(kye-shah moe-chee day)*

company goals 企業目標 **kigyō mokuhyō** *(k'gyoe moe-kuu-h'yoe)*

company owned by foreign interests 外資系会社 **gaishikei gaisha** *(guy-she-kay guy-shah)*

company pension 厚生年金 **kōsei nenkin** *(koe-say nane-keen)*

company policy 会社の方針 **kaisha no hōshin** *(kye-shah no hoe-sheen)*

company recreational trip 慰安旅行 **ian ryokō** *(ee-ahn rio-koe)*

company union 企業別(内)組合 **kigyōbetsu (nai) kumiai** *(kee-g'yoe-bait-sue (nah-ee) kuu-me-eye)*

company villa (may also be private) 別荘 **bessō** *(base-so)*; 保養所 **hoyō-jo** *(hoe-yoe-joe)*

company with limited liability 有限会社 **yūgen gaisha** *(yuu-gen guy-shah)*

company with foreign equity 外資系企業 **gaishikei kigyō** *(guy-she-kay kee-g'yoe)*

compensation 補償 **hōshū** *(hoe-shuu)*

compensation trade 求償貿易 **kyūshō bōeki** *(cue-show boe-ay-kee)*

compete 競う **kisou** *(kee-soh-uu)*

competition 競争 **kyōsō** *(k'yoe-so)*
▪ There is no competition in this industry. この業界に競争はありません。**Kono gyōkai ni kyōsō wa arimasen.** *(koe-no g'yoe-kye nee k'yoe-so wah ah-ree-mah-sen.)*

competitive advantage 競争上の利点 **kyōsō jō no riten** *(k'yoe-so jo no ree-ten)*; セールスポイント **sērusu pointo** *(say-rue-sue point-oh)*

competitive bidding 競争入札 **kyōsō nyūsatsu** *(k'yoe-so n'yuu-sah-t'sue)*

competitive edge 競争上の優位性 **kyōsō-jō no yūi-sei** *(k'yoe-so joe-no yuu-ee-say)*

competitive price 競争価格 **kyōsō kakaku** *(k'yoe-so kah-kah-kuu)*

competitive strategy 競争戦略 **kyōsō senryaku** *(k'yoe-so sen-ree-yah-kuu)*

competitor 競争相手 **kyōsō aite** *(k'yoe-so eye-tay)*

competitor analysis 競争者分析 **kyōsō sha bunseki** *(k'yoe-so shah boon-say-kee)*

competitors (company) 競争相手 **kyōsō aite** *(k'yoe-so ah-ee-tay)*; 競合他社 **kyōgō tasha** *(k'yoe-go-tah-shah)*

complain (ぐちを)こぼす **(guchi wo) kobosu** *((guu-chee wo) koe-boe-sue)*; nothing to complain about こぼすことはない **kobosu koto wa nai** *(koe-boe-sue koe-toe wah nigh)*; 不平を言う **fuhei wo iu** *(fuu-hay oh yuu)*; 苦情を言う **kujō wo iu** *(kuu-joe oh yuu)*
▪ He is always complaining to me. あの人はいつも私にこぼしています。**Ano hito wa watashi ni itsumo koboshite imasu.** *(ah-no shtoe wah wah-tah-she nee eat-sue-moe koe-boe shtay-mahss.)*

complaint (grievance) 苦情 **kujō** *(kuu-joe)*
▪ What is your complaint this time? 今度の苦情は何ですか。**Kondo no kujō wa nan désu ka?** *(cone-doe no kuu-joe wah nahn dess kah?)*

complete (accomplish) 完成する **kansei suru** *(kahn-say sue-rue)*; 大成 **taisei** *(tie-say)*

compliance 承諾 **shōdaku** *(show-dah-kuu)*

compliment お褒め **ohome** *(oh-hoe-may)*
▪ Thank you for the compliment. お褒めに預かり恐縮です。**Ohome ni azukari kyōshuku désu.** *(oh-hoe-may nee ah-zuu-kah-ree k'yoe-shuu-kuu dess.)*

compliments 賛辞 **sanji** *(sahn-jee)*
▪ Please give my compliments to the (company) president. 社長によろしくお伝えください。**Shachō ni yoroshiku otsutae kudasai.** *(shah-choh nee yoe-roe-she-kuu oh-t'sue-tah-ay kuh-dah-sigh.)*

complimentary copy 贈呈本 **zōtei bon** *(zoe-tay bone)*

component 構成要素 **kōsei yōso** *(koe-say yoe-so)*; コンポ **konpo** *(cone-poe)*

component (part) 部分 **bubun** *(buu-boon)*

composite materials 複合材料 **fukugō zairyō** *(fuu-kuu-go zye-rio)*

compound interest 複利 **fukuri** *(fuu-kuu-ree)*

compound semiconductor 化合物半導体 **kagōbutsu handōtai** *(kah-go-boot-sue hahn-doe-tie)*

compromise 遠慮しあう **enryo shiau** *(en-rio she-ow)*; 妥協する **dakyō suru** *(dah-k'yoe sue-rue)*
▪ Unfortunately, there is no room for compromise. あいにく、妥協の余地はありません。**Ainiku, dakyō no yochi wa arimasen.** *(eye-nee-kuu, dah-k'yoe no yoe-chee wah ah-ree-mah-sen.)*

comptroller 会計監査役 **kaikei kansa-yaku** *(kye-kay kahn-sah-yah-kuu)*

computer コンピュータ **konpyūta** *(kome-pyuu-tah)*

computer bank コンピュータバンク **konpyūta banku** *(kome-pyuu-tah bahn-kuu)*

computer center コンピュータセンター **konpyūta sentā** *(kome-pyuu-tah sen-tah)*

computer input コンピュータ入力 **konpyūta nyūryoku** *(kome-pyuu-tah n'yuu-rio-kuu)*

computerized numerical control コンピュータ内蔵数値制御 **konpyūta naizō sūchi seigyo** *(kome-pyuu-tah nigh-zo suu-chee say-g'yoe)*

computer language コンピュータ 言語 **konpyūta gengo** *(kome-pyuu-tah gen-go)*

computer memory メモリ **memorii** *(may-moe-ree)*

computer output コンピュータ出力 **konpyūta shutsuryoku** *(kome-pyuu-tah shoot-sue-rio-kuu)*

computer program コンピュータプログラム **konpyūta puroguramu** *(kome-pyuu-tah puu-roe-guu-rah-muu)*

computer storage コンピュータ ストレージ **konpyūta sutorēji** *(kome-pyuu-tah stow-ray-jee)*

computer terminal コンピュータ ターミナル **konpyūta tāminaru** *(kome-pyuu-tah tah-me-nah-rue)*

conclusion (concluding remarks) 結論 **ketsuron** *(kate-sue-roan)*; 締結 **teiketsu** *(tay-kate-sue)*; final results 結末 **ketsumatsu** *(kate-sue-mah-t'sue)*

condition (aspect) 状態 **jōtai** *(joe-tie)*

conditional acceptance 条件付き引受け **jōken-tsuki hikiuke** *(joe-ken-ski he-kee-uu-kay)*

conditional sales contract 条件付き売買契約 **jōken-tsuki baibai keiyaku** *(joe-ken-ski by-by kay-yah-kuu)*

conditions (terms) 条件 **jōken** *(joe-ken)*

conference 会談 **kaidan** *(kye-dahn)*; 会議 **kaigi** *(kye-ghee)*; 話し合い **hanashi-ai** *(hah-nah-she-eye)*
▪ What time will the conference begin? 会議は何時に始まりますか。**Kaigi wa nanji ni hajimarimasu ka?** *(kye-ghee wah nahn-jee nee hah-jee-mah-ree-mahss kah?)*

conference room 会議室 **kaigi shitsu** *(kye-ghee sheet-sue)*

confidential 機密の **kimitsu no** *(kee-meet-sue no)*; 内密の **naimitsu no** *(nie-meet-sue no)*

confirm 確認する **kakunin suru** *(kah-kuu-neen sue-rue)*; 確かめる **tashikameru** *(tah-she-kah-may-rue)*
▪ Please confirm my airline reservations. 飛行機の予約を確認してください。**Hikōki no yoyaku wo kakunin shite kudasai.** *(he-koe-kee no yoe-yah-kuu oh kah-kuu-neen shtay kuh-dah-sigh.)*

confirmation of order 注文確認 **chūmon kakunin** *(chew-moan kah-kuu-neen)*

confirmation slip; receipt 確認書 **kakunin sho** *(kah-kuu-neen show)*

confiscate 没収する **bosshū suru** *(boe-shuu sue-rue)*

conflict of interest 利益の衝突 **rieki no shōtotsu** *(ree-ay-kee no show-tote-sue)*; 利害の対立 **rigai no tairitsu** *(ree-guy no tah-ree-t'sue)*

confrontation 対立 **tairitsu** *(tah-ree-t'sue)*
▪ Let us avoid a confrontation. 対立を避けましょう。**Tairitsu wo sakemashō.** *(tie-ree-t'sue oh sah-kay-mah-show)*

conglomerate 複合企業 **fukugō kigyō** *(fuu-kuu-go kee-g'yoe)*

connecting flight 乗り継ぎ便 **noritsugi bin** *(no-ree-t'sue-ghee-bean)*
▪ What time does your connecting flight leave? あなたの乗り継ぎ便は何時ですか。**Anata no noritsugi bin wa nanji dess ka?** *(ah-nah-tah no no-ree-t'sue-ghee bean wah nahn-jee dess kah?)*

consent (accept, agree) 承知する **shōchi suru** *(show-chee sue-rue)*
▪ I consent (accept). 承知しました。**Shōchi shimashita.** *(show-chee she-mah-shtah.)*

conservative (in color, style) 地味な **jimi na** *(jee-me nah)*
▪ I want a suit that is very conservative. とても無難なスーツが欲しいです。**Totemo bunan na sūtsu ga hoshii désu.** *(toe-tay-moe buu-nahn nah suit-sue gah hoe-she dess.)*

consideration 考える **kangaeru** *(kahn-guy-rue)*
▪ I will give your proposal serious consideration. あなたの提案を真剣に考えてみます。**Anata no teian wo shinken ni kangaete mimasu.** *(ah-nah-tah no tay-an oh sheen-kane nee kahn-guy-tay me-mahss.)*

consignee 受託者 **jutaku sha** *(juu-tah-kuu shah)*; 荷受人 **niuke nin** *(nee-uu-kay neen)*

consignment note 委託貨物運送状 **itaku kamotsu unsō-jō** *(ee-tah-kuu kah-moat-sue uun-so-joe)*

consignment sales 委託販売 **itaku hanbai** *(ee-tah-kuu hahn-by)*; goods on consignment 委託品 **itaku hin** *(ee-tah-kuu heen)*

consolidate 強める **tsuyomeru** *(t'sue-yoh-may-rue)*; 統合する **tōgō suru** *(toe-goe sue-rue)*; 合併する **gappei suru** *(gahp-pay sue-rue)*

consolidated accounting 連結決算 **renketsu kessan** *(rane-kay-t'suu case-sahn)*

consolidated financial statement 連結財務諸表 **renketsu zaimu shohyō** *(ren-kate-sue zye-muu show-h'yoe)*

consolidated shipment 連結出荷 **renketsu shukka** *(ren-kate-sue shuuk-kah)*

consortium 国際借款団 **kokusai shakkan-dan** *(coke-sigh shock-kahn-dahn)*

construction 建築 **kenchiku** *(ken-chee-kuu)*; 建設 **kensetsu** *(ken-say-t'sue)*; 工事 **kōji** *(koe-jee)*
▪ Construction will start on the new building in January next year. 新しいビルの建設は来年の1月から始まります。**Atarashii biru no kensetsu wa rainen no ichigatsu kara hajimarimasu.** *(ah-tah-rah-she bee-rue no ken-say-t'sue wah rye-nen no ee-chee-got-sue kah-rah hah-jee-mah-ree-mahss.)*

consul (diplomatic) 領事 **ryōji** *(re-yohh-jee)*

consular invoice 領事送り状 **ryōji okurijō** *(rio-jee oh kuu-ree-joe)*

consulate 領事館 **ryōjikan** *(re-yohh-jee-kahn)*

consult (with you) 相談する **sōdan suru** *(so-dahn sue-rue)*
▪ I would like to consult with Mr. Kawahara about this matter. この件を川原さんに相談したいです。**Kono ken wo Kawahara-san ni sōdan shitai désu.** *(koe-no ken oh kah-wah-hah-rah sahn nee so-dahn she-tie dess.)*

consultant 相談役 **sōdanyaku** *(so-dahn-yah-kuu)*
▪ He is a consultant for Mitsui Trading company. あの方は三井物産の相談役です。**Ano-kata wa Mitsui Bussan no sōdanyaku désu.** *(ah-no-kah-tah wah meet-sue-ee buse-sahn no so-dahn-yah-kuu dess.)*

consultation 相談 **sōdan** *(sohh-dahn)*

consumer 消費者 **shōhisha** *(show-he-shah)*

consumer acceptance 需要者承認 **juyōsha shōnin** *(juu-yoe-shah show-neen)*

consumer credit 消費者信用 **shōhisha shin'yō** *(show-he-shah sheen-yoe)*; 消費者金融 **shōhisha kin'yū** *(show-he-shah keen-yuu)*

consumer goods 消費財 **shōhi zai** *(show-he zye)*

consumer price index 消費者物価指数 **shōhisha bukka shisū** *(show-he-shah buu-kah she-sue)*

consumer research 消費者調査 **shōhisha chōsa** *(show-he-shah choe-sah)*

consumer satisfaction 顧客満足 **kokyaku manzoku** *(koe-k'yah-kuu mahn-zoe-kuu)*

contact (get in touch with) 連絡する **renraku suru** *(ren-rah-kuu sue-rue)*
▪ Please contact me next month. 来月連絡してください。**Raigetsu renraku shite kudasai.** *(rye-gate-sue ren-rah-kuu shtay kuu-dai-sigh.)*
▪ May I contact you next week? 来週連絡してもいいですか。**Raishū**

renraku shite mo ii désu ka? *(rye-shuu ren-rah-kuu shtay moe ee dess kah?)*

contact (someone you know) コネ **kone** *(koe-nay)*; 接触 **sesshoku** *(say-show-kuu)*; personal contact 個人的なつながり **kojin teki na tsunagari** *(koe-jeen tay-kee nah t'sue-nah-gah-ree)*
▪ I have no contacts in that company. 私はその会社にはコネがありません。**Watashi wa sono kaisha ni wa kone ga nai désu.** *(wah-tah-she wah so-no kye-shah nee wah cone-nay gah ah-ree-mah-sen.)*

container コンテナ **kontena** *(cone-tay-nah)*

content (of medical preparation) 容量 **yōryō** *(yoe-rio)*

contents (of box, etc.) 内容 **naiyō** *(nigh-yoe)*; 中身 **nakami** *(nah-kah-mee)*
▪ What is the contents of this box? この箱の中身は何ですか。**Kono hako no nakami wa nan désu ka?** *(koe-no hah-koe no nah-kah-mee wah nahn dess kah?)*

contingencies 不測の事態 **fusoku no jitai** *(fuu-so-kuu no jee-tie)*

contingency funds 緊急用積立金 **kinkyū-yō tsumitate kin** *(keen-cue-yoe t'sue-me-tah-tay keen)*; 臨時費 **rinji hi** *(reen-jee hee)*

contingent liability 偶発債務 **gūhatsu saimu** *(guu-hot-sue sigh-muu)*

contraband 密輸品 **mitsuyuhin** *(meet-sue-yuu-heen)*

contract 契約 **keiyaku** *(kay-yah-kuu)*; long-term contract 長期契約 **chōki keiyaku** *(choe-kee kay-yah-kuu)*
▪ The contract expires on April 1 next year. 契約は来年の4 月1 日に切れます。**Keiyaku wa rainen no shigatsu tsuitachi ni kiremasu.** *(kay-yah-kuu wah rye-nen no she-got-sue t'sue-ee-tah-chee nee kee-ray-mahss.)*

contract carrier 契約輸送業者 **keiyaku yusō gyōsha** *(kay-yah-kuu yuu-so g'yoe-shah)*

contract month 契約月 **keiyaku zuki** *(kay-yah-kuu zuu-kee)*

contractor 請負人 **ukeoinin** *(uu-kay-oh-e-neen)*; 契約人 **keiyakunin** *(kay-yah-kuu-neen)*

contribution; donation 寄付 **kifu** *(kee-fuu)*

contributor 寄付者 **kifusha** *(kee-fuu-shah)*

control 支配 **shihai** *(she-hie)*; 管理 **kanri** *(kahn-ree)*

control by management 支配する **shihai suru** *(she-high sue-rue)*

control by rules 統制する **tōsei suru** *(toe-say sue-rue)*

controllable costs 管理可能費 **kanri-kanō hi** *(kahn-ree-kah-no he)*

controller 会計監査役 **kaikei kansayaku** *(kye-kay kahn-sah-yah-kuu)*

controlling interest 支配権 **shihai ken** *(she-high ken)*

convene 集まる **atsumaru** *(aht-sue-mah-rue)*; 開く **hiraku** *(he-rah-kuu)*

conventional; habit; customary 習慣 **shūkan** *(shuhh-kahn)*; 慣習 **kanshū** *(kahn-shuhh)*

converter コンバーター **konbātā** *(kone-bahh-tahh)*

converter (electrical) 変換機 **henkanki** *(hen-kahn-kee)*

convertible currency 交換可能通貨 **kōkan kanō tsūka** *(koe-khan kah-no-t'sue-kah)*

convertible debentures 転換社債 **tenkan shasai** *(ten-kahn shah-sigh)*

convertible preferred stock 転換優先株 **tenkan yūsen kabu** *(ten-kahn yuu-sen kah-buu)*

cookie (java computer program) クッキー **kukkii** *(kuu-kee)*

cooperate 協力する **kyōryoku suru** *(k'yohh-rio-kuu sue-rue)*

cooperation (collaboration) 協力 **kyōryoku** *(k'yoe-rio-kuu)*

cooperative 協同組合 **kyōdō kumiai** *(k'yoe-doe kuu-me-eye)*

cooperative advertising 共同広告 **kyōdō kōkoku** *(k'yoe-doe koe-koe-kuu)*

co-ownership 共同所有権 **kyōdō shoyūken** *(k'yoe-doe show-yuu-ken)*

copier コピー機 **kopii-ki** *(koh-pee-kee-kie)*

copy コピー **kopii** *(koe-pee)*; 複写 **fukusha** *(fuu-kuu-shah)*
▪ Please make ten copies of this report. このレポートのコピーを10枚とってください。**Kono ripōto no kopii wo jūmai totte kudasai.** *(koe-no ree-poe-toe no koe-pee oh juu-my toe-tay kuu-dah-sigh.)*

copy (for advertising) 広告文案 **kōkoku bun-an** *(koe-koe-kuu boon-ahn)*; 宣伝文句 **senden monku** *(sen-den moan-kuu)*

copy (editorial manuscript) 原稿 **genkō** *(gen-koe)*

copy testing 現行調査 **genkō chōsa** *(gen-koe choe-sah)*

copyright 版権 **hanken** *(hahn-ken)*; 著作権 **chosaku ken** *(choe-sha-kuu ken)*; copyright reserved 版権所有 **hanken shoyū** *(hahn-ken sho-yuu)*

cordless phone コードレスホン **kōdoresu hon** *(koe-doe-ray-sue hone)*

core 核 **kaku** *(kah-kuu)*; 主軸 **shujiku** *(shuu-jee-kuu)*

core business 主力事業 **shuryoku jigyō** *(shuu-rio-kuu jee-g'yoe)*

corporate growth 企業成長 **kigyō seichō** *(kee-g'yoe say-choe)*

corporate image 企業イメージ **kigyō imēji** *(kee-g'yoe ee-may-jee)*

corporate income tax 法人所得税 **hōjin shotoku zei** *(hoe-jeen show-toe-kuu zay)*

corporate planning 企業計画 **kigyō keikaku** *(kee-g'yoe kay-kah-kuu)*

corporate; project 企業 **kigyō** *(kee-g'yohh)*

corporate structure 事業形態 **jigyō keitai** *(jee-g'yoe kay-tie)*

corporate tax 法人税 **hōjin zei** *(hoe-jeen zay)*

corporation (stock company) 株式会社 **kabushiki gaisha** *(kah-buu-she-kee guy-shah)*

corporation tax law 法人税法 **hōjin zei hō** *(hoe-jeen zay hoe)*

correspondence 通信 **tsūshin** *(t'sue-sheen)*; 文書 **bunsho** *(boon-show)*

correspondent bank 代理銀行 **dairi ginkō** *(dah-ee-ree gheen-koe)*

cosmopolitan 世界的 **sekai-teki** *(say-kie-tay-kee)*; 国際人 **kokusai-jin** *(coke-sigh-jeen)*

cost 原価 **genka** *(gen-kah)*

cost (expense) 費用 **hiyō** *(he-yoe)*; コスト **kosuto** *(cost-oh)*; 経費 **keihi** *(kay-he)*

cost accounting 原価計算 **genka keisan** *(gen-kah kay-sahn)*

cost analysis 原価分析 **genka bunseki** *(gen-kah boon-say-kee)*

cost and freight 運賃込み値段 **unchin komi nedan** *(uun-cheen koe-me nay-dahn)*

cost-benefit analysis 費用便益分析 **hiyō-ben'eki bunseki** *(he-yoe-ben-eh-kee boon-say-kee)*

cost control 原価管理 **genka kanri** *(gen-kah kahn-ree)*

cost-effectiveness 費用効率 **hiyō kōritsu** *(he-yoe koe-ree-t'sue)*

cost factor 費用予想 **genka yosō** *(gen-kah yoe-so)*; コスト要因 **kosuto yōin** *(cost yoe-een)*

cost of capital 資本コスト **shihon kosuto** *(she-hone cost-oh)*

cost of goods sold 売上原価 **uriage genka** *(uu-ree-ah-gay gen-kah)*

cost-of-living 生活費 **seikatsu hi** *(say-cot-sue he)*
▪ The cost of living is rising. 生活費は上がっています。**Seikatsu hi wa agatte imasu.** *(say-cot-sue he wah ah-got-tay ee-mahss.)*

cost of production 生産費 **seisan hi** *(say-sahn he)*; 製造原価 **seizō genka** *(say-zoe gen-kah)*

cost-plus 原価加算方式 **genka kasan hōshiki** *(gen-kah kah-sahn hoe-she-kee)*

cost-plus contract 原価加算契約 **genka kasan keiyaku** *(gen-kah kah-sahn kay-yah-kuu)*

cost-price squeeze 原価引き締め **genka hikishime** *(gen-kah he-kee-she-may)*

cost reduction 経費削減 **keihi sakugen** *(kay-he sah-kuu-gen)*

counter check 預金引出し票 **yokin hikidashi hyō** *(yoe-keen he-kee-dah-she h'yoe)*

counterfeit 偽造品 **gizō-hin** *(ghee-zoe-heen)*

countermeasures 対策 **taisaku** *(tie-sah-kuu)*; take countermeasures 対策を立てる **taisaku wo tateru** *(tie-sah-kuu oh tah-tay-rue)*
▪ We must take countermeasures. 対策を立てなければなりません。**Taisaku wo tatenakereba narimasen.** *(tie-sah-kuu oh tah-tay-nah-kay-ray-bah nah-ree-mah-sen.)*

country 国 **kuni** *(kuu-nee)*

country of origin 原産国 **gensan koku** *(gen-sahn koe-kuu)*

countryside 田舎 **inaka** *(ee-nah-kah)*

county 郡 **gun** *(guun)*

coup お手柄 **otegara** *(ohh-tay-gah-rah)*

coupon (bond interest) 利札 **rifuda** *(ree-fuu-dah)*; クーポン **kūpon** *(kuu-pone)*; 割引券 **waribiki-ken** *(wah-ree-bee-kee-ken)*

courier service 国際宅配便 **kokusai takuhai bin** *(coke-sigh tah-kuu-high bean)*

courtesy visit あいさつ回り **aisatsu mawari** *(eye-sah-t'sue mah-wah-ree)*
▪ I have come to pay a courtesy visit to Mr. Sato. 佐藤さんへごあいさつに伺いました。**Satō-san e go-aisatsu ni ukagaimashita.** *(sah-toe-sahn ay go-eye-sah-t'sue nee uu-kah-guy-mahsh-tah.)*

court of law 法廷 **hōtei** *(hoe-tay)*; 裁判所 **saibansho** *(sigh-bahn-show)*

cover (of magazine) 表紙 **hyōshi** *(h'yoe-she)*

cover charge サービス料 **sābisu ryō** *(sah-bee-sue rio)*; 席料 **seki ryō** *(say-kee rio)*

cover letter 添え状 **soe jō** *(so-eh joe)*

craftsman, craftsmen 職人 **shokunin** *(show-kuu-neen)*

craftsmanship 職人芸 **shokuningei** *(show-kuu-neen-gay-ee)*

creative 創造的 **sōzō-teki** *(sohh-zohh-tay-kee)*

creativity 創造力 **sōzō-ryoku** *(sohh-zohh-rio-yoh-kuu)*; 創作性 **sōsaku-sei** *(sohh-sah-kuu say)*

credentials 証明書 **shōmeisho** *(shohh-may-e-show)*

credit (financial) 信用 **shin'yō** *(sheen-yoe)*; クレジット **kurejitto** *(kuu-ray-jeet-toe)*

credit balance 貸方残高 **kashikata zandaka** *(kah-she-kah-tah zahn-dah-kah)*

credit bank 信用銀行 **shin'yō ginkō** *(sheen-yoe gheen-koe)*

credit bureau 商業興信所 **shōgyō kōshin-jo** *(show-g'yoe koe-sheen-joe)*; 信用調査所 **shinyō chōsa-jo** *(sheen-yoe choe-sah-joe)*

credit card クレジットカード **kurejitto kādo** *(kuu-ray-jeet-toe kah-doe)*
▪ Do you accept credit cards? クレジットカードは使えますか。**Kurejitto kādo wa tsukae masu ka?** *(kuu-ray-jeet-toe kahh-doe wah t'sue-kie mahss kah?)*

credit line 信用限度額 **shin'yō gendo-gaku** *(sheen-yoe gen-doe-gah-kuu)*; 融資枠 **yūshi waku** *(yuu-she-wah-kuu)*

creditor 債権者 **saikensha** *(sigh-ken-shah)*

credit rating 信用格付け **shin'yō kakuzuke** *(sheen-yoe kah-kuu-zuu-kay)*

credit reference 信用照会 **shin'yō shōkai** *(sheen-yoe show-kye)*

credit terms 支払条件 **shiharai jōken** *(she-hah-rye joe-ken)*

credit union 信用組合 **shin'yō kumiai** *(sheen-yoe kuu-me-eye)*

criminal matter 刑事事件 **keiji jiken** *(kay-jee jee-ken)*

crisis 危機 **kiki** *(kee-kee)*

criterion 規準 **kijun** *(kee-june)*

critical 厳しい **kibishii** *(kee-bee-sheee)*; 批判的な **hihan teki na** *(hee-hahn tay-kee nah)*

criticism; critique 批評 **hihyō** *(hee-h'yohh)*

cross-licensing 特許権交換 **tokkyo ken kōkan** *(toke-k'yoe ken-koe-kahn)*

crude oil 原油 **genyu** *(gane-yuu)*

cultivate; develop (a market) 開発する **kaihatsu suru** *(kye-hot-sue sue-rue)*

cultural property 文化財 **bunka zai** *(boon-kah zie)*

culture (arts; civilization) 文化 **bunka** *(boon-kah)*

cumulative 累積的 **ruiseke-teki** *(rue-ee-say-kee-tay-kee)*

curfew 門限 **mongen** *(moan-gane)*

currency 通貨 **tsūka** *(t'sue-kah)*

currency band 通貨変動幅 **tsūka**

hendō haba *(t'sue-kah hen-doe hah-bah)*

currency clause 通貨条項 **tsūka jōkō** *(t'sue-kah joe-koe)*

currency conversion 通貨転換 **tsūka tenkan** *(t'sue-kah ten-kahn)*

currency exchange rate 為替相場 **kawase sōba** *(kah-wah-say so-bah)*

current account 当座勘定 **tōza kanjō** *(toe-zah kahn-joe)*

current assets 流動資産 **ryūdō shisan** *(r'yuu-doe she-shan)*

current checking account 当座預金 **tōza yokin** *(toe-zah yoe-keen)*

current liabilities 流動負債 **ryūdō fusai** *(r'yuu-doe fuu-sigh)*

current ratio 流動比率 **ryūdō hiritsu** *(r'yuu-doe he-ree-t'sue)*

current yield 現行利回り **genkō rimawari** *(gen-koe ree-mah-wah-ree)*

curriculum vitae (resumé) 履歴書 **rirekisho** *(ree-ray-kee-show)*

custodian (caretaker) 管理人 **kanrinin** *(kahn-ree-neen)*

customer 顧客 **kokyaku** *(koe-k'yah-kuu)*

customer service 顧客サービス **kokyaku sābisu** *(koe-k'yah-kuu sah-bee-sue)*

custom (behavior, practice) 習慣 **shūkan** *(shuu-kahn)*

customs 税関 **zeikan** *(zay-kahn)*

customs broker 通関業者 **tsūkan gyōsha** *(t'sue-kahn g'yoe-shah)*

customs duties 関税 **kanzei** *(kahn-zay)*

customs entry 通関手続 **tsūkan tetsuzuki** *(t'sue-kahn tate-sue-zuu-kee)*

customs invoice 税関送り状 **zeikan okurijō** *(zay-kahn oh-kuu-ree-joe)*

cutback 削減 **sakugen** *(sah-kuu-gen)*

cutting edge 最先端 **saisentan** *(sigh-sen-tahn)*
▪ That company specializes in cutting-edge technology for computers. その企業は、最先端のコンピュータ技術を専門にしている。 **Sono kigyō wa saisentan no konpyūta gijutsu wo senmon ni shite iru.** *(soe-no kee-g'yoe wa sie-sen-tahn no kon-p'yuu-ta gee-juu-t'sue wo sen-moan nee shtay iru.)*

cyberspace サイバースペース **saibā supēsu** *(sie-bah suu-pay-suu)*

cycle (long period of time) 周期 **shūki** *(shuu-kee)*; cycle of events 事件の連鎖 **jiken no rensa** *(jee-ken no rane-sah)*; cycle of seasons 季節の移り変わり **kisetsu no utsurikawari** *(key-sate-sue no uu-t'sue-ree-kah-wah-ree)*

cycle billing 請求書の分割発行 **seikyūsho no bunkatsu hakkō** *(say-cue-show no boon-cot-sue hock-koh)*

cyclical 周期的 **shūki-teki** *(shuu-kee-tay-kee)*

D

daily 毎日 **mainichi** *(my-nee-chee)*

daily necessities 日用品 **nichiōhin** *(nee-chee-ohhh-heen)*

daily pay 日給 **nikkyū** *(neek-cue)*

dairy products 酪農製品 **rakunō seihin** *(rah-kuu-no say-heen)*; 乳製品 **nyū seihin** *(n'yee say-heen)*

damage; loss 損害 **songai** *(soan-guy)*
▪ The rain caused a lot of damage. 雨でだいぶ損をしました。 **Ame de daibu**

son wo shimashita. *(ah-may day dye-buu soan oh she-mahsh-tah.)*

dangerous 危ない **abunai** *(ah-buu-nigh)*; 危険な **kiken na** *(kee-ken nah)*; dangerous condition 危険な状態 **kiken na jōtai** *(kee-ken nah joe-tie)*
▪ Driving in Japanese cities is dangerous because of the narrow streets. 日本の狭い道で運転するのは危険です。**Nihon no semai michi de unten suru no wa kiken désu.** *(nee-hone no say-my me-chee day uun-ten sue-rue no wah kee-ken dess.)*

data (information materials) 資料 **shiryō** *(she-rio)*
▪ We do not yet have enough data to make a decision. 決定するにはまだ資料が足りない。**Kettei suru ni wa mada shiryō ga tarinai.** *(kate-tay sue-rue nee wah mah-dah she-rio gah tah-ree-nigh.)*

data (other) データ **dēta** *(day-tah)*
▪ This data appears to be wrong. このデータは間違っているようです。**Kono dēta wa machigatteiru yō désu.** *(koh-no day-tah wah mah-chee-guy-tay-ee-rue yoh dess.)*

data acquisition データ収集 **dēta shūshū** *(day-tah shuu-shuu)*

data bank データバンク **dēta banku** *(day-tah bahn-kuu)*

data base データベース **dēta bēsu** *(day-tah bay-sue)*

date (of the month) 日付 **hizuke** *(he-zuu-kay)*
▪ What is today's date? 今日は何日ですか。**Kyō wa nan-nichi désu ka?** *(k'yoe wa nahn-nee-chee dess kah?)*

date of delivery 受け渡し日 **ukewatashi bi** *(uu-kay-wah-tah-she bee)*; 納期 **nōki** *(nohh-kee)*
▪ When is the delivery date? 納期はいつですか。**Nōki wa itsu désu ka?** *(nohh-kee wah eet-sue dess kah?)*

day 日 **hi** *(he)*; 日 **nichi** *(nee-chee)*; what day 何日 **nan nichi** *(nahn nee-chee)*
▪ How many days will it take? 何日ぐらいかかりますか。**Nan nichi gurai kakarimasu ka?** *(nahn nee-chee guu-rye kah-kah-ree-mahss kah?)*

dead freight 空荷運賃 **kara-ni unchin** *(kah-rah-nee uun-cheen)*

deadline 最終期限 **saishū kigen** *(sigh-shuu kee-gen)*

deadlock 行き詰まり **ikizumari** *(ee-kee-zuu-mah-ree)*

deal (business) 取引 **torihiki** *(toe-ree-he-kee)*

dealer ディーラー **diirā** *(dee-rah)*

dealership 販売権 **hanbai-ken** *(hanh-by-ken)*; 販売特約店 **hanbai tokuyaku ten** *(hanh-by toe-kuu-yah-kuu ten)*

deal with 取引する **torihiki suru** *(toe-ree-he-kee sue-rue)*
▪ I do not want to deal with that company. その会社とは取引したくない。**Sono kaisha to wa torihiki shitaku nai.** *(so-no kye-shah toe wah toe-ree-he-kee she-tah-kuu nigh.)*

debate 討論 **tōron** *(tohh-roan)*

debentures 社債 **shasai** *(shah-sigh)*

debit 借方 **karikata** *(kah-ree-kah-tah)*

debit card デビットカード **debitto kādo** *(day-beet-toh kah-doh)*
▪ Is this a debit card? これはデビットカードですか。**Kore wa debitto kādo désu ka?** *(koe-ray wah day-beet-toe kah-doe dess kah?)*

debt 借金 **shakkin** *(shock-keen)*; 負債 **fusai** *(fuu-sigh)*

debt; liabilities 負債 **fusai** *(fuu-sai)*

debtor 負債者 **fusaisha** *(fuu-sie-shah)*; 債務者 **saimusha** *(sie-muu-shah)*

debug (computer program) デバッグする **debaggu suru** *(day-bug-guu sue-rue)*

debut デビュー **debyū** *(day-b'yuu)*

decentralize 分散する **bunsan suru** *(buun-sahn sue-rue)*

decision 決定 **kettei** *(kate-tay)*; prompt decision 即断 **sokudan** *(so-kuu-dahn)*
▪ When will you make a decision? いつ決定しますか。**Itsu kettei shimasu ka?** *(eat-sue kate-tay she-mahss kah?)*

decline (decay) 衰退する **suitai suru** *(sue-ee-tie sue-rue)*
▪ That industry is now declining. その産業は今、衰退しています。**Sono sangyō wa ima suitai shiteimasu.** *(so-no sahn-g'yoe wah ee-mah sue-ee-tye shtay-mahss.)*

decrease 減らす **herasu** *(hay-rah-sue)*
▪ Our profits have been decreasing since last year. 会社の利益は去年から減っています。**Kaisha no rieki wa kyonen kara hette imasu.** *(kye-shah no ree-ay-kee wah k'yoe-nen kah-rah hate-tay ee-mahss.)*

decree 命令 **meirei** *(may-e-ray-e)*

deductible 控除(できる) **kōjō (dekiru)** *(koe-joe (day-kee-rue))*; 免責金額 **menseki kingaku** *(men-say-kee keen gah-kuu)*

deduction 控除 **kōjō** *(koe-joe)*

deed 証書 **shōsho** *(show-show)*

deed of sale 売り渡し証書 **uriwatashi shōsho** *(uu-ree-wah-tah-she show-show)*

deed of transfer 譲渡証書 **jōto shōsho** *(joe-toe show-show)*

deed of trust 信託証書 **shintaku shōsho** *(sheen-tah-kuu show-show)*

default 債務不履行 **saimu furikō** *(sigh-muu fuu-ree-koe)*

defect 欠陥 **kekkan** *(cake-kahn)*

defective 欠陥がある **kekkan ga aru** *(cake-kahn gah ah-rue)*; defective product 欠陥商品 **kekkan shōhin** *(cake-kahn show-heen)*

defendant (accused) 被告 **hikoku** *(he-koh-kuu)*

deferred annuities 据置年金 **sueoki nenkin** *(sway-oh-kee nen-keen)*

deferred assets 繰延べ資産 **kurinobe shisan** *(kuu-ree-no-bay she-sahn)*

deferred charges 繰延べ費用 **kurinobe hiyō** *(kuu-ree-no-bay he-yoe)*

deferred delivery 延べ渡し **nobe watashi** *(no-bay wah-tah-she)*

deferred income 繰り延べ収益 **kurinobe shūeki** *(kuu-ree-no-bay shuu-ay-kee)*

deferred liabilities 繰延べ負債 **kurinobe fusai** *(kuu-ree-no-bay fuu-sigh)*

deferred tax 繰延べ税 **kurinobe zei** *(kuu-ree-no-bay zay)*

deficit 赤字額 **akaji gaku** *(ah-kah-jee gah-kuu)*

deficit financing 赤字財政 **akaji zaisei** *(ah-kah-jee zye-say)*

deficit spending 超過支出 **chōka shishutsu** *(choe-kah she-shoot-sue)*

deflation 通貨収縮 **tsūka shūshuku** *(t'sue-kah shuu-shuu-kuu)*

degree (grade) 程度 **teido** *(tay-doe)*

delay 延滞 **entai** *(en-tie)*

delete 消す **kesu** *(kay-sue)*
▪ Please delete this sentence. この文章を消してください。**Kono bunshō wo keshite kudasai.** *(koe-no boon-shohh oh kay-ssh-tay kuu-dah-sie.)*

delinquent account 延滞金 **entai kin** *(en-tie keen)*

deliver (small things) 届ける **todokeru** *(toe-doe-kay-rue)*
▪ Please deliver this package to Mr. Fujimoto. この荷物を藤本さんに届けてください。**Kono nimotsu wo Fujimoto-san ni todokete kudasai.** *(koe-no nee-moat-sue oh fuu-jee-moe-toe-sahn nee toe-doe-kay-tay kuu-dah-sigh.)*

deliver goods 納品する **nōhin suru** *(no-heen sue-rue)*; statement of delivery 納品書 **nōhin sho** *(no-heen show)*
▪ Please deliver (these goods) to the warehouse. 倉庫へ納品してください。**Sōko e nōhin shite kudasai.** *(so-koe ay no-heen shtay kuu-dah-sigh.)*

delivery 引き渡し **hikiwatashi** *(he-kee-wah-tah-she)*; 納品 **nōhin** *(no-heen)*; 配達 **haitatsu** *(high-tah-t'sue)*

delivery date 納期 **nōki** *(no-kee)*

delivery notice 引き渡し通知書 **hikiwatashi tsūchi-sho** *(he-kee-wah-tah-she t'sue-chee-show)*; 配達証明 **haitatsu shōmei** *(high-tah-t'sue show-may)*

delivery price (shipping) 運賃込値段 **unchin komi nedan** *(uun-cheen koe-me nay-dahn)*; 引き渡し価格 **hikiwatashi kakaku** *(he-kee-wah-tah-she kah-kah-kuu)*

demand deposit 要求払預金 **yōkyū barai yokin** *(yoe-cue bah-rye yoe-keen)*

demographic 人口統計学上の **jinkō tōkei gaku-jō no** *(jeen-koe toe-kay gah-kuu-joe no)*

demonstrate; demonstration 示す **shimesu** *(she-may-sue)*; 実演 **jitsuen** *(jee-t'sue-en)*

department 部門 **bumon** *(buu-moan)*

department manager (in a company) 部長 **buchō** *(buu-choe)*

department store デパート **depāto** *(day-pah-toe)*

departure 出発 **shuppatsu** *(shupe-paht-sue)*

departure gate 搭乗口 **tōjō guchi** *(toe-joe guu-chee)*
▪ Let's meet at the departure gate. 搭乗口で会いましょう。**Tōjō guchi de aimashō.** *(toe-joe guu-chee day eye-mah-show.)*

deposit (bank account) 銀行預金 **ginkō yokin** *(gheen-koe yoe-keen)*

deposit (for security purposes) 保証金 **hoshō kin** *(hoe-show keen)*

deposit (in advance) 頭金 **atama kin** *(ah-tah-mah keen)*

deposit (when renting a house or apartment) (returnable) 敷金 **shikikin** *(she-kee-keen)*

deposit (when renting a house or apartment) (not returnable) 権利金 **kenrikin** *(ken-ree-keen)*

depreciation 価値低下 **kachi teika** *(kah-chee tay-kah)*

depreciation allowance 減価償却引当金 **genka shōkyaku hikiate kin** *(gen-kah show-k'yah-kuu he-kee-ah-tay keen)*

depreciation of currency 通貨下落 **tsūka geraku** *(t'sue-kah gay-rah-kuu)*

depression (economic) 不景気 **fukeiki** *(fuu-kay-kee)*; 不況 **fukyō** *(fuu-k'yoe)*

deputy (agent) 代理 **dairi** *(dye-ree)*

deputy chairperson 副会長 **fuku kaichō** *(fuu-kuu kye-choe)*

deputy manager 副支配人 **fuku shihainin** *(fuu-kuu she-high-neen)*

deregulation 規制緩和 **kisei kanwa** *(kee-say kahn-wah)*

design デザイン **dezain** *(day-zine)*

design engineering デザイン工学 **dezain kōgaku** *(day-zine koe-gah-kuu)*

designer デザイナー **dezainā** *(day-zine-nah)*

desktop calculator 電卓 **dentaku** *(den-tah-kuu)*

destination 行先 **ikisaki** *(ee-kee-sah-kee)*; 行き先 **yukisaki** *(yuu-kee-sah-kee)*; 目的地 **mokutekichi** *(moe-kuu-tay-kee-chee)*
▪ Where is your final destination? 最終目的地はどこですか。**Saishū mokutekichi wa doko désu ka?** *(sigh-shuu moe-kuu-tay-kee-chee wah doe-koe dess-kah?)*

details 細部 **saibu** *(sigh-buu)*; 詳細 **shōsai** *(show-sigh)*
▪ Please explain the details of the contract. 契約内容を説明してください。**Keiyaku naiyō wo setsumei shite kudasai.** *(kay-yah-kuu nigh-yoe oh say-t'sue-may shtay kuu-dah-sigh.)*

devaluation 平価切下げ **heika kirisage** *(hay-kah kee-ree-sah-gay)*

develop (photograph) 現像する **genzō suru** *(gen-zoe sue-rue)*

develop (reclaim) 開拓する **kaitaku suru** *(kye-tah-kuu sue-rue)*
▪ The factory is on developed land. 工場は開拓された土地にあります。**Kōjō wa kaitaku sareta tochi ni arimasu.** *(koe-joe wah kye-tah-kuu sah-ray-tah toe-chee nee-ah-ree-mahss.)*

developing country 後進国 **kōshin koku** *(koe-sheen koe-kuu)*; 開発途上国 **kaihatsu tojō-koku** *(kye-hot-sue toe-joe-coke)*

development; growth 開発 **kaihatsu** *(kye-hot-sue)*; gradual progress 発展する **hatten suru** *(hot-ten sue-rue)*; expansion 拡張 **kakuchō** *(kah-kuu-choe)*; development cost 開発費 **kaihatsu hi** *(kie-hot-sue he)*

dialogue 対話 **taiwa** *(tie-wah)*

dictation 書き取り **kakitori** *(kah-kee-toe-ree)*; 口述 **kōjutsu** *(koe-juu-t'sue)*; ディクテーション **dikutēshon** *(deek-tay-shone)*

diesel (engine) ディーゼル **diizeru** *(dee-zay-rue)*

digital デジタル **dejitaru** *(day-jee-tah-rue)*

digital audio disc デジタル・オーディオ・ディスク **dejitaru ōdio disuku** *(day-jee-tah rue oh-dee-oh disk-uu)*

digital audio taperecorder デジタルオーディオ・テープレコーダー **dejitaru ōdio tēpu rekōda** *(day-jee-tah-rue oh-dee-oh tay-puu ray-koe-dah)*

digital broadcasting service デジタル放送 **dejitaru hōsō** *(day-jee-tah-rue hoe-so)*
▪ Is this television ready for digital broadcasting? このテレビはデジタル放送対応ですか。**Kono terebi wa dejitaru hōsō taiō désu ka?** *(koe-no tay-ray-bee wa day-jee-tah-rue hohh-sohh tie-ohh dess kah?)*

digitalize デジタル化する **dejitaru-ka suru** *(day-jee-tah-rue-kah sue-rue)*

dignitary 名士 **meishi** *(may-e-she)*

diligent 勤勉(な) **kinben (na)** *(keen-bane)*
▪ He is a very diligent man. 彼はとても勤勉な人です。**Kare wa totemo kinben na hito désu.** *(kah-ray wah toe-tay-moe keen-bane nah he-toe dess.)*

dilution of equity 持ち株比率の低下 **mochi-kabu hiritsu no teika** *(moe-chee-kah-buu he-ree-t'sue no tay-kah)*

diplomacy (between nations) 外交 **gaikō** *(guy-kohh)*; tactful dealing, tactics, strategy 駆け引き **kakehiki** *(kah-kay-hee-kee)*

diplomat 外交官 **gaikōkan** *(guy-kohh-kahn)*

diplomatic 外交上 **gaikōjō** *(guy-kohh-johh)*

direct access storage 直接アクセスストレージ **chokusetsu akusesu sutorējī** *(choke-say-t'sue ah-kuu-say-sue stow-ray-jee)*

direct cost 直接費 **chokusetsu hi** *(choke-say-t'sue he)*

direct expense 直接経費 **chokusetsu keihi** *(choke-say-t'sue kay-he)*

direct investment 直接投資 **chokusetsu tōshi** *(choke-say-t'sue toe-she)*

direct line 直通 **choku tsū** *(choke t'sue)*
▪ When you call, use the direct line. 電話を掛ける時は直通を使ってください。**Denwa wo kakeru toki wa chokutsū wo tsukatte kudasai.** *(den-wah oh kah-kay-rue toe-kee wah choke-t'suu oh scot-tay kuu-dah-sigh.)*

direct mail ダイレクトメール **dairekuto mēru** *(dye-reck-toe may-rue)*

director of a company 取締役 **torishimariyaku** *(toe-ree-she-mah-ree-yah-kuu)*

direct quotation 直接相場 **chokusetsu sōba** *(choke-say-t'sue so-bah)*

direct sales shop/store 直売店 **choku bai ten** *(choke by ten)*

direct selling 直接販売 **chokusetsu hanbai** *(choke-say-t'sue hahn-by)*

direct tax 直接税 **chokusetsu zei** *(choke-say-t'sue zay)*

disbursement 支払い **shiharai** *(she-hah-rye)*

discharge; fire 解雇する **kaiko suru** *(kye-koe sue-rue)*

discipline 鍛錬 **tanren** *(tahn-rane)*

disclose 明らかにする **akiraka ni suru** *(ah-kee-rah-kah nee sue-rue)*; 公開する **kōkai suru** *(koe-kye sue-rue)*

discount 割引 **waribiki** *(wah-ree-bee-kee)*; 割引率 **waribiki ritsu** *(wah-ree-bee-kee ree-t'sue)*

discount rate 手形割引歩合 **tegata waribiki buai** *(tay-gah-tah wah-ree-bee-kee buu-eye)*

discount tour 格安ツアー **kakuyasu tsuā** *(kah-kuu-yah-suu t'suu-yah)*
▪ Can you recommend a discount tour? おすすめの格安ツアーはありますか。**Osusume no kakuyasu tsuā wa arimasu ka?** *(oh-sue-sue-may noh kah-kuu-yah-suu t'suu-yah wa ah-ree-mahss kah?)*

discretionary income 仲買人所得 **nakagai nin shotoku** *(nah-kah-guy ee-neen show-toe-kuu)*

discretionary order 成り行き注文 **nariyuki chūmon** *(nah-ree-yuu-kee chew-moan)*

disk (磁気)ディスク **(jiki) disuku** *(jee-kee disk-uu)*

dismiss; let go 解散させる **kaisan saseru** *(kye-sahn sah-say-rue)*; 解雇 **kaiko** *(kye-koe)*
▪ Business is slow so I let him go. 業績不振のため彼を解雇しました。**Gyōseki fushin no tame kare wo kaiko shimashita.** *(g'yoe-say-kee fuu-sheen noh tah-may kah-ray oh kye-koe she-mahsh-tah.)*

dispatch; send (shipment; goods) 出荷する **shukka suru** *(shuuk-kah sue-rue)*; 発送する **hassō suru** *(hot-so sue-rue)*

display unit ディスプレー装置 **disupurei sōchi** *(dis-puu-ray so-chee)*

disposable income 可処分所得 **kashobun shotoku** *(kah-show-boon-show-toe-kuu)*; 手取り収入 **tedori shūnyū** *(tay-doe-ree shuu-n'yuu)*

dispute 争議 **sōgi** *(so-ghee)*; to dispute something 論争する **ronsō suru** *(roan-so sue-rue)*

distribution 分配 **bunpai** *(boon-pie)*; 配給 **haikyū** *(hie-cue)*; 流通 **ryūtsū** *(r'yuu-t'sue)*
▪ When will distribution start? 配給はいつ始まりますか。**Haikyū wa itsu hajimarimasu ka?** *(hie-cue wa eet-sue hah-jee-mah-ree-mahss kah?)*

distribution channel 流通経路 **ryūtsū keiro** *(r'yuu-t'sue kay-roe)*; 流通チャネル **ryūtsū chaneru** *(r'yuu-t'sue chah-nay-rue)*

distribution costs 流通コスト **ryūtsū kosuto** *(r'yuu-t'sue cost-oh)*

distribution network 流通網 **ryūtsū mō** *(r'yuu-t'sue moe)*

distribution policy (goods) 流通政策 **ryūtsū seisaku** *(r'yuu-t'sue say-sah-kuu)*

distributor (of goods) 販売業者 **hanbai gyōsha** *(hahn-by g'yoe-shah)*; 配給業者 **haikyu gyōsha** *(high-cue g'yoe-shah)*

diversification (business) 多角経営化 **takaku keiei-ka** *(tah-kah-kuu kay-ee-kah)*

diversify 多様化する **tayōka suru** *(tah-yohh-kah sue-rue)*
▪ We must diversify our products. 当社の商品を多様化しなければなりません。**Tōsha no shōhin wo tayōka shinakereba narimasen.** *(toe-shah no shohh-heen oh tah-yohh-kah she-nah-kay-ray-bah nah-ree-mah-sen.)*

divestment 負の投資 **fu no tōshi** *(fuu-no-toe-she)*

dividend 配当 **haitō** *(high-toe)*

dividend yield 配当利回り **haitō rimawari** *(high-toe ree-mah-wah-ree)*

division of labor 分業 **bungyō** *(boon-g'yoe)*

dock handling charges 貨物取扱費 **kamotsu toriatsukai hi** *(kah-moat-sue toe-ree-ah-t'sue-kay he)*

dock receipt 貨物受取書 **kamotsu uketori-sho** *(kah-moat-sue uu-kay-toe-ree-show)*

doctorate, Ph.D. 博士 **hakase** *(hah-kah-say)*; Doctor Ito 伊藤博士 **Ito Hakase** *(ee-toe hah-kah-say)*

documentary ドキュメンタリー **dokyumentarii** *(doh-que-men-tah-ree)*

documents (official papers) 書類 **shorui** *(show-rue-ee)*; 文書 **bunsho** *(buun-show)*
▪ Are these all the documents that are needed? 必要な書類はこれで全部ですか。**Hitsuyō na shorui wa kore de**

zenbu désu ka? *(heat-sue-yoe nah show-ruu-ee wah koe-ray day zem-buu dess kah?)*

dollar cost averaging (dollar average method) ドル平均法 **doru heikin hō** *(doe-rue hay-keen hoe)*

domain name ドメインネーム **domein nēmu** *(doh-may-nuu nay-muu)*
▪ Have you registered that domain name? そのドメインネームを登録しましたか。**Sono domein nēmu wo tōroku shimashita ka?** *(soh-no doh-may-nuu nay-muu oh toe-roe-kuu she-mah-ssh-tah kah?)*

domestic 国内 **kokunai** *(koe-kuu-nigh)*
▪ This product is not sold in the domestic market. この品物は国内のマーケットでは売られていません。**Kono shinamono wa kokunai no māketto de wa urareteimasen.** *(koe-no she-nah-moe-no wah koe-kuu-nigh no mah-ket-toe day wah uu-rah-ray-tay-mah-sen.)*

domestic bill 国内手形 **kokunai tegata** *(coe-kuu-nigh tay-gah-tah)*; 内国為替 **naikoku kawase** *(nigh-coe-kuu kah-wah-say)*

domestic company 国内企業 **kokunai kigyō** *(coe-kuu-nigh kee-g'yoe)*

door-to-door sales 戸別訪問販売 **kobetsu hōmon hanbai** *(koe-bay-t'sue hoe-moan hahn-by)*

dormitory 寮 **ryō** *(ree-ohhh)*

double-entry bookkeeping 複式簿記 **fuku-shiki boki** *(fuu-kuu she-kee boe-kee)*

double pricing 二重価格 **nijū kakaku** *(nee-juu kah-kah-kuu)*

double taxation 二重課税 **nijū kazei** *(nee-juu kah-zay)*

double time pay 賃金倍額支給 **chingin baigaku-shikyū** *(cheen-gheen by-gah-kuu she-cue)*

download ダウンロード **daunrōdo** *(down-roh-doh)*
▪ Please download that file for me. そのファイルをダウンロードしてください。**Sono fairu wo daunrōdo shite kudasai.** *(so-no fie-ruu oh down-roh-doh ssh-tay kuu-dah-sie.)*

down payment 頭金 **atama kin** *(ah-tah-mah keen)*

down period 閉鎖期間 **heisa kikan** *(hay-sah kee-khan)*

down-time 中断時間 **chūdan-jikan** *(chew-dahn-jee-kahn)*

down-turn 沈滞 **chintai** *(cheen-tie)*

draft (bank) 振出手形 **furidashi tegata** *(fuu-ree-dah-she tay-gah-tah)*

draft (of document) 下書き **shita-gaki** *(she-tah-gah-kee)*

drawback (money) 戻し税 **modoshi zei** *(moe-doe-she zay)*

draw down 引き下ろす **hiki orosu** *(he-kee oh-roe-sue)*

drawee (of draft) 手形名宛人 **tegata na-ate nin** *(tay-gah-tah nah-ah-tay neen)*

drawer (of draft) 手形振出人 **tegata furidashi nin** *(tay-gah-tah fuu-ree-dah-she neen)*

drop-shipment (生産者)直送 **(seisan-sha) chokusō** *((say-sahn-shah) choke-so)*

dry cargo 乾貨物 **kan kamotsu** *(kahn kah-moat-sue)*

dry goods (grain) 穀類 **koku rui** *(koe-kuu rue-ee)*

dry goods (textiles) 織物 **ori mono** *(oh-ree moe-no)*

due date 支払い期日 **shiharai kijitsu** *(she-hah-rye kee-jee-t'sue)*

dummy (mockup of a printing project) 体裁見本 **teisai mihon** *(tay-sigh me-hone)*; ダミー **damii** *(dah-mee)*

dumping ダンピング **danpingu** *(dahm-peen-guu)*; 投げ売り **nageuri** *(nah-gay uu-ree)*

dun (for payment) しつこく催促する **shitsukoku saisoku suru** *(she-t'sue-koe-kuu sigh-so-kuu sue-rue)*

durable 丈夫な **jōbu na** *(joe-buu nah)*; 長持ちする **nagamochi suru** *(nah-gah-moh-chee sue-rue)*

durable goods 耐久消費財 **taikyū shōhi zai** *(tie-cue show-he zye)*

Dutch (person) オランダ人 **Orandajin** *(Oh-rahn-dah-jeen)*

duty (honor bound, obligation) 義務 **gimu** *(ghee-muu)*; 責任 **sekinin** *(say-kee-neen)*

duty (customs fees) 関税 **kanzei** *(kahn-zay)*

duty-free 免税で **menzei de** *(men-zay day)*

duty-free goods 免税品 **menzei hin** *(men-zay heen)*

DVD DVD **Dii-Bui-Dii** *(D-B-D, pronouncing the V like a B)*
▪ How many films are on this DVD? このDVD には、いくつ映画が入ってますか。**Kono DVD niwa ikutsu eiga ga haittemasu ka?** *(koe-no DBD nee wah ee-koot-sue eigh-gah gah hight-tay-mahss kah?)*

E

earnest money 手付金 **tetsuke kin** *(tay-t'sue-kay keen)*

earnings (profit) 利益 **rieki** *(ree-ay-kee)*; 収益 **shūeki** *(shuu-ay-kee)*
▪ We will not make a profit this year. 今年は利益がでません。**Kotoshi wa rieki ga demasen.** *(koe-toe-she wah ree-ay-kee gah day-mah-sen.)*

earnings on assets 資産所得 **shisan shotoku** *(she-sahn show-toe-kuu)*

earnings per share 一株あたりの利益 **hito-kabu atari no rieki** *(he-toe-kah-buu ah-tah-ree no ree-ay-kee)*

earnings/price ratio 収益株価率 **shūeki kabu-ka ritsu** *(shuu-ay-kee kah-buu-kah ree-t'sue)*

earnings report 業績報告 **gyōseki hōkoku** *(g'yoe-say-kee hoe-koe-kuu)*

earnings retained 保留利益 **horyū rieki** *(hoe-r'yuu ree-ay-kee)*; 剰余金 **jōyo kin** *(joe-yoe keen)*

earphone イヤホン **iyahon** *(ee-yah-hone)*

earplugs 耳栓 **mimisen** *(me-me-sane)*

ebook e-book **ii-buku** *(ee-buu-kuu)*
▪ Ebooks are the next generation's publication style. イーブックは、次世代の出版スタイルです。**Ēbukku wa jisedai no shuppan sutairu désu.** *(ee-buuk-kuu wa jee-say-die no shupe-pan sue-tie-rue dess.)*

economical 経済的 **keizai-teki** *(kay-zye-tay-kee)*

economic barometer 経済観測指標 **keizai kansoku shihyō** *(kay-zye kahn-so-kuu she-h'yoe)*

economic indicators 経済指標 **keizai shihyō** *(kay-zye she-h'yoe)*

economic mission 経済使節団 **keizai shisetsu dan** *(kay-zye she-say-t'sue dahn)*

economic prospects 経済見通し **keizai mitōshi** *(kay-zye me-toe-she)*
▪ What are the economic prospects for that country? その国の経済見通しはどうですか。**Sono kuni no keizai mitōshi wa dō désu ka?** *(so-no kuu-nee no kay-zye me-toe-she wah doe dess kah?)*

economics 経済学 **keiza gaku** *(kay-zye gah-kuu)*

economic trend 経済動向 **keizai dōkō** *(kay-zye doe-koe)*
▪ There is some concern about future economic trends. 今後の経済動向が気になります。**Kongo no keizai dōkō ga ki ni narimasu.** *(cone-go no kay-zye doe-koe gah nee nah-ree-mahss.)*

economize 節約する **setsuyaku suru** *(say-t'sue-yah-kuu sue-rue)*

economy 経済 **keizai** *(kay-zye)*

economy of scale 規模の経済 **kibo no keizai** *(kee-boe no kay-zye)*

edit 編集する **henshū suru** *(hane-shuuu sue-rue)*
▪ Please edit this copy. このコピーを編集してください。**Kono kopii wo henshū shite kudasai.** *(koe-no koe-pee oh hane-shuuu ssh-tay kuu-dah-sie.)*

editor 編集者 **henshūsha** *(hen-shuu-shah)*; エディター **editā** *(eh-dee-tahh)*; chief editor 編集長 **henshū chō** *(hane-shuu-choh)*

editorial (in newspaper) 社説 **shasetsu** *(shah-sate-sue)*

educate; train 教育する **kyōiku suru** *(k'yoe-ee-kuu sue-rue)*

efficiency 効率 **kōritsu** *(koe-ree-t'sue)*; improvement in efficiency 効率化する **kōritsu-ka suru** *(koe-ree'tsue-kah sue-rue)*

effort (exertion; attempt) 努力 **doryoku** *(doe-rio-kuu)*

effort, make an (make an effort) 力を尽くす **chikara wo tsukusu** *(chee-kah-rah oh t'sue-kuu-sue)*
▪ I will extend my best effort. できるだけ努力します。**Dekiru dake doryoku shimasu.** *(day-kee-rue day-kay doe-rio-kuu she-mahss.)*

Egypt エジプト **Ejiputo** *(eh-jeep-toe)*

Egyptian (person) エジプト人 **Eijputojin** *(eh-jeep-toe-jeen)*

eight-hour-a-day system 8 時間労働制 **hachi-ji-kan rōdō sei** *(hah-chee-jee-kahn roe-doe say)*

elasticity (supply/demand) 弾力性 **danryoku sei** *(dahn-rio-kuu say)*

elections 選挙 **senkyo** *(sen-k'yoe)*

electric 電気の **denki no** *(den-kee no)*

electrical engineering 電気工学 **denki kōgaku** *(den-kee koe-gah-kuu)*

electrically conductive 導電性 **dōden sei** *(doe-den say)*

electrical product 電気製品 **denki seihin** *(den-kee say-heen)*

electrical resistance 電気抵抗 **denki teikō** *(den-kee tay-koe)*

electric circuit 電気回路 **denki kairo** *(den-kee kye-roe)*

electric heater 電気ストーブ **denki sutōbu** *(den-kee sue-toe-buu)*; ヒーター **hiitā** *(he-tah)*

electricity 電気 **denki** *(den-kee)*

electric power 電力 **denryōku** *(dane-r'yohh-kuu)*

electric shaver 電気かみそり **denki higesori** *(den-kee he-gay-soe-ree)*

electric tools 電気工具 **denki kōgu** *(den-kee koe-guu)*

electronic desk calculator 電卓 **dentaku** *(den-tah-kuu)*

electronic publishing 電子出版 **denshi shuppan** *(dane-she shupe-pahn)*; electronic publisher 電子出版社 **denshi shuppansha** *(dane-she shupe-pahn-shah)*
▪ I'm looking for an electronic publisher. 電子出版社を探しています。**Denshi shuppansha wo sagashite imasu.** *(dane-she shupe-pahn oh sah-gah-shtay-mahss.)*

electronics 電子工学 **denshi kōgaku** *(den-she koe-gah-kuu)*

eliminate 除く **nozoku** *(no-zoh-kuu)*

elimination; exclusion; removal 排除 **haijō** *(hi-johh)*

email Eメール **iimeru** *(ee-may-ruu)*
▪ I will email you tomorrow. 明日、Eメールします。**Ashita iimeru shimasu.** *(ah-ssh-tah ee-may-ruu she-mahss.)*

embargo 通商禁止 **tsūshō kinshi** *(t'sue-show keen-she)*

embassy 大使館 **taishikan** *(tie-she-kahn)*
▪ Please go to the American Embassy. アメリカ大使館に行ってください。**Amerika Taishikan ni itte kudasai.** *(ah-may-ree-kah Tie-she-kahn nee eet-tay kuu-dah-sie.)*

embezzle 横領する **ōryō suru** *(ohh-r'yohh sue-rue)*

embezzlement 横領 **ōryō** *(oh-rio)*

embryo 胎児 **taiji** *(tie-jee)*

emergency 非常時 **hijōji** *(he-joe-jee)*

emergency measures 緊急措置 **kinkyū sochi** *(kee-n-cue so-chee)*

emigrant 移住者 **ijūsha** *(ee-juuu-shah)*

emotional 情緒的 **jōcho-teki** *(joe-choe-tay-kee)*

employ 雇う **yatou** *(yah-toe-uu)*

employee 従業員 **jūgyō-in** *(juu-g'yoe-een)*; office employee 事務員 **jimu-in** *(jee-muu-een)*

employee relations 従業員関係 **jūgyō-in kankei** *(juu-g'yoe-een kahn-kay)*

employment 雇用 **koyō** *(koe-yoe)*; employment terms 雇用条件 **koyō jōken** *(koe-yoe joe-ken)*

employment agency 職業安定所 **shokugyō antei-jo** *(show-kuu-g'yoe ahn-tay-joe)*; 派遣会社 **haken gaisha** *(hah-ken guy-shah)*

encounter; oppose 対決する **taiketsu** *(tie-kay-t'sue)*

end of period 期末 **kimatsu** *(kee-mot-sue)*

endorse 裏書きする **uragaki suru** *(uu-rah-gah-kee sue-rue)*
▪ Please endorse this check. この小切手に裏書きしてください。**Kono kogitte ni uragaki shite kudasai.** *(koe-no koe-gheet-tay nee uu-rah-gah-kee shtay kuu-dah-sigh.)*

endorsee 被裏書人 **hi-uragaki-nin** *(he-uu-rah-gah-kee-neen)*

endorsement 裏書き **uragaki** *(uu-rah-gah-kee)*

endorser 裏書人 **uragaki-nin** *(uu-rah-gah-kee-neen)*

endow 与える **ataeru** *(ah-tie-rue)*; 寄付する **kifu suru** *(kee-fuu sue-rue)*

endowment 寄贈 **kizō** *(kee-zoe)*

end-use certificate 最終用途者証明書 **saishū yōto sha shōmeisho** *(sigh-shuu yoe-toe shah show-may-show)*

energy エネルギー **enerugii** *(eh-nay-rue-ghee)*

engineer 技師 **gishi** *(ghee-she)*; エンジニア **enjinia** *(en-jee-nee-ahh)*

engineering 工学 **kōgaku** *(koe-gah-kuu)*

engineering design department 技術設計部門 **gijutsu sekkei bumon** *(ghee-jute-sue sake-kay-buu-moan)*

England イギリス **Igirisu** *(ee-ghee-ree-sue)*

English (person) イギリス人 **Igirisujin** *(ee-ghee-ree-sue-jeen)*

engrave (for printing) 彫る **horu** *(hoe-rue)*

enlarge 拡大する **kakudai suru** *(kah-kuu-dye sue-rue)*
▪ Can you enlarge this copy? このコピーを拡大する事ができますか。**Kono kopii wo kakudai suru koto ga dekimasu ka?** *(koe-no koe-pee oh kah-kuh-dye sue-rue koe-toe gah day-kee-mahss kah?)*

enlarge (a photograph) 引き延ばす **hikinobasu** *(he-kee-no-bah-sue)*

enterprise 企業 **kigyō** *(kee-g'yoe)*; enterprising 積極的 **sekkyoku-teki** *(sake-yoe-kuu-tay-kee)*

enterprise taxes 事業税 **jigyō zei** *(jee-g'yoe zay)*

enterprise union 企業内組合 **kigyō nai kumiai** *(kee-g'yoe nigh kuu-me-eye)*

entertainment 余興 **yokyō** *(yoe-k'yoe)*; 遊び **asobi** *(ah-so-bee)*; 娯楽 **goraku** *(go-rah-kuu)*; 催し **moyōshi** *(moe-yoe-she)*

entertainment expense 交際費 **kōsai hi** *(koe-sigh he)*; 接待費 **settai hi** *(set-tie he)*

entertainment industry エンターテイメント業界 **entāteimento gyōkai** (*een-tah-tain-men-toh g'yoh-kai)*
▪ The entertainment industry in Japan is very large. 日本のエンターテイメント業界は、とても大きいです。**Nihon no entāteimento gyōkai wa totemo okii désu.** *(nee-hone noh een-tah-tain-men-toh g'yoh-kai wah toe-tay-moh ohh-kee dess.)*

entrepreneur 起業家 **kigyō-ka** *(kee-g'yoe-kah)*; アントロプレナー **antoro-purenā** *(ahn-toe-roe-puu-ray-nuu-ah)*

entry permit 通関免許 **tsūkan menkyo** *(t'sue-kahn men-k'yoe)*; 入国許可 **nyūkoku kyoka** *(n'yuu-koe-kuu k'yoe-kah)*

entry visa 入国ビザ **nyūkoku biza** *(n'yuu-koe-kuu bee-zah)*

environment 環境 **kankyō** *(kahn-k'yoe)*

equal 同一 **dōitsu** *(doe-eat-sue)*

equalize 均等にする **kintō ni suru** *(keen-toe nee sue-rue)*

equal pay for equal work 同一(労働同一)賃金 **dōitsu (rōdō dōitsu) chingin** *(doe-eat-sue (roe-doe doe-eat-sue) cheen-gheen)*

equipment 設備 **setsubi** *(say-t'sue-bee)*
▪ New equipment was introduced into the factory. 工場に新しい設備を導入しました。**Kōjō ni atarashii setsubi wo dōnyū shimashita.** *(kohh-johh nee ah-tah-rah-shee sate-sue-bee oh doan-yuu she-mahssh-tah.)*

equipment; device; installation 装置 **sōchi** *(sohh-chee)*

equity 持ち分 **mochibun** *(moe-chee-boon)*; 自己資本 **jiko shihon** *(jee-koe she-hon)*

equity investments 直接出資 **chokusetsu shusshi** *(choke-say-t'sue shuu-she)*

error エラー **erā** *(eh-rah)*; 間違い **machigai** *(mah-chee-guy)*

escalator clause エスカレーター条項 **esukarētā jōkō** *(es-kah-ray-tah joe-koe)*

escape clause 免責条項 **menseki jōkō** *(men-say-kee joe-koe)*
▪ Is there an escape clause in the contract? 契約に免責条項がありますか。**Keiyaku ni menseki jōkō ga arimasu ka?** *(kay-yah-kuu nee men-say-kee joe-koe gah ah-ree-mahss kah?)*

escrow account エスクロウ・アカウント **esukurō akaunto** *(ess-kuu-roe ah-count-oh)*

escrow bond 条件付譲渡証書 **jōken tsuki jōto shōsho** *(joe-ken ski joe-toe show-show)*

establish 設立する **setsuritsu suru** *(say-t'sue-ree-t'sue sue-rue)*
▪ I/We will establish a new company. 新しい会社を設立します。**Atarashii kaisha wo setsuritsu shimasu.** *(ah-tah-rah-she kye-shah oh say-t'sue-ree-t'sue she-mahss.)*

estate 資産 **shisan** *(she-sahn)*; 遺産 **isan** *(ee-sahn)*; 財産 **zaisan** *(zye-sahn)*

estate agent 財産管理人 **zaisan kanri nin** *(zye-sahn kahn-ree neen)*

estate tax 遺産相続税 **isan sōzoku zei** *(ee-sahn so-zoe-kuu zay)*

estimate 見積もり **mitsumori** *(meet-sue-moe-ree)*; written estimate 見積書 **mitsumori sho** *(meet-sue-moe-ree show)*; to estimate 見積もる **mitsumoru** *(meet-sue-moe-rue)*

estimate cost 見積原価 **mitsumori genka** *(meet-sue-moe-ree gen-kah)*

estimated price 見積価格 **mitsumori kakaku** *(meet-sue-moe-ree kah-kah-kuu)*

estimated time of arrival 到着予定時刻 **tōchaku yotei jikoku** *(toe-chah-kuu yoe-tay jee-koe-kuu)*

estimated time of departure 出発予定時刻 **shuppatsu yotei jikoku** *(shuup-pot-sue yoe-tay jee-koe-kuu)*

ethics 道徳 **dōtoku** *(doe-toe-kuu)*

EU; European Union 欧州連合 **ōshū rengō** *(oh-shoe ren-go)*

Eurobond ユーロ債 **Yūro sai** *(yuu-roe sigh)*

Eurocurrency ユーロカレンシー **Yūro karenshii** *(yuu-roe kah-ren-she)*

Eurodollar ユーロダラー **Yūro darā** *(yuu-roe dah-rah)*

Europe ヨーロッパ **Yōroppa** *(yoe-roe-pah)*; Europe-oriented ヨーロッパ向け **Yōroppa-muke** *(yoe-roe-pah-muu-kay)*; European Community EC **Ii-Shi** *(ee-she)*

European ヨーロッパ人 **Yōroppajin** *(yohh-rope-pah-jeen)*

evaluate 評価する **hyōka suru** *(h'yohh-kah sue-rue)*
▪ I cannot evaluate this project. この事業を評価することができません。**Kono jigyō wo hyōka suru koto ga dekimasen.** *(koe-no jee-g'yohh oh h'yohh sue-rue koe-toe gah day-kee-mah-sen.)*

evaluation 評価(額) **hyōka(gaku)** *(h'yoe-kah gah-kuu)*

event イベント **ibento** *(e-ben-toe)*

evidence 証拠 **shōko** *(shohh-koh)*
▪ Where is the evidence? 証拠はどこにありますか。**Shōko wa doko ni arimasu ka?** *(shohh-koe wah doe-koe nee ah-ree-mahss kah?)*

examine; study; consider 検討する **kentō suru** *(ken-toe sue-rue)*
▪ I will consider your idea. あなたの考えを検討します。**Anata no kangae wo kentō shimasu.** *(ah-nah-tah no kahn-guy oh ken-toe she-mahss.)*

example (for) 例えば **tatoeba** *(tah-toh-a-bah)*

excess demand 超過需要 **chōka juyō** *(choe-kah juu-yoe)*

exchange (barter/swap) 交換 **kōkan** *(koe-kahn)*

exchange controls 外国為替管理 **gaikoku kawase kanri** *(guy-koe-kuu kah-wah-say kahn-ree)*

exchange discount 為替割引 **kawase waribiki** *(kah-wah-say wah-ree-bee-kee)*

exchange loss 為替差損 **kawase sason** *(kah-wah-say sah-soan)*

exchange market (foreign) 外国為替市場 **gaikoku kawase shijō** *(guy-koe-kuu kah-wah-say she-joe)*

exchange name cards 名刺交換 **meishi kōkan** *(may-she koe-kahn)*

exchange rate 外国為替相場 **gaikoku kawase sōba** *(guy-koe-kuu kah-wah-say so-bah)*
▪ What is today's exchange rate? 今日の為替相場はどうですか。**Kyō no gaikoku kawase sōba wa dō désu ka?** *(k'yoe no guy-koe-kuu kah-wah-say so-bah wah doe dess kah?)*

exchange risk 為替リスク **kawase risuku** *(kah-wah-say risk-uu)*

exchange value 交換価値 **kōkan kachi** *(koe-kahn kah-chee)*

excise duty 消費税 **shōhi zei** *(show-he zay)*

excise license (license tax (fee)) 免許税 **menkyo zei** *(men-k'yoe zay)*

exclude 除く **nozoku** *(noe-zoe-kuu)*; 除いて **nozoite** *(no-zoe-ee-tay)*

exclusive 専属 **senzoku** *(sen-zoe-kuu)*; 独占的 **dokusen teki** *(doe-kuu-sen tay-kee)*

exclusive agency 専属特約店 **senzoku tokuyakuten** *(sen-zoe-kuu toe-kuu-yah-kuu-ten)*

exclusive agent 一手代理店 **itte dairi ten** *(eat-tay dye-ree ten)*

ex-dividend 配当落ち **haitō ochi** *(high-toe oh-chee)*

ex dock 埠頭渡し **futō watashi** *(fuu-toe wah-tah-she)*

executive 経営幹部 **keiei kanbu** *(kay-ee kahn-buu)*; 重役 **jūyaku** *(juu-yah-kuu)*

executive board (常任)理事会 **(jōnin) riji kai** *((joe-neen) ree-jee kye)*

executive committee (常務)執行委員会 **(jōmu) shikkō i'in-kai** *((joe-muu) sheek-koe ee-een-kye)*

executive compensation 役員報酬 **yakuin hōshū** *(kahn-buu yah-kuu-een hoe-shuu)*

executive director 専務/常務取締役 **senmu/jōmu torishimariyaku** *(sem-muu/joe-muu toe-ree-she-mah-ree-yah-kuu)*

executive secretary 事務局長 **jimu kyokuchō** *(jee-muu k'yoe-kuu-choe)*

executive session 実行委員会議 **jikkō i'in kaigi** *(jee-koe ee-een kye-ghee)*

executive staff 幹部 **kanbu** *(kahm-buu)*

executor 遺言執行人 **yuigon shikkō nin** *(yuu-ee-goan sheek-koe neen)*

exempt from taxes 免税 **men zei** *(men zay)*

exemption 免除 **menjo** *(men-joe)*

ex factory 工場渡し **kōjō watashi** *(koe-joe wah-tah-she)*; 現場 **genba watashi** *(gane-bah wah-tah-she)*

exhibition 展示 **tenji** *(tane-jee)*; public showing 展覧会 **tenrankai** *(tane-rahn-kie)*

expectation; aspect 予想 **yosō** *(yoe-so)*

expected profits 期待利益 **kitai rieki** *(kee-tie ree-eh-kee)*

expedite 早める **hayameru** *(hah-yah-may-rue)*

expenditures 支出 **shishutsu** *(she-shoot-sue)*

expense 費用 **hiyō** *(he-yohh)*

expense account 接待費 **settai hi** *(set-tie he)*; 経費勘定 **keihi kanjō** *(kay-he kahn-joe)*

expenses 経費 **keihi** *(kay-he)*

expenses for eating and drinking 飲食費 **inshoku hi** *(een-show-kuu he)*

expensive 高い **takai** *(tah-kie)*

experience 経験 **keiken** *(kay-kane)*
▪ Do you have any experience? 経験がありますか。**Keiken ga arimasu ka?** *(kay-kane gah ah-ree-mahss kah?)*

experiment 実験 **jikken** *(jeek-kane)*

experimental 実験的 **jikken-teki** *(jeek-kane-tay-kee)*

expert (technical or scientific) 専門家 **senmonka** *(sem-moan-kah)*; expert in doing things 玄人 **kurōto** *(kuu-roe-toe)*
▪ He is a computer expert. あの人はコンピュータの専門家です。**Ano hito wa konpyūta no senmonka désu.** *(ah-no shtoe wah kome-pew-tah no sem-moan-kah dess.)*

expertise 専門知識 **senmon chishiki** *(sane-moan-chee-she-kee)*

explain 説明する **setsumei suru** *(say-t'sue-may sue-rue)*

exploitation 開発 **kaisetsu** *(kye-say-t'sue)*; 開拓 **kaitaku** *(kye-tah-kuu)*; 売り込み **urikomi** *(uu-ree-koe-mee)*

export 輸出(する) **yushutsu (suru)** *(yuu-shoot-sue (sue-rue))*

export agent 輸出代理店 **yushutsu dairiten** *(yuu-shoot-sue dye-ree-ten)*

export ban 輸出禁止 **yushutsu kinshi** *(yuu-shoot-sue keen-she)*

export broker 輸出ブローカー **yushutsu burōkā** *(yuu-shoot-sue buu-roe-kah)*

export company 輸出商社 **yushutsu shōsha** *(yuu-shoot-sue show-shah)*

export credit 輸出信用状 **yushutsu shin'yō jō** *(yuu-shoot-sue sheen-yoe joe)*

export duty 輸出税 **yushutsu zei** *(yuu-shoot-sue zay)*

export entry 輸出申告書 **yushutsu shinkoku sho** *(yuu-shoot-sue sheen-koe-kuu show)*

export-import bank 輸出入銀行 **yushutsunyū ginkō** *(yuu-shoot-sue-n'yuu gheen-koe)*

export license 輸出許可証 **yushutsu kyokashō** *(yuu-shoot-sue k'yoe-kah-show)*

▪ Do you have an export license? 輸出許可証を持っていますか。**Yushutsu kyokashō wo motte imasu ka?** *(yu-shoot-sue k'yoe-kah-show oh-moat-tay ee-mahss kah?)*

export manager 輸出マネージャー **yushutsu manējā** *(yuu-shoot-sue mah-nay-jah)*; 輸出責任者 **yushutsu sekininsha** *(yuu-shoot-sue say-kee-neen-shah)*

export permit 輸出許可書 **yushutsu kyoka sho** *(yuu-shoot-sue k'yoe-kah show)*

export quota 輸出割り当て **yushutsu wariate** *(yuu-shoot-sue wah-ree-ah-tay)*
▪ There is no export quota on wooden products. 木製品には輸出割り当てはありません。**Moku seihin ni wa yushutsu wariate wa arimasen.** *(moe-kuu say-heen nee wah yuu-shoot-sue wah-ree-ah-tay wah ah-ree-mah-sen.)*

export regulations 輸出規則 **yushutsu kisei** *(yuu-shoot-sue kee-say)*

export restrictions 輸出制限 **yushutsu seigen** *(yuu-shoot-sue say-gen)*

export sales contract 輸出売買契約 **yushutsu baibai keiyaku** *(yuu-shoot-sue by-by kay-yah-kuu)*

export tax 輸出税 **yushutsu zei** *(yuu-shoot-sue zay)*

express train 急行列車 **kyūkō ressha** *(cue-koe ray-shah)*

expropriation 徴収 **chōshū** *(choe-shuu)*

ex rights 権利落ち **kenri ochi** *(ken-ree oh-chee)*

ex ship 着船渡し **chakusen watashi** *(chock-sen wah-tah-she)*; 本船渡し **honsen watashi** *(hon-sen wah-tah-she)*

extend; extension of time 延長する **enchō suru** *(en-choe sue-rue)*

ex warehouse 倉庫渡し **sōko watashi** *(so-koe wah-tah-she)*

F

face value 額面価格 **gakumen kakaku** *(gah-kuu-men kah-kah-kuu)*

facilities 設備 **setsubi** *(say-t'sue-bee)*

factor 要因 **yōin** *(yoe-een)*

factory 工場 **kōjō** *(koe-joe)*
▪ Where is your factory located? 工場の場所はどこですか。**Kōjō no basho wa doko désu ka?** *(koe-joe no bah-show wah doe-koe dess kah?)*

factory manager 工場長 **kōjō chō** *(koe-joe choe)*

factory overhead 製造間接費 **seizō kansetsu-hi** *(say-zoe kahn-say-t'sue-he)*

factory price 工場渡し値段 **kōjō watashi nedan** *(koe-joe wah-tah-she nay-dahn)*

factory worker 工員 **kō in** *(koe een)*

fail (business) 倒産する **tōsan suru** *(toe-sahn sue-rue)*; 破綻する **hatan suru** *(hah-tan-sue-rue)*

fair 公正 **kōsei** *(koe-say)*; fair-minded 公平な **kōhei na** *(koe-hay-nah)*

fair market value 適正市場価格 **tekisei shijō kakaku** *(tay-kee-say she-joe kah-kah-kuu)*

fair return 適性利潤 **tekisei rijun** *(tay-kee-say ree-juun)*

fair trade 公正貿易 **kōsei bōeki** *(koe-*

say boe-eh-kee); 公正取引 **kōsei torihiki** *(koe-say toe-ree-he-kee)*

fake 偽物 **nisemono** *(nee-say-moh-no)*
▪ This wrist-watch is a fake. この腕時計は偽物です。**Kono ude-dokei wa nisemono désu.** *(koe-no uu-day-doe-kay-ee wah nee-say-moe-no dess.)*

family 家族 **kazoku** *(kah-zoe-kuu)*

family allowance 家族手当 **kazoku teate** *(kah-zoe-kuu tay-ah-tay)*

FAQ (frequently asked questions) よくある質問と答え **yoku aru shitsumon to kotae** *(yoe-kuu ah-rue she-t'sue-moan toe koe-tah-ay)*
▪ The FAQ page helps when you have problems. なにか問題があるときは、FAQのページが役に立ちます。**Nani ka mondai ga aru toki wa FAQ no pēji ga yakuni tachi masu.** *(nah-nee-kah mone-die gah ah-rue toe-kee wah FAQ no pay-gee gah yah-kuu-nee tah-chee mah-sue.)*

Far East 極東 **Kyokutō** *(k'yoh-kuu-tohhh)*

farewell party 送別会 **sōbetsu kai** *(so-bait-sue kye)*

farmer 農民 **nōmin** *(no-mean)*

farm out (send work out) 外注する **gaichū suru** *(guy-chew sue-rue)*

fashion 流行 **ryūkō** *(r'yuu-koe)*; ファッション **fasshon** *(fah-shone)*

fashionable 流行(の) **ryūkō (no)** *(r'yuu-kohh (no))*

fast 速い **hayai** *(hah-yie)*

fast food ファースト・フード **fāsuto fūdo** *(fahhs-toe fuu-doh)*

fast food providers 外食産業 **gaishoku sangyō** *(guy-show-kuu shan-g'yoe)*; ファーストフード業 **fāsuto fūdo gyōkai** *(fahhs-toe fuu-doh g'yoe-kye)*

faulty; defective 欠陥のある **kekkan no aru** *(cake-kahn no ah-ruu)*

favorable business conditions, prosperity 好景気 **kōkeiki** *(koh-kay-kee)*

favorite bar 行きつけのバー **iki-tsuke no bā** *(ee-kee-skay no bah)*
▪ Do you have a favorite bar? 行きつけのバーがありますか。**Iki-tsuke no bā ga arimasu ka?** *(ee-kee-skay no bah gah ah-ree-mahss-kah?)*

fax ファックス(する) **fakkusu (suru)** *(fah-kuu-suu (sue-rue))*
▪ Please fax this document immediately. この書類を今すぐファックスしてください。**Kono shorui wo ima sugu fakkusu shite kudasai.** *(koh-no show-ruu-ee oh ee-mah suu-guu fahk-kuu-suu ssh-tay kuu-dah-sie.)*

fax machine ファックスマシーン **fakkusu mashiin** *(fah-kuu-suu mah-sheen)*

Federation of Economic Organizations (a key business group) 経団連 **Keidanren** *(kay-dahn-ren)*

fee; charge 料金 **ryōkin** *(rio-keen)*
▪ How much is the fee? 料金はいくらですか。**Ryōkin wa ikura désu ka?** *(rio-keen wah ee-kuu-rah dess kah?)*

feedback フィードバック **fiido bakku** *(fee-doe bahk-kuu)*

fiber-optic communication 光通信 **hikari tsūshin** *(he-kah-ree t'sue-sheen)*

fibers; textiles 繊維 **seni** *(sen-ee)*

field warehousing 委託倉庫(業務) **itaku sōko (gyōmu)** *(ee-tah-kuu so-koe g'yoe-muu)*

figure; number 数字 **sūji** *(sue-jee)*

figurehead 名前だけの(人) **namae dake no (hito)** *(nah-my dah-kay no ssh-toe)*
▪ He is just a figurehead. あの人は名前だけの人です。**Anohito wa namae dake no hito désu.** *(Ah-no-ssh-toe wah nah-my dah-kay no ssh-toe dess.)*

file ファイル **fairu** *(fie-ruu)*
▪ Which file did you put it in? どのファイルに入れましたか。**Dono fairu ni iremashita ka?** *(do no fie-ruu nee ee-ray-mahssh-tah kah?)*

fill out (a form) 書き込む **kaki komu** *(kah-kee koe-muu)*

film フィルム **firumu** *(fee-rue-muu)*

filter フィルター **firutā** *(fee-rue-tah)*

finalize 最終化する **saishū-ka suru** *(sigh-shuu-kah sue-rue)*

finance 融資する **yūshi suru** *(yuu-she sue-rue)*

finance company 金融会社 **kin'yū gaisha** *(keen-yuu guy-shah)*

Finance Ministry 財務省 **zaimushō** *(zye-muu show)*

financial affairs 財務 **zaimu** *(zye-muu)*

financial aid/assistance 金融支援 **kinyū shien** *(keen-yuu-she-en)*

financial analysis 財務分析 **zaimu bunseki** *(zye-muu boon-say-kee)*

financial appraisal 財政評価 **zaimu hyōka** *(zye-muu h'yoe ka)*

financial base 財務基盤 **zaimu kiban** *(zye-muu kee-bahn)*

financial condition/status 財務状態 **zaimu jōtai** *(zye-muu joe-tie)*

financial control 財務統制 **zaimu tōsei** *(zye-muu toe-say)*

financial crisis 経営危機 **keiei kiki** *(kay-ee kee-kee)*

financial difficulties 財政難 **zaiseinan** *(zye-say nahn)*

financial director 財務部長 **zaimu buchō** *(zye-muu buu-choe)*

financial incentive 金銭的誘因 **kinsen teki yūin** *(keen-sen-tay-kee yuu-een)*

financial leverage ファイナンシャルレバレッジ **fainansharu rebarejji** *(fie-nahn-shah-rue ray-bah-ray-jee)*

financial management 財務管理 **zaimu kanri** *(zye-muu kahn-ree)*

financial period 会計期間 **kaikei kikan** *(kye-kay kee-kahn)*

financial planning 財務計画 **zaimu keikaku** *(zye-muu kay-kah-kuu)*

financial report 財務報告 **zaimu hōkoku** *(zye-muu hoe-koe-kuu)*

financial services ファイナンシャルサービス **fainansharu sābisu** *(fie-nahn-shah-rue sah-bee-sue)*

financial statements 財務諸表 **zaimu shohyō** *(zye-muu show-h'yoe)*

financial year 会計年度 **kaikei nendo** *(kye-kay nen-doe)*

financier 資本家 **shihonka** *(she-hone-kah)*

financing (a loan) 融資 **yūshi** *(yuu-she)*

fine (penalty) 罰金 **bakkin** *(bahk-keen)*

finished goods 在庫 **zaiko** *(zye-koe)*; 製品 **seihin** *(say-heen)*

finished goods inventory 製品在庫 **seihin zaiko** *(say-heen zye-koe)*

fire (dismiss) 解雇する **kaiko suru** *(kye-koe sue-rue)*

firm stand 強気 **tsuyoki** *(t'sue-yoe-kee)*

first-class goods 一流品 **ichi-ryū hin** *(ee-chee-r'yuu heen)*

first-class company 一流企業 **ichi-ryū kigyō** *(ee-chee r'yuu kee-g'yoe)*

first-class school 名門校 **meimonkō** *(may-moan-koe)*

first-class ticket 一等席の切符 **ittō seki no kippu** *(eat-toe sah-kee no keep-puu)*

first edition 初版 **shohan** *(show-hahn)*

first half of the fiscal year 上半期 **kami hanki** *(kah-me hahn-kee)*

First Section of the Tokyo Stock Exchange 東証一部 **tōshō ichibu** *(toe-show ee-chee-buu)*

fiscal agent 財務代理人 **zaimu dairinin** *(zye-muu dye-ree-neen)*

fiscal year 会計年度 **kaikei nendo** *(kye-kay nen-doe)*

fishing industry 漁業 **gyogyō** *(g'yohh-g'yohh)*; 水産業 **suisan gyō** *(sue-ee-sahn-g'yohh)*

fission 分裂 **bunretsu** *(boon-rate-sue)*

fix (repair) 直す **naosu** *(nah-oh-sue)*; 直せる **naoseru** *(nah-oh-say-rue)*

fixed assets 固定資産 **kotei shisan** *(koe-tay she-sahn)*

fixed capital 固定資本 **kotei shihon** *(koe-tay she-hone)*

fixed charges (business) 確定費 **kakutei hi** *(kah-kuu-tay he)*

fixed costs; expenses 固定費 **kotei hi** *(koe-tay he)*

fixed investment 固定資本投資 **kotei shihon tōshi** *(koe-tay she-hone toe-she)*

fixed liability 固定負債 **kotei fusai** *(koe-tay fuu-sigh)*

fixed price 定価 **teika** *(tay-kah)*

fixed rate of exchange 為替低率 **kawase teiritsu** *(kah-wah-say tay-ree-t'sue)*

fixed term 定期 **teiki** *(tay-kee)*

fixed terms 確定条件 **kakutei jōken** *(kah-kuu-tay joe-ken)*

flagship product 主力商品 **shuryoku shōhin** *(shuu-rio-kuu show-heen)*; 目玉商品 **medama shōhin** *(may-dah-mah show-heen)*

flat panel monitor/display フラットパネルモニター/ディスプレー **furatto paneru monitā/disupurē** *(fuu-raht-toh pah-nay-ruu moh-nee-tah/dee-sue-puu-ray)*
▪ I want to buy a flat panel monitor. フラットパネルモニターを買いたいです。 **Furatto paneru monitā wo kaitai désu.** *(fuu-raht-toh pah-nay-ruu moh-nee-tah oh kie-tie dess.)*

flat rate 均一料金 **kin'itsu ryōkin** *(keen-eat-sue rio-keen)*

flat yield 均一利回り **kin'itsu rimawari** *(keen-eat-sue ree-mah-wah-ree)*

flexible tariff 伸縮関税 **shinshuku kanzei** *(sheen-shuu-kuu kahn-zay)*

flextime 時差勤務 **jisa kinmu** *(jee-sah keen-muu)*; フレックスタイム **furekkusu taimu** *(fuu-ray-kuu-suu tah-ee-mee)*
▪ As of this year onwards our company also introduced the flextime system.今年から当社もフレックスタイム制を導入しました。 **Kotoshi kara tōsha mo furekkusu taimu sei wo dōnyū shimashita.** *(koe-to-she kah-rah toe-shah mo fuu-*

rake-kuu-sue tie-muu say oh dohhn-yuu she-mah-ssh-tah.)

flight number 便名 **bin mei** *(bean may)*; フライトナンバー **furaito nanba** *(fuu-rye-toe-nahm-bah)*

float (outstanding checks; stock) フロート **furōto** *(fuu-roe-toe);* 変動相場 **hendō sōba** *(hen-doe so-bah)*

float (issue stock) 起債する **kisai suru** *(kee-sigh sue-rue)*; 債券を発行する **saiken wo hakkō suru** *(sigh-ken wo hock-koh sue-rue)*

floating asset 流動資産 **ryūdō shisan** *(r'yuu-doe she-sahn)*

floating charge 浮動担保 **fudō tanpo** *(fuu-doe tahm-poe)*

floating debt 一時借入金 **ichiji kari-ire kin** *(ee-chee-jee kah-ree-ee-ray keen)*

floating exchange rate 変動為替相場 **hendō kawase sōba** *(hen-doe kah-wah-say so-bah)*

floating exchange system 変動相場制 **hendō sōba sei** *(hen-doe so-bah say)*

floating rate 変動相場 **hendō sōba** *(hen-doe so-bah)*

floor of stock exchange 立会所 **tachiai jo** *(tah-chee-eye joe)*

floppy disk フロッピーディスク **furoppii disku** *(fuu-roe-pee disk-uu)*

flow chart 業務運行票 **gyōmu unkō-hyō** *(g'yoe-muu uun-koe-h'yoe)*; フローチャート **furōchāto** *(fuu-roe-chaah-toe)*

flow chart (production) 生産工程順序一覧表 **seisan kōtei junjo ichiran-hyō** *(say-sahn koe-tay june-joe ee-chee-rahn-h'yoe)*; 製造工程表 **seizō kōtei hyō** *(say-zoe koe-tay-h'yoe)*

fluctuate (go up and down) 上がり下がり(する) **agari-sagari (suru)** *(ah-gah-ree-sah-gah-ree (sue-rue))*

folder (including computer) ホルダー **horudā** *(hoh-rue-dahh)*
▪ Open a new folder for this newsletter. このニュースレターの新しいホルダーを開けてみて。**Kono nyūsuretā no atarashii horudā wo akete kudasai.** *(koe-no nuu-suu-ray-tahh no ah-tah-rah-shee hoh-rue-dahh oh ah-kay-tay me-tay.)*

follower 子分 **kobun** *(koe-boon)*; 弟子 **deshi** *(day-she)*; 部下 **buka** *(buu-kah)*

follow-up 追跡調査 **tsuiseki chōsa** *(t'sue-ee-say-kee choe-sah)*

font (type style) フォント **fonto** *(fone-toe)*; 書体 **shotai** *(show-tie)*

food additives 食品添加物 **shokuhin tenkabutsu** *(show-kuu-heen ten-kah-buu-t'sue)*

food processor フードプロセッサー **fūdo purosessā** *(fuu-doe pro-say-sahh)*

foods 食品 **shokuhin** *(shohh-kuu-heen)*

foodstuffs 食料 **shokuryō** *(show-kuu-rio)*

forecast 予測 **yosoku** *(yoe-so-kuu)*; as expected 予想通り **yosō dōri** *(yoe-so doe-ree)*; weather forecast 天気予報 **tenki yohō** *(ten-kee yoe-hoe)*

foreign (abroad; overseas) 海外(の) **kaigai (no)** *(kye-guy (no))*; 外国(の) **gaikoku (no)** *(guy-koe-kuu (no))*

Foreign Affairs, Ministry of 外務省 **Gaimushō** *(guy-muu-show)*

foreign agency 在外代理店 **zaigai dairiten** *(zah-ee-guy-koe-kuu dye-ree-ten)*

foreign bill of exchange 外国為替手形 **gaikoku kawase tegata** *(guy-koe-kuu kah-wah-say tay-gah-tah)*

foreign capital; funds 外資 **gaishi** *(guy-she)*

foreign company 外資系企業 **gaishi kei kigyō** *(guy-she-kay kee-g'yoe)*

foreign correspondent bank 外国取引銀行 **gaikoku torihiki ginkō** *(guy-koh-kuu toe-ree he-kee gheen-koe)*

foreign currency 外貨 **gaika** *(guy-kah)*

foreign debt 外債 **gaisai** *(guy-sigh)*

foreign demand 外需 **gaiju** *(guy-juu)*

foreigner 外国人 **gaikoku-jin** *(guy-koe-kuu-jeen)*

foreign exchange 外国為替 **gaikoku kawase** *(guy-koe-kuu kah-wah-say)*

foreign exchange bank 外国為替銀行 **gaikoku kawase ginkō** *(guy-koe-kuu kah-wah-say gheen-koe)*

foreign exchange rate 外国為替相場 **gaikoku kawase sōba** *(guy-koe-kuu kah-wah-say so-bah)*

foreign investment 海外投資 **kaigai tōshi** *(kye-guy toe-she)*

foreign minister 外務大臣 **Gaimu daijin** *(guy-muu die-jeen)*; 外相 **gai shō** *(guy show)*

foreign securities 外国証券 **gaikoku shōken** *(guy-koe-kuu show-ken)*

foreign tax credit 外国税額控除 **gaikoku zeigaku kōjo** *(guy-koe-kuu zay-gah-kuu koe-joe)*

foreign trade 外国貿易 **gaikoku bōeki** *(guy-koe-kuu boe-ay-kee)*

foreman 職長 **shoku-chō** *(show-kuu-choe)*; 主任 **shunin** *(shuu-neen)*; 親方 **oyakata** *(oh-yah-kah-tah)*

foresight 先見の明 **senken no mei** *(sane-kane no may-ee)*
▪ The company president is a man of great foresight. 社長は先見の明がある人です。**Shachō wa senken no mei ga aru hito désu.** *(shah-choh wa sane-kane no may-ee gah ah-rue he-toe dess.)*

for export 輸出用 **yushutsu yō** *(yuu-shoot-sue yoe)*

forgery 偽造 **gizō** *(ghee-zoe)*

form of printing layouts 組み版 **kumihan** *(kuu-me-hahn)*

form (shape) 形 **katachi** *(kah-tah-chee)*

formalities; proceedings 形式 **keishiki** *(kay-she-kee)*; formalities (documents) 手続き **tetsuzuki** *(tay-t'sue-zuu-kee)*

format (layout for printing) 体裁 **teisai** *(tay-sigh)*

form letter 形どおりの書簡 **katadōri no shokan** *(kah-tah doe-ree no show-kahn)*

formula (method) 方式 **hōshiki** *(hoe-she-kee)*

forum フォーラム **fōramu** *(fohh-rume)*

forward contract 先物契約 **sakimono keiyaku** *(sah-kee-moe-no kay-yah-kuu)*

forward/future margin 先物マージン **sakimono mājin** *(sah-kee-moe-no ma-jeen)*

forwarding agent 運送業者 **unsō gyōsha** *(uun-so g'yoe-shah)*

forward market 先物市場 **sakimono shijō** *(sah-kee-moe-no she-joe)*

forward purchase 先物買い **sakimono gai** *(sah-kee-moe-no guy)*

forward shipment 先積み **saki zumi** *(sah-kee zuu-me-she)*

foundation; basis 基礎 **kiso** *(kee-so)*

founder 設立者 **setsuritsu-sha** *(sate-sue-reet-sue-shah)*
▪ Is the company founder still alive? 会社の設立者はまだご存命すか。**Kaisha no setsuritsusha wa mada go-zonmei désu ka?** *(kie-sha no sate-sue-reet-sue-shah wah mah-dah go zoe-may dess kah?)*

four-color printing 4色刷り **yon shoku zuri** *(yoan show-kuu zuu-ree)*

four-wheel drive 四輪駆動 **yonrin kudō** *(yoan-reen kuu-doe)*

France フランス **Furansu** *(fuu-rahn-sue)*

franchise 独占販売権 **dokusen hanbai ken** *(doe-kuu-sen hahn-by ken)*; フランチャイズ **furanchaizu** *(fuu-run-chah-ee-zuu)*

franchise sales 一手販売 **itte hanbai** *(eat-tay hahn-by)*

fraud (swindle) 詐欺 **sagi** *(sah-ghee)*

free of charge 無料で **muryō de** *(muu-rio day)*
▪ This sample is free. この見本は無料です。**Kono mihon wa muryō désu.** *(koe-no me-hone wah muu-rio dess.)*

free alongside ship 船側渡し **sensoku watashi** *(sen-so-kuu wah-tah-she)*

free and clear 抵当に入っていない **teitō ni haitte inai** *(tay-toe nee height-tay ee-nigh)*

free enterprise 自由企業 **jiyū kigyō** *(jee-yuu kee-g'yoe)*

freelancer 自由契約者 **jiyū-keiyaku sha** *(jee-yuu kay-yah-kuu sha)*

free list (commodities without customs duty) 免税品リスト **menzei hin risuto** *(men-zay heen ree-sue-toe)*

free market 自由市場 **jiyū shijō** *(jee-yuu she-joe)*

free on board (FOB) 本船渡し **honsen watashi** *(hone-sen wah-tah-she)*

free on rail (FOR) 貨車渡し **kasha watashi** *(kah-shah wah-tah-she)*

free port 自由貿易港 **jiyū bōeki kō** *(jee-yuu boe-eh-kee koe)*

free trade 自由貿易 **jiyū bōeki** *(jee-yuu boe-eh-kee)*

free trade zone 自由貿易圏 **jiyū bōeki ken** *(jee-yuu boe-eh-kee ken)*

freight 貨物 **kamotsu** *(kah-moat-sue)*

freight collect 運賃到着地払い **unchin tōchakuchi barai** *(uun-cheen toe-chah-kuu-chee bah-rye)*

freighter (vessel) 貨物船 **kamotsu-sen** *(kah-moat-sue-sen)*
▪ On which day will the freighter arrive? 貨物船は何日に到着しますか。**Kamotsu-sen wa nan nichi ni tōchaku shimasu ka?** *(kah-moat-sue-sen wah nahn nee-chee nee toe-chah-kuu she-mahss kah?)*

freight forwarder 貨物取扱業者 **kamotsu toriatsukai gyōsha** *(kah-moat-sue toe-ree-ah-t'sue-kye g'yoe-shah)*; 乙仲 **otsu naka** *(oh-t'sue nah-kah)*

freight included 運賃込み **unchin komi** *(uun-cheen koe-me)*

freight insurance 運賃保険 **unchin hoken** *(uun-cheen hoe-ken)*

freight prepaid 運賃前払い **unchin mae barai** *(uun-cheen my bah-rye)*

French (person) フランス人 **Furansujin** *(fuu-rahn-sue-jeen)*

fringe benefits 付加給付 **fuka kyūfu** *(fuu-kah cue-fuu)*

fringe market 二次的市場 **niji-teki shijō** *(nee-jee-tay-kee she-joe)*

front-end fee 先取り手数料 **sakidori tesūryō** *(sah-kee doe-ree tay-sue-rio)*

front-wheel drive 前輪駆動 **zenrin kudō** *(zen-reen kuu-doe)*

frozen assets 凍結資産 **tōketsu shisan** *(toe-kate-sue she-sahn)*

FTP (File Transfer Protocol) FTP **FTP** *(E-fuu-Tee-Pee)*
▪ Which FTP program are you using? どのFTPプログラムを使っていますか? **Dono FTP puroguramu wo tsukatte imasu ka?** *(doh-no E-fuu-Tee-Pee puu-roh-guu-rah-muu oh t'su-kaht-tay ee-mahss kah?)*

fuel (for combustion engines) 燃料 **nenryō** *(nen-rio)*

fuel consumption 燃料消費量 **nenryō shōhiryō** *(nen-rio show-hee-rio)*

full page "bleed" ad 裁ち切り **tachikiri** *(tah-chee-kee-ree)*

full scale 本格的 **honkaku teki** *(hone-kah-kuu tay-kee)*

full settlement 総決算 **sō kessan** *(so case-sahn)*

full-time employee/worker 正社員 **seishain** *(say-shah-een)*
▪ Are all of your employees full-time? 従業員はすべて正社員ですか。**Jūgyōin wa subete seishain désu ka?** *(juu-g'yoe-een wah sue-bay-tay say-shah-een dess kah?)*

functional analysis 機能分析 **kinō bunseki** *(kee-no boon-say-kee)*

funds (capital) 資金 **shikin** *(she-keen)*; 資本金 **shihonkin** *(she-hone-keen)*; 基金 **kikin** *(kee-keen)*

fuse 導火線 **dōkasen** *(dohh-kah-sen)*; ヒューズ **hyūzu** *(h'yee-zuu)*

fusion フュージョン **fyūjon** *(few-jone)*

futures (finance) 先物取引 **sakimono torihiki** *(sah-kee-moe-no toe-ree-hee-kee)*

futures (securities) 先物契約 **sakimono keiyaku** *(sah-kee-moe-no kay-yah-kuu)*

futures option 先物オプション **sakimono opushon** *(sah-kee-moe-no op-shone)*

G

gain 利益 **rieki** *(ree-ay-kee)*

gains and losses 損益 **soneki** *(saon-ay-kee)*

gap 開き **hiraki** *(he-rah-kee)*; ギャップ **gyappu** *(gahp-puu)*

garnishment 債券差し押さえ **saiken sashiosae** *(sigh-ken sah-she-oh-sigh)*

gas ガス **gasu** *(gah-sue)*

gasoline ガソリン **gasorin** *(gah-so-reen)*

GAT (General Agreement on Tariffs and Trade) ガット **GATTO** *(Gah-Toe)*; 関税と貿易に関する一般協定 **kanzei to bōeki ni kansuru ippan kyōtei** *(kahn-zye toe boe-ay-kee nee kahn sue-rue eep-pahn k'yoe-tay)*

geek, computer (computer geek) コンピュータオタク **konpyūta otaku** *(kome-p'yuu-tah oh-tah-kuu)*

gene 遺伝子 **idenshi** *(ee-dane-she)*

general acceptance 普通引き受け **futsū hikiuke** *(fuu-t'sue he-kee-uu-kay)*

general affairs (business) 総務 **sōmu** *(so-muu)*

general affairs department (company) 総務部 **sōmu bu** *(so-muu buu)*
▪ I have an appointment with the manager of the general affairs department. 総務部長と約束があります。**Sōmu buchō to yakusoku ga arimasu.** *(so-muu buu-choe toe yahk-so-kuu gah ah-ree-mahss.)*

general expenditures 一般歳出 **ippan saishutsu** *(eep-pahn sigh-shee-t'sue)*

general manager 総支配人 **sō shihainin** *(so she-high-neen)*

general meeting 総会 **sōkai** *(so-kye)*

general partnership company 合名会社 **gōmei gaisha** *(go-may guy-shah)*

general shareholders' meeting 株主総会 **kabunushi sōkai** *(kah-buu-nuu-she so-kye)*

general strike ゼネスト **zenesuto** *(zay-nay-sue-toe)*

generation 世代 **sedai** *(say-die)*

generator (for electricity) 発電機 **hatsuden ki** *(hot-t'seu den kee)*; ジェネレーター **jenerētā** *(jay-nay-ray-tah)*

genetics 遺伝学 **idengaku** *(ee-dane-gah-kuu)*

gentleman's agreement 紳士協定 **shinshi kyōtei** *(sheen-she k'yoe-tay)*

German language ドイツ語 **Doitsugo** *(doh-eet-sue-go)*

German (person) ドイツ人 **Doitsujin** *(doh-eet-sue-jeen)*

Germany ドイツ **Doitsu** *(doh-eet-sue)*

gift (present) お土産 **omiyage** *(oh-me-yah-gay)*; 贈り物 **okurimono** *(oh-kuu-ree-moe-no)*; ギフト **gifuto** *(gift-oh)*
▪ Thank you very much for the gift. お土産をどうもありがとうざいました。**Omiyage wo dōmo arigatō gozaimashita.** *(oh-me-yah-gay oh doe-moe ah-ree-gah-toe go-zye-mah-shtah.)*

global 世界的 **sekai-teki** *(say-kie-tay-kee)*

global standard 世界基準 **sekai kijun** *(say-kye kee-june)*; グローバルスタンダード **gurōbaru sutandādo** *(guu-roe-bah-rue suu-tahn-dah-doe)*
▪ The company aims to achieve success by setting the global standard. 事業を成功させるためグローバルスタンダードを目指します。**Jigyō wo seikō saseru tame gurōbaru sutandādo wo mezashimasu.** *(jeeg-yohhh oh say-kohh sah-say-rue tah-may guu-rohh-bah-rue sue-tahn-dahh-doh oh may-zah-she mah-sue.)*

glossy (photo on coated paper) つや出しの **tsuya dashi no** *(t'sue-yah dah-she no)*

glut (excess supply) 供給過剰 **kyōkyū kajō** *(k'yoe-cue-kah-joe)*

GNP (Gross National Product) 国民総生産 **kokumin sō-seisan** *(koe-kuu-meen so-say-sahn)*

go-between in business 仲介者 **chūkai-sha** *(chew-kye-shah)*
▪ I am looking for a go-between. 仲介者を探しています。**Chūkai-sha wo sagashite imasu.** *(chew-kye-shah oh sah-gah-shtay-mahss.)*

godown (warehouse) 倉庫 **sōko** *(so-koe)*

going rate (price) 現行歩合 **genkō buai** *(gen-koe buu-eye)*

golf ゴルフ **gorufu** *(go-rue-fuu)*; have a passion for golf ゴルフ好き **gorufu-zuki** *(go-rue-fuu-zuu-kee)*

good luck 幸運 **kōun** *(koe-uun)*

good-luck day 大安 **tai-an** *(tie ahn)*

goods (merchandise) 物資 **busshi** *(boosh-she)*; 商品 **shōhin** *(show-heen)*

goods, capital (capital goods) 資本財 **shihon zai** *(she-hone zye)*

goods, consumer (consumer goods) 消費材 **shōhi zai** *(show-hee zye)*

goods, durable (durable goods) 耐久消費財 **taikyū shōhi zai** *(tie-cue show-hee zye)*

goods, industrial (industrial goods) 生産資材 **seisan shizai** *(say-sahn she-zye)*

goods in stock 在庫品 **zaikohin** *(zye-koe-boon)*

good weather いい天気 **ii tenki** *(ee tane-kee)*

goodwill (with customers) 営業権 **eigyō ken** *(eh-ee-g'yoe ken)*

Google グーグル **Gūguru** *(Guu-guu-ruu)*
▪ Look for it on Google! グーグルで探して! **Gūguru de sagashite!** *(Guu-guu-ruu day sah-gah-ssh-tay!)*
▪ You can find almost anything on Google. グーグルで大抵、何でも見つかります。**Gūguru de taitei nandemo mitsukari masu.** *(Guu-ruu-ruu day tie-tay-ee nahn-day-moe meet-sue-kah- ree mahss.)*
▪ I found you on Google! あなたをグーグルで見つけました。**Anata wo Gūguru de mitsukemashita!** *(Ah-nah-tah oh guu-guu-ruu day wah meet-sue-kay-mah-ssh-tah!)*

go public with stock 株式公開する **kabushiki kōkai suru** *(kah-buu-she-kee koe-kye sue-rue)*

go to meet 迎えに行く **mukae ni iku** *(muu-kye nee ee-kuu)*
▪ Don't worry. I will (go to) meet you. ご心配はいりません。お迎えに参ります。**Go-shimpai wa irimasen. O-mukae ni mairimasu.** *(go-sheem-pie wah ee-ree-mah-sen oh-muu-kye nee mah-ee-ree-mahss.)*

government 政府 **seifu** *(say-fuu)*; Japanese government 日本政府 **Nihon seifu** *(nee-hone say-fuu)*

government agency 政府機関 **seifu kikan** *(say-fuu kee-kahn)*

government bank (central bank) 中央銀行 **Chūō Ginkō** *(chew-oh gheen-koe)*

government bonds 国債 **koku sai** *(coke sigh)*

government leader 政府指導者 **seifu shidō sha** *(say-fuu she-doe sha)*; 首脳 **shunō** *(shuu-nohh)*

government policy 政府の政策 **seifu no seisaku** *(say-fuu no say-sah-kuu)*
▪ Do you always follow government policy? 政府の政策にいつも従いますか。**Seifu no seisaku ni itsumo shitagaimasu ka?** *(say-fuu no say-sah-kuu nee eat-sue-moe shtah-guy-mahss kah?)*

grace period 猶予期間 **yūyo kikan** *(yuu-yoe kee-kahn)*

grade, commercial (commercial grade) 商業格付け **shōgyō kakuzuke** *(show-g'yoe kah-kuu-zuu-kay)*

grade (stage) 段階 **dankai** *(dahn-kye)*

graft 収賄 **shūwai** *(shuu-why)*

grain 穀物 **kokumotsu** *(koe-kuu-moat-sue)*

grain (of photo or piece of art or film) 木目 **kime** *(kee-may)*

gram グラム **guramu** *(guu-rah-muu)*

grant (subsidy) 助成金 **josei kin** *(joh-say-keen)*

graph グラフ **gurafu** *(guu-rah-puu)*

gratuity (tip) チップ **chippu** *(cheap-puu)*
▪ Isn't it necessary to tip here? ここでチップは必要ですか。**Koko de chippu wa hitsuyō ka?** *(koe-koe day cheap-puu wah he-t'sue-yoe dess kah?)*

gray market グレーマーケット **gurē māketto** *(guu-ray mah-ket-toe)*

Great Britain イギリス **Igirisu** *(ee-ghee-ree-sue)*

great number (majority) 多数 **tasū** *(tah-sue)*

Greece ギリシャ **Girisha** *(ghee-ree-shah)*

Greek (person) ギリシャ人 **Girishajin** *(ghee-ree-shah-jeen)*

greenhouse 温室 **onshitsu** *(own-sheet-sue)*

greetings (greeting visitors in your office or visiting someone's office and greeting them is a very important part of Japanese protocol) あいさつ **aisatsu** *(eye-sah-t'sue)*

grievance 不服のもと **fufuku no moto** *(fuu-fuu-kuu no moh-toe)*

grievance procedure 苦情処理手続き **kujō shori tetsuzuki** *(kuu-joe show-ree tay-t'sue-zuu-kee)*

gross income 総所得 **sō shotoku** *(so show-toe-kuu)*

gross investment 総投資 **sō tōshi** *(so toe-she)*

gross loss 総損失 **sō sonshitsu** *(so soan-sheet-sue)*

gross margin 売上総利益 **uriage sō rieki** *(uu-ree-ah-gay so ree-eh-kee)*

gross national product (GNP) 国民総生産 **kokumin sō-seisan** *(koe-kuu-meen so-say-sahn)*

gross profit 売上総利益 **uriage sō rieki** *(uu-ree-ah-gay so ree-eh-kee)*

gross sales 総売上高 **sō uriage daka** *(so uu-ree-ah-gay dah-kah)*

gross spread 値ザヤ **ne zaya** *(nay zah-yah)*; 価格差 **kakaku sa** *(kah-kah-kuu sah)*

gross weight 総重量 **sō jūryō** *(so juu-rio)*

gross yield 総利回り **sō rimawari** *(so ree-mah-wah-ree)*

ground (earth) 地面 **jimen** *(jee-men)*

group accounts 連結財務諸表 **renketsu zaimu shohyō** *(ren-kate-sue zye-muu show-h'yoe)*

group discussion 話し合い **hanashiai** *(hah-nah-she-eye)*; 討論 **tōron** *(toe-roan)*

group dynamics グループダイナミクス **gurūpu dainamikusu** *(guu-ruu-puu dye-nah-mee-kue-sue)*

group insurance 団体保険 **dantai hoken** *(dahn-tie hoe-ken)*

group spirit 集団意識 **shūdan ishiki** *(shuu-dahn ee-shee-kee)*

group training 集団訓練 **shūdan kunren** *(shuu-dahn coon-ren)*

grow; raise (crop) 栽培する **saibai suru** *(sigh-by sue-rue)*

grow; raise (child) 育つ **sodatsu** *(so-dah-t'sue)*

growth 成長 **seichō** *(say-choe)*

growth, corporate (corporate growth) 企業成長 **kigyō seichō** *(kee-g'yoe say-choe)*

growth index 成長指標 **seichō shihyō** *(say-choe she-h'yoe)*

growth industry 成長産業 **seichō sangyō** *(say-choe sahn-g'yoe)*

growth potential 成長の可能性 **seichō no kanōsei** *(say-choe no kah-no-say)* ▪ Do you think this business has growth potential? この事業は成長の可能性があると思いますか。**Kono jigyō wa seichō no kanōsei ga aru to omoimasu ka?** *(koe-no jee-g'yoe wah say-choe no kah-no-say gah ah-rue toe oh-moe-ee-mahss kah?)*

growth rate 成長率 **seichō ritsu** *(say-choe ree-t'sue)*

growth stock 成長株 **seichō kabu** *(say-choe kah-buu)*

guarantee 保証します **hoshō shimasu** *(hoe-show she-mahss)* ▪ I will guarantee payment. 支払いを保証します。**Shiharai wo hoshō shimasu.** *(she-hah-rye oh hoe-show she-mahss.)*

guarantee deposit/payment 保証金 **hoshō kin** *(hoe-show keen)*

guaranteed salary 固定給 **kotei kyū** *(koe-tay cue)*

guaranty bond 保証書 **hoshō sho** *(hoe-show show)*

guaranty company 保証会社 **hoshō gaisha** *(hoe-show guy-shah)*

guard (person) ガードマン **gādoman** *(gahh-doh-mahn)*

guess 推察 **suisatsu** *(sue-ee-saht-sue)*; 当て推量 **ate suiryō** *(ah-tay suu-ee-rio)*

guest ゲスト **gesuto** *(gess-toh)*; 来客 **raikyaku** *(righ-k'yah-kuu)*

guide (lead) 案内 **annai** *(ahn-nigh)*; 案内する **annai suru** *(ahn-nigh sue-rue)*

guided missile 誘導ミサイル **yūdō misairu** *(yuu-dohh me-sigh-rue)*

guidelines ガイドライン **gaido rain** *(guy-doe rine)*

H

hacker ハッカー **hakkā** *(hahk-kah)*

half 半分 **hanbun** *(hahn-boon)*; 半期 **hanki** *(hahn-kee)* ▪ Just half will be enough. 半分で十分です。**Hanbun de jūbun désu.** *(hahn-boon day juu-boon dess.)*

half a year 半年 **hantoshi** *(hahn-toe-she)* ▪ I have been in Japan for half a year. 半年日本に居ます。**Hantoshi Nihon ni imasu.** *(hahn-toe-she nee-hone nee ee-mahss.)*

half-finished goods 半製品 **han-sei hin** *(hahn-say heen)*

hand-clapping (to mark an auspicious event) 手締め **te-jime** *(tay-jee-may)*

handicap 不利な条件 **furi na jōken** *(fuu-ree-nah joe-ken)*

handicrafts 工作 **kōsaku** *(kohh-sah-kuu)*; 手芸 **shugei** *(shuu-gay)*

handling 取扱い **tori atsukai** *(toe-ree ah-t'sue-kye)*

handling charge 手数料 **tesūryō** *(tay-sue-rio)* ▪ About how much will the handling charge be? 手数料はだいたいいくらになりますか。**Tesūryō wa daitai ikura ni narimasu ka?** *(tay-sue-rio wah dye-tie ee-kuu-rah nee nah-ree-mahss kah?)*

hand-made 手作りの **te-zukuri no** *(tay-zuu-kuu-ree no)*

hand-painted 手塗りの **te-nuri no** *(tay*

nuu-ree no); 手描きの **tegaki no** *(tay-gah-kee no)*

handset ハンドセット **hando-setto** *(hahn-doe-set-toe)*; 電話機 **denwa ki** *(dane-wah kee)*
▪ Where did you buy this cell-phone's handset? この携帯電話機はどこで買ったの。**Kono keitai denwa ki wa doko de kattano?** *(koh-no kay-tie dane-wah kee wah doh-koh day kot-tah-no?)*

Haneda Airport 羽田空港 **Haneda Kūkō** *(hah-nay-dah kuu-koe)*

hard (to the touch) 堅い **katai** *(kah-tie)*; difficult 難しい **muzukashii** *(muu-zuu-kah-she)*
▪ This work is very hard. この仕事はとても大変です。**Kono shigoto wa totemo taihen désu.** *(koe-no she-gah-toe wah toe-tay-moe tai-hen dess.)*

hard copy ハードコピー **hādo kopii** *(hah-doe koe-pee)*
▪ Please make a hardcopy. ハードコピーを出力してください。**Hādo copii wo shutsuryoku shite kudasai.** *(hah-doh koh-pee oh shuu-t'sue-rio-kuu ssh-tay kuu-dah-sie.)*

hardcover (as in book) ハードカバー **hādo kabā** *(hah-doe kah-bah)*; 上製本 **jōsei bon** *(joe-say bone)*

hard currency 交換可能通貨 **kōkan kanō tsūka** *(koe-kahn kah-no t'sue kah)*

hard-drive ハードドライブ **hādo-doraibu** *(hah-doh doh-rie-buu)*
▪ I want the large capacity of a hard-drive. 容量の大きいハードドライブが欲しいです。**Yōryō no ōkii hādo doraibu ga hoshii désu.** *(yoh-rio no ooh-kee hah-doh doh-rie-buu gah hoh-shee dess.)*
▪ What is the capacity of this hard-drive? このハードドライブの容量はどのくらいですか。**Kono hādo-doraibu no yōryō wa dono kurai désu ka?** *(koh-no hah-doh doh-rie-buu no yoh-rio wah doh-no kuu-rie dess kah?)*

hard sell ハードセール **hādo sēru** *(hah-doe say-rue)*

hardware ハードウエア **hādo wea** *(hah-doe way-ah)*

harmony 和 **wa** *(wah)*; 調和 **chō wa** *(choe-wah)*

hazardous 危険(な) **kiken (na)** *(kee-kane)*

headhunter (new employee scout) 人材スカウト **jinzai sukauto** *(jeen-zye scout-oh)*

headline 見出し **midashi** *(me-dah-she)*; ヘッドライン **heddo rain** *(hay-doe rine)*
▪ The headlines of sport journals are always exaggerated. スポーツ新聞の見出しはいつも大げさです。**Supōtsu shinbun no midashi wa itsumo ōgesa désu.** *(suu-pote-sue sheem-boon no mee-dah-she way eet-sue-moh ohh-gay-sah dess.)*

head office 本社 **honsha** *(hone-shah)*
▪ (Our) head office has moved to Shinjuku. 本社は新宿に移りました。**Honsha wa Shinjuku ni utsurimashita.** *(hone-shah wah sheen-juu-kuu nee uu-t'sue-ree mah-shtah.)*

headquarters 本部 **honbu** *(hone-buu)*

heavy 重い **omoi** *(oh-moy)*

heavy industry 重工業 **jū kōgyō** *(juu koe-g'yoe)*

heavy labor 力仕事 **chikara shigoto** *(chee-kah-rah she-go-toe)*
▪ I am not used to heavy labor/work. 力仕事には慣れていません。**Chikara shigoto ni wa narete imasen.** *(chee-

kah-rah she-go-toe nee wah nah-ray-tay ee-mah-sen.)

heavy penalty tax 重加算税 **jū kasan zei** *(juu kah-sahn-zye)*

hectare (2.471 acres) ヘクタール **hekutāru** *(hay-kuu-tah-rue)*

hedge (one's position) つなぐ **tsunagu** *(t'sue-nah-guu)*

hedge fund ヘッジファンド **heggi fando** *(hayg-gee-fan-doe)*

height 高さ **takasa** *(tah-kah-sah)*
▪ What is the height of that building? そのビルの高さはどのぐらいですか。 **Sono biru no takasa wa dono gurai désu ka?** *(so-no bee-rue no tah-kah-sah wah doh-no guu-rye dess kah?)*

help (care) お世話 **o-sewa** *(oh-say-wah)*
▪ Thanks for your help. お世話になっています。 **O-sewa ni natte imasu.** *(oh-say-wah nee nah-tay ee-mahss)*

help wanted (advertisement) 求人広告 **kyūjin kōkoku** *(cue-jeen koe-coke)*

hidden assets 隠匿資産 **intoku shisan** *(een-toe-kuu she-sahn)*

hidden assets (securities) 含み資産 **fukumi shisan** *(fuu-kuu-me she-sahn)*

high 高い **takai** *(tah-kye)*

high-end 高級志向の **kokyū shikō no** *(koe-k'yuu she-koh no)*

high-end user ハイエンドユーザー **haiendo yūzā** *(hie-een-doe yuu-zaa)*
▪ The sale of high-end user products is going well. ハイエンドユーザー向けの商品の売れ行きが好調です。 **Haiendo yūzā muke no shōhin no ureyuki ga kōchō désu.** *(hie-en-doe yuu-zaa muu-kay no shohh-heen no uu-ray-yuu-kee ga kohh-chohh dess.)*

high fidelity ハイファイ **haifai** *(hie-fie)*

highlight ハイライト **hairaito** *(hie-rie-toh)*

high quality 優秀な **yūshū na** *(yuu-shuu nah)*; 上質な **jōshitsu na** *(joe-she-t'sue na)*

high-resolution television ハイビジョン **haibijon** *(hie-bee-john)*
▪ When I get my bonus I'm going to buy a high-resolution television set. 今度のボーナスでハイビジョンテレビを買うつもりです。 **Kondo no bōnasu de haibijon terebi wo kau tsumori désu.** *(kone-doh no bohh-nah-sue day hie-bee-jone tay-ray-bee oh kow t' sue-moe-ree dess.)*

high-speed dial-up ハイスピード通信 **hai-supiido tsūshin** *(hie-suu-pee-doe t'sue-sheen)*
▪ Is this cell-phone high-speed dial-up? この携帯電話はハイスピード通信対応ですか。 **Kono keitai denwa wa hai-supiido tsūshin taiō désu ka?** *(koh-no kay-tie dane-wah wah hie-spee-doh t'sue-sheen tie-oh dess kah?)*
▪ How much does it cost to have high-speed dial-up per month? ハイスピード通信の利用料は月額いくらですか。 **Hai-supiido tsūshin no riyō ryō wa getsugaku ikura désu ka?** *(hie-spee-doh t'sue-sheen no ree-yoh rio wah gate-sue-gah-kuu ee-kuu-rah dess kah?)*

high technology ハイテク **haiteku** *(hie-tay-kuu)*

high tech product ハイテク製品 **haiteku seihin** *(hie-take-kuu say-heen)*

high yen 円高 **en daka** *(en dah-kah)*

highest bidder 最高入札者 **saikō nyūsatsu-sha** *(sigh-koe n'yuu-sah-t'sue-shah)*

▪ Who was the highest bidder? 最高入札者はどなたでしたか。**Saikō nyūsatsu-sha wa donata déshita ka?** *(sigh-koe n'yuu-sah-t'sue-shah wah doe-nah-tah desh-tah kah?)*

hijack ハイジャックする **haijakku suru** *(hie-jahk-kuu sue-rue)*

hijacker 乗っ取り犯 **nottori han** *(note-toh-ree hahn)*; ハイジャック犯 **haijakku han** *(hie-jahk-kuu hahn)*

hobby 趣味 **shumi** *(shuu-me)*

holding company 持ち株会社 **mochikabu gaisha** *(moe-chee-kah-buu guy-shah)*; 親会社 **oya gaisha** *(oh-yah guy-shah)*
▪ Who is the president of your holding company? あなたの持ち株会社の社長はどなたですか。**Anata no mochikabu gaisha no shachō wa donata désu ka?** *(ah-nah-tah no moe-chee-kah-buu guy-shah no shah-choe wah doe-nah-tah dess kah?)*

holding period 保有期間 **hoyū kikan** *(hoe-yuu kee-kahn)*

holdings 持ち株 **mochikabu** *(moe-chee-kah-buu)*

holiday (day off) 休み **yasumi** *(yah-sue-me)*; 休暇 **kyūka** *(cue-kah)*; take a day or days off 休みを取る **yasumi wo toru** *(yah-sue-me oh toe-rue)*

Holland オランダ **Oranda** *(oh-rahn-dah)*

homemaker 主婦 **shufu** *(shuu-fuu)*

home market 国内市場 **kokunai shijō** *(koe-kuu-nigh she-joe)*

home page ホームページ **hōmu pēji** *(hoh-muu pay-jee)*
▪ Show me your home page. ホームページを見せてください。**Hōmu pēji wo misete kudasai.** *(hoe-muu pay-jee oh me-say-tay kuu-dah-sie.)*
▪ I don't have a home page. ホームページを持っていません。**Hōmu pēji wo motteimasen.** *(hoe-muu pay-jee oh mote-tay-ee-mah-sen.)*
▪ Will you design a home page for me? ホームページをデザインしてくれますか。**Hōmu pēji wo dezain shite kuremasu ka?** *(hoh-muu pay-jee oh design ssh-tay kuu-ray-mahss kah?)*

hometown ふるさと **furusato** *(fuu-ruu-sah-toh)*; 出身地 **shusshinchi** *(shuu-sheen chee)*
▪ Where is your hometown? 出身地はどこですか。**Shusshinchi wa dóko désu ka?** *(shuu-sheen chee wah dohh-koe dess kah?)*

hope 見込み **mikomi** *(me-koe-me)*; hope (yours) ご希望 **go-kibō** *(go-kee-boe)*

horsepower 馬力 **bariki** *(bah-ree-kee)*

host (person who receives guests) ホスト **hosuto** *(hoh-suu-toh)*

hostage 人質 **hitojichi** *(ssh-toh-jee-chee)*

hostess (nightclub/cabaret) ホステス **hosutesu** *(hohss-tay-suu)*

hot 暑い/熱い **atsui** *(ah-t'sue-ee)*

hot line ホットライン **hotto rain** *(hoht-toh rine)*

hot money ホットマネー **hotto manē** *(hoe-toe mah-nay)*; 不正な金 **fusei na kane** *(fuu-say nah kane)*

hourly earnings 時間収入 **jikan shūnyū** *(jee-kahn-shuu-n'yuu)*

hourly pay 時間給 **jikan kyū** *(jee-kahn cue)*

hours of operation 稼働時間 **kadō jikan** *(kah-doe jee-kahn)*; 営業時間 **eigyō jikan** *(eh-ee-g'yoe jee-kahn)*
▪ What are the business hours of

Mitsukoshi Department Store? 三越デパートの営業時間は何時から何時までですか。**Mitsukoshi Depāto no eigyō jikan wa nanji kara nanji made désu ka?** *(meet-sue-koe-she day-pah-toe no eh-ee-g'yoe jee-kahn wah nahn-jee kah-rah nan-jee mah-day dess kah?)*

household; housekeeping 所帯 **shotai** *(show-tie)*; 世帯 **setai** *(say-tie)*

household (family) 家族 **kazoku** *(kah-zoh-kuu)*; 家庭 **katei** *(kah-tay)*

household electrical appliances 家電 **kaden** *(kah-dane)*

housewife 主婦 **shufu** *(shuu-fuu)*

housework 家事 **kaji** *(kah-jee)*

House of Councillors 参議院 **Sangi-in** *(sahn-ghee-een)*; councillor 参議院議員 **Sangi-in giin** *(sahn-ghee-een ghee-een)*

House of Representatives 衆議院 **Shūgi-in** *(shuu-ghee-een)*; representative 衆議院議員 **Shūgi-in giin** *(shuu-ghee-een ghee-een)*

house phone 内線電話 **naisen denwa** *(nah-ee-sen dane-wah)*
▪ Where are the house phones? 内線電話はどこにありますか。**Naisen denwa wa doko ni arimasu ka?** *(nah-ee-sen dane-wah wah doe-koe nee ah-ree-mahss kah?)*

human affairs; personnel affairs 人事 **jinji** *(jeem-jee)*

human resources 人材 **jinzai** *(jeen-zye)*

human rights 人権 **jin ken** *(jeen ken)*

hybrid car ハイブリッドカー **haiburiddo kā** *(high-buu-rid kahh)*
▪ I think I will buy a hybrid car for my parents. 両親のためにハイブリッドカーを買おうと思う。**Ryōshin no tame ni hybrid car wo kaō to omou.** *(rio-sheen no tah-may nee hybrid car oh kah-oh to oh-mohh.)*

hybrid materials ハイブリッド材料 **haiburiddo zairyō** *(high-buu-reed-doe zye-rio)*

hygiene; sanitation 衛生 **eisei** *(eh-ee-say)*

I

idea (thought) 考え **kangae** *(kahn-guy)*; アイデア **aidea** *(aye-deer)*
▪ He always proposes unique ideas. 彼はいつもユニークなアイデアを提案します。**Kare wa itsumo yuniiku na aidea wo teian shimasu.** *(kah-ray wah eet-suu-moh yuu-neek-nah aye-deer oh tay-ahn she-mahss.)*

ideal 理想 **risō** *(ree-so)*; **ideally** 理想として **risō to shitei** *(ree-so toe shtay)*

identification (I.D.) (card) 身分証明証 **mibun shōmei shō** *(me-boon show-may show)*
▪ Please let me see some identification. 身分証明証を見せてください。**Mibun shōmei shō wo misete kudasai.** *(me-boon show-may show oh me-say-tay kuu-dah-sigh.)*

identification (I.D.) (number) 識別番号 **shikibetsu bangō** *(she-kee-bay-t'sue bahn-go)*

identity アイデンティティ **aidentiti** *(aye-den-tee-tee)*; 個性 **kosei** *(koe-say)*; 意識 **ishiki** *(ee-she-kee)*
▪ Today's young people do not have enough personal identity. 最近の若者はアイデンティティが足りない。**Saikin no wakamono wa aidentiti ga tarinai.** *(sie-keen no wah-kah-moe-no wah aye-den-tee-tee gah tah-ree-nie.)*

idle capacity (facilities) 遊休施設 **yūkyū shisetsu** *(yuu-cue she-say-t'sue)*

idol (TV performer/entertainer) アイドル **aidoru** *(aye-doh-rue)*

ignition イグニッション **igunisshon** *(ee-guu-nee-shone)*

ignore (disregard) 無視する **mushi suru** *(muu-she sue-rue)*

illegal 不法の **fuhō-no** *(fuu-hoe-noh)*

illegal dumping 不法投棄 **fuhō tōki** *(fuu-hoe toe-kee)*

illegal lending ヤミ金融 **yami kinyū** *(yah-me keen-yuu)*

illegal shipments 違法出荷 **ihō shukka** *(ee-hoe shuuk-kah)*

illegal trade 不正取引 **fusei torihiki** *(fuu-say toe-ree-hee-kee)*

illustration イラスト **irasuto** *(ee-rah-stow)*

imagination 想像 **sōzō** *(so-zoe)*

imitation product 模造品 **mozō hin** *(moe-zoe heen)*; 偽物 **nisemono** *(nee-say-moe-no)*
▪ This looks like an imitation. これは偽物のようです。**Kore wa nisemono no yō désu.** *(koe-ray wah nee-say-moe-no no yoe dess.)*

immediately 大至急 **dai-shikyū** *(dye-she-cue)*

impatient せっかちな **sekkachi na** *(sake-kah-chee nah)*

impending changes 差し迫った変化 **sashisematta henka** *(sah-she-say-maht-tah hen-kah)*

implied agreement 黙諾 **moku daku** *(moe-kuu dah-kuu)*

import 輸入 **yunyū** *(yuun-yuu)*; to import 輸入する **yunyū suru** *(yuun-yuu sue-rue)*
▪ What kind of merchandise do you import? どんな品物を輸入していますか。**Donna shinamono wo yunyū shite imasu ka?** *(doan-nah she-nah-moe-no oh yuun-yuu shtay-mahss kah?)*

important point 重点 **jūten** *(juu-ten)*

import company; importer 輸入業者 **yunyū gyōsha** *(yuun-yuu g'yoe-shah)*

import declaration 輸入申告 **yunyū shinkoku** *(yuun-yuu sheen-koe-kuu)*

import deposit 輸入担保 **yunyū tanpo** *(yuun-yuu tahn-poe)*

import duty 輸入税 **yunyū zei** *(yuun-yuu zay)*

import entry 輸入手続 **yunyū tetsuzuki** *(yuun-yuu tay-t'sue-zuu-kee)*

import license/permit 輸入許可(証) **yunyū kyoka (shō)** *(yuun-yuu k'yoe-kah (show))*

import quota 輸入割り当て **yunyū wariate** *(yuun-yuu wah-ree-ah-tay)*
▪ Does Japan have an import quota for Western-style wearing apparel? 日本は洋服の輸入割り当てがありますか。**Nihon wa yōfuku no yunyū wariate ga arimasu ka?** *(nee-hone wah yoe-fuu-kuu no yuun-yuu wah-ree-ah-tay gah ah-ree-mahss kah?)*
▪ How much did the percentage rise for import quotas? 輸入割り当ては何パーセントアップしましたか。**Yunyū wariate wa nan pāsento appu shimashita ka?** *(yuun-yuu wah-ree-ah-tay wah nahn pah-cent-oh up she-mah-she-tah kah?)*

import regulations 輸入規則 **yunyū kisoku** *(yuun-yuu kee-so-kuu)*

import tariff (list) 輸入関税表 **yunyū kanzei-hyō** *(yuun-yuu kahn-zay-h'yoe)*

import tariffs 輸入税率 **yunyū zeiritsu** *(yuun-yuu zay-ree-t'sue)*

import tax 輸入税 **yunyū zei** *(yuun-yuu zay)*

impound 差し押さえる **sashi osaeru** *(sah-she oh-sigh-rue)*; 没収する **bosshū suru** *(bohs-shuu sue-rue)*

impressed, impressive 感動する **kandō suru** *(kahn-doe sue-rue)*; 感心 **kanshin suru** *(kahn-sheen sue-rue)*
▪ I was very impressed with Mr. Obata. 小畑さんに大変感心させられました。**Obata-san ni taihen kanshin saseraremashita.** *(oh-bah-tah-san nee tie-hen kahn-sheen sah-say-rah-ray-mah-shtah.)*

impression 印象 **inshō** *(en-show)*; first impression 第一印象 **dai-ichi inshō** *(dye-ee-chee een-show)*

improvement 改善 **kaizen** *(kye-zen)*

impulse buying 衝動買い **shōdō gai** *(show-doe guy)*

in addition to (besides) 他に **hoka ni** *(hoe-kah nee)*
▪ Do you have any sizes besides this? この他にサイズがありますか。**Kono hoka ni saizu ga arimasu ka?** *(koe-no hoe-kah nee sigh-zuu gah ah-ree-mahss kah?)*

inadequate 不適切な **futekisetsu na** *(fuu-tay-kee-say-t'sue nah)*

in advance 前もって **maemotte** *(my-moat-tay)*; 前払い金 **maebarai kin** *(my bah-rye keen)*; advance payment 内金 **uchi kin** *(uu-chee-keen)*

incentive 誘因 **yūin** *(yuu-een)*; きっかけ **kikkake** *(kee-kah-kay)*
▪ He will not move without an incentive. きっかけが無かったら彼は動かないでしょう。**Kikkake ga nakattara kare wa ugokanai deshō.** *(kee-kah-kay gah nah-kah-tah-rah kah-ray wah uu-go-kah-nigh day-show.)*

incidental expenses 臨時費 **rinji hi** *(reen-jee hee)*

include 含む **fukumu** *(fuu-kuu-muu)*

income 所得 **shotoku** *(show-toe-kuu)*; 収入 **shūnyū** *(shuun-yuu)*; gross income 総収入 **sō shūnyū** *(so shuun-yuu)*; net income 準所得 **jun shotoku** *(june show-toe-kuu)*

income bracket 所得階層 **shotoku kaisō** *(show-toe-koe kye-so)*

income/revenue increase 増収 **zōshū** *(zohh-shuu)*

income statement 所得計算書 **shotoku keisan sho** *(show-toe-kuu kay-sahn show)*; 損益計算書 **son'eki keisan sho** *(soan-eh-kee kay-sahn show)*

income tax 所得税 **shotoku zei** *(show-toe-kuu zay)*

income tax, corporate (corporate income tax) 法人所得税 **hōjin shotoku zei** *(hoe-jeen show-toe-kuu zay)*

income tax, personal (personal income tax) 個人所得税 **kojin shotoku zei** *(koe-jeen show-toe-kuu zay)*

income yield 集計利回り **shūkei rimawari** *(shuu-ay-kee ree-mah-wah-ree)*

inconstant 変わりやすい **kawari yasui** *(kah-wah-ree yah-sue-ee)*

incorporate 会社を法人化する **kaisha wo hōjin ka suru** *(kye-shah wo hoe-jeen kah sue-rue)*
▪ Is your company incorporated? あなたの会社は法人組織ですか。**Anata**

no kaisha wa hōjin soshiki désu ka? *(ah-nah-tah no kye-shah wah hoe-jeen so-she-kee dess kah?)*

increase 増える **fueru** *(f'way-rue)*; 増やす **fuyasu** *(fuu-yah-sue)*

increase (in business, population, weight) 増加 **zōka** *(zoe-kah)*; to increase 増加する **zōka suru** *(zoe-kah sue-rue)*

incremental cash flow 増分キャッシュフロー **zōbun kyasshu furō** *(zoe-buun k'yah-shuu fuu-roe)*

indebtedness 負債 **fusai** *(fuu-sigh)*

indemnity 保障 **hoshō** *(hoe-show)*

independent (self-supporting) 独立 **dokuritsu** *(doe-kuu-ree-t'sue)*

independent administrative institution 独立行政法人 **dokuritsu gyōsei hōjin** *(doe-kuu-ree-t'sue g'yoe-say-hoe-jeen)*

independent suspension 独立懸架 **dokuritsu kenka** *(doe-kuu-reet-t'sue ken-kah)*

index (indicator) 指数 **shisū** *(she-sue)*

index 索引 **sakuin** *(sah-kuu-een)*

indexing; indexation 物価スライド制 **bukka suraido sei** *(buu-kah sue-rye-doe say)*

India インド **Indo** *(een-doh)*

Indian (person) インド人 **Indojin** *(een-doh-jeen)*

indirect claim 間接要求 **kansetsu yōkyū** *(kahn-say-t'sue yoe-cue)*

indirect cost 間接費 **kansetsu hi** *(kahn-say-t'sue hee)*

indirect expenses 一般経費 **ippan keihi** *(eep-pahn kay-he)*; 間接費 **kansetsu hi** *(kahn-say-t'sue he)*
▪ Indirect expenses are eating into our profits. 間接費は利益を浸食しています。**Kansetsu hi wa rieki wo shinshoku shiteimasu.** *(kahn-say-t'sue he wah ree-ay-kee oh sheen-show-kuu shtay-mahss.)*

indirect labor 間接労働 **kansetsu rōdō** *(kahn-say-t'sue roe-doe)*

indirect tax 間接税 **kansetsu zei** *(kahn-say-t'sue zay)*

individual 個人 **kojin** *(koe-jeen)*
▪ Should I join the old age individual annuity insurance program? 老後のために個人年金保険に入ったほうがよいでしょうか。**Rōgo no tame ni kojin nenkin hoken ni haitta hō ga yoi deshō ka?** *(roh-goh no tah-may nee koh-jeen nane-keen hoh-ken nee hite-tah hoh gah yoy day-show kah?)*

individual consumption 個人消費 **kojin shōhi** *(koe-jeen show-hee)*

individualism 個人主義 **kojin-shugi** *(koe-jeen-shuu-ghee)*

industrial 産業 **sangyō** *(sahn-g'yoe)*; 工業 **kōgyō** (koe-g'yoe)

industrial accidents 労働災害 **rōdō saigai** *(roe-doe sigh-guy)*; 労災 **rōsai** *(roe-sigh)*

industrial arbitration 労働調停 **rōdō chōtei** *(roe-doe choe-tay)*

industrial goods 生産資財 **seisan shizai** *(say-sahn she-zye)*

industrialist 資本家 **shihon-ka** *(she-hone-kah)*

industrial insurance 簡易保険 **kan-i hoken** *(kah-nee hoe-ken)*

industrialize 工業化 **kōgyōka** *(koe-g'yoe-kah)*

industrial park 工業団地 **kōgyō danchi** *(koe-g'yoe dahn-chee)*

▪ Is your factory in an industrial park? あなたの工場は工業団地の中にありますか。**Anata no kōjō wa kōgyō danchi no naka ni arimasu ka?** *(ah-nah-tah no koe-joe wah koe-g'yoe dahn-chee no nah-kah nee ah-ree-mahss kah?)*

industrial planning/project 産業計画 **sangyō keikaku** *(sahn-g'yoe kay-kah-kuu)*

industrial relations 労使関係 **rōshi kankei** *(roe-she kahn-kay)*

industrial robot 産業ロボット **sangyō robotto** *(sahn-g'yoe roe-boat-toe)*

industrial union 産業別労働組合 **sangyō-betsu rōdō-kumiai** *(sahn-g'yoe-bay-t'sue roe-doe-kuu-me-eye)*

industrial waste product 産業廃棄物 **sangyō haiki butsu** *(sahn-g'yoe high-kee-buu-t'sue)*

industry 産業 **sangyō** *(sahn-g'yoe)*

industrywide 産業全体の **sangyō zentai no** *(sahn-g'yoe zen-tie no)*; 業界全体の **gyōkai zentai no** *(g'yoe-kye zen-tie no)*

inefficient 非効率的な **hi kōritsuteki na** *(he-koe-reet-stay-kee nah)*

inexperience 未経験 **mi-keiken** *(me-kay-ken)*
▪ The new person is completely inexperienced. 新入社員は全く未経験です。**Shinnyū shain wa mattaku mi-keiken désu.** *(sheen-n'yuu shah-een wah mah-tah-kuu muu-kay-ken dess.)*

inferior parts 不良部品 **furyō buhin** *(fuu-rio buu-heen)*

inflation インフレ **infure** *(een-fuu-ray)*

inflationary インフレの **infure no** *(een-fuu-ray no)*

influence 影響 **eikyō** *(eh-ee-k'yoe)*

influential 有力な **yūryoku na** *(yuu-rio-kuu nah)*

inform (notify) 知らせる **shiraseru** *(she-rah-say-rue)*
▪ I will inform you tomorrow. 明日、知らせます。**Ashita shirasemasu.** *(ah-shtah she-rah-say-mahss.)*

information (report) 情報 **jōhō** *(joe-hoe)*; 報道 **hōdō** *(hoe-doe)*

information desk/counter 案内所 **annai sho** *(ahn-nigh show)*; 受付 **uketsuke** *(uu-kate-sue-kay)*
▪ Please ask at the information desk. 受付で聞いてください。**Uketsuke de kiite kudasai.** *(uu-kate-sue-kay day kee-tay kuu-dah-sigh.)*

information technology (IT) 情報技術 **joho gijutsu** *(joe-hoe gee-juu-t'sue)*; IT **Ai Tii** *(aye-tea)*
▪ Are IT stocks making money? IT株は儲かりますか。**IT kabu wa mōkari masu ka?** *(eye-tee kah-buu wa mohh-kah-ree mah-sue kah?)*

infrared 赤外線の **sekigai-sen no** *(say-kee-guy-sen no)*

infrastructure (economic) 経済基盤 **keizai kiban** *(kay-zye kee-bahn)*

infringement; violation; invade 侵害 **shingai** *(sheen-guy)*; 違反 **ihan** *(ee-hahn)*

ingredient 材料 **zairyō** *(zie-r'yohh)*

inheritance 相続 **sōzoku** *(so-zoe-kuu)*

inheritance tax 遺産相続税 **isan sōzoku zei** *(ee-sahn so-zoe-kuu zay)*

injunction 強制命令 **kyōsei meirei** *(k'yoe-say may-ray)*; 差し止め命令 **shashitome meirei** *(sah-she-toe-may may-ray)*

injustice 不当 **futō** *(fuu-tohh)*

ink インク **inku** *(een-kuu)*

inland bill of lading 国内船荷証券 **kokunai funani shōken** *(koe-kuu-nigh fuu-nah-nee show-ken)*

innovation 技術革新 **gijutsu kakushin** *(ghee-jute-sue kah-kuu-sheen)*

input インプット **inputto** *(een-pute-toe)*

inquiry 問い合わせ **toiawase** *(toe-ee-ah-wah-say)*; 引合い **hikiai** *(he-kee-aye)*
▪ We receive more than one hundred inquiries every day. 毎日、百件以上の問い合わせがあります。**Mainichi hyakken ijō no toiawase ga arimasu.** *(my-nee-chee h'yah-kuu-ken ee-joe no toe-ee-ah-wah-say gah ah-ree-mahss.)*

insert (as used in printing) 挿入 **sōnyū** *(soan-yuu)*; 差し込み **sashikomi** *(sah-she-koe-me)*

inside 内側 **uchigawa** *(uu-chee-gah-wah)*; 内面 **naimen** *(nigh-men)*

inside cover (magazine) 中表紙 **naka byōshi** *(nah-kah b'yoe-she)*

insider trading インサイダー取引 **insaidā torihiki** *(een-sigh-dah toe-ree-hee-kee)*

insolvent (company or person) 支払不能者 **shiharai funōsha** *(she-hah-rye fuu-no-shah)*; 倒産した **tosan shita** *(toe-sahn shtah)*; 破綻した **hatan shita** *(hah-tahn shtah)*

inspect (check) 検査する **kensa suru** *(ken-sah sue-rue)*; inspection 点検 **tenken** *(tane-kane)*
▪ I must inspect this baggage. この荷物を検査しなければなりません。**Kono nimotsu wo kensa shinakereba narimasen.** *(koh-no nee-moat-sue oh ken-sah she-nah-kay-ray-bah nah-ree-mah-sen.)*

inspector 検査官 **kensa-kan** *(ken-sah-kahn)*

instability 不安定な **fuantei na** *(fuu-ahn-tay nah)*

install (equipment or something) 取り付ける **toritsukeru** *(toe-ree-t'sue-kay-rue)*; installation 敷設 **fusetsu** *(fuu-say-t'sue)*; installation cost 敷設費 **fusetsu hi** *(fuu-say-t'sue he)*

install (computer) インストールする **insutōru suru** *(een-suu-toe-rue sue-rue)*
▪ Have you installed a new (computer) application? 新しいアプリケーションをインストールしましたか。**Atarashii apurikēshon wo insutōru shimashita ka?** *(ah-tah-rah-shee ah-puu-ree-kay-shown oh ean-sue-toe-rue she-mah-ssh-tah kah?)*

installment credit 分割払い信用 **bunkatsubarai shin'yō** *(buun-kah-t'sue-bah-rye sheen-yoe)*

installment plan 分割払い方式 **bunkatsu barai hōshiki** *(boon-kah-t'sue bah-rye hoe-she-kee)*

instant message インスタントメッセージ **insutanto messēji** *(inns-tahn-toh may-say-jee)*
▪ Which instant message program do you use? どのインスタントメッセージプログラムを使いますか。**Dono insutanto messēji puroguramu wo tsukaimasu ka?** *(doe-no inns-than-toh may-say-jee no puu-roh-guu-rah-muu oh t'sue-kai-mahss kah?)*
▪ I get many instant messages every day. 毎日たくさんのインスタントメッセージを受け取ります。**Mainichi takusan no insutanto messēji wo uketorimasu.** *(my-nee-chee tahk-sahn inns-tahn-toh no may-say-jee oh uu-kay-toh-ree-mahss.)*

instant messaging インスタントメッセージング **insutanto messējingu** *(inns-tahn-toh may-say-jeen-guu)*

▪ I don't use instant messaging. インスタントメッセージを使いません。**Insutanto messējingu wo tsukaimasen.** *(inns-tahn-toh may-say-jeen-guo oh t'sue-kie-mah-sen.)*

institutional advertising 企業広告 **kigyō kōkokū** *(kee-g'yoe koe-koe-kuu)*

institutional investor 機関投資家 **kikan tōshi ka** *(kee-kahn toe-she kah)*

instruction 指図 **sashizu** *(sah-she-zoo)*; instruction manual 解説書 **kaisetsu sho** *(kye-sate-sue show)*

insurance 保険 **hoken** *(hoe-ken)*
▪ Have you taken out insurance for something? 何か保険に加入していますか。**Nani ka hoken ni kanyū shite imasu ka?** *(nah-nee kah hoh-kane nee kahn-yuu shtay-mahss kah?)*

insurance benefits 保険給付金 **hoken kyufū kin** *(hoe-ken k'yuu-fuu keen)*

insurance company 保険会社 **hoken gaisha** *(hoe-ken guy-shah)*

insurance fund 保険資金 **hoken shikin** *(hoe-ken she-keen)*

insurance policy 保険証券 **hoken shōken** *(hoe-ken show-ken)*

insurance premium 保険料 **hoken ryō** *(hoe-ken rio)*

insurance underwriter 保険業者 **hoken gyōsha** *(hoe-ken g'yoe-shah)*

insure 保険を付ける **hoken wo tsukeru** *(hoe-ken oh t'sue-kay-rue)*

intangible assets 無形資産 **mukei shisan** *(muu-kay she-sahn)*

integrate 総合する **sōgō suru** *(so-go sue-rue)*; 統合 **tōgō suru** *(toe-go sue-rue)*

integrated circuit 集積回路 **shūseki kairo** *(shuu-say-kee kye-roe)*

integration 統合 **tōgō** *(toe-go)*

intellectual 知的 **chiteki** *(chee-tay-kee)*

intellectual property (rights) 知的所有権 **chiteki shoyūken** *(chee-tay-kee show-yuu ken)*

intelligence 知能 **chinō** *(chee-no)*; 知性 **chisei** *(chee-say)*

intelligent robot 知能ロボット **chinō robotto** *(chee-no roe-boat-toe)*

interbank 銀行間の **ginkō-kan no** *(gheen-koe-kahn no)*

interchangeable lenses 交換レンズ **kōkan renzu** *(koe-kahn ren-zuu)*

interest (profit) 利息 **risoku** *(ree-so-kuu)*; interest rate 金利 **kinri** *(keen-ree)*; interest yield 利回り **rimawari** *(ree-mah-wah-ree)*

interest 利子 **rishi** *(ree-she)*

interest, compound (compound interest) 複利 **fukuri** *(fuu-kuu-ree)*

interest income 利子所得 **rishi shotoku** *(ree-she show-toe-kuu)*

interest period 金利期間 **kinri kikan** *(keen-ree kee-kahn)*; 利息計算期間 **rishoku keisan kikan** *(ree-so-kuu kay-sahn kee-kahn)*

interest rate 利率 **riritsu** *(ree-ree-t'sue)*
▪ What is the interest rate? 利率はどのくらいですか。**Riritsu wa dono kurai désu ka?** *(ree-ree-t'sue wah doh-no kuu-rie dess kah?)*

interface インターフェース **intāfēsu** *(een-tah-fay-sue)*

interim 仮の **kari no** *(kah-ree no)*

interim budget 暫定予算 **zantei yosan** *(zahn-tay yoe-sahn)*

interim statement 仮計算書 **kari keisan sho** *(kah-ree kay-sahn show)*

interlocking directorate 兼任重役 **kennin jūyaku** *(ken-neen juu-yah-kuu)*

intermediary 仲介者 **chūkai sha** *(chew-kye shah)*

internal (inside a company) 内部の **naibu no** *(nigh-buu no)*

internal (domestic) 国内 **kokunai** *(koe-kuu-nigh)*

internal audit 内部監査 **naibu kansa** *(nigh-buu kahn-sah)*

internal finance 自己金融 **jiko kin'yū** *(jee-koe keen-yuu)*

internal rate of return 内部収益率 **naibu shūeki ritsu** *(nigh-buu shuu-ay-kee ree-t'sue)*

internal revenue 内国税収入 **naikoku zei shūnyū** *(nigh-koe-kuu zay shuun-yuu)*

international 国際(的) **kokusai (teki)** *(coke-sigh (tay-kee))*

international date line 国際日付変更線 **kokusai hizuke henkō-sen** *(coke-sigh he-zuu-kay hen-koe-sen)*

international driver's license 国際運転免許証 **kokusai unten menkyo shō** *(coke-sigh uun-ten men-k'yoe show)*
▪ It is necessary to have an international driver's license to drive a car in foreign countries. 海外で車を運転するには、国際運転免許証が必要です。**Kaigai de kuruma wo unten suru ni wa kokusai unten menkyo shō ga hitsuyō désu.** *(kie-guy day kuu-ruu-mah oh uun-tane sue-rue nee wah koke-sie uuntane mane-k'yoh shohh gah heet-sue-yoh dess.)*
▪ Do you have an international driver's license? 国際運転免許証を持っていますか。**Kokusai unten menkyo shō wo motte imasu ka?** *(kohh-kuu-sie uun-tane mane-k'yoh shohh oh mote-tay ee-mahss kah?)*

internationalize 国際化 **kokusai-ka** *(coke-sigh-kah)*

Internet インターネット **Intānetto** *(een-tah-net-toe)*
▪ I use the Internet every day! 私は毎日インターネットを使います。**Watakushi wa mainichi Intānetto wo tsukaimasu.** *(wah-tahk-she wah my-nee-chii Een-tah-net-toe oh t'suu-kie-mahss.)*
▪ The Internet has become a necessary tool for daily life. インターネットは日常生活に書かせないツールになりました。**Intānetto wa nichijō seikatsu ni kakasenai tsūru ni narimashita.** *(en-tah-net-toh wa nee-chee-joh say-kot-sue nee kah-kay-say-nigh t'sue-rue nee nah-ree-mahssh-tah.)*

Internet bank ネット銀行 **netto ginkō** *(net geen-koe)*; ネットバンク **netto banku** *(net-toe bahn-kuu)*
▪ Internet banking is very convenient. ネットバンクシステムはとても便利です。**Netto banku system wa totemo benri désu.** *(net-toe bahn-kuu system wah toe-tay-moe bane-ree dess.)*

Internet connection インターネット接続 **intānetto setsuzoku** *(een-tah-net-toh sate-suu-zoh-kuu)*
▪ Is this the Internet connection? これはインターネットの接続ですか。**Kore wa Intānetto no setsuzoku désu ka?** *(koe-ray wah Een-tah-net-toe no sate-sue-zoh-kuu dess kah?)*
▪ It is now possible to connect to the Internet by cell-phone. 携帯電話でもインターネット接続が可能になりました。**Keitai denwa demo Intānetto setsuzoku ga kanō ni narimashita.** *(kay-tie dane-wah day-moh Een-tah-net-toh sate-suu-zoh-kuu ga kah-no nee nah-ree-mah-ssh-tah.)*

Internet host インターネットホスト **intānetto hosto** *(een-tah-net-toe hohss-toe)*
▪ Where is your Internet host? インターネットのホストはどこにありますか。**Intānetto no hosto wa doko ni arimasu ka?** *(een-tah-net-toh no hohss-toh wa doh-koh nee ah-ree-mahss kah?)*

Internet link (インターネット)リンク **(intānetto) rinku** *((een-tah-net-toh) reen-kuu)*
▪ Do you have an Internet link to that site? そのサイトに(インターネット)リンクがありますか。**Sono saito ni (Intānetto) rinku ga arimasu ka?** *(soh-no sie-toh nee (een-tah-net-toh) reen-kuu gah ah-ree-mahss kah?)*
▪ How many Internet links do you have? どのぐらいリンクがありますか。**Dono gurai rinku ga arimasu ka?** *(doh-no guu-rie reen-kuu gah ah-ree-mahss kah?)*

Internet protocol telephone service IP 電話サービス **aipii denwa sābisu** *(aye pee den-wah sah-bee-sue)*
▪ I want to sign up with an Internet Protocol telephone service. IP 電話の契約をしたいです。**IP denwa no keiyaku wo shitai désu.** *(eye-pee dane-wah no kay-yah-kuu oh she-tie dess.)*

interpretation 解釈 **kaishaku** *(kye-shah-kuu)*; 通訳 **tsūyaku** *(t'sue-yah-kuu)*

interpreter 通訳(者) **tsūyaku (sha)** *(t'sue-yah-kuu (sha))*
▪ Please call an interpreter. 通訳を呼んでください。**Tsūyaku wo yonde kudasai.** *(t'sue-yah-kuu oh-yoan-day kuu-dah-sigh.)*

interruption 停止 **teishi** *(tay-she)*; 中断 **chūdan** *(chuu-dahn)*; 妨害 **bōgai** *(bow-guy)*

inter-state commerce 州際通商 **shū-sai tsūshō** *(shuu-sigh t'sue-show)*

interview 会見 **kaiken** *(kye-ken)*; インタビュー **intabyū** *(een-tah-b'yuu)*; for story 面会 **menkai** *(main-kye)*; for employment 面接 **mensetsu** *(men-say-t'sue)*

in the red 赤字で **akaji de** *(ah-kah-jee day)*

in transit 輸送中 **yusō chū** *(yuu-so chew)*

intrinsic value 本質的価値 **honshitsu teki kachi** *(hone-sheet-sue tay-kee kah-chee)*

introduce 紹介する **shōkai suru** *(show-kye sue-rue)*
▪ I will introduce you to Mr. Smith. スミスさんに紹介します。**Sumisu-san ni shōkai shimasu.** *(sue-mee-sue-sahn nee show-kye she-mahss.)*

introduction (in book) 序 **jo** *(joe)*;序文 **jo-bun** *(joe-buun)*

invalidate 無効にする **mukō ni suru** *(muu-koe nee sue-rue)*

invent 発明する **hatsumei suru** *(hot-sue-may sue-rue)*
▪ That new product was invented last year. その新製品は去年発明されました。**Sono shin seihin wa kyonen hatsumei saremashita.** *(soh-no sheen say-heen wa k'yoh-nane hot-sue-may sah-ray-mah-ssh-tah.)*

invention 発明 **hatsumei** *(hot-sue-may)*

inventor 発明家 **hatsumeika** *(hot-sue-may-kah)*
▪Do you know the name of the inventor? その発明家の名前を知っていますか。**Sono hatsumeika no namae wo shitte imasu ka?** *(so-no hot-sue-may-kah no nah-my oh sheet-tay ee-mahss kah?)*

inventory 在庫(品) **zaiko (hin)** *(zye-koe (heen))*

inventory control 在庫管理 **zaiko kanri** *(zye-koe kahn-ree)*

inventory turnover 棚卸資産回転率 **tana oroshi shisan kaiten ritsu** *(tah-nah oh-roe-she she-sahn kye-ten ree-t'sue)*; 在庫品回転率 **zaiko hin kaiten ritsu** *(zye-koe heen kye-ten ree-t'sue)*

invest 投資する **tōshi suru** *(toe-she sue-rue)*

invested capital 投下資本 **tōka shihon** *(toe-kah she-hone)*

investigation; inquiry 調査 **chōsa** *(choe-sah)*; 取り調べ **torishirabe** *(toe-ree-she-rah-bay)*

investment 投資 **tōshi** *(toe-she)*

investment analysis 投資分析 **tōshi bunseki** *(toe-she boon-say-kee)*

investment appraisal 投資査定 **tōshi satei** *(toe-she sah-tay)*

investment bank 投資銀行 **tōshi ginkō** *(toe-she gheen-koe)*

investment budget 投資予算 **tōshi yosan** *(toe-she yoe-sahn)*

investment company 投資信託会社 **tōshi shintaku gaisha** *(toe-she sheen-tah-kuu guy-shah)*

investment criteria 投資基準 **tōshi kijun** *(toe-she kee-june)*

investment fund 投資ファンド **tōshi fando** *(toe-she fund)*

investment policy 投資政策 **tōshi seisaku** *(toe-she say-sah-kuu)*

investment program 投資計画 **tōshi keikaku** *(toe-she kay-kah-kuu)*

investment return 投資収益 **tōshi shūeki** *(toe-she shoe-ay-kee)*

investment strategy 投資戦略 **tōshi senryaku** *(toe-she sen-r'yah-kuu)*

investment trust 投資信託 **tōshi shintaku** *(toe-she sheen-tah-kuu)*

invitation to bid 入札勧誘 **nyūsatsu kan'yū** *(n'yuu-sah-t'sue kahn-yuu)*

invite 招待する **shōtai suru** *(show-tie sue-rue)*; **omaneki** (very polite) お招き *(oh-mah-nay-kee)*
▪ I want to invite you to a nightclub. ナイトクラブにお招きしたいです。**Naitokurabu ni omaneki shitai désu.** *(night-kuu-rah-buu nee oh-mah-nay-kee she-tie dess.)*

invoice 送り状 **okurijō** *(oh-kuu-ree-joe)*; 請求書 **seikyū-sho** *(say-cue-show)*
▪ What items must be included in the invoice? 送り状にはどんな項目を記載しますか。**Okurijō ni wa donna kōmoku wo kisai shimasu ka?** *(oh-kuu-ree-joe nee wah doan-nah koe-moe-kuu oh kee-sigh she-mahss kah?)*

invoice, commercial (commercial invoice) 商業送り状 **shōgyō okurijō** *(show-g'yoe oh-kuu-ree-joe)*; コマーシャルインボイス **komāsharu inboisu** *(koe-mah-shan-rue een-boe-ee-sue)*

invoice, consular (consular invoice) 領事送り状 **ryōji okurijō** *(rio-jee oh-kuu-ree-joe)*

invoice, pro forma (pro forma invoice) 見積り送り状 **mitsumori okurijō** *(meet-sue-moe-ree oh-kuu-ree-joe)*

iPod iPod **aippodo** *(i-Pah-doe)*
▪ All of my friends have iPods. 私の友達はみんなiPodを持っています。**Watakushi no tomodachi wa minna iPod wo motte imasu.** *(wah-tahk-she no toh-moh-dah-chee wah meen-nah ai-ppo-do oh mote-tay ee-mahss.)*

Ireland アイルランド **Airurando** *(aye-ruu-rahn-doh)*

Irish (person) アイルランド人 **Airuandojin** *(aye-ruu-rahn-doh-jeen)*

Islam イスラム教 **Isuramu-kyō** *(ee-suu-rah-muu-k'yohh)*

ISP (Internet Service Provider) ISP **AiSP** *(aye-S-P)*; プロバイダー **purobaidā** *(provider)*
▪ Which company is your ISP? あなたのISP(プロバイダー)はどこですか。 **Anata no ISP (purobaidā) wa doko désu ka?** *(ah-nah-tan no Aye-S-P (provider) wah doko dess kah?)*

issue; stock; brand 銘柄 **meigara** *(may-gah-rah)*; 株 **kabu** *(kah-buu)*

issue (of a publication or stock) 発行 **hakkō** *(hock-koh)*

issue; publish 発行する **hakkō suru** *(hock-koh sue-rue)*

issued stocks 発行済株式 **hakkō zumi kabushiki** *(hock-koh zuu-me kah-buu-she-kee)*

Italian イタリア人 **Itariajin** *(ee-tah-ree-ah-jeen)*

italics (type style) イタリック体 **itarikku tai** *(ee-tah-ree-kuu tie)*

Italy イタリア **Itaria** *(ee-tah-ree-ah)*

item 項目 **kōmoku** *(koe-moe-kuu)*; 品目 **hinmoku** *(heen-moe-kuu)*

itemize 明細化する **meisaika suru** *(may-sigh-kah sue-rue)*

itemized account 明細精算書 **meisai seisansho** *(may-sigh say-sahn-show)*

J

jacket (book cover) カバー **kabā** *(kah-bah)*

Japan 日本 **Nihon** *(Nee-hone)*/**Nippon** *(neep-pone)*

Japan Agriculture and Forestry Standard (JAS) JAS **JASU** *(jah-sue)*

Japan Chamber of Commerce & Industry 日本商工会議所 **Nihon Shōkō Kaigisho** *(nee-hone show-koe kye-ghee-show)*

Japan Economic Federation 日経連 **Nikkei Ren** *(neek-kay-ren)*

Japan Economic Journal 日本経済新聞 **Nihon Keizai Shinbun** *(nee-hone kay-zye sheem-boon)*; 日経 **Nikkei** *(neek-kay)*

Japanese (person) 日本人 **Nihonjin** *(nee-hone-jeen)*

Japanese food 日本食 **Nihon shoku** *(nee-hone show-kuu)*; 和食 **washoku** *(wah-show-kuu)*
▪ This is the first time I've had Japanese food. 和食は初めてです。 **Washoku wa hajimete désu.** *(wah-show-kuu wah hah-jee-may-tay dess.)*

Japanese language 日本語 **Nihongo** *(nee-hone-go)*

Japanese language edition 日本語版 **Nihongo ban** *(nee-hone-go bahn)*

Japanese style 日本的な **Nihonteki na** *(nee-hone-tay-kee nah)*; 和風の **wafū no** *(wah-fuu-no)*; 和式の **wa shiki no** *(wah-she-kee no)*

"Japanese telepathy" 以心伝心 **ishin denshin** *(ee-sheen den-sheen)*

Japan External Trade Organization (JETRO) 日本貿易振興機構 **Nihon**

Bōeki Shinkōkikō *(nee-hone boe-ay-kee sheen-koe-kee-koe)*

Japan Industrial Standards (JIS) JIS **JISU** *(jee-sue)*; 日本工業規格 **Nihon Kōgyō Kikaku** *(nee-hone koe-g'yoe kee-kah-kuu)*

Japan-oriented (toward Japan, for Japan) 日本向け **Nihon muke** *(nee-hone muu-kee)*

jet lag 時差ぼけ **jisa boke** *(jee-sah boe-kay)*
▪ I'm really suffering from jet lag. ひどく時差ぼけをしています。**Hidoku jisa boke wo shiteimasu.** *(he-doe-kuu jee-sah boe-kay oh shtay-mahss.)*

Jew; Jewish ユダヤ人 **Yudayajin** *(yuu-dah-yah-jeen)*; イスラエル人 **Isurarerujin** *(ees-rah-ray-ruu-jeen)*

job/position 職 **shoku** *(show-kuu)*; 仕事 **shigoto** *(she-go-toe)*
▪ I am seeking a job. 求職中です。**Kyūshoku chū désu.** *(cue-show-kuu chuu dess.)*

job analysis 業務分析 **gyōmu bunseki** *(g'yoe-muu boon-say-kee)*

jobber (wholesaler) 卸商 **oroshishō** *(oh-roe-she-show)*

job classification 職務級 **shokumu-kyū** *(show-kuu-muu cue)*

job description 職務記述書 **shokumu kijutsu-sho** *(show-kuu-muu kee-jute-sue-show)*

job evaluation 職務評定 **shokumu hyōtei** *(show-kuu-muu h'yoe-tay)*

job-hopper 常習転職者 **jōshū tenshoku sha** *(joe-shuu ten-show-kuu shah)*

job security 雇用保障 **koyō hoshō** *(koe-yoe hoe-show)*

join 加盟する **kamei suru** *(kah-may sue-rue)*; 入社する **nyūsha suru** *(n'yuu-sha sue-rue)*

joint account 共同預金口座 **kyōdō yokin kōza** *(k'yoe-doe yoe-keen koe-zah)*
▪ I have a joint account with my wife. 家内と共同預金口座を持っています。**Kannai to kyōdō yokin kōza wo motte imasu.** *(kah-nigh toe k'yoe-doe yoe-keen koe-zah oh moat-tay ee-mahss.)*

joint liability 連帯責任 **rentai sekinin** *(ren-tie say-kee-neen)*

joint owners 共有者 **kyōyū sha** *(k'yoe-yuu shah)*

joint stock company 株式会社 **kabushiki gaisha** *(kah-buu-she-kee guy-shah)*

joint venture (JV) 合弁 **gōben** *(go-ben)*; 共同企業体 **kyōdō kigyō tai** *(k'yoe-doe kee-g'yoe tie)*

joint venture company 合弁会社 **gōben gaisha** *(go-ben guy-shah)*
▪ I want to form a joint venture company. 合弁会社をつくりたいです。**Gōben gaisha wo tsukuritai désu.** *(go-ben guy-shah oh t'sue-kuu-ree-tie dess.)*

judge (official) 裁判官 **saibankan** *(sigh-bahn-kahn)*; to judge 判断する **handan suru** *(hahn-dahn sue-rue)*

judgement 審判 **shinpan** *(sheem-pahn)*

junior (subordinate) 後輩 **kōhai** *(koe-high)*
▪ This is my junior. (usually used in reference to graduates of the same school) こちらは私の後輩です。**Kochira wa watakushi no kōhai désu.** *(koe-chee-rah wah wah-tah-she no koe-high dess.)*

jurisdiction 司法権 **shihō ken** *(she-hoe ken)*; 裁判権 **saiban ken** *(sie-bahn ken)*

just (tight, close) ぎりぎり **giri giri** *(ghee-ree ghee-ree)*

justice 正義 **seigi** *(say-ghee)*

justify (lines of type) 行の左右をそろえる **gyō no sayū wo soroeru** *(g'yoe no sah-yuu oh so-roe-ay-rue)*; ジャスティファイ **jasutifai** *(justify)*

just-in-time かんばん方式 **kanban hōshiki** *(kahn-bahn hoe-she-kee)*; ジャストインタイム方式 **jasuto in taimu hōshiki** *(jah-sue-toe-ee-n tah-ee-muu hoe-she-kee)*
▪ Do you use the just-in-time-parts system? かんばん方式を使いますか。 **Kanban hōshiki wo tsukaimasu ka?** *(kahn-bahn hoe-she-kee oh t'ski-mahss kah?)*

K

karaoke カラオケ **karaoke** *(kah-rah-oh-kay)*
▪ Let's go to a karaoke bar tonight. 今晩、カラオケバーに行きましょう。 **Konban karaoke bā ni ikimashō.** *(comb-bahn kah-rah-oh-kay bah nee ee-kee-mah-show.)*

keep one waiting 待たせる **mataseru** *(mah-tah-say-rue)*
▪ I'm sorry I kept you waiting. おまたせ致しました。 **O-matase itashimashita.** *(oh-mah-tah-say ee-tah-she-mahsh-tah.)*

keyboard (computer) キーボード **kii bōdo** *(kee boe-doe)*

key currency 基軸通貨 **kijiku tsūka** *(kee-jee-kuu-t'sue-kah)*; 国際通貨 **kokusai tsūka** *(coke-sigh t'sue-kah)*

key industry 基幹産業 **kikan sangyō** *(kee-kahn sahn-g'yoe)*
▪ Are you buying key industry stocks? 基幹産業株に投資していますか。 **Kikan sangyō kabu ni tōshi shite imasu ka?** *(ke-kahn sahn-g'yoh kah-buu nee toh-see shtay-mahss kah?)*

key (interest) rate 政策金利 **seisaku kinri** *(say-sah-kuu keen-ree)*

keyman insurance 事業家保険 **jigyō-ka hoken** *(jee-g'yoe-kah hoe-ken)*

key word キーワード **kii wādo** *(kee waah-doh)*
▪ About how many key words did you put in? いくつぐらいのキーワードを入れましたか。 **Ikutsu gurai no kii wādo wo iremashita ka?** *(ee-kuut-sue guu-rie no kee waah-doh woe e-ray-mah-ssh-tah kah?)*

kickback リベート **ribēto** *(ree-bay-toe)*

kilogram キロ **kiro** *(kee-roe)*

kilometer キロメートル **kiromētoru** *(kee-roh-may-toh-ruu)*

kind (type) 種類 **shurui** *(shuu-rue-ee)*
▪ How many kinds do you have? 何種類ありますか。 **Nan shurui arimasu ka?** *(nahn shuu-rue-ee ah-ree-mahss kah?)*

kiting (checks) 融通手形の振り出し **yūzū tegata no furidashi** *(yuu-zuu tay-gah-tah no fuu-ree-dah-she)*

knockdown (unassembled) 組立式 **kumitate-shiki** *(kuu-me-tah-tay-she-kee)*
▪ I want to buy the desk knocked-down. 組立式の机を買いたいです。 **Kumitate-shiki no tsukue wo kaitai désu.** *(kuu-me-tah-tay-she-kee no t'sue-kuu-eh oh kie-tie dess.)*

knockdown exports 現地組立輸出

genchi kumitate yushutsu *(gen-chee kuu-me-tah-tay yuu-shoot-sue)*

knockdown prices 最低価格 **saitei kakaku** *(sigh-tay kah-kah-kuu)*; 底値 **soko ne** *(so-koe-nee)*

knot (nautical mile) ノット **notto** *(not-toe)*

knowhow ノウハウ **nou hau** *(no how)*

knowledge 知識 **chishiki** *(chee-she-kee)*

Korea (North) 北朝鮮 **Kita Chōsen** *(kee-tah Chohh-sen)*

Korea (South) 韓国 **Kankoku** *(kahn-koh-kuu)*

Korean 韓国人 **Kankokujin** *(kahn-koh-kuu-jeen)*

Kyoto protocol 京都議定書 **Kyōto gitei sho** *(kyoto gee-tay show)*

L

label ラベル **raberu** *(rah-bay-ruu)*

labeling 表示 **hyōji** *(h'yoe-jee)*

labor 労働 **rōdō** *(roe-doe)*

laboratory 研究所 **kenkyūjo** *(ken-cue-joe)*

labor code 労働規約 **rōdō kiyaku** *(roe-doe kee-yah-kuu)*

labor dispute 労働争議 **rōdō sōgi** *(roe-doe so-ghee)*

laborer (worker) 労働者 **rōdō-sha** *(roe-doe-shah)*

labor force 労働力 **rōdō ryoku** *(roe-doe rio-kuu)*

labor-intensive industry 労働集約産業 **rōdō shūyaku sangyō** *(roe-doe shuu-yah-kuu sahn-g'yoe)*

labor laws 労働法 **rōdō hō** *(roe-doe hoe)*

labor market 労働市場 **rōdō shijō** *(roe-doe she-joe)*

labor relations 労使関係 **rōshi kankei** *(roe-she kahn-kay)*

labor-saving 省力(化) **shōryoku ka** *(show-rio-kuu kah)*

labor turnover 労働異動 **rōdō idō** *(roe-doe ee-doe)*

labor union 労働組合 **rōdō kumiai** *(roe-doe kuu-me-eye)*

labor union leaders 労働組合幹部 **rōdō kumiai kanbu** *(roe-doe kuu-me-eye kahn-buu)*

land 土地 **tochi** *(toe-chee)*

landed certificate 陸揚げ証明書 **rikuage shōmei sho** *(ree-kuu-ah-gay show-may show)*

landing charges 陸揚げ費 **rikuage hi** *(ree-kuu-ah-gay he)*; 荷揚げ料 **niage ryō** *(nee-ah-gay rio)*

landed cost 陸揚げ費込値段 **rikuage hi komi nedan** *(ree-kuu-ah-gay he koe-me nay-dahn)*

land owner 地主 **ji nushi** *(jee nuu-she)*

land tax 地租 **chi so** *(chee so)*

laptop computer ラップトップ(コンピュータ) **rapputoppu (konpyūta)** *(rahp-tope-puu (kome-p'yuu-tah))*; ノートパソコン **nōto pasokon** *(noh-toh pah-soh-kone)*
▪ I also take the laptop computer with me on business trips. 私は、出張にもノートパソコンを持って行きます。**Watashi wa shutchō ni mo nōto pasokon wo motte ikimasu.** *(wah-tah-she way shoot-toh nee moh noh-toh pah-soh-kone oh moe-tay-ee-kee-mahss.)*

large-scale 大口 **ōguchi** *(oh-guu-chee)*

largest 最大 **saidai** *(sigh-dye)*

laser レーザー **rēzā** *(ray-zah)*

laser beam printer レーザープリンター **rēzā purintā** *(ray-zah puu-reen-tah)*

laser processing レーザー加工 **rēzā kakō** *(ray-zah kah-koe)*

last ten days of the month 下旬 **gejun** *(gay-june)*

latent gains or losses 含み損益 **fukumi son eki** *(fuu-kuu-me soan-ay-kee)*

latent gains/profit 含み益 **fukumi eki** *(fuu-kuu-me ay-kee)*

Latin (South) America 南アメリカ **Minami Amerika** *(me-nah-me Ah-may-ree-kah)*

launch (新)発売 **(shin) hatsubai** *((sheen) hah-t'sue-by)*
▪ The plan is to launch the new product next month. 新商品は、来月発売される予定です。**Shin shōhin wa raigetsu hatsubai sareru yotei désu.** *(sheen shoh-heen wah rie-gate-sue hot-sue-by sah-ray-rue yoh-tay-ee dess.)*

law 法規 **hōki** *(hoe-kee)*; 法律 **hōritsu** *(hoe-ree-t'sue)*

lawsuit 訴訟 **soshō** *(so-show)*

lawyer 弁護士 **bengoshi** *(ben-go-she)*
▪ Japanese companies usually do not use lawyers. 日本の会社はあまり弁護士を使いません。**Nihon no kaisha wa amari bengoshi wo tsukaimasen.** *(nee-hone no kye-shah wah ah-mah-ree ben-go-she oh sky-mah-sen.)*

layoff レイオフ **reiofu** *(ray-oh-fuu)*; 一時解雇 **ichiji kaiko** *(ee-chee-jee kye-koe)*

layout (for ad or page makeup) 配置 **haichi** *(high-chee)*; レイアウト **reiauto** *(layout)*

leader 指導者 **shidō sha** *(she-doe shah)*; 首脳 **shunō** *(shuu-nohh)*

leadership 指導(力) **shidō(ryoku)** *(she-doe rio-kuu)*

learn a lesson from (be instructive) 勉強になる **benkyō ni naru** *(ben-k'yoe nee nah-rue)*

lease リース **riisu** *(ree-sue)*

leave to (someone else) 任せる **makaseru** *(mah-kah-say-ruu)*

lecture 講演 **kōen** *(koe-en)*
▪ I'm going to a lecture on environmental protection tomorrow. 明日、環境保護の講演を聞きに行きます。**Ashita, Kankyō hogo no kōen wo kiki ni ikimasu.** *(ahssh-tah, kahn-k'yoh hoh-go no koh-enn oh kee-kee nee ee-kee-mahss.)*

lecture hall (auditorium) 講堂 **kōdō** *(koe-doe)*

ledger 元帳 **moto-chō** *(moe-toe-choe)*

legal 法律的 **hōritsu-teki** *(hoe-ree-t'sue-tay-kee)*; 法律の **hōritsu no** *(hoe-ree-t'sue no)*; 正当な **seitō na** *(say-toe nah)*

legal advisor 顧問弁護士 **komon bengoshi** *(koe-moan ben-go-she)*

legal case – fine; monetary sanction 罰金 **bakkin** *(bahk-keen)*

legal case – hearing; trial 裁判 **saiban** *(sie-bahn)*

legal case – legal action; lawsuit 訴訟 **soshō** *(soh-shohh)*

legal case – losing 敗訴 **haiso** *(hie-soh)*

legal case – official advice; counsel 勧告 **kankoku** *(kahn-koh-kuu)*

legal case – prosecution; indictment 起訴 **kiso** *(kee-soh)*

legal case – reconciliation; peaceful settlement 和解 **wakai** *(wah-kie)*

legal case – winning 勝訴 **shōso** *(shohh-soh)*

legal entity 法的実態 **hō-teki jittai** *(hoe-tay-kee jeet-tie)*

legal holiday 公休日 **kōkyū bi** *(koe-cue bee)*
▪ The day after tomorrow is a legal holiday. 明後日は公休日です。**Asatte wa kōkyū bi désu.** *(ah-sah-tay wah koe-cue bee dess.)*

legal monopoly 合法的独占 **gōhōteki dokusen** *(go-hoe-tay-kee doke-sen)*

legislation (bill) 案 **an** *(ahn)*; 立法 **rippō** *(rip-pow)*

lend 融資する **yūshi suru** *(yee-she sue-rue)*

lessee 賃借人 **chinshaku-nin** *(cheen-shah-kuu-neen)*; 借り主 **karinushi** *(kah-ree-nuu-she)*

lesson 稽古 **keiko** *(kay-koe)*

lessor 賃貸人 **chintai-nin** *(cheen-tie-neen)*

less than 以下 **ika** *(ee-kah)*

letter 手紙 **tegami** *(tah-gah-me)*

letter of credit (L/C) LC **eru shii** *(eh-rue she)*; 信用状 **shin'yō jō** *(sheen-yoe joe)*; letter-of-credit payable at sight LC一回払い **eru shii ikkai barai** *(eh-rue she-ee ee-kye bah-rye)*

letter of indemnity 念書 **nen sho** *(nen show)*

letter of introduction 紹介状 **shōkai jō** *(show-kye joe)*
▪ I have a letter of introduction from Mr. Shimizu. 清水さんの紹介状を持っています。**Shimizu-san no shōkai jō wo motte imasu.** *(she-me-zuu sahn no show-kye joe oh moat-tay ee-mahss.)*

letter of resignation 辞表 **jihyō** *(jee-h'yoe)*

liability 債務 **saimu** *(sigh-muu)*

liability, actual (actual liability) 実質債務 **jisshitsu saimu** *(jeesh-sheet-sue sigh-muu)*

liability, assumed (assumed liability) 継承債務 **keishō saimu** *(kay-show sigh-muu)*

liability, contingent (contingent liability) 偶発債務 **gūhatsu saimu** *(guu-hot-sue sigh-muu)*

liability, current (current liability) 流動負債 **ryūdo fusai** *(r'yuu-doe fuu-sigh)*

liability, fixed (fixed liability) 固定負債 **kotei fusai** *(koe-tay fuu-sigh)*

liability, insurance (insurance liability) 責任保険 **sekinin hoken** *(say-kee-nee hoe-ken)*

liability, secured (secured liability) 担保付負債 **tanpo tsuki fusai** *(tahn-poe ski fuu-sigh)*

liability, unsecured (unsecured liability) 無担保債務 **mu-tanpo saimu** *(muu-tahn-poe sigh-muu)*

liaison 連携 **renkei** *(rane-kay)*

libel 名誉毀損 **meiyo kison** *(may-yoe kee-soan)*

liberalization 自由化 **jiyū-ka** *(jee-yuu kah)*; 規制緩和 **kisei kanwa** *(kee-say kahn-wah)*

license 免許 **menkyo** *(men-k'yoe)*
▪ Did you bring your license? 免許証を持って来ましたか。**Menkyo shō wo motte kimashita ka?** *(men-k'yoe show oh moat-tay kee-mah-shtah kah?)*

license fees 特許権使用料 **tokkyo ken shiyō ryō** *(toke-yoe ken she-yoe rio)*

licensing agreement ライセンス契約 **raisensu keiyaku** *(rye-sen-sue kay-yah-kuu)*

lien 差し押さえ **sashiosae ken** *(sah-she-oh-sigh ken)*; 抵当権 **teitō ken** *(tay-toe ken)*

life cycle (of product) 製品寿命 **seihin jumyō** *(say-heen jume-yoe)*

life expectancy 平均寿命 **heikin jumyō** *(hay-keen juu-m'yohh)*

life insurance 生命保険 **seimei hoken** *(say-may hoe-ken)*

life insurance policy 生命保険証券 **seimei hoken shōken** *(say-may hoe-ken show-ken)*

lifestyle ライフスタイル **raifusutairu** *(rie-fuu-sty-ruu)*

lifetime 生涯 **shōgai** *(show-guy)*; 一生 **isshō** *(it-show)*

lifetime employment 終身雇用 **shūshin koyō** *(shuu-sheen koe-yoe)*

lifetime of a patent 特許権存続期間 **tokkyo ken sonzoku kikan** *(toke-yoe ken soan-zoe-kuu kee-kahn)*

light (weight) 軽い **karui** *(kah-rue-ee)*

limit; limits 限り **kagiri** *(kah-ghee-ree)*; 制限 **seigen** *(say-gen)*

limited liability 有限責任 **yūgen sekinin** *(yuu-gen say-kee-neen)*

limited liability company 有限会社 **yūgen gaisha** *(yuu-gen guy-shah)*

limited partnership 合資会社 **gōshi gaisha** *(go-she guy-shah)*

line (limit) 線 **sen** *(sen)*

line drawing 線画 **sen ga** *(sen gah)*

line executive ライン部門幹部職員 **rain bumon kanbu shokuin** *(rine buu-moan kahn-buu show-kuu-een)*

line of business 営業品目 **eigyō hinmoku** *(eh-ee-g'yoe heen-moe-kuu)*

line of management ライン部門管理 **rain bumon kanri** *(rine buu-moan kahn-ree)*

line of type 行 **gyō** *(g'yoe)*

line printer ラインプリンター **rain purintā** *(rine print-ah)*

liner (ship) 汽船 **kisen** *(kee-sane)*

link 連動させる **rendō saseru** *(ren-doe sah-say-rue)*; リンクさせる **rinku saseru** *(ree-kuu sah-say-rue)*

liquid assets 流動資産 **ryūdō shisan** *(r'yuu-doe she-sahn)*

liquidate 弁済する **bensai suru** *(bane-sigh sue-rue)*; 清算する **seisan suru** *(say-sahn sue-rue)*

liquidation 清算 **seisan** *(say-sahn)*; 売却 **baikyaku** *(by-k'yah-kuu)*

liquidation value 清算価額 **seisan kagaku** *(say-sahn kah-gah-kuu)*

liquid crystal 液晶 **ekishō** *(eh-kee-shohh)*; liquid crystal display 液晶画面 **ekishō gamen** *(eh-kee-shohh gah-men)*

liquidity 流動性 **ryūdō sei** *(r'yuu-doe say)*

list (of names) 名簿 **meibo** *(may-bow)* ▪ Please send invitations to all members on the customer list. 顧客名簿の全員に案内状を送ってください。 **Kokyaku meibo no zen'in ni annaijō wo okutte kudasai.** *(koh-k'yah-kuu may-boh no zen-een nee ahn-nie-joh oh oh-koot-day kuu-dah-sie.)*

list (compile, write down) 記入する **kinyū suru** *(keen-yuu sue-rue)*

list (chart, timetable) 表 **hyō** *(he-yoe)*

listed securities 上場証券 **jōjō shōken** *(joe-joe show-ken)*

list price 表示価格 **hyōji kakaku** *(h'yoe-jee kah-kah-kuu)*

litigation 訴訟 **soshō** *(so-show)*
▪ We are now involved in litigation. 今、訴訟をしています。**Ima soshō wo shiteimasu.** *(ee-mah so-show oh shtay-mahss.)*

livelihood 生計 **seikei** *(say-kay)*

loading; embarking 搭載 **tōsai** *(tohh-sie)*

loan 借金 **shakkin** *(shock-keen)*; ローン **rōn** *(roan)*; 貸し **kashi** *(kah-she)*

loan loss 貸し倒れ **kashi daore** *(kah-she dah-oh-ray)*

lobby (of hotel) ロビー **robii** *(roe-bee)*
▪ I'll meet you in the lobby. ロビーで会いましょう。**Robii de aimashō.** *(roe-bee day eye-mah-show.)*

lobbyist ロビースト **robiisuto** *(roe-bee-ee-stow)*; to lobby 陳情する **chinjō suru** *(cheen-joe sue-rue)*

local 地方の **chihō no** *(chee-hoe no)*

local corporate tax 法人事業税 **hōjin gigyō zei** *(hoe-jeen jee-g'yoe-zye)*

local customs (tax authorities) 現地の税関 **genchi no zeikan** *(gen-chee no zay-kahn)*

local hire (personnel hired locally) 現地採用 **genchi saiyō** *(gen-chee sigh-yoe)*

local tax 地方税 **chihō zei** *(chee-hoe zay)*

log-in ログイン **rogu-in** *(roh-guu-in)*
▪ First, you have to log-in. 最初にログインしなければなりません。**Saisho ni rogu-in shinakereba narimasen.** *(sie-show ni roh-in she-nah-kay-ray-bah nah-ree-man-sin.)*
▪ The server was unable to log-in with the password provided. 入力されたパスワードではログインできませんでした。**Nyūryoku sareta pasuwādo de wa rogu-in dekimasen déshita.** *(n'yuu-rio-kuu sah-ray-tah pahss-waah-doh day roh-guu enn day-kee-mah-sen desh-tah.)*

log-off ログオフ **rogu-ofu** *(roh-guu-oh-fuu)*
▪ Please be sure to log-off when you leave the system. システムから外れる時は、必ずログオフしてください。**Shisutemu kara hazureru toki wa kanarazu rogu-ofu shite kudasai.** *(shees-tay-muu kah-rah hah-zuu-ray-rue toh-kee wah kah-nah-rah-zuu roh-guu-oh-fuu ssh-tay kuu-dah-sie.)*

logo ロゴ **rogo** *(roe-go)*; シンボルマーク **shinboru māku** *(sheen-boe-rue mah-kuu)*
▪ Does your company have a logo? 会社のシンボルがありますか。**Kaisha no shinboru ga arimasu ka?** *(kie-shah no sheen-boh-rue gah ah-ree-mahss kah?)*

long-range planning 長期計画 **chōki keikaku** *(choe-kee kay-kah-kuu)*

long-term 長期の **chōki no** *(choe-kee no)*

long-term debt 長期借入金 **chōki kari-ire kin** *(choe-kee kah-ree-ee-ray keen)*

long-term interest rate 長期金利 **chōki kinri** *(choe-kee keen-ree)*

loss 損失 **sonshitsu** *(soan-sheet-sue)*; 損をする **son wo suru** *(soan oh sue-rue)*

▪ Last month (we) suffered a lot of losses. 先月は多くの損失が出ました。**Sengetsu wa ookuno sonshitsu ga demashita.** *(sane-gate-sue wa ooh-kuu-no soan-sheet-sue gah day-mah-ssh-tah.)*

loss leader 目玉商品 **medama shōhin** *(may-dah-mah show-heen)*

lot (quite a bit) たくさん **takusan** *(tock-sahn)*

low 低い **hikui** *(he-kuu-ee)*; 安値 **yasu ne** *(yah-sue-nee)*

lower yen quotation 円安 **en yasu** *(en yah-sue)*

low income 低所得 **tei shotoku** *(tay show-toe-kuu)*

low interest loan 低金利ローン **tei kinri rōn** *(tay-keen-ree roan)*

low-yield bonds 低利回り債券 **tei rimawari saiken** *(tay ree-mah-wah-ree sigh-ken)*

loyalty 忠義 **chūgi** *(chew-ghee)*; loyalty to one's self, company, country 忠誠 **chūsei** *(chew-say)*

lump-sum 総額 **sōgaku** *(so-gah-kuu)*; 一括払い **ikkatsu barai** *(eek-cot-sue bah-rye)*

luxurious 贅沢 **zeitaku** *(zay-tah-kuu)*; 豪華 **gōka** *(go-kah)*
▪ Your home is really luxurious. あなたのお家は本当に豪華ですね。**Anata no o-uchi wa hontō ni gōka désu ne.** *(ah-nah-tah no oh-uu-chee wah hone-toe nee go-kah dess nee.)*

luxury goods 贅沢品 **zeitaku hin** *(zay-tah-kuu heen)*

luxury tax 奢侈税 **shashi zei** *(shah-she zay)*

M

machine 機械 **kikai** *(kee-kye)*

machine tools 工作機械 **kōsaku kikai** *(koe-sah-kuu kee-kye)*

machinery and tools 機器 **kiki** *(kee-kee)*

magazine 雑誌 **zasshi** *(zahsh-she)*; monthly magazine 月刊誌 **gekkan shi** *(gay-kahn she)*
▪ Do you subscribe to Fortune magazine? フォーチュン誌を定期購読していますか。**Fōchun shi wo teiki kōdoku shite imasu ka?** *(fohh-chuun she oh tay-kee koh-doh-ku shtay-mahss kah?)*

magnet (natural) 磁鉄 **jitetsu** *(je-tate-sue)*, instrument 磁石 **jishaku** *(jee-sha-kuu)*; マグネット **magunetto** *(mah-guu-net-toe)*

mailing list 郵送先名簿 **yusō saki meibo** *(yu-so sah-kee may-boe)*

mail order メールオーダー **mēru ōdā** *(may-rue oh-dah)*; 通信販売 **tsūshin hanbai** *(t'sue-sheen hahn-by)*

main goal (purpose) 主要目的 **shuyō mokuteki** *(shuu-yoe moe-kuu-tay-kee)*

main road (main highway) 本道 **hōn dō** *(hone doe)*

mainstay (product) 主力商品 **shuryoku shōhin** *(shuu-rio-kuu shoh-heen)*; 大黒柱 **daikoku-bashira** *(die-koh-kuu-bah-she-rah)*
▪ What is your mainstay (most important product)? 主力商品は何でしょうか。**Shuryoku shōhin wa nan déshō ka?** *(shuu-rio-kuu shoh-heen wah nahn day-shohh kah?)*

mainstream 主流 **shuryū** *(shuu-r'yuu)*

maintenance 維持 **iji** *(ee-jee)*; 保守 **hoshu** *(hoe-shuu)*

maintenance contract 保守契約 **hoshu keiyaku** *(hoe-shuu kay-yah-kuu)*

majority interest 過半数持ち分 **kahansū mochibun** *(kah-han-sue moe-chee-boon)*

maker (manufacturer) メーカー **mēkā** *(may-kah)*; 生産者 **seisansha** *(say-sahn-shah)*; 製造業者 **seizō gyōsha** *(say-zoe g'yoe-shah)*

manage 経営する **keiei suru** *(kay-ee sue-rue)*

managed costs マネージドコスト **manējido kosuto** *(mah-nay-jee-doe cost-oh)*

managed economy 管理経済 **kanri keizai** *(kahn-ree kay-zye)*

management 管理 **kanri** *(kahn-ree)*; 経営 **keiei** *(kay-ee)*

management by objectives 目標管理 **mokuhyō kanri** *(moe-kuu-h'yoe kahn-ree)*

management chart 管理活動表 **kanri katsudō hyō** *(kahn-ree cot-sue-doe h'yoe)*

management consultant 経営コンサルタント **keiei konsarutanto** *(kay-ee cone-sah-rue-tahn-toe)*

management group マネージメントグループ **manējimento gurūpu** *(mah-nay-jee-men-toe guu-rue-puu)*

manager 経営者 **keiei sha** *(kay-ee shah)*; 支配人 **shihainin** *(she-high-neen)*

man-hours (一人あたりの)のべ時間 **(hitori atari no) nobe jikan** *((hee-toe-ree ah-tah-ree no) no-bay jee-kahn)*

manner 物腰 **monogoshi** *(moe-no-go-she)*; 礼儀作法 **reigi sahō** *(ray-ghee sah-hoe)*; マナー **manā** *(mah-nah)*

manpower 人的資源 **jinteki shigen** *(jeen-tay-kee she-gen)*;人材 **jinzai** *(jeen-zye)*

manual labor 肉体労働 **nikutai rōdō** *(nee-kuu-tie roe-doe)*

manual workers 肉体労働者 **nikutai rōdōsha** *(nee-kuu-tie roe-doe-shah)*

manufacture (produce) 製造 **seizō** *(say-zoe)*

manufacture for trial 試作する **shisaku suru** *(she-sah-kuu sue-rue)*

manufactured goods 製品 **seihin** *(say-heen)*; 物産 **bussan** *(buu-sahn)*

manufacturer 製造業者 **seizō gyōsha** *(say-zoe g'yoe-shah)*; 生産者 **seisansha** *(say-sahn-shah)*

manufacturer's representative 製造業者代理店 **seizō gyōsha dairiten** *(say-zoe g'yoe-shah dye-ree-ten)*

manufacturing capacity 生産能力 **seisan nōryoku** *(say-sahn no-rio-kuu)*

manufacturing control 生産管理 **seisan kanri** *(say-sahn kahn-ree)*

manufacturing expense 製造間接費 **seizō kansetsu-hi** *(say-zoe kahn-say-t'sue-he)*

manufacturing industry 工業 **kōgyō** *(koe-g'yoe)*; 製造業 **seizō gyō** *(say-zoe g'yoe)*

margin 余白 **yohaku** *(yoh-hah-kuu)*; 利ざや **rizaya** *(ree-zah-yah)*
▪ There is no margin in that price. その価格では、利ざやが無い。**Sono kakaku de wa rizaya ga nai.** *(soe-no kah-kah-kuu day wah ree-zah-yah gah nie.)*

marine cargo insurance 貨物海上保険 **kamotsu kaijō hoken** *(kah-moat-sue kye-joe hoe-ken)*

mark down 値下げする **nesage suru** *(nay-sah-gay sue-rue)*

market (marketplace) 市場 **shijō** *(she-joe)*

market access 市場への接近 **shijō e no sekkin** *(she-joe ay no sake-keen)*

market appraisal 市場評価 **shijō hyōka** *(she-joe h'yoe-kah)*

market concentration 市場集中 **shijō shūchū** *(she-joe shuu-chew)*

market forces 市場の実力 **shijō no jitsuryoku** *(she-joe no jee-t'sue-rio-kuu)*

market forecast 市場見通し **shijō mitōshi** *(she-joe me-toe-she)*
▪ We are now preparing a market forecast. いま市場の見通しを測っています。**Ima shijō no mitōshi wo hakatte imasu.** *(ee-mah she-joe no mee-toe-she oh hock-kah-tay-ee-mahss.)*

market index 市場指数 **shijō shisū** *(she-joe she-sue)*

marketing マーケテイング **māketingu** *(mah-kay-teen-guu)*; 市場調査 **shijō chōsa** *(she-joe choe-sah)*

marketing budget 市場開拓費 **shijō kaitaku hi** *(she-joe kye-tah-kuu he)*

marketing concept マーケテイングコンセプト **mākketingu konseputo** *(mah-kay-ting-uu cone-sepp-toe)*

marketing network 販売網 **hanbai mō** *(hahn-by moe)*
▪ Our company has a worldwide marketing network. 当社は世界的な販売網を持っています。**Tōsha wa sekai teki na hanbai mō wo motteimasu.** *(tohh-shah wa say-kie tay-kee nah hahn-by mohh oh mote-tay-ee-mahss.)*

marketing plan マーケテイング計画 **mākketingu keikaku** *(mah-kay-ting-uu kay-kah-kuu)*

marketing strategy マーケテイング戦略 **mākkettingu senryaku** *(mah-kay-ting-guu sen-r'yah-kuu)*

market intervention 市場介入 **shijō kainyū** *(she-joe kye-n'yuu)*

market management 市場管理 **shijō kanri** *(she-joe kahn-ree)*

market manipulation 市場操作 **shijō sōsa** *(she-joe so-sah)*

market penetration 市場浸透 **shijō shintō** *(she-joe sheen-toe)*

market plan 市場計画 **shijō keikaku** *(she-joe kay-kah-kuu)*

market position 市況 **shikyō** *(she-k'yoe)*

market potential 販売可能量 **hanbai kanō ryō** *(hahn-by kahn-no rio)*

market price 相場 **sōba** *(so-bah)*; 市価 **shika** *(she-kah)*

market report 市況報告 **shikyō hōkoku** *(she-k'yoe hoe-koe-kuu)*

market research 市場調査 **shijō chōsa** *(she-joe choe-sah)*
▪ First, market research is important for the development of a new product. 新製品の開発のために、まず市場調査が重要です。**Shinseihin kaihatsu no tame ni, mazu shijō chōsa ga juyō désu.** *(sheen-say-heen kie-hot-sue no tah-may nee, mah-zuu she-joh choh-sah gah juu-yohh dess.)*

market saturation 市場飽和 **shijō hōwa** *(she-joe hoe-wah)*

market share 市場占有率 **shijō sen'yū ritsu** *(she-joe sen-yuu ree-t'sue)*

market survey 市場調査 **shijō chōsa** *(she-joe choe-sah)*

market trends 市場動向 **shijō dōkō** *(she-joe doe-koe)*

market value 市場価格 **shijō kakaku** *(she-joe kah-kah-kuu)*

markup 値上げ **neage** *(nay-ah-gay)*
▪ We will mark everything up in January. 一月に全て値上げします。**Ichigatsu ni subete neage shimasu.** *(ee-chee-got-sue nee sue-bay-tay nay-ah-gay she-mahss.)*

marriage ties 縁結び **enmusubi** *(en-muu-sue-bee)*

mass communications マスコミ **masukomi** *(mah-sue-koe-me)*

mass marketing 大量販売 **tairyō hanbai** *(tie-rio hahn-by)*

mass media マスメディア **masu media** *(mah-sue may-dee-ah)*

mass meeting (rally) 大会 **taikai** *(tie-kye)*

mass production 大量生産 **tairyō seisan** *(tie-rio say-sahn)*

master of ceremonies 司会者 **shikaisha** *(she-kye-shah)*

match (game, bout) 試合 **shiai** *(she-eye)*

materials (data, information) 資料 **shiryō** *(she-rio)*

materials, natural (natural materials) 天然素材 **tennen sozai** *(tane-nane soh-zie)*
▪ Natural materials are good for the people as well as the environment. 天然素材は人にも環境にもやさしい。**Tennen sozai wa hito ni mo kankyō ni mo yasashii.** *(tane-nane soh-zie wa ssh-toh nee-moh kahn-k'yoh nee-moh yah-sah-shee.)*

materials, raw (raw materials) 材料 **zairyō** *(zye-rio)*

materials; resources; supplies 資材 **shizai** *(she-zie)*

maternity leave 出産休暇 **shussan kyūka** *(shuu-sahn cue-kah)*

maturity date 支払期日 **shiharai kijitsu** *(she-hah-rye kee-jee-t'sue)*

mayor 市長 **shichō** *(she-choe)*
▪ I would like to meet the mayor. 市長にお会いしたいです。**Shichō ni o-ai shitai désu.** *(she-choe nee oh-eye she-tie dess.)*

maximize 最大限に(活用)する **saidaigen ni (katsuyō) suru** *(sigh-dye-gen nee (cot-sue-yoe) sue-rue)*

maximum 最高 **saikō** *(sigh-koe)*

means (way) 手段 **shudan** *(shuu-dahn)*

measure(s) 対策 **taisaku** *(tie-sah-kuu)*; 政策 **seisaku** *(say-sah-kuu)*; 測定 **sokutei** *(soe-kuu-tay)*

measure 計る **hakaru** *(hah-kah-rue)*

media 媒体 **baitai** *(by-tie)*; メディア **media** *(me-dii-ah)*

mediate 調停する **chōtei suru** *(chohh-tay sue-rue)*

mediation 調停 **chōtei** *(chohh-tay)*

mediator 調停者 **chōteisha** *(chohh-tay-shah)*

medicine; pharmaceutical goods 医薬品 **iyaku-hin** *(ee-yah-kuu-heen)*

medium and small enterprises 中小企業 **chū shō kigyō** *(chew show kee-g'yoe)*

meeting 会合 **kaigō** *(kye-go)*; 会議 **kaigi** *(kye-ghee)*

meeting of board of directors 取締役会議 **torishimari yaku kaigi** *(toe-ree-she-mah-ree yah-kuu kye-ghee)*

member firm (of group) 加盟企業 **kamei kigyō** *(kah-may kee-g'yoe)*

memo メモ **memo** *(may-moe)*
▪ Please prepare a memo of the meeting by tomorrow afternoon. 明日の午後までに打ち合わせのメモを用意してください。**Ashita no gogo made ni uchiawase no memo wo yōi shite kudasai.** *(ah-ssh-tah no go-go mah-day nee uu-chee-ah-way-say no may-moh oh yoh-ee ssh-tay kuu-dah-sie.)*

memory メモリー **memorii** *(may-moe-ree)*
▪ How much memory does this computer have? このコンピュータはどのぐらいのメモリーがありますか。**Kono konpyūta wa dono gurai no memorii ga arimasu ka?** *(koe-no kome-p'yuu-tah wah doe-no guu-rye no may-moe-ree gah ah-ree-mahss kah?)*
▪ I need a new memory chip. 新しいメモリーチップは必要ですか。**Atarashii no memori chippu wah hitsuyō désu ka.** *(ah-tah-rah-she no may-moe-ree cheep-puu wah hee-t'sue-yoe dess kah.)*

merchandise (goods) 商品 **shōhin** *(show-heen)*

merge 合併する **gappei suru** *(gahp-pay sue-rue)*

merger and acquisition (M&A) 吸収合併 **kyūshū gappei** *(cue-shuu gahp-pay)*

merit 実力 **jitsuryoku** *(jee-t'sue-rio-kuu)*; 価値 **kachi** *(kah-chee)*

merits and demerits 得失 **tokushitsu** *(toe-kuu-sheet-sue)*

message お言付け **okotozuke** *(oh-koe-toe-zuu-kay)*; メッセージ **messēji** *(may-say-jee)*

metal, metals 金属 **kinzoku** *(keen-zoe-kuu)*

method (way) 方法 **hōhō** *(hoe-hoe)*

Mexican メキシコ人 **Mekishikojin** *(Meck-she-koh-jeen)*

Mexico メキシコ **Mekishiko** *(Meck-she-koh)*

micro camera マイクロカメラ **maikuro kamera** *(my-kuu-roe kah-may-rah)*

micro cassette recorder マイクロカセットレコーダー **maikuro kasetto rekōdā** *(myu-kuu-roe kah-say-toe ray-koe-dah)*

micro chip マイクロチップ **maikuro chippu** *(my-kuu-roe cheap-puu)*

microwave oven 電子レンジ**denshi renji** *(den-she rain-jee)*
▪ Can I heat this in the microwave? これをレンジで温められますか。**Kore wo renji de atatameraremasu ka?** *(koe-ray oh rain-jee day ah-tah-tah-may-rah-ray-mahss kah?)*

mid-career recruitment 中途採用 **chūto saiyō** *(chew-toe sigh-yoe)*

middle (between minimum and maximum) 中間 **chūkan** *(chew-kahn)*, 真ん中 **man naka** *(man-nah-kah)*

middleman 中間業者 **chūkan gyōsha** *(chew-kahn g'yoe-shah)*

middle management ミドルマネージメント **midoru manējimento** *(me-doe-rue mah-nay-jee-men-toe)*; 部課長 **bukachō** *(buu-kah-choe)*; 中間管理職 **chūkan kanrishoku** *(chew-kahn kahn-ree-show-kuu)*

middle of the month 中旬 **chūjun** *(chew-june)*

midterm account settlement 中間決算 **chūkan kessan** *(chew-kahn case-sahn)*

mile マイル **mairu** *(my-rue)*

mileage 走行マイル数 **sōkō mairu sū** *(so-koe my-rue sue)*; マイレージ **mairēji** *(migh-ray-jee)*

millionaire 百万長者 **hyakumanchōja** *(h'yan-kuu-mahn-choe-jah)*; 大富豪 **dai fugō** *(die-fuu-go)*

mini computer ミニコンピュータ **mini konpyūta** *(me-nee kome-p'yuu-tah)*

minimum 最低 **saitei** *(sigh-tay)*

minimum charge 最低料金 **saitei ryōkin** *(sigh-tay rio-keen)*
▪ How much is the minimum charge? 最低料金はいくらですか。**Saitei ryōkin wa ikura désu ka?** *(sigh-tay rio-keen wah ee-kuu-rah dess kah?)*

minimum wage 最低賃金 **saitei chingin** *(sigh-tie cheen-gheen)*

mining; mining industry 鉱業 **kōgyō** *(kohh-g'yohh)*

Ministry of Defense 防衛省 **Bōei shō** *(boe-aye show)*

Ministry of Economy, Trade & Industry 経済産業省 **Keizai Sangyō shō** *(kee-zah-ee sahn-g'yoe-show)*

Ministry of Education, Culture, Sports, Science and Technology 文部科学省 **Monbu Kagaku shō** *(moan-buu kah-gah-kuu show)*

Ministry of Finance 財務省 **Zaimu shō** *(zye-muu show)*

Ministry of Foreign Affairs 外務省 **Gaimu shō** *(guy-muu show)*

Ministry of Health, Labor and Welfare 厚生労働省 **Kōsei Rōdō shō** *(koe-say roe-doe show)*

Ministry of Justice 法務省 **Hōmu shō** *(hoe-muu show)*

Ministry of Land, Infrastructure and Transport 国土交通省 **Kokudo Kōtsū shō** *(koe-kue-doe koe-t'sue show)*

minority interest 少数株主持ち分 **shōsū kabunushi mochibun** *(show-sue kah-buu-nuu-she moe-chee-boon)*

miscellaneous (items) 雑多な **zatta na** *(zaht-tah nah)*

miscellaneous expenses 雑費 **zappi** *(zaph-pee)*

miscellaneous goods 雑貨 **zakka** *(zahk-kah)*

missile ミサイル **misairu** *(me-sie-ruu)*

misunderstand 誤解する **gokai suru** *(go-kye sue-rue)*
▪ I'm sorry, I misunderstood. すみません、誤解していしました。**Sumimasen, gokai shite imashita.** *(suu-me-mah-sen, go-kie ssh-tay ee-mah-ssh-tah.)*

misunderstanding 誤解 **gokai** *(go-kye)*
▪ There seems to have been a misunderstanding. 誤解があったようです。**Gokai ga atta yō désu.** *(go-kie gah aht-tah yoh dess.)*

mobile phone 携帯電話 **keitai denwa** *(kay-ee-tie dane-wah)*; 携帯 **keitai** *(kay-ee-tie)*
▪ I want to rent a mobile phone. 携帯電話を貸りたいです。**Keitai denwa wo karitai désu.** *(kay-ee-tie dane-wah oh kah-ree-tie dess.)*
▪ How much does it cost to rent a mobile phone for a week? 携帯のレンタル料は一週間でいくらですか。**Keitai no rental ryō wa isshūkan da ikura désu ka?** *(kay-ee-tie noh rental rio wah ees-shuu-kahn day ee-kuu-rah dess kah?)*

mobility of labor 労働力の移動性 **rōdō ryoku no idōsei** *(roe-doe rio-kuu-no ee-doe-say)*

mode モード **mōdo** *(moe-doe)*

model (vehicle, etc.) モデル **moderu** *(moe-day-rue)*; 型式 **kata shiki** *(kah-tah she-kee)*

modem モデム **modemu** *(moe-day-muu)*

modern 近代的な **kindai-teki na** *(keen-dye-tay-kee nah)*; モダンな **modan na** *(moe-dahn nah)*

monetary authorities 金融当局 **kinyū tōkyoku** *(keen-yuu toe-k'yoe-kuu)*

monetary base 財政基盤 **zaisei kiban** *(zye-say kee-bahn)*

monetary easing policy 金融緩和政策 **kinyū kanwa seisaku** *(keen-yuu kahn-wah say-sah-kuu)*

monetary policy 金融政策 **kin'yū seisaku** *(keen-yuu say-sah-kuu)*

money お金 **okane** *(oh-kah-nay)*; 通貨 **tsūka** *(t'sue-kah)*

money laundering 不正資金の洗浄 **fusei shikin no senjō** *(fuu-say she-keen no sen-joe)*

money market 金融市場 **kin'yū shijō** *(keen-yuu she-joe)*

money order 郵便為替 **yūbin kawase** *(yuu-bean kah-wah-say)*

monitor (computer/TV) モニター **monitā** *(moh-nee-tahh)*

monkey business (lie, cheat, unfair practices) インチキ **in-chiki** *(een-chee-kee)*; illegitimate business インチキ商売 **inchiki shōbai** *(een-chee-kee show-by)*

monopoly 独占 **dokusen** *(doke-sen)*
▪ Do you have a monopoly on this item? この品物に独占権がありますが。**Kono shinamono ni dokusen ken ga arimasu ka?** *(Koh-no shee-nah-moh-no nee doke-sen ken gah ah-ree-mahss kah?)*

monthly payment 月賦 **geppu** *(gape-puu)*

monthly salary 月給 **gekkyū** *(gake-cue)*

moonlighting 副業 **fukugyō** *(fuu-kuu-g'yoe)*

morale 勤労意欲 **kinrō iyoku** *(keen-roe ee-yoe-kuu)*; 士気 **shiki** *(she-kee)*

morality (ethics) 道徳 **dōtoku** *(doe-toe-kuu)*

moratorium (on payment) 支払停止 **shiharai teishi** *(she-hah-rye tay-she)*

more than 以上 **ijō** *(eee-joe)*

morning meeting 朝礼 **chōrei** *(choe-ray)*

mortgage 抵当権 **teitō ken** *(tay-toe-ken)*

mortgage bank 担保貸し銀行 **tanpo gaishi ginkō** *(tahn-poe-gah-she gheen-koe)*

mortgage bond 担保付き債券 **tanpo tsuki saiken** *(tahn-poe ski sigh-ken)*

mortgage debenture 担保付き社債券 **tanpo tsuki shasai ken** *(tahn-poe ski shah-sigh ken)*

mortgage finance company 住宅金融会社 **jūtaku kinyū gaisha** *(juu-tah-kuu keen-yuu guy-shah)*

most-favored nation 最恵国 **saikei koku** *(sigh-kay koe-kuu)*

motor モーター **mōtā** *(moe-tah)*

motor drive (camera, etc.) モータードライブ **mōtā doraibu** *(moe-tah doe-rye-buu)*

moving expenses 引っ越し費用 **hikkoshi hiyō** *(heek-koe-she he-yoe)*
▪ Is your company going to pay moving expenses? 会社が引っ越し費用を払いますか。**Kaisha ga hikkoshi hiyō wo haraimasu ka?** *(kye-shah gah heek-koe-she he-yoe oh hah-rye-mahss kah?)*

multilateral agreement 多国間協定 **takoku kan kyōtei** *(tah-koe-kuu kahn k'yoe-tay)*

multilateral trade 多角貿易 **takaku bōeki** *(tah-kah-kuu boe-ay-kee)*

multinational corporation 多国籍企業 **takokuseki kigyō** *(tah-koe-kuu-say-kee kee-g'yoe)*

multiple debtor 多重債務者 **tajū saimu sha** *(tah-juu sigh-muu-shah)*

multiple exchange rate 複数為替相場 **fukusū kawase sōba** *(fuu-kuu-sue kah-wah-say so-bah)*

multiple taxation 副税 **fuku zei** *(fuu-kuu zay)*

multi-unit apartment 団地 **danchi** *(dahn-chee)*

mutual fund 投資信託 **tōshi shintaku** *(toe-she sheen-tah-kuu)*

mutual responsibility 対外の責任 **taigai no sekinin** *(tie-guy no say-kee-neen)*

mutual understanding 相互理解 **sōgo rikai** *(so-go ree-kye)*

N

name (nominate; designate) 指名する **shimei suru** *(she-may sue-rue)*

name card 名刺 **meishi** *(may-she)*
▪ I would like to order some new name cards. 新しい名刺を注文したいです。**Atarashii meishi wo chūmon shitai désu.** *(ah-tah-rah-she may-she oh chew-moan she-tie dess.)*

named point of destination 指定到着地 **shitei tōchaku chi** *(she-tay toe-cha-kuu chee)*

named point of exportation 指定輸出地点 **shitei yushutsu chiten** *(she-tay yuu-shoot-sue chee-ten)*

named port of importation 指定輸入港 **shitei yunyū kō** *(she-tay yuun-yuu koe)*

named point of (product) origin 指定原産地 **shitei gensanchi** *(she-tay gen-sahn-chee)*

named point of origin 指定原産地点 **shitei gensan chiten** *(she-tay gen-sahn chee-ten)*

name seal/stamp はんこ **hanko** *(hahn-koe)*; (registered seal used when signing official documents) 実印 **jitsu-in** *(jee-t'sue-een)*
▪ Do you need (my) registered seal? 実印が必要ですか。**Jitsuin ga hitsuyō désu ka?** *(jeet-sue-een gah heet-sue-yoh dess kah?)*
▪ I don't have a name stamp. Will a signature do? はんこを持っていません。サインでいいですか。**Hanko wo motteimasen. Sain de ii désu ka?** *(hahn-koe oh moat-tay-mah-sen sign day ee dess kah?)*

NASDAQ ナスダック **nasudakku** *(nah-sue-dahk-kuu)*; 米店頭株式市場 **bei tentō kabushiki shijō** *(bay ten-toe kah-buu-she-kee she-joe)*

national bank 国立銀行 **kokuritsu ginkō** *(koe-kuu-ree-t'sue gheen-koe)*

national bond 国債 **kokusai** *(koe-kuu-sigh)*

national debt 国家債務 **kokka saimu** *(coke-kah sigh-muu)*

National Diet building 国会議事堂 **Kokkai Gijidō** *(coke-kye ghee-jee-doe)*

nationalization 国有化 **kokuyūka** *(koe-kuu-yuu-kah)*

national pension premium 国民年金保険料 **kokumin nenkin hoken ryō** *(koe-kuu-mean nane-keen hoe-ken-rio)*

national pension system 国民年金 **kokumin nenkin** *(koe-kuu-mean nane-keen)*

national tax 国税 **koku zei** *(koe-kuu zay)*

National Tax Agency 国税庁 **Koku Zei Chō** *(koe-kuu zay choe)*

nation-wide 全国 **zenkoku** *(zen-koe-kuu)*
▪ We are doing business nation-wide. 全国的に取引をしています。**Zenkoku teki ni torihiki wo shite imasu.** *(zen-koe-kuu tay-kee nee toe-ree-he-kee oh shtay-mahss.)*

natural resources 天然資源 **tennen shigen** *(ten-nen she-gen)*

needs 需要 **juyō** *(juu-yoe)*; ニーズ **niizu** *(nee-zuu)*
▪ The aim is to develop products that meet the needs of consumers. 消費者のニーズにあった商品開発を目指します。**Shōhisha no niizu ni atta shōhin kaihatsu wo mezashimasu.** *(shoh-he-shah no nee-suu nee aht-tah shohh-heen kie-hot-sue wo may-zah-she-mahss.)*

negative (film for printing) ネガ **nega** *(nay-gah)*

negative cash flow 負のキャッシュフロー **fu no kyasshu furō** *(fuu no k'yah-shuu fuu-roe)*

negative factor マイナス要因 **mainasu yōin** *(my-nah-sue yoe-in)*

negative net worth 債務超過 **saimu chōka** *(sigh-muu choe-kah)*

negotiable 譲渡できる **jōto dekiru** *(joe-toe day-kee-rue)*

negotiate 交渉する **kōshō suru** *(koe-show sue-rue)*

negotiated sale 商談による販売 **shōdan ni yoru hanbai** *(show-dahn nee yoe-rue hahn-by)*

negotiations 交渉 **kōshō** *(koe-show)*; 商談 **shōdan** *(show-dahn)*
▪ We are now in the midst of negotiations. ただいま、交渉中です。**Tadaima kōshō chū désu.** *(tah-dah-ee-mah koe-show chew dess.)*

net 正味 **shōmi** *(show-me)*

net assets 純資産 **jun shisan** *(june she-sahn)*

net cash flow ネットキャッシュフロー **netto kyasshu furō** *(net-toe k'yah-shuu fuu-roe)*

Netherlands オランダ **Oranda** *(Oh-rahn-dah)*

net income 純所得 **jun shotoku** *(june show-toe-kuu)*; 手取り **tedori** *(tay-doe-ree)*

net investment 純投資 **jun tōshi** *(june toe-she)*

net liabilities 債務超過額 **saimu chōka gaku** *(sigh-muu choe-kah gah-kuu)*

net profit 純益 **jun eki** *(june ay-kee)*
▪ We will split the net profits fifty-fifty. 純益は半分ずつ分けましょう。**Jun eki wa hanbun zoe-t'sue wakemashō.** *(june ay-kee wah hahn-boon-hahn-boon wah-kay-mah-show.)*

net sales 純売上高 **jun uriage daka** *(june uu-ree-ah-gay dah-kah)*

network ネットワーク **nettowāku** *(net-toh-wah-kuu)*

network operating system ネットワークOS **netto wāku ōesu** *(net-toh-wah-kuu oh-ay-suu)*

net worth 正味資産 **shōmi shisan** *(show-me she-sahn)*

new model (type) 新型 **shingata** *(sheen-gah-tah)*

new product 新製品 **shin seihin** *(sheen say-heen)*

new-product development 新製品開発 **shin seihin kaihatsu** *(sheen say-heen kye-hot-sue)*

news ニュース **nyūsu** *(nuu-sue)*; (お)知らせ **(o-)shirase** *((oh) she-rah-say)*

news group ニュースグループ **nūsu gurūpu** *(nuu-suu guu-ruu-puu)*
▪ You can obtain a variety of information when you belong to news groups. ニュースグループに入るといろいろな情報を得られます。**Nyūsu gurūpu ni hairu to iroiro na jōhō wo eraremasu.** *(n'yuu-sue guu-ruu-puu nee high-rue toh ee-roh-ee-roh nah joo-hoh oh eh-rah-ray-mahss.)*

newspaper 新聞 **shinbun** *(sheem-boon)*
▪ Do you carry (stock) *The New York Times*? ニューヨークタイムスをお持ちですか。**Nyū Yōku Taimuzu wo o-mochi désu ka?** *(nyuu-yoe-kuu time-zuu oh oh-moe-chee dess kah?)*

newsprint 新聞用紙 **shinbun yō shi** *(sheem-boon yoe she)*

niche 特定分野 **tokutei bunya** *(toe-kuu-tay buun-yah)*; ニッチ **nitchi** *(neet-chee)*

night club ナイトクラブ **naito kurabu** *(night-oh kuu-rah-buu)*

night depository 夜間金庫 **yakan kinko** *(yah-kahn keen-koe)*

Nikkei Index 日経平均株価 **Nikkei heikin kabuka** *(neek-kay hay-keen kah-buu-kah)*

nondurable goods 非耐久財 **hi-taikyū zai** *(he-tie-cue zye)*

nonferrous metals 非金属 **hi-kinzoku** *(he-keen-zoe-kuu)*

nonlife insurance policy 損害保険(証券) **songai hoken (shōken)** *(soan-guy hoe-ken (show-ken))*

nonmanufacturers 非製造業 **hi seizō gyō** *(he say-zoe-g'yoe)*

nonmember 非会員 **hi-kai'in** *(he kye-een)*

nonpayment; dishonor 不渡り **fuwatari** *(fuu-wah-tah-ree)*

nonperforming loan 不良債権 **furyō saiken** *(fuu-rio sigh-ken)*

nonprofit company 非営利企業 **hi-eiri kigyō** *(he-eh-ee-ree kee-g'yoe)*

nonresident 非居住者 **hi-kyojūsha** *(he-k'yoe-juu-shah)*

nontaxable write-off 無税償却 **muzei shōkyaku** *(muu-zye show-k'yah-kuu)*

nonvoting stock 無議決権株 **mugiketsuken kabu** *(muu-ghee-kate-sue-ken kah-buu)*

no par value 無額面の **mugakumen no** *(muu-gah-kuu-men no)*

nosedive 暴落する **bōraku suru** *(boe-rah-kuu sue-rue)*

notary public 公証人 **kōshō nin** *(koe-show neen)*
▪ Can you introduce me to a good notary public? しっかりした公証人を紹介していただけますか。**Shikkaishita kōshō nin wo shōkai shite**

itadakemasu ka? *(sit-kah-ree she-tah koe-show neen oh show-kye shtay ee-tah-dah-kee-mahss kah?)*

notary public office 公証役場 **kōshō yakuba** *(koe-show yah-kuu-bah)*

note (money) 紙幣 **sihei** *(she-hay)*; 札 **satsu** *(sah-t'sue)*

note; bill; draft 手形 **tegata** *(tay-gah-tah)*

notebook computer ノートパソコン **nōto pasokon** *(note-pah-soh-kone)*
▪ Where are your notebook computers? ノートパソコンはどこですか。**Nōto pasokon wa doko désu ka?** *(note-pah-soh-kone wah doh-koh dess kah?)*
▪ How much is that notebook computer? そのノートパソコンはいくらですか。**Sono nōto pasokon wa ikura désu ka?** *(soe-no note-pah-soh-kone wah ee-kuu-rah dess kah?)*

notes payable 手形借入金 **tegata kari ire kin** *(tay-gah-tah kah-ree-ee-ray keen)*

notice 通知 **tsūchi** *(t'sue-chee)*

nuclear power 原子力 **genshi ryoku** *(gen-she rio-kuu)*

nuclear reactor 原子炉 **genshi ro** *(gen-she roe)*

nuisance e-mail 迷惑メール **meiwaku mēru** *(may-wah-kuu may-rue)*
▪ I am tormented by nuisance e-mails. 迷惑メールに悩まされています。**Meiwaku mēru ni nayamasareteimasu.** *(may-ee-wah-kuu maay-rue nee nah-yah-may-sah-ray-tay ee-mahss.)*

null and void 無効の **mukō no** *(muu-koe nah)*

nullify (cancel) 取り消す **torikesu** *(toe-ree-kay-sue)*

▪ Please cancel my order. 注文を取消して下さい。**Chūmon wo torikeshite kudasai.** *(chew-moan oh toe-ree-kay-shtay kuu-dah-sigh.)*

nursing care insurance 介護保険 **kaigo hoken** *(kye-go hoe-ken)*

O

objections 異存 **izon** *(ee-zone)*; 異論 **iron** *(ee-ron)*
▪ I have no objections. 異存はありません。**Izon wa arimazen.** *(ee-zone wah ah-ree-mah-sen.)*

objective (policy) 方針 **hōshin** *(hoe-sheen)*

obligation (debt) 債務 **saimu** *(sigh-muu)*; duty 義務 **gimu** *(ghee-muu)*

obligation to secrecy 守秘義務 **shuhi gimu** *(shuu-he ghee-muu)*
▪ Doctors are obligated to keep confidential the medical condition of their patients. 医者は患者に対して守秘義務がある。**Isha wa kanja ni taishite shuhi gimu ga aru.** *(ee-shah wa kahn-jah ni tie-ssh-tay shu-hee ghee-muu gah ah-rue.)*

obsolescence 陳腐 **chinpu** *(cheen-puu)*

obsolete 不要の **fuyō no** *(fuu-yoe no)*; もう使わない **mō tsukawanai** *(moe t'sue-kah-wah-nigh)*
▪ That machine is obsolete. その機械はもう使いません。**Sono kikai wa mō tsukaimasen.** *(so-no kee-kye wah moe t'sue-kye-mah-sen.)*

occupation 職業 **shokugyō** *(show-kuu-g'yoe)*
▪ What is your occupation? ご職業はなんですか。**Go-shokugyō wa nan désu ka?** *(go-show-kuu-g'yoe wah nahn dess kah?)*

occupational hazard 職業上の危険 **shokugyō jō no kiken** *(show-kuu'g-yoe joe no kee-ken)*; 労働災害 **rōdō saigai** *(roe-doe sigh-guy)*

occupation risk allowance 危険手当 **kiken teate** *(kee-ken tay-ah-tay)*

odometer (automobile) 走行距離計 **sōkō kyori kei** *(so-koe k'yoe-ree kay)*

off duty 非番 **hiban** *(he-bahn)*

offer 提供する **teikyō suru** *(tay-k'yoe sue-rue)*; 申し出る **mōshi deru** *(moe-she-day-rue)*

offer for sale 売りに出す **uri ni dasu** *(uu-ree nee dah-sue)*

offering 募集 **boshū** *(boe-shuu)*; 発行 **hakkō** *(hock-koh)*

offer price 呼び値 **yobi ne** *(yoe-bee nay)*

offer rate オファードレート **ofādo rēto** *(oh-fah-doe ray-toe)*

office オフィス **ofisu** *(oh-fee-sue)*; 事務所 **jimusho** *(jeem-show)*
▪ What floor is your office on? オフィスは何階ですか。**Ofisu wa nan kai désu ka?** *(oh-fee-sue wah nahn kye dess kah?)*

office branch 支店 **shiten** *(she-ten)*

office management 事務管理 **jimu kanri** *(jee-muu kahn-ree)*

officer (company) 役員 **yakuin** *(yah-kuu-in)*

official (government representative) 公 **ōyake** *(oh-yah-kay)*; 公式の **kōshiki no** *(koe-she-kee no)*

official; formal (wear, etc.) 正式の **seishiki no** *(say-she-kee no)*

official business 公務 **kōmu** *(koe-muu)*

official business trip 出張 **shutchō** *(shuu-choe)*
▪ Mr. Honda is away on a business trip. 本田さんは出張しています。**Honda-san wa shutchō shiteimasu.** *(hone-dah-sahn wah shuu-choe shtay-mahss.)*

official discount rate 公定歩合 **kōtei buai** *(koe-tay buu-aye)*

official employment 本採用 **hon saiyō** *(hone sigh-yoe)*; 正式採用 **seishiki saiyō** *(say-she-kee sigh-yoe)*

off-line (computer) オフライン **ofu rain** *(oh-fuu rine)*

off-season 季節外れ **kisetsu hazure** *(kee-say-t'sue hah-zoo-ray)*

offset 相殺(する) **sōsai (suru)** *(saw-sigh (sur-rue))*

offset printing オフセット印刷 **ofusetto insatsu** *(oh-fuu-set-toe een-sah-t'sue)*

offshore company オフショアカンパニー **ofushoa kanpanii** *(oh-fuu-show-ah kahn-pah-nee)*

oil (for autos, etc.) 石油 **sekiyu** *(say-kee-yuu)*; 原油 **genyu** *(gen-yuu)*

okay 大丈夫 **daijōbu** *(dye-joe-buu)*
▪ Is this schedule okay? この予定で大丈夫ですか。**Kono yotei de daijōbu désu ka?** *(koe-no yoe-tay day dye-joe-buu dess kah?)*

omit 省略する **shōryaku suru** *(show-r'yah-kuu sue-rue)*

on account sales 掛売りで **kakeuri de** *(kah-kay-uu-ree day)*

on consignment 委託販売で **itaku hanbai de** *(ee-tah-kuu hahn-by day)*

on demand 要求に応じて **yōkyū ni ōjite** *(yoe-cue nee oh-jee-tay)*; オンデマンドで **ondemando de** *(on-dee-man-doe day)*

one hundred million 一億 **ichi oku** *(ee-chee oh-kuu)*

one-thousand-yen note 千円札 **sen en satsu** *(sen en sought-sue)*
▪ Would you please change this into one-thousand-yen notes? 千円札にしてもらえますか。**Sen en satsu ni shite moraemasu ka?** *(sen en sah-t'sue nee shtay moe-rah-ay-mahss kah?)*

online オンライン **onrain** *(on-rine)*
▪ Are you on line now? 今オンライン中ですか。**Ima onrain chū désu ka?** *(ee-mah on-rine chuu dess kah)* Also: 今オンラインにつながっていますか。**Ima onrain ni tsunagatte imasu ka?** *(ee-mah on-rine nee t'sue-nah-got-tay ee-mahss kah?)*
▪ I want to buy it online. インターネットで買いたい。**Intānetto de kaitai.** *(in-tah-net-toh day kie-tie.)*
▪ I can't get online. インタネットにつながらない。**Intānetto ni tsunagaranai.** *(in-tah-net-toh nee t'sue-nah-gah-ray-nigh.)*

on-the-job training 職場訓練 **shokuba kunren** *(show-kuu-bah coon-ren)*

open (doors; office) 開く **hiraku** *(he-rah-kuu)*

open account オープン勘定 **ōpun kanjō** *(oh-puun kahn-joe)*

open-door policy 門戸開放政策 **monko kaihō seisaku** *(moan-koe kye-hoe say-sah-kuu)*

opening balance 期首残高 **kishu zandaka** *(kee-shuu zahn-dah-kah)*

opening price 寄付き値段 **yoritsuki nedan** *(yoe-ree-tsue-kee nay-dahn)*

open market 公開市場 **kōkai shijō** *(koe-kye she-joe)*

operate 経営する **keiei suru** *(kay-ee sue-rue)*

operating budget 運営予算 **unei yosan** *(uun-ay yoe-sahn)*
▪ Have you already settled on an operating budget? 運営予算をもう決めましたか。**Unei yosan wo mō kimemashita ka?** *(uun-ay yoe-sahn oh moe kee-may-mah-shtah kah?)*

operating expenses 営業費 **eigyō hi** *(eh-ee-g'yoe he)*; 経常経費 **keijō keihi** *(kay-joe kay-kee)*

operating income 営業収益 **eigyō shūeki** *(eh-ee-g'yoe shuu-ay-kee)*

operating profit 営業利益 **eigyō rieki** *(eh-ee-g'yoe ree-ay-kee)*

operating manual 業務マニュアル **gyōmu manyuaru** *(g'yoe-muu mah-n'yuu-ah-rue)*
▪ Please read that operating manual carefully. その業務マニュアルをよく読んでおいてください。**Sono gyōmu manual wo yoku yonde oite kudasai.** *(so-no ghee-yoh-muu manual oh yoe-kuu yone-day oh-ee-tay kuu-dah-sie.)*

operating performance 営業成績 **eigyō seiseki** *(eh-ee-g'yoe say-say-kee)*

operating revenue 営業収益 **eigyō shūeki** (*eh-ee-g'yoe shuu-ay-kee)*

operating system OS **O Esu** *(OS)*; 基本ソフト **kihon sofuto** *(kee-hoen so-fuu-toe)*

operation 経営 **keiei** *(kay-ee)*; 業務 **gyōmu** *(g'yoe-muu)*

operations management 業務管理 **gyōmu kanri** *(g'yoe-muu kahn-ree)*

operator オペレーター **operētā** *(oh-pay-ray-tah)*

opportunity 機会 **kikai** *(kee-kye)*
▪ I think it will be a wonderful business opportunity. それは絶好のビ

ジネスチャンスになるだろう。**Sore wa zekkō no bijinesu chansu ni naru darō.** *(soh-ray way zeck-koh no be-jee-nay-suu chahn-suu nee nah-rue dah-roh.)*

oppose 反対する **hantai suru** *(hahn-tie sue-rue)*

optical cable 光ケーブル **hikari kēburu** *(he-kah-ree kay-buu-rue)*

optical communications 光通信 **hikari tsūshin** *(he-kah-ree t'sue-sheen)*

optical computer 光コンピュータ **hikari konpyūta** *(he-rah-ree comb-pew-tah)*

optical disc 光ディスク **hikari disuku** *(he-kah-ree disk-uu)*

optical equipment (for auto) オプション部品 **opushon buhin** *(ope-shone buu-heen)*

optical fiber 光ファイバー **hikari faibā** *(he-kah-ree fye-bah)*

option オプション **opushon** *(ope-shone)*

optional (choice) 自由選択の **jiyū sentaku no** *(jee-yuu sen-tah-kuu no)*

oral bid 口頭入札 **kōtō nyūsatsu** *(koe-toe nuu-sah-t'sue)*

order (for merchandise/goods) 注文する **chūmon suru** *(chew-moan sue-rue)*; 発注する **hatchū suru** *(hot-chew sue-rue)*

order form 注文書 **chūmon sho** *(chew-moan show)*

order number 注文番号 **chūmon bangō** *(chew-moan bahn-go)*

ordinary 普通 **futsū** *(fuu-t'sue)*

ordinary deposit 普通預金 **futsū yokin** *(fuu-t'sue yoe-keen)*

organization 組織 **soshiki** *(so-she-kee)*

organization chart 組織機構図 **soshiki kikōzu** *(soe-she-kee kee-koe-zuu)*

organize (form) 組織する **soshiki suru** *(so-she-kee sue-rue)*

orientation オリエンテーション **orientēshon** *(orien-tay-shone)*

original (copy) 原文 **genbun** *(gen-boon)*; 原本 **genpon** *(gen-poon)*

original (work) 原初 **gensho** *(gen-show)*; 原型 **genkei** *(gen-kay)*

original cost 取得原価 **shutoku genka** *(shuu-toe-kuu gen-kah)*

outdated; obsolete 時代遅れ **jidaiokure** *(jee-die-oh-kuu-ray)*
▪ Your computer is obsolete. あなたのコンピュータは時代遅れです。**Anata no konpyūta wa jidaiokure désu.** *(Ah-nah-tah no kome-pyuu-tahh wah jee-die-oh-kuu-ray dess.)*

outlay 支出 **shishutsu** *(she-shoot-sue)*

outlet 販路 **hanro** *(hahn-roe)*; 小売店 **kouri ten** *(koe-uu-ree ten)*; アウトレット **autoretto** *(outlet)*

outline あらまし **aramashi** *(ah-rah-mah-she)*; 概要 **gaiyō** *(guy-yoe)*

outlook 見通し **mitōshi** *(me-toe-she)*

out-of-date 期限切れ **kigengire** *(kee-gane-ghee-ray)*

out of order 故障 **koshō** *(koe-show)*

out-of-pocket expenses 経費の一時立替 **keihi no ichiji tatekae** *(kay-he no ee-chee-jee tah-tay-kye)*

outside pressure 外圧 **gai-atsu** *(guy-ah-t'sue)*

outsourcing 外注 **gaichū** *(guy-chew)*

outstanding balance 未払い残高 **mibarai zandaka** *(me-bah-rye zahn-dah-kah)*

outstanding debt 未払い負債額 **miharai fusaigaku** *(me-hah-rye fuu-sigh-gah-kuu)*

outstanding shares 発行済株式 **hakkō zumi kabushiki** *(hock-koh zuu-me kah-buu-she-kee)*

outstanding stock 社外株 **shagai kabu** *(shah-guy kah-buu)*

overage 供給過剰 **kyōkyū kajō** *(k'yoe-cue kah-joe)*; 過剰生産 **kajō seisan** *(kah-joe say-sahn)*

overbuy 買い過ぎる **kaisugiru** *(kye-sue-ghee-rue)*

overcharge 法外な代金請求 **hōgai na daikin seikyū** *(hoe-guy nah dye-keen say-cue)*; 過剰請求 **kajō seikyū** *(kah-joe say-cue)*

overdraft 当座貸越 **tōza kashikoshi** *(toe-zah kah-she-koe-she)*

overdue (payment) (支払)期限が過ぎた **(shiharai) kigen ga sugita** *((she-hah-rye) kee-gen gah sue-ghee-tah)*

overhead 諸経費 **shokeihi** *(show-kah-ee he)*

overpaid 払い過ぎの **haraisugi no** *(hah-rye-sue-ghee no)*

overproduction 過剰生産 **kajō seisan** *(kah-joe say-sahn)*

overseas (in a foreign country) 海外 **kaigai** *(kye-guy)*; foreign location 外地 **gaichi** *(guy-chee)*

overseas phone call 国際電話 **kokusai denwa** *(coke-sigh den-wah)*
▪ Can I make an overseas call from this telephone? この電話から国際電話できますか。**Kono denwa kara kokusai denwa dekimasu ka?** *(koe-no dane-wah kah-rah koe-kuu-sigh dane-wah day-kee-mahss kah?)*
▪ Mr. Sato, you have an overseas phone call. 佐藤さん、国際電話です。**Sato-san, kokusai denwa désu.** *(sah-toe-sahn coke-sigh den-wah dess.)*

oversell 過大評価する **kadai hyōka suru** *(kah-dye h'yoe-kah sue-rue)*

overstock 在庫過剰 **zaiko kajō** *(zye-koe kah-joe)*

oversubscribed 申し込み超過の **mōshikomi chōka no** *(moe-she-koe-me choe-kah no)*

oversupply 供給過剰 **kyōkyū kajō** *(k'yoe-cue kah-joe)*

over-the-counter quotation 店頭取引相場 **tentō torihiki sōba** *(ten-toe toe-ree-he-kee so-bah)*

overtime 超過勤務 **chōka kinmu** *(choe-kah keen-muu)*; 残業 **zangyō** *(zahn-g'yohh)*

overtime allowance 超過勤務手当て **chōka kinmu teate** *(choe-kah keen-muu tay-ah-tay)*; 残業手当て **zangyō teate** *(zahn-g'yohh tay-ah-tay)*

overtime work 残業 **zangyō** *(zahn-g'yohh)*

overvalued 過大評価された **kadai hyōka sareta** *(kah-dye h'yoe-kah sah-ray-tah)*

overwork 働きすぎ **hatarakisugi** *(hah-tah-rah-kee-sue-ghee)*; 過労 **karō** *(kah-roe)*

owner 所有者 **shoyūsha** *(show-yuu-shah)*; 持ち主 **mochinushi** *(moe-chee-nuu-she)*; オーナー **ōnā** *(oh-nahh)*
▪ Who is the owner of that shop? その店のオーナーはどなたですか。**Sono mise no ōnā wa donata désu ka?** *(so-no me-say no oh-nahh wah doe-nah-tah dess kah?)*

owner's equity 所有者持分 **shoyūsha**

mochibun *(show-yuu-shah moe-chee-boon)*

ownership 所有権 **shoyūken** *(show-yuu-ken)*

P

pack (bags) 荷造りする **nizukuri suru** *(nee-zuu-kuu-ree sue-rue)*
▪ Hurry! Pack your bags! 急いで荷造りして！ **Isoide nizukuri shite!** *(ee-soy-day nee-zuu-kuu-ree shtay!)*

package (parcel) 小包 **kozutsumi** *(koe-zute-sue-me)*
▪ Does this package belong to you? この小包はあなたのですか。**Kono kozutsumi wa anata no désu ka?** *(koe-no koe-zute-sue-me wah ah-nah-tah no dess kah?)*
▪ I want to mail this package. この小包を郵便で送りたいです。**Kono kozutsumi wo yūbin de okuritai désu.** *(koe-no koe-zute-sue-me oh yuu-bean day oh-kuu-ree-tie dess.)*

package deal 一括取引 **ikkatsu torihiki** *(eek-cot-sue toe-ree-he-kee)*; 一括購入 **ikkatsu kōnyū** *(eek-cot-sue koe-n'yuu)*

packaging 包装 **hōsō** *(hoe-so)*

packing case 輸送用包装箱 **yusō-yō hōsō bako** *(yuu-so-yoe hoe-so bah-koe)*

packing list 包装証明書 **hōsō meisaisho** *(hoe-so may-sigh-show)*; 納品書 **nōhinsho** *(noh-heen-show)*; パッキングリスト **pakkingu risuto** *(pahk-keen-gue ree-sue-toe)*
▪ Let me see the packing list. パッキングリストを見せてください。**Pakkingu risuto wo misete kudasai.** *(pahk-keen-gue ree-sue-toe oh me-say-tay kuu-dah-sigh.)*

page ページ **pēji** *(pay-jee)*

paid holiday 有給休暇 **yūkyū kyūka** *(you-cue cue-kah)*

paid in full 全額支払済み **zengaku shiharaizumi** *(zen-gah-kuu she-hah-rye-zuu-me)*

paid-in surplus 払い込み剰余金 **haraikomi jōyokin** *(hah-rye-koe-me joe-yoe-keen)*

paid-up 支払済み **shiharaizumi** *(she-hah-rie-zuu-me)*

paid-up capital 払込済み資本金 **haraikomizumi shihonkin** *(hah-rye-koe-me-zuu-me she-hone-keen)*

paid-up shares 払込済み株式 **haraikomizumi kabushiki** *(hah-rye-koe-me-zuu-me kah-buu-she-kee)*

pallet パレット **paretto** *(pah-rate-toe)*

palletized freight/shipment パレット輸送 **paretto yusō** *(pah-rate-toe yuu-so)*

pamphlet パンフレット **panfuretto** *(pahn-fuu-rate-toe)*

paper 紙 **kami** *(kah-me)*

paperback (book) ペーパーバック **pēpābakku** *(pay-pah-back-kuu)*

par 平価 **heika** *(hay-kah)*

par, above (above par) 額面以上で **gakumen ijō de** *(gah-kuu-men ee-joe day)*

paradigm 枠組み **waku gumi** *(wah-kuu guu-me)*

par, below (below par) 額面以下で **gakumen ika de***(gah-kuu-men ee-kah day)*

parcel post 小包郵便 **kozutsumi yūbin** *(koe-zute-sue-me yuu-bean)*
▪ I will send it to you by parcel post. 小包で送ります。**Kozutsumi de**

okurimasu. *(koe-zute-sue-me day oh-kuu-ree-mahss.)*
▪ How much is the charge to send a parcel post to America? アメリカまで、小包郵便はいくらですか。**Amerika made kozutsumi yubin wa ikura désu ka?** *(ah-may-ree-kah mah-day koh-zuut-sue-me yuu-been wah ee-kuu-rah dess kah?)*

parent company 親会社 **oya gaisha** *(oh-yah guy-shah)*

parity 等価 **tōka** *(toe-kah)*

part (portion) 一部 **ichibu** *(ee-chee-buu)*

partial payment 分割払い **bunkatsu barai** *(boon-cot-sue bah-rye)*; 内払い **uchibarai** *(uu-chee-bah-rye)*
▪ Will partial payment be all right? 分割払いでよろしいですか。**Bunkatsu barai de yoroshii désu ka?** *(boon-cot-sue bah-rye day yoe-roe-she dess kah?)*

participation 参加 **sanka** *(sahn-kah)*

participation fee 参加費 **sanka hi** *(sahn-kah hee)*

participation loan 共同融資 **kyōdō yūshi** *(k'yoe-doe yuu-she)*

partner (business) パートナー **pātonā** *(pah-toe-nah)*; other party 相手 **aite** *(eye-tay)*

partnership (company) 合名会社 **gōmei gaisha** *(goe-may guy-shah)*; 共同経営 **kyōdō keiei** *(k'yoe-doe kay-ee)*

parts (of products) 部品 **buhin** *(buu-heen)*

part-time work アルバイト **arubaito** *(ah-rue-by-toe)*; パート **pāto** *(pah-toe)*
▪ Have you done part-time work? アルバイトをしたことがありますか。**Arubaito wo shita koto ga arimasu ka?** *(ah-ruu-by-toh oh ssh-tah koh-toh gah ah-ree-mahss kah?)*

party (Japanese style) 宴会 **enkai** *(en-kye)*

party (political) 政党 **seitō** *(say-toe)*
▪ I don't know which political party will win the next election. 次の選挙でどの政党が勝つかわかりません。**Tsugi no senkyo de dono seitō ga katsu ka wakarimasen.** *(t'sue-ghee no sane-k'yoh day doe-no say-ee-toe gah kot-sue kah wah-kah-ree-mah-sen.)*

par value 額面価格 **gakumen kakaku** *(gah-kuu-men kah-kah-kuu)*

passbook (bank) 預金通帳 **yokin tsūchō** *(yoe-keen t'sue-choe)*

passport control 入国審査 **nyūkoku shinsa** *(n'yee coke sheen-sah)*

password パスワード **pasu wādo** *(pah-suu wah-doh)*
▪ I forgot my password. パスワードを忘れてしまいました。**Pasu wādo wo wasureteshimaimashita.** *(pah-suu wah-doh oh wah-suu-ray-mah-ssh-tah.)*

past due 期限経過の **kigen keika no** *(kee-gen kay-kah noh)*

patent 特許 **tokkyo** *(toke-k'yoe)*
▪ Is this patented? 特許を取ってありますか。**Tokkyo wo totte arimasu ka?** *(toke-k'yoe oh tote-tay ah-ree-mahss kah?)*

patent application 特許出願 **tokkyo shutugan** *(toke-k'yoe ken sheen-say)*

patented process 特許を持つ生産方法 **tokkyo wo motsu seisan hōhō** *(toke-k'yoe oh moat-sue say-sahn hoe-hoe)*

patent law 特許法 **tokkyo hō** *(toke-k'yoe hoe)*

patent pending 特許出願中 **tokkyo shutsugan chū** *(toke-k'yoe shuu-t'sue-gahn chew)*

patent royalty 特許使用料 **tokkyo shiyō ryō** *(toke-k'yoe she-yoe-rio)*

paternalism 温情主義 **onjōshugi** *(own-joe-shuu-ghee)*

patience (perseverance) 辛抱 **shinbō** *(sheen-boe)*; (forbearance) 我慢 **gaman** *(gah-mahn)*
▪ Please be patient. 辛抱してください。**Shinbō shite kudasai.** *(sheen-boe shtay kuu-dah-sigh.)*

pattern (design) 模様 **moyō** *(moe-yoe)*

pattern recognition (electronically) パターン認識 **patān ninshiki** *(pah-tahn neen-she-kee)*

pay 支払う **shiharau** *(she-hah-rah-uu)*

pay (wages) 給料 **kyūryō** *(cue-rio)*

payable on demand 要求払い **yōkyū barai** *(yoe-cue bah-rye)*

payable to bearer 持参人払い **jisan nin barai** *(jee-sahn neen bah-rye)*

pay-as-you-go system 現金払い主義 **genkin-barai shugi** *(gen-keen-bah-rye shuu-ghee)*

payback period 回収期間 **kaishū kikan** *(kye-shuu kee-kahn)*; 返済期間 **hensai kikan** *(hen-sigh kee-kahn)*

payee 受取人 **uketori nin** *(uu-kay-toe-ree neen)*

payer 支払人 **shiharai nin** *(she-hah-rye neen)*

pay in full 全額支払い **zengaku shiharai** *(zen-gah-kuu she-hah-rye)*

paymaster 会計部長 **kaikei buchō** *(kye-kay buu-choe)*

payment 支払 **shiharai** *(she-hah-rye)*; 支給 **shikyū** *(she-cue)*
▪ When will payment be made? 支払いはいつになさいますか。**Shiharai wa itsu ni nasaimasu ka?** *(she-hah-rye wah eat-sue nee nah-sigh-mahss kah?)*

payment in full 全額払い **zengaku barai** *(zen-gah-kuu bah-rye)*

payment in kind 現物払い **genbutsu barai** *(gen-boot-sue bah-rye)*

payment of taxes 納税 **nō zei** *(no zay)*

payoff (illegal action) 贈賄 **zōwai** *(zoe-wie)*

payout period 回収期間 **kaishū kikan** *(kye-shuu kee-kahn)*

payroll 給与支払簿 **kyūryō shiharai bo** *(cue-rio she-hah-rye boe)*

payroll tax 給与税 **kyūyo zei** *(cue-yoe zay)*

peak load ピークロード **piiku rōdo** *(pee-kuu roe-doe)*

peer 同業者 **dōgyōsha** *(doe-g'yoe-shah)*

pegged price 固定価格 **kotei kakaku** *(koe-tay kah-kah-kuu)*

penalty 罰金 **bakkin** *(bahk-keen)*

penalty clause 違約条項 **iyaku jōkō** *(ee-yah-kuu joe-koe)*

penalty tax 追徴税 **tuichō zei** *(t'sue-ee-choe zye)*

pension (company) 厚生年金 **kōsei nenkin** *(koe-say nane-keen)*; national (government) pension 国民年金 **kokumin nenkin** *(koe-kuu-mean nane-keen)*

pension fund 年金基金 **nenkin kikin** *(nane-keen kee-keen)*

pension system 年金制度 **nenkin seido** *(nane-keen say-doe)*

per あたり **atari** *(ah-tah-ree)*

per capita 一人あたりの **hitori atari no** *(htoe-ree ah-tah-ree no)*

percent パーセント **pāsento** *(pah-sen-toe)*
▪ How about a ten percent discount? １０パーセントの割引でいかがですか。**Juppāsento no waribiki de ikaga désu ka?** *(joop-pah-sen-toe no wah-ree-bee-kee day ee-kah-gah dess kah?)*

percentage earnings 歩合収入 **buai shūnyū** *(buu-eye shuun-yuu)*

percentage of profits 利益率 **rieki ritsu** *(ree-ay-kee ree-t'sue)*

per diem 日当 **nittō** *(neat-toe)*

perfect (complete) 完全 **kanzen** *(kahn-zen)*; 完璧 **kanpeki** *(kahn-pay-kee)*

performance 実績 **jisseki** *(jeet-say-kee)*; 業績 **gyōseki** *(g'yoe-say-kee)*
▪ His performance having been recognized, the youthful person was promoted to company director. 彼は、実績が認められてあの若さで取締役に就任した。**Kare wa jisseki ga mitomerarete ano wakasa de torishimari-yaku ni shūnin shita.** *(kah-ray wah jeese-say-kee gah me-toe-may-rah-ray-tay ah-no wah-kah-sah day toe-ree-she-mah-ree-yah-kuu nee shuu-neen sshta.)*

performance evaluation 考課 **kōka** *(kohh-kah)*

period (term) 期間 **kikan** *(kee-kahn)*

periodic checkup 定期検査 **teiki kensa** *(tay-kee ken-sah)*

periodic inventory 定期棚卸 **teiki tanaoroshi** *(tay-kee tah-nah-oh-roe-she)*

peripheral (equipment) 周辺機器 **shūhen kiki** *(shu-hen kee-kee)*

perks 臨時手当 **rinji teate** *(reen-jee tay-ah-tay)*

permanent 恒久 **kōkyū** *(coke-yuu)*

permit (permission) 許可 **kyoka** *(k'yoe-kah)*
▪ A permit is necessary. 許可が必要です。**Kyoka ga hitsuyō désu.** *(k'yoe-kah gah heat-sue-yoe dess.)*

perpetual inventory 継続的棚卸 **keizoku tanaoroshi** *(kay-zoe-kuu tah-nah-oh-roe-she)*

per piece per piece 一個に付き **ikko ni tsuki** *(eek-koe nee t'sue-kee)*; 一つあたりの **hitotsu atari no** *(htoe-t'sue ah-tah-ree no)*

per share 一株あたりの **hitokabu atari no** *(shtoe-kah-buu ah-tah-ree-no)*

personal computer パソコン **pasokon** *(pah-so-cone)*

personal computer network パソコン通信 **pasokon tsūshin** *(pah-soh-kohn t'sue-sheen)*

personal connections コネ **kone** *(koe-nay)*
▪ In Japan personal connections are especially important. 日本ではコネが特に重要です。**Nihon de wa kone ga toku ni jūyō désu.** *(nee-hone day wah koe-nay gah toe-kuu nee juu-yoe dess.)*

personal consumption/spending 個人消費 **kojin shōhi** *(koe-jeen show-he)*

personal history record (biographical resume) 履歴書 **rireki sho** *(ree-ray-kee show)*
▪ Please send your personal history and references. 履歴書と紹介状を送ってください。**Rirekisho to shōkaijō wo okutte kudasai.** *(ree-rake-shoh to shoh-kie-joh oh oh-koot-tay kuu-dah-sie.)*

personal income tax 個人所得税

kojin shotoku zei *(koe-jeen show-toe-kuu-zay)*

personality 性格 **seikaku** *(say-kah-kuu)*; 人格 **jinkaku** *(jean-kah-kuu)*; 人柄 **hitogara** *(shtoe-gah-rah)*

personal liability 個人的責任 **kojin teki sekinin** *(koe-jeen tay-kee say-kee-neen)*

personal property 動産 **dōsan** *(doe-sahn)*

person concerned 本人 **hon nin** *(hone neen)*
▪ The person concerned is not here today. 本人は今日居りません。**Hon nin wa kyō orimasen.** *(hone neen wah k'yoe ee-mah-sen.)*

person in charge 担当者 **tantō sha** *(tahn-toe-shah)*; 係り **kakari** *(kah-kah-ree)*
▪ Who is the person in charge? ご担当者はどなたでしょうか。**Go-tantō sha wa donata deshō ka?** *(go-tahn-toe shah wah doe-nah-tah day-show-kah?)*

personnel 人員 **jin'in** *(jeen-een)*

personnel administration 人事管理 **jinji kanri** *(jeen-jee kahn-ree)*

personnel affairs 人事 **jinji** *(jeen-jee)*

personnel costs 人件費 **jinken hi** *(jeen-ken he)*

personnel department 人事部 **jinji bu** *(jeen-jee buu)*

personnel expense (salaries, wages) 人件費 **jinken hi** *(jeen-ken he)*

personnel transfer 人事異動 **jinji idō** *(jeen-jee ee-dohh)*

person-to-person 指名通話 **shimei-tsūwa** *(she-may-t'sue-wah)*

petroleum 石油 **sekiyu** *(say-kee-yuu)*

pharmacist 薬剤師 **yakuzai-shi** *(yah-kuu-zye-she)*

pharmacy 薬局 **yakkyoku** *(yahk-k'yoe-kuu)*

phase-in 段階的に組み入れる **dankai-teki ni kumiireru** *(dahn-kye tay-kee nee kuu-me-ee-ray-rue)*

phase-out 段階的に取り除く **dankai-teki ni torinozoku** *(dahn-kye tay-kee nee toe-ree-no-zoe-kuu)*

phone 電話 **denwa** *(den-wah)*; return phone call 折り返しの電話 **ori-kaeshi no denwa** *(oh-ree-kye-she no den-wah)*; call back コールバック **kōru bakku** *(koe-rue bah-kuu)*

phone answering machine 留守番電話 **rusuban denwa** *(rue-sue-bahn den-wah)*

photographer カメラマン **kameraman** *(kah-may-rah-mahn)*

physical inventory 実地棚卸 **jitchi tanaoroshi** *(jee-chee tah-nah-oh-roe-she)*

physician 医者 **isha** *(ee-shah)*; 医師 **ishi** *(ee-she)*

pickup (meet at airport or station) 迎えに行く **mukae ni iku** *(muu-kye nee ee-kuu)*
▪ I will meet you (pick you up) at the airport. 空港にお迎えに参ります。**Kūkō ni o-mukae ni mairimasu.** *(kuu-koe nee oh-muu-kye nee my-ree-mahss.)*

pickup and delivery 集配(サービス) **shūhai (sābisu)** *(shuu-high (sah-bee-sue))*

piecework 出来高払い **dekidakabarai** *(day-kee-dah-kah bah-rah-ee)*

pie chart 円グラフ **en gurafu** *(en guu-rah-fuu)*

piggyback service ピギーバックサー

ビス **pigii bakku sābisu** *(pee-ghee bahk-kuu sah-bee-sue)*

pilferage こそ泥 **kosodoro** *(koe-so doe-roe)*

pill (medicinal) 錠剤 **jōzai** *(joe-zye)*

place an order 発注する **hatchū suru** *(hot-chew sue-rue)*; (in a restaurant) 注文する **chūmon suru** *(chew-moan sue-rue)*

placement office 就職指導部 **shūshoku shidō bu** *(shuu-shoh-ku she-doe buu)*

place of business 営業所 **eigyō sho** *(eh-ee-g'yoe show)*

place of origin 原産地 **gensan chi** *(gen-shah chee)*

place of work 職場 **shokuba** *(show-kuu-bah)*

plagiarize 剽窃する **hyōsetsu suru** *(h'yohh-sate-suu sue-rue)*; 盗作する **tōsaku suru** *(toe-sah-kuu sue-rue)*

plaintiff 原告 **genkoku** *(gane-koh-kuu)*

plan (planning, project) 計画 **keikaku** *(kay-kah-kuu)*; 企画 **kikaku** *(kee-kah-kuu)*

planned obsolescence 計画的旧式化 **keikaku-teki kyūshiki ka** *(kay-kah-kuu cue-she-kee kah)*

planning department 企画部 **kikaku bu** *(kee-kah-kuu buu)*

plant 工場 **kōjō** *(koe-joe)*

plant capacity 工場生産能力 **kōjō seisan nōryoku** *(koe-joe say-sahn no-rio-kuu)*

plant location 工場の立地 **kōjō no ritchi** *(koe-joe no rit-chee)*

plant manager 工場長 **kōjō chō** *(koe-joe choe)*

platform (subway/train boarding) ホーム **hōmu** *(hoh-muu)*
▪ Your train leaves from the first platform. あなたが乗る電車は１番ホームから出ます。**Anata ga noru densha wa ichban hōmu kara demasu.** *(ah-nah-tah gah no-rue dane-shah wa ee-chee-bah-n hoh-muu kah-rah day-mahss.)*
▪ What is the number of the platform for Kyoto? 京都行きは何番ホームですか。**Kyoto iki wa nanban hōmu désu ka?** *(kyoto i-kee wah nah-bahn no hoh-muu dess kah?)*
▪ Please take me to platform number eight. ８番ホームまで案内して下さい。**Hachi ban hōmu made annai shite kudasai.** *(hah-chee bahn hoh-muu mah-day ahn-nie ssh-tay kuu-dah-sie.)*

pledge 担保 **tanpo** *(tahn-poe)*; 抵当 **teitō** *(tay-toe)*

plot of land (lot) 土地 **tochi** *(toe-chee)*

plug-in 差込み口 **sashikomi guchi** *(sah-she koe-me guu-chee)*
▪ Where is the plug-in? コンセントはどこですか。**Konsento wa doko désu ka?** *(kone-sen-to wah doh-koh dess kah?)*

plug-in (computer) プラグイン **puragu in** *(puu-rah-guu een)*
▪ Plug-in software is necessary to improve the function of the computer. パソコンの機能を高めるにはプラグインソフトが必要です。**Pasokon no kinō wo takameru ni wa puragu in sofuto ga hitsuyō désu.** *(pah-soh-kone no kee-noh wo tah-kah-may-rue nee wa puu-rah-guu een so-fuu-toh ga heet-sue-yoh dess.)*

Pocket PC (or PDA) ポケットPC **Poketto P-Shii** *(poh-ket-toh P-She)*
▪ The pocket PC is a computer terminal unit of the palmtop. ポケットPCは手のひらサイズの情報端末機で

す。**Poketto piishii wa tenohira saizu no jōhō tanmatsu ki désu.** *(poh-ket-toh pee-shee wah tane-no-hee-rah sie-zuu no joh-hoh than-mot-sue kee dess.)*

pocket TV ポケットテレビ **poketto terebi** *(poe-ket-toe tay-ray-bee)*

podcasting ポッドキャスティング **poddo-kasutingu** *(pah-doe-kah-suu-teen-guu)*
▪ If you use podcasting, you can download music and video anytime. ポッドキャスティングを使えば、いつでも音楽や映像をダウンロードできます。**Poddo kyasutingu wo tsukaeba itsu demo ongaku ya eizō wo daunrōdo dekimasu.** *(pod-doh k'yas-teen-guu oh t'sue-kie-bah eet-sue day-moh own-gah-kuu yah eh-ee-zoh oh down-roh-doh day-kee-mahss.)*

point of sale 販売時点 **hanbai jiten** *(hahn-by jee-ten)*

polar coordinates robot 極座標ロボット **kyoku zahyō robotto** *(k'yoe-kuu zah-h'yoe roe-boat-toe)*

policy 政策 **seisaku** *(say-sah-kuu)*; 方針 **hōshin** *(hoe-sheen)*

policy (insurance) 保険証券 **hoken shōken** *(hoe-ken show-ken)*

policyholder 保険契約者 **hoken keiyaku sha** *(hoe-ken kay-yah-kuu shah)*

polite, be (be polite) (ご)遠慮する **(go-) enryo suru** *((go)-en-rio sue-rue)*

politicians 政治家 **seijika** *(say-jee-kah)*

politics 政治 **seiji** *(say-jee)*

pollution 公害 **kōgai** *(koe-guy)*

poor performance 業績悪化 **gyōseki akka** *(g'yoe-say-kee ahk-kah)*

popular 流行 **ryūkō** *(ree-you-koe)*; 人気がある **ninki ga aru** *(neen-kee gah ah-rue)*

population 人口 **jinkō** *(jeen-koe)*

portable telephone 携帯電話 **keitai denwa** *(kay-tie dane-wah)*

portable TV ポータブルテレビ **pōtaburu terebi** *(poe-tah-buu-rue tay-ray-bee)*

portfolio 資産内容 **shisan naiyō** *(she-sahn nigh-yoe)*

possession 所有 **shoyū** *(show-yuu)*

position (place) 位置 **ichi** *(ee-chee)*

position/(job) hunt 求職中 **kyūshoku chū** *(cue-show-kuu chuu)*

position seeker's guide 求人案内 **kyūjin annai** *(cue-jeen ahn-nigh)*

positive 積極的 **sekkyoku teki** *(say-k'yoe-kuu tay-kee)*

positive (film) ポジ **poji** *(poe-jee)*

positive cash flow 正のキャッシュフロー **sei no kyasshufurō** *(say no k'yah-shuu fuu-roe)*

possibility 可能性 **kanōsei** *(kah-no-say)*
▪ Is there any possibility (it will happen, etc.)? 可能性がありますか。**Kanōsei ga arimasu ka?** *(kah-no-say gah ah-ree-mahss kah?)*

postage (cost) 郵便代 **yūbin-dai** *(yuu-bean-dye)*

postal money order 郵便為替 **yūbin kawase** *(yuu-bean kah-wah-say)*

postdated 先日付の **saki hizuke no** *(sah-kee he-zuu-kay no)*

postpone 延期する **enki suru** *(en-kee sue-rue)*

potential buyer 見込み客 **mikomi kyaku** *(me-koe-me k'yah-kuu)*

potential sales 販売の可能性 **hanbai no kanōsei** *(hahn-by no kah-no-say)*

power of attorney 委任権 **inin ken** *(ee-neen ken)*
▪ Do you have power of attorney? 委任権を持っていますか。**Inin ken wo motteimasu ka?** *(ee-neen ken oh moe-tay-mahss kah?)*

power steering (vehicle) パワーステアリング **pawā sutearingu** *(pah-wah sue-tay-ah-reen-guu)*

practical 実際的な **jissai tekina** *(jeece-sigh tay-kee-na)*; 実用的な **jitsuyō-teki na** *(jee-t'sue-yoe tay-kee nah)*

practice 実行 **jikkō** *(jeek-koh)*; 実践 **jissen** *(jeet-sen)*

precision machinery 精密機械 **seimitsu kikai** *(say-meet-sue kee-kye)*

prediction 予言 **yogen** *(yoe-gen)*

preface (in book, etc.) 前書き **maegaki** *(my-gah-kee)*

prefectural governor 知事 **chiji** *(chee-jee)*

prefecture 県 **ken** *(ken)*

preferential right 優先権 **yūsen ken** *(yuu-sen ken)*

preferential treatment 優遇 **yūgū** *(yuu-guu)*; 優待 **yūtai** *(yuu-tie)*

preferred stock 優先株 **yūsen kabu** *(yuu-sen kah-buu)*

preferred tariff 特恵関税 **tokkei kanzei** *(toke-kay kahn-zay)*

preliminary prospectus 仮趣意書 **kari shui sho** *(kah-ree shuu-ee show)*

premium 保険料 **hoken ryō** *(hoe-ken rio)*

premium payment 保険料支払 **hoken ryō shiharai** *(hoe-ken rio she-hah-rye)*

prepay 前払いする **maebarai suru** *(my-bah-rye sue-rue)*

prescription (medical) 処方箋 **shohō-sen** *(show-hoe-sen)*

presence 影響力 **eikyō ryoku** *(ay-ee-k'yoe-rio-kuu)*; 地位 **chii** *(chee-ee)*

presentation; lecture 講演 **kōen** *(koe-en)*; 講義 **kōgi** *(koe-ghee)*

presentation; contribution 寄贈 **kizō** *(kee-zoh)*

present condition 現状 **genjō** *(gen-joe)*

president (of a company) 社長 **shachō** *(shah-choe)*
▪ What is the president's name? 社長のお名前は。**Shachō no o-namae wa?** *(shah-choe no oh-nah-my wah?)*

press conference 記者会見 **kisha kaiken** *(kee-shah kie-ken)*
▪ Let's hold a press conference. 記者会見を行いましょう。**Kisha kaiken wo okonaimashō.** *(kee-shah kie-ken oh oh-koe-nie-mah-show.)*

pressure; oppression 圧迫 **appaku** *(ahp-pah-kuu)*

pre-tax loss/profit 経常損失／利益 **keijō sonshitsu/rieki** *(kay-joe soan-she-t'sue/ree-ay-kee)*

preventive maintenance 予防保全 **yobō hozen** *(yoe-boe hoe-zen)*

price (put price on) 値段をつける **nedan wo tsukeru** *(nay-dahn oh t'sue-kay-rue)*

price (value) 価格 **kakaku** *(kah-kah-kuu)*; 値段 **nedan** *(nay-dahn)*; original price 元値 **moto ne** *(moe-toe nay)*

price competition 価格競争 **kakaku kyōso** *(kah-kah-kuu k'yoe-so)*

price-cutting 値下げ **nesage** *(nay-sah-gay)*

price differential 価格格差 **kakaku kakusa** *(kah-kah-kuu kah-kuu-sah)*

price-earnings ratio 株価収益率 **kabuka shūeki ritsu** *(kah-buu-kah shuu-eh-kee ree-t'sue)*

price increase 値上げ **neage** *(nay-ah-gay)*

price index 物価指数 **bukka shisū** *(buuk-kah she-sue)*

price limit 指し値 **sashine** *(sah-she-nay)*

price list 価格表 **kakaku hyō** *(kah-kah-kuu h'yoe)*
▪ Let me see the price list. 価格表を見せて下さい。**Kakaku hyō wo misete kudasai.** *(kah-kah-kuu h'yoe wo me-say-tay kuu-dah-sigh.)*

price of goods 物価 **bukka** *(buu-kah)*

price range 価格帯 **kakaku tai** *(kah-kah-kuu tie)*

price support 価格維持 **kakaku iji** *(kah-kah-kuu e-jee)*

price war 値下げ競争 **nesage kyōsō** *(nay-sah-gay k'yoe-so)*

pride 誇り **hokori** *(hoe-koe-ree)*; プライド **puraido** *(puu-rye-doe)*
▪ He is a man of great pride. あの人はプライドが高いです。**Ano hito wa praido ga takai désu.** *(ah-no shtoe wah puu-rye-doe ga tah-kye dess.)*

primary market 主要市場 **shuyō shijō** *(shuu-yoe she-joe)*

primary reserves 第一支払い準備金 **dai ichi shiharai junbi kin** *(dye-ee-chee she-hah-rye juum-bee-keen)*

prime rate プライムレート **puraimu rēto** *(puu-rye-muu ray-toe)*

prime time プライムタイム **puraimu taimu** *(puu-rah-ee-muu tah-ee-muu)*; 最好調期 **sai kōchō ki** *(sigh koe-choe kee)*

principal (key individual) 本人 **hon nin** *(hone neen)*; 主役 **shuyaku** *(shoe-yah-kuu)*

principle 原則 **gensoku** *(gen-so-kuu)*; 主義 **shugi** *(shuu-ghee)*

print 印刷する **insatsu suru** *(een-sah-t'sue sue-rue)*

printed matter 印刷物 **insatsu butsu** *(een-sah-t'sue boot-sue)*
▪ Please send this (mail) as printed matter. これを印刷物扱いで送って下さい。**Kore wo insatsu butsu atsukai de okutte kudasai.** *(koe-ray oh een-sah-t'sue boot-sue day oh-coot-tay kuu-dah-sigh.)*

printer 印刷屋 **insatsuya** *(een-sah-t'sue-yah)*; プリンタ **purinta** *(puu-reen-tah)*

printout (computer) プリントアウト **purinto auto** *(puu-reen-toe out-oh)*

print-run (number of copies) 出版部数 **shuppan bussū** *(shuup-pahn buuse-sue)*

priority 優先権 **yūsen ken** *(yuu-sen ken)*

private (not public) 私用の **shiyō no** *(she-yohh no)*

private (personal) 個人 **kojin** *(koe-jeen)*
▪ Let's take a private taxi. 個人タクシーに乗りましょう。**Kojin takushii ni norimashō.** *(koe-jeen tahk-she nee no-ree-mah-show.)*

private label 自家商標 **jika shōhyō** *(jee-kah show-h'yoe)*; 自社ブランド **jisha burando** *(jee-shah brand)*

private management 民営 **minei** *(meen-eh-ee)*; 個人経営 **kojin keiei** *(koe-jeen kay-ee)*

private matter 私的な事 **shiteki na koto** *(she-tay-kee nah koe-toe)*; 私事 **watakushi goto** *(wah-tah-kuu-she goe-toe)*

private placement (of stock) 私募 **shibo** *(she-boe)*

private secretary 私設秘書 **shisetsu hisho** *(she-say-t'sue he-show)*

private sector 民間部門 **minkan bumon** *(meen-kahn buu-moe-n)*

privatization 民営化 **min-ei ka** *(meen-ay-ee kah)*
▪ In 2007 the Japan Post was privatized. 郵政公社は2007年に民営化されました。 **Yusei kōsha wa 2007 nen ni min-ei ka saremashita.** *(yuu-say kohh-shah wa 2007 nane nee meen-eh kah sah-ray-mah-shh-tah.)*

privilege 特典 **tokuten** *(toe-kuu-ten)*

prize 賞 **shō** *(show)*; 賞品 **shōhin** *(show-heen)*

problem (question) 問題 **mondai** *(moan-dye)*
▪ Is there a problem? 何か問題がありますか。 **Nani ka ondai ga arimasu ka?** *(nah-nee kah moan-dye gah ah-ree-mahss-kah?)*

problem analysis 問題分析 **mondai bunseki** *(moan-dye boon-say-kee)*

problem occurs 問題が起きる **mondai ga okiru** *(moan-dye gah oh-kee-rue)*

problem solving 問題解決 **mondai kaiketsu** *(moan-dye kye-kate-sue)*

procedure 手続き **tetsuzuki** *(tay-t'sue-zuu-kee)*
▪ How should I do the proper procedure? 正しい手続きはどのようにすべきですか。 **Tadashii tetsuzuki wa dono yō ni subeki désu ka?** *(tah-dah-shee tate-sue-zuu-kee wah doh-no yohh nee sue-bay-kee dess kah?)*

process 処理する **shori suru** *(show-ree sue-rue)*

procurement 調達 **chōtatsu** *(choe-tot-sue)*

produce 生産する **seisan suru** *(say-shan sue-rue)*; 製作する **seisaku suru** *(say-sah-kuu sue-rue)*

product 製品 **seihin** *(say-heen)*

product analysis 製品分析 **seihin bunseki** *(say-heen boon-say-kee)*

product design 製品設計 **seihin sekkei** *(say-heen sake-kay)*; 商品デザイン **shōhin dezain** *(show-heen design)*

product development 製品開発 **seihin kaihatsu** *(say-heen kye-hot-sue)*

product group 製品グループ **seihin gurūpu** *(say-heen guu-ruu-puu)*

production 生産 **seisan** *(say-sahn)*; 生産高 **seisandaka** *(say-sahn-dah-kah)*; 製作物 **seisakubutsu** *(say-sah-kuu-buu-t'sue)*

production control 生産管理 **seisan kanri** *(say-sahn kahn-ree)*
▪ Who is responsible for production control? 生産管理の責任者はどなたですか。 **Seisan kanri no sekinin sha wa donata désu ka?** *(say-sahn kahn-ree no say-kee-neen shah wah doe-nah-tah dess kah?)*

production costs 生産費 **seisan hi** *(say-sahn he)*; 製造原価 **seizō genka** *(say-zoe gen-kah)*

production line 流れ作業 **nagare sagyō** *(nah-gah-ray sah-g'yoe)*

production process 生産工程 **seisan kōtei** *(say-sahn koe-tay)*

production schedule 製造予定表 **seizō yotei hyō** *(say-zoe yoe-tay h'yoe)*

productivity 生産性 **seisan sei** *(say-sahn-say)*

product life 製品寿命 **seihin jumyō** *(say-heen juum-yoe)*

product line 製品種目 **seihin shumoku** *(say-heen shuu-moe-kuu)*

product management 製品管理 **seihin kanri** *(say-heen kahn-ree)*

profession 専門職 **senmon shoku** *(sen-moan-show-kuu)*

profit 利潤 **rijun** *(ree-june)*; 儲け **mōke** *(moe-kay)*; 収益 **shūeki** *(shuu-ay-kee)*; 利益 **rieki** *(ree-ay-kee)*

profitability 収益性 **shūeki sei** *(shuu-ay-kee say)*

profitability analysis 収益性分析 **shūeki sei bunseki** *(shuu-eh-kee-say boon-say-kee)*

profitable 有利な **yūri na** *(yuu-ree nah)*

profit and loss 損益 **soneki** *(soan-eh-kee)*

profit-and-loss statement 損益計算書 **son-eki keisan sho** *(soan-eh-kee kay-sahn show)*

profit forecast 収益予測 **shūeki yosoku** *(shuu-ay-kee yoe-so-kuu)*

profit increase 増益 **zōeki** *(zohh-eh-kee)*

profitless 利益のない **rieki no nai** *(ree-eh-kee no nigh)*

profit margin 利鞘 **rizaya** *(ree-zah-yah)*

profit point 採算ベース **saisan bēsu** *(sigh-sahn bay-sue)*

profit reduction 減益 **geneki** *(gane-eh-kee)*

profit sharing 利潤分配 **rijun bunpai** *(ree-june boon-pie)*

profit-taking 利食い **rigui** *(ree-gooey)*

pro forma invoice 見積り送り状 **mitsumori okurijō** *(meet-sue-more-ree oh-kuu-ree-joe)*
▪ Please send a pro forma invoice. 見積り送り状を送って下さい。**Mitsumori okurijō wo okutte kudasai.** *(meet-sue-more-ree oh-kuu-ree-joe oh oh-kuu-tay kuu-dah-sigh.)*

pro forma statement 見積り財務諸表 **mitsumori zaimu shohyō** *(meet-sue-more-ree zah-ee-moe show-h'yoe)*

program (plan) 計画 **keikaku** *(kay-kah-kuu)*

program (computer) プログラム **puroguramu** *(puu-roe-guu-rah-muu)*

progress 進歩 **shinpo** *(sheem-poe)*; make progress 進歩する **shinpo suru** *(sheem-poe sue-rue)*; 上達する **jōtatsu suru** *(joe-tot-sue sue-roe)*; go ahead, go forward 進む **susumu** *(sue-sue-muu)*

prohibited 禁止 **kinshi** *(keen-she)*

prohibited goods 禁制品 **kinsei hin** *(keen-say heen)*

project 企画 **kikaku** *(kee-kah-kuu)*; 事業 **jigyō** *(jee-g'yoe)*
▪ Are you working on a new project now? 今新しい企画をやっていますか。**Ima atarashii kikaku wo yatte imasu ka?** *(ee-mah ah-tah-rah-she kee-kah-ku oh yaht-tay ee-mahss kah?)*

projector 映写機 **eisha-ki** *(eh-shah-kee)*

project proposal in writing 稟議書 **ringi sho** *(reen-ghee show)*

promise (appointment) 約束 **yakusoku** *(yah-kuu-so-kuu)*

promissory note 約束手形 **yakusoku tegata** *(yah-kuu-so-kuu tay-gah-tah)*

promote (to higher position/rank) 昇進させる **shōshin saseru** *(show-sheen sah-say-rue)*

promotion 昇進 **shōshin** *(show-sheen)*
▪ Congratulations on your promotion. ご昇進おめでとうございます。**Go-shōshin omedetō gozaimasu.** *(go-show-sheen oh-may-day-toe go-zye-mahss)*

promotion for sales 販売促進 **hanbai sokushin** *(hahn-by so-kuu-sheen)*; 振興 **shinkō** *(sheen-koe)*

prompt answer 速答 **sokutō** *(so-kuu-toe)*

prompt decision 速断 **sokudan** *(so-kuu-dahn)*

proof 確証 **kakushō** *(kah-kuu-show)*; 証拠 **shōko** *(show-koe)*

proof of loss 損害証明書 **songai shōmei sho** *(soan-guy show-may-show)*

proofread 校正する **kōsei suru** *(koe-say sue-rue)*

proofreading 校正 **kōsei** *(koe-say)*

property 財産 **zaisan** *(zye-sahn)*

proposal (proposition) 提案 **teian** *(tay-ahn)*; 申し込み **mōshikomi** *(moe-she-koe-me)*

proprietary 所有者の **shoyū sha no** *(show-yuu shah no)*

proprietary rights 所有権 **shoyū ken** *(show-yuu ken)*

proprietor 所有者 **shoyū sha** *(show-yuu shah)*

prospect (outlook) 見通し **mitōshi** *(me-toe-she)*

prospective client 見込み客 **mikomi kyaku** *(me-koe-me k'yack-uu)*

prospectus 趣意書 **shui sho** *(shuu-ee show)*; 案内書 **annai sho** *(ahn-nie show)*
▪ May I see your business prospectus? 事業案内を拝見してもよろしいですか。**Jigyō annai wo haiken shite mo yoroshii désu ka?** *(jeeg-yoh ahn-nie oh hi-kane ssh-tay-moh yoh-roh-shee dess kah?)*

prosperity 繁栄 **han'ei** *(hahn-eh)*; to thrive 隆盛な **ryūsei na** *(r'yuu-say nah)*

protectionism 保護貿易主義 **hogo bōeki shugi** *(hoe-go boe-eh-kee shuu-ghee)*

protective tariff 保護関税 **hogo kanzei** *(hoe-go kahn-zay)*

provocative 刺激的 **shigeki-teki** *(she-gay-kee-tay-kee)*

prove (verify) 証明する **shōmei suru** *(show-may sue-rue)*

provider プロバイダー **purobaidā** *(provider)*

provision 規定 **kitei** *(kee-tay)*; 条項 **jōkō** *(joe-koe)*

proxy 代理 **dairi** *(dye-ree)*

proxy statement 委任状 **inin jō** *(ee-neen joe)*

public 公 **ōyake** *(oh-yah-kay)*; 公共 **koukyuo** *(koe-k'yoe-uu)*

publication 出版 **shuppan** *(shuup-pahn sha)*; 出版物 **shuppan butsu** *(shuup-pahn buu-t'sue)*

public auction 競売 **kyōbai** *(k'yoe-by)*; 公売 **kōbai** *(koe-by)*

public domain (patent) 権利消滅状態 **kenri shōmetsu jōtai** *(ken-ree show-mate-sue joe-tie)*

public funds 公金 **kōkin** *(koe-keen)*

public investment 公共投資 **kōkyō tōshi** *(koe-k'yoe toe-she)*

publicity 宣伝 **senden** *(sen-den)*

public offering 公募 **kōbo** *(koe-boe)*

public opinion poll 世論調査 **yoron chōsa** *(yoe-roan choe-sah)*

public property 公有財産 **kōyū zaisan** *(koe-yuu zye-sahn)*

public relations 渉外活動 **shōgai katsudō** *(show-guy kah-t'sue-doe)*; PR活動 **pii-āru katsudō** *(pee-ah-rue kah-t'sue-doe)*

public relations department 広報部（室／課）**kōhō bu(shitsu/ka)** *(koe-hoe buu (sht'sue/kah)*

public utilities 公益事業 **kōeki jigyō** *(koe-ay-kee jee-g'yoe)*

public works 公共事業 **kōkyō jigyō** *(koe-k'yoe jee-g'yoe)*

publish 発行する **hakkō suru** *(hock-koh sue-rue)*; 出版する **shuppan suru** *(shuup-pahn sue-rue)*

publisher 出版社 **shuppansha** *(shuup-pahn-shah)*

pulse パルス **parusu** *(pah-rue-sue)*; 脈 **myaku** *(m'yah-kuu)*

punishment; sanction 制裁 **seisai** *(say-sie)*

purchase 購入する **kōnyū suru** *(cone-yuu sue-rue)*; 買う **kau** *(cow)*

purchase order 発注書 **hatsuchu sho** *(hot-chew-chuu show)*

purchase order (for securities) 買い注文 **kai chūmon** *(kye chew-moan)*

purchase price 仕入れ価格 **shi-ire kakaku** *(she-ee-ray kah-kah-kuu)*

purchasing agent 購買担当者 **kōbai tantōsha** *(koe-by tan-toe shah)*

purchasing manager 購買主任 **kōbai shunin** *(koe-by shuu-neen)*

purchasing power 購買力 **kōbai ryoku** *(koe-by rio-kuu)*

pyramid selling マルチ商法 **maruchi shōhō** *(mah-rue-chee show-hoe)*

Q

qualifications 資格 **shikaku** *(she-kah-kuu)*

quality 品質 **hinshitsu** *(heen-sheet-sue)*
▪ Quality is very important to Japanese consumers. 日本の消費者にとって品質は大切なことです。**Nihon no shōhi sha ni totte hinshitsu wa taisetsu na koto désu.** *(nee-hone no show-he shah ni tote-tay heen-sheet-sue wa tie-say-t'sue nah koe-toe dess.)*

quality control 品質管理 **hinshitsu kanri** *(heen-sheet-sue kahn-ree)*

quality control circle QCサークル **kyū shii sākuru** *(cue she-ee sah-kuu-rue)*

quality goods 優良品 **yūryō hin** *(yuu-rio heen)*; 高級品 **kōkyū hin** *(koe-cue heen)*

quantity (number) 数量 **sūryō** *(sue-rio)*; (amount) 分量 **bunryō** *(boon-rio)*

quantity discount 数量割引 **sūryō waribiki** *(sue-rio wah-ree-bee-kee)*
▪ How many do I need to order to get a quantity discount? いくつ以上の注文で(数量)割引になりますか。**Ikutsu ijō no chūmon de (sūryō) waribiki ni narimasu ka?** *(ee-kute-sue ee-joh no chuu-moan day (suu-rio) wah-ree-bee-kee nee nah-ree-mahss kah?)*

quantity order 大量注文 **tairyō chūmon** *(tie-rio chew-moan)*

quarter (quarterly period) 四半期 **shihanki** *(she-hahn-kee)*

quarterly (publication) 季刊誌 **kikanshi** *(kee-kahn-she)*

quasi-public company 準公共企業体 **jun-kōkyō kigyō-tai** *(june-koe-k'yoe kee-g'yoe-tie)*

question 質問 **shitsumon** *(sheet-sue-moan)*
▪ Does anyone have any questions? 誰か質問がありますか。**Dare ka shitsumon ga arimasu ka?** *(dah-ray kah sheet-sue-moan gah ah-ree-mahss kah?)*

quit-claim deed 権利放棄(証書) **kenri hōki (shōsho)** *(ken-ree hoe-kee (show-show))*

quorum 定足数 **teisoku sū** *(tay-so-kuu sue)*

quota 割り当て **wariate** *(wah-ree-ah-tay)*

quota system 割当制 **wariate sei** *(wah-ree-ah-tay say)*

quotation 相場 **sōba** *(so-bah)*
▪ What is today's [market price] quotation? 今日の相場はなんですか。**Kyō no sōba wa nan désu ka?** *(k'yoe no so-bah wah nahn dess kah?)*

quotation (estimate) 見積(書) **mitsumori (sho)** *(meet-sue-moh-ree-shoh)*
▪ Please submit a written quotation by tomorrow afternoon. 明日の午後までに見積書を提出してください。**Asu no gogo made ni mitsumori sho wo teishutsu shite kudasai.** (*ah-sue no go-go mah-day nee meet-sue-moh-ree-shoh oh tay-shoot-sue ssh-tay kuu-dah-sie.*)

R

race (contest) 競争 **kyōsō** *(k'yoe-so)*

race (human) 人種 **jinshu** *(jeen-shuu)*

radar レーダー **rēdā** *(ray-dah)*

radial tire ラジアルタイヤ **rajiaru taiya** *(rah-jee-ah-rue tie-yah)*

radiator ラジエーター **rajiētā** *(rah-jee-eh-tah)*

radio ラジオ **rajio** *(rah-jee-oh)*

radioactive 放射性(の) **hōshasei (no)** *(hohh-shah-say)*

radio cassette player ラジカセ **rajikase** *(rah-jee-kah-say)*

railroad 鉄道 **tetsudō** *(tay-t'sue-doe)*

rail shipment 鉄道輸送 **tetsudō yusō** *(tay-t'sue-doe yuu-so)*

railway(s), private 私鉄 **shitetsu** *(she-tate-sue)*

rain check 引換券 **hikikae ken** *(he-kee-kye ken)*; 振替券 **furikae ken** *(fuu-ree-kye ken)*; 延期 **enki** *(ayn-kee)*

raise 上げる **ageru** *(ah-gay-rue)*

raise capital 資金調達 **shikin chōtatsu** *(she-keen choe-tot-sue)*

raise; grow (crops) 栽培する **saibai suru** *(sigh-by sue-rue)*
▪ Are soybeans raised in Japan? 日本で大豆を栽培していますか。**Nihon de daizu wo saibai shite imasu ka?** *(nee-hone day dye-zuu oh sigh-by shtay-mahss kah?)*

raise; grow (child) 育つ **sodatsu** *(so-dah-t'sue)*
▪ Where were you raised? どこで育ちましたか。**Doko de sodachimashita ka?** *(doe-koe day so-dye-chee-mahsh-tah kah?)*

rally 本当 **hantō** *(hahn-toe)*

rally, recovery (recovery rally) (in stock prices) 反騰相場 **hantō sōba** *(hahn-toe so-bah)*

Random Access Memory (RAM) ランダムアクセスメモリー **randamu akusesu memorii** *(rahn-dah-muu ah-kuu-say-sue may-moe-ree)*; RAM **RAMU** *(rah-muu)*
▪ How much RAM does this computer have? このコンピュータはどのぐらいのRAMがありますか? **Kono konpyūta wa dono gurai no RAMU ga arimasu ka?** *(koh-no kome-p'yuu-tah wah doh-no guu-rie rah-muu gah ah-ree-mahss kah?)*

random sample 無作為抽出見本 **musakui chūshutsu mihon** *(muu-sah-kuu-ee chew-shoot-sue me-hone)*; ランダムサンプル **randamu sanpuru** (*rahn-dah-muu sahn-puu-rue)*

rank (military) 階級 **kaikyū** *(kye-cue)*

rate 率 **ritsu** *(ree-t'sue)*; 割合 **wariai** *(wah-ree-eye)*

rate of exchange 為替相場 **kawase sōba** *(kah-wah-say so-bah)*

rate of growth 成長率 **seichō ritsu** *(say-choe ree-t'sue)*
▪ That company's rate of growth has expanded rapidly. その会社の成長率は急速に伸びています。**Sono kaisha no seichō ritsu wa kyūsoku ni nobite imasu.** *(soh-no kie-shah no say-chohh reet-sue way k'yuu-soh-kuu nee no-bee-tay ee-mahss.)*

rate of increase 増加率 **zōka ritsu** *(zoe-kah ree-t'sue)*

rate of interest 利率 **ri ritsu** *(ree ree-t'sue)*

rate of return 収益率 **shūeki ritsu** *(shuu-eh-kee ree-t'sue)*

ratio 比率 **hiritsu** *(he-ree-t'sue)*

ration 配給する **haikyū suru** *(high-cue sue-rue)*

raw materials 原材料 **gen zairyō** *(gen zye-rio)*

reaction (response) 反応 **hannō** *(hahn-no)*
▪ I kept talking while watching her reaction. 私は、彼女の反応を見ながら話し続けた。**Watashi wa kanojo no hannō wo minagara hanashi tsuzuketa.** *(wah-tock-she wah kah-no-joh no hahn-no oh me-nah-gah-rah hah-nah-she t'sue-zuu-kay-tah.)*

reactor (atomic) 原子炉 **genshiro** *(gane-she-roh)*

reading 数値 **sūchi** *(suu-chee)*; 指標 **shihyō** *(she-h'yoe)*

ready cash 即金払い **sokkin barai** *(soak-keen bah-rye)*

ready-to-wear 既製服 **kisei fuku** *(kee-say fuu-kuu)*

real estate 不動産 **fudōsan** *(fuu-doe-sahn)*

real income 実質所得 **jisshitsu shotoku** *(jee-sheet-sue show-toe-koe)*

reality 現実 **genjitsu** *(gane-jee-t'sue)*

real price 実質価格 **jisshitsu kakaku** *(jee-sheet-sue kah-kah-kuu)*

real thing (genuine) 現物 **genbutsu** *(gane-boot-sue)*

real time リアルタイム **rearu taimu** *(ray-ah-rue tie-muu)*

real wages 実質賃金 **jisshitsu chingin** *(jee-sheet-sue cheen-gheen)*

reasonable care 相当な注意 **sōtō na chūi** *(so-toe nah chew-ee)*

reassignment; reshuffle 配置転換

haichi tenkan *(hi-chee ten-kahn)*; 配転 **haiten** *(hi-tane)*

rebate 割り戻し **wari modoshi** *(wah-ree moe-doe-she)*; リベート **ribēto** *(ree-bay-ee-toe)*

rebate on sales 払い戻し **harai modoshi** *(hah-rye moe-doe-she)*

rebound 回復する **kaifuku suru** *(kye-fuu-kuu sue-rue)*

recapitalization 資本再構成 **shihon saikōsei** *(she-hone sigh-koe-say)*

receipt 受領書 **juryō shō** *(juu-rio-sho)*; 領収書 **ryōshū sho** *(rio-shuu show)*
▪ A receipt, please. 領収書お願いします。**Ryōshū shō onegai shimasu.** *(rio-shuu show oh-nay-guy she-mahss.)*

reception レセプション **resepushon** *(ree-sep-shone)*

recession 景気後退 **keiki kōtai** *(kay-kee koe-tie)*

rechargeable 充電式の **jūden shiki no** *(juu-den she-kee no)*

reciprocal trade 互恵貿易 **gokei bōeki** *(go-kay boe-eh-kee)*

recommend 推薦する **suisen suru** *(sue-ee-sen sue-rue)*
▪ Can you recommend that company? その会社を推薦できますか。**Sono kaisha wo suisen dekimasu ka?** *(so-no kye-shah oh sue-ee-sen day-kee-mahss kah?)*

record player レコードプレーヤー **rekōdo purēyā** *(ray-koe-doe puu-ray-yah)*

recovery (economic) 回復 **kaifuku** *(kye-fuu-kuu)*

recovery of expenses 費用の回収 **hiyō no kaishū** *(he-yoe-no kuy-shuu)*

recruitment 求人 **kyūjin** *(k'yuu-jeen)*; 採用 **saiyō** *(sigh-yoe)*

rectifier 整流器 **seiryū-ki** *(say-r'yuu-kee)*

recur 繰返す **kurikaesu** *(kuu-ree-kye-sue)*

recycle リサイクルする **risaikuru suru** *(ree-sie-kuu-ruu sue-rue)*

redemption 償還 **shōkan** *(show-kahn)*; 解約 **kaiyaku** *(kye-yah-kuu)*

red figure (as in the red) 赤字 **aka ji** *(ah-kah jee)*

red tape お役所仕事 **o-yakusho shigoto** *(oh-yahk-show she-go-toe)*; 形式主義 **keishikishugi** *(kay-she-kee-shuu-ghee)*

re-export 再輸出 **sai-yushutsu** *(sigh-yuu-shoot-sue)*

reference 証明書 **shōmei sho** *(show-may show)*

reference, for your (for your reference) ご参考までに **go-sankō made ni** *(go-sahn-koe mah-day nee)*

reference number 整理番号 **seiri bangō** *(say-ree bahn-go)*

refinance リファイナンス **rifainansu** *(ree-fie-nahn-sue)*; 借り換え **kari kae** *(kah-ree kah-ay)*

reflex camera リフレックスカメラ **refurekkusu kamera** *(ray-fuu-rake-suu kah-may-rah)*

refund 払い戻し **harai modoshi** *(hah-rye moe-doe-she)*; 返金 **henkin** *(hen-kin)*
▪ I have not yet received a refund. まだ返金してもらっていません。**Mada henkin shitemorattemasen.** *(mah-dah hen-kin shtay-moe-rah-tay-mah-sen.)*

refuse acceptance 引き受けを拒絶する **hikiuke wo kyozetsu suru** *(he-kee-uu-kay oh k'yoe-zay-t'sue sue-rue)*

refuse payment 支払いを拒絶する

shiharai wo kyozetsu suru *(she-hah-rye oh k'yoe-zay-t'sue sue-rue)*

register (patent, etc.) 登録する **tōroku suru** *(toe-roe-kuu sue-rue)*

registered agent 顧客係 **kokyaku gakari** *(koe-k'yah-kuu gah-kah-ree)*

registered check 登録小切手 **tōroku kogitte** *(toe-roe-kuu koe-gheet-tay)*

registered design 登録意匠 **tōroku ishō** *(toe-roe-kuu ee-show)*

registered mail 書留郵便 **kakitome yūbin** *(kah-kee-toe-may yuu-bean)*

registered securities 記名証券 **kimei shōken** *(kee-may show-ken)*

registered trademark 登録商標 **tōroku shōhyō** *(toe-roe-kuu show-h'yoe)*

registration 登録 **tōroku** *(toe-roe-kuu)*
▪ Have you completed the registration for the trademark of the new product? 新製品の商標登録は済みましたか。**Shin seihin no shōhyō tōroku wa sumimashita ka?** *(sheen say-heen no shohh-h'yohh toe-roe-kuu wah sue-me-mah-ssh-tah kah?)*

regular pay 基本給 **kihon kyū** *(kee-hone cue)*

regulation 規則 **kisoku** *(kee-so-kuu)*

regulation (control) 規定 **kitei** *(kee-tay)*

regulations (prospectus) 規則書 **kisoku sho** *(kee-so-kuu show)*

rehabilitation 回復 **kaifuku** *(kye-fuu-kuu)*; 再建 **saiken** *(sigh-ken)*

reimburse 払い戻す **harai modosu** *(hah-rye moe-doe-sue)*

re-insurer 再保険者 **sai-hoken sha** *(sigh-hoe-ken shah)*

relationship 関係 **kankei** *(kahn-kay)*

remainder (sell off at discount) たたき売り **tataki uri** *(tah-tah-kee uu-ree)*

remedy (medical) 治療法 **chiryō hō** *(chee-rio hoe)*

reminder 催促状 **saisoku jō** *(sigh-so-kuu joe)*
▪ The reminder from the bank came late. 銀行からの催促状が送られてきました。**Ginko kara no saisoku jō ga okurarete kimashita.** *(gheen-koe kah-rah no sie-soe-kuu johh gah oh-kuu-rah-ray-tay kee-mah-ssh-tah.)*

remission of tax 税免除 **zei menjo** *(zay men-joe)*; 免税 **menzei** *(men-zay)*

remit money 送金する **sōkin suru** *(so-keen sue-rue)*
▪ I will remit the money tomorrow. 明日送金します。**Ashita sōkin shimasu.** *(ah-shtah so-keen she-mahss.)*

remittance 送金 **sōkin** *(so-keen)*

remodel 改造する **kaizō suru** *(kye-zoe sue-rue)*; モデルチェンジする **moderu chenji suru** *(moe-day-rue chen-jee sue-rue)*

remote control リモートコントロール **rimōto kontorōru** *(ree-moe-toe cone-toe-roe-rue)*; remote controller リモコン **rimokon** *(ree-moe-kon)*

remuneration 報酬 **hōshū** *(hoe-shuu)*

renegotiate 再交渉する **sai kōshō suru** *(sigh koe-show sue-rue)*
▪ I want to renegotiate my contract. 契約を再交渉したいです。**Keiyaku wo saikōshō shitai désu.** *(kay-yah-kuu oh sigh-koe-show she-tie dess.)*

renew (subscription) 継続する **keizoku suru** *(kay-zoe-kuu sue-rue)*; 更新する **kōshin suru** *(koe-sheen sue-rue)*

renewal (renovate) 更新 **kōshin** *(koe-sheen)*

renew contract 契約を更新する **keiyaku wo kōshin suru** *(kay-yah-kuu oh koe-sheen sue-rue)*

rent (obtain for a fee) 借りる **kariru** *(kah-ree-rue)*; rent paid for living quarters 家賃 **yachin** *(yah-cheen)*

rental (rented house) 借家 **shaku-ya** *(shah-kuu-yah)*; 貸家 **kashi-ya** *(kah-she-yah)*

rent received (by landlord) 賃貸料 **chin-tai ryō** *(cheen-tie rio)*

reorder 再注文する **sai-chūmon suru** *(sigh-chew-moan sue-rue)*

reorganize 再編成する **sai-hensei suru** *(sigh-hen-say sue-rue)*

repair 直す **naosu** *(nah-oh-sue)*

repairs 修理 **shūri** *(shuu-ree)*

repay 返済する **hensai suru** *(hen-sigh sue-rue)*

repeat order 再注文 **sai-chūmon** *(sigh-chew-moan);* 追加注文 **tsuika chūmon** *(t'sue-ee-kah chew-moan)*

replace 取り替える **torikaeru** *(toe-ree-kye-rue)*

replacement 取替え **torikae** *(toe-ree-kye)*

replacement costs 代替え費用 **daigae hiyō** *(dye-gye hee-yoe)*

replacement parts 交換部品 **kōkan buhin** *(koe-kahn buu-heen)*

report (written) 報告する **hōkoku sho** *(hoe-koe-kuu show)*

representative (agency, proxy) 代理(人) **dairi(nin)** *(dye-ree (neen))*; 代表者 **daihyōsha** *(dye-h'yoe shah)*

reproduction copy (for printing) 清刷り **kiyozuri** *(kee-yoe-zuu-ree)*

reproduction costs 再生産費 **sai-seisan hi** *(sigh-say-sahn he)*

reputation 評判 **hyōban** *(h'yoe-bahn)*; have a good reputation 評判が良い **hyōban ga ii** *(h'yoe-bahn gah ee)*
▪ Does he (that person) have a good reputation? その人は評判がいいですか。**Sono hito wa hyōban ga ii désu ka?** *(so-no shtoe wah h'yoe-bahn gah ee dess kah?)*

request for bid 入札請求 **nyūsatsu seikyū** *(n'yuu-sah-t'sue say-cue)*

requirement (demand; claim) 要求 **yōkyū** *(yoe-cue)*

requirements 必要条件 **hitsuyō jōken** *(heat-sue-yoe joe-ken)*
▪ Please write down your requirements. 必要条件を書いて下さい。**Hitsuyō jōken wo kaite kudasai.** *(heat-sue yoe joe-ken oh kye-tay kuu-dah-sigh.)*

requisition 請求 **seikyū** *(say-k'yuu)*

resale 転売 **tenbai** *(ten-by)*

resale price 再販価格 **sai-han kakaku** *(sigh-hahn kah-kah-kuu)*
▪ What is your resale price? 再販価格はいくらですか。**Sai-han kakaku wa ikura désu ka?** *(sigh-hahn kah-kah-kuu wah ee-kuu-rah dess kah?)*

research 研究 **kenkyū** *(ken-cue)*

research department (room) 研究室 **kenkyū shitsu** *(ken-cue sheet-sue)*

research and development (R&D) 研究開発 **kenkyū kaihatsu** *(ken-cue kye-hot-sue)*

research expenses 研究費 **kenkyū hi** *(ken-cue he)*

research institute 研究所 **kenkyū jo** *(ken-cue-joe)*

resell 再販する **saihan suru** *(sigh-hahn sue-rue)*

reservation 予約 **yoyaku** *(yoe-yah-kuu)*
▪ I want to confirm my reservations. 予約の確認をしたいです。**Yoyaku no kakunin wo shitai désu.** *(yoe-yah-kuu no kah-kuu-neen wo she-tie dess.)*

reserved (not aggressive or forward) 遠慮 **enryo** *(en-rio)*
▪ Don't be so shy (reserved). 遠慮しないで下さい。**Enryo shinaide kudasai.** *(en-rio she-nigh-day kuu-dah-sigh.)*

reserves (money) 準備金 **junbi kin** *(juum-bee keen)*

resident buyer 産地仕入れ人 **sanchi shiire nin** *(sahn-chee she-ee-ray neen)*

residents (inhabitants, population) 住民 **jūmin** *(juu-meen)*

resign 辞職する **jishoku suru** *(jee-show-kuu sue-rue)*
▪ Mr. Baker resigned last year. ベイカーさんは去年辞職しました 。**Beikā-san wa kyonen jishoku shimashita.** *(bay-kah-sahn wah k'yoe-nen jee-show-kuu she-mah-shtah.)*

resolution (legal declaration) 決議 **ketsugi** *(kate-sue-ghee)*

resort 行楽地 **kōrakuchi** *(koe-rah-kuu-chee)*

resources 資材 **shizai** *(she-zye)*; 資源 **shigen** *(she-gen)*

resources allocation 資源配分 **shigen haibun** *(she-gen high-boon)*

respect 尊敬する **sonkei suru** *(soan-kay sue-rue)*

response 返事 **henji** *(hen-jee)*
▪ I will wait for your response. あなたのご返事をお待ちします。**Anata no go-henji wo o-machi shimasu.** *(ah-nah-tah no go-hen-jee oh oh-mah-chee she-mahss.)*

responsibility 責任 **sekinin** *(say-kee-neen)*; take responsibility 責任を待つ **sekinin wo motsu** *(say-kee-neen oh moat-sue)*

responsible person 責任者 **sekinin sha** *(say-kee-neen shah)*
▪ Who is the responsible person? 責任者はどなたですか。**Sekinin sha wa donata désu ka?** *(say-kee-neen shah wah doe-nah-tah dess kah?)*

restrictions 制限 **seigen** *(say-gen)*; 規制 **kisei (***kee-say)*

restrictions on exports 輸出規制 **yushutsu kisei** *(yuu-shoot-sue kee-say)*

restrictions on imports 輸入規制 **yunyū kisei** *(yuun-yuu kee-say)*

restrictions on trade 貿易規制 **bōeki kisei** *(boe-eh-kee kee-say)*

restrictive labor practices 拘束的労働慣習 **kōsoku-teki rōdō kanshū** *(koe-so-kuu-tay-kee roe-doe kahn-shuu)*

restructure 再構成する **sai-kōsei suru** *(sigh-koe-say sue-rue)*; リストラする **risutora suru** *(ree-suu-toe-rah sue-rue)*

restructuring リストラ **risutora** *(ree-suu-toe-rah)*
▪ The number of companies undergoing restructuring has decreased. リストラによる失業者は減りました。**Risutora ni yoru shitsugyō sha wa herimashita.** *(ree-sue-toe-rah nee yoe-rue sheet-sue-ghee-yoh shah wah hay-ree-mah-ssh-tah.)*

results (consequences) 結果 **kekka** *(cake-kah)*
▪ Have the results come out (been announced)? 結果はもうでましたか。

Kekka wa mō demashita ka? *(kay-kah wah moe day-mah-shtah kah?)*

resumé (for job application) 履歴書 **rireki sho** *(ree-ray-kee show)*

retail dealer/outlet 小売店 **kouri ten** *(koe-uu-ree ten)*

retail merchandise 小売商品 **kouri shōhin** *(koe-uu-ree show-heen)*

retail price 小売価格 **kouri kakaku** *(koe-uu-ree kah-kah-kuu)*
▪ What is the retail price? 小売価格はいくらですか。**Kouri kakaku wa ikura désu ka?** *(koe-uu-ree kah-kah-kuu wah ee-kuu-rah dess kah?)*

retail sales 小売 **kouri** *(koe-uu-ree)*

retail sales tax 小売売上税 **kouri uriage zei** *(koe-uu-ree uu-ree-ah-gay zay)*

retail trade 小売業 **kouri gyō** *(koe-uu-ree g'yoe)*

retained earnings 留保利益 **ryūho rieki** *(r'yuu-hoe ree-ay-kee)*

retainer (fee) 顧問料 **komon ryō** *(koe-moan rio)*; コンサルタント料 **konsarutanto ryō** *(cone-sah-rue-tahn-toe rio)*

retire 退職する **taishoku suru** *(tie-shohh-kuu sue-rue)*; 引退する **intai suru** *(een-tie sue-rue)*

retirement; resignation 退職 **taishoku** *(tie-shohh-kuu)*

retirement age 定年 **teinen** *(tay-nane)*
▪ What is the retirement age (in your company)? 定年は何歳ですか。**Teinen wa nan-sai désu ka?** *(Tay-nane wah nahn-sigh dess kah?)*

retirement allowance 退職金 **taishoku kin** *(tie-show-kuu keen)*

retirement fund 退職基金 **taishoku kikin** *(tie-show-kuu kee-keen)*

retract 取り消す **torikesu** *(toe-ree-kay-sue)*

retroactive さかのぼって効力を発する **sakanobotte kōryoku wo hassuru** *(sah-kah-no-boat-tay koe-r'yoe-kuu oh hah-sue-rue)*

return; profit 利益 **rieki** *(ree-ay-kee)*; 収益 **shūeki** (*shuu-eh-kee)*

return; recovery; rebound (stock prices) 戻る **modoru** *(moh-doh-ruu)*

return on capital 資本収益(率) **shihon shūeki(ritu)** *(she-hone shuu-eh-kee (ree-t'sue))*

return on equity (ROE) 株主資本利益率 **kabushiki shihon rieki-ritsu** *(kah-buu she-kee-hon ree-ay-kee-ree-t'sue)*

return on investment 投資収益率 **tōshi shūeki-ritsu** *(toe-she shuu-eh-kee-ree-t'sue)*

return on sales 販売利益率 **hanbai rieki ritsu** *(hahn-by ree-ay-kee-ree-t'sue)*

returns (unsold products) 返品 **henpin** *(hen-peen)*

revenue 収入 **shūnyū** *(shuun-yuu)*; 収益 **shūeki** *(shuu-ay-kee)*

revenue bonds 歳入担保債 **sainyū tanpo sai** *(sigh-n'yuu tahn-poe sigh)*

revenue stamp 収入印紙 **shūnyū inshi** *(shuun-yuu een-she)*

revise 修正する **shūsei suru** *(shuu-say sue-rue)*; 訂正する **teisei suru** *(tay-say sue-rue)*; 改訂する **kaitei suru** *(kye-tay sue-rue)*
▪ You must revise this contract. この契約を修正しなければなりません。**Kono keiyaku wo shūsei shinakereba narimasen.** *(koe-no kay-yah-kuu oh shuu-say she-nah-kay-ray-bah nah-ree-mah-sen.)*

revise downward/upward 下方/上方修正する **kahō/johō shusei suru** *(kah-hoe/joe-hoe shuu-say sue-rue)*

revision (alteration) 改正 **kaisei** *(kye-say)*

revocable trust 撤回可能信託 **tekkai kanō shintaku** *(tech-kye kah-no sheen-tah-kuu)*

revolving credit リボルビング式借金 **revolving shiki shakkin** *(revolving she-kee shah-keen)*

revolving fund 回転資金 **kaiten shikin** *(kye-ten she-keen)*

revolving letter of credit 回転信用状 **kaiten shin'yō jō** *(kye-ten sheen-yoe joe)*

reward 報酬 **hōshū** *(hoe-shuu)*

rewrite 書き換え **kakikae** *(kah-kee-kye)*
▪ I will rewrite the agreement by next week. 来週までに協定書を書き換えます。**Raishū made ni kyōtei sho wo kakikaemasu.** *(rye-shuu mah-day nee k'yoe-tay show oh kah-kee-kye-mahss.)*

rich 裕福な **yūfuku na** *(yuu-fuu-kuu nah)*
▪ Mr. Saito is very rich. 佐藤さんは、とても裕福です。**Saito-san wa totemo yūfuku désu.** *(sigh-toe-sahn wah toe-tay-moe yuu-fuu-kuu dess.)*

rider (stipulation on contract) 付帯条項 **futai jōkō** *(fuu-tie joe-koe)*

right of recourse 償還請求権 **shōkan seikyū ken** *(show-kahn say-cue ken)*

rise あげる **agaru** *(ah-gah-rue)*

rise in prices 値上げ **neage** *(nay-ah-gay)*
▪ There has been a rise in prices. 値上げがありました。**Neage ga arimashita.** *(nay-ah-gay gah ah-ree-mah-shtah.)*

risk (danger) 危険 **kiken** *(kee-kane)*

risk analysis 危険分析 **kiken bunseki** *(kee-kane boon-say-kee)*

risk assessment 危険査定 **kiken satei** *(kee-kane sah-tay)*; リスク評価 **risuku hyōka** *(risk h'yoe-kah)*

risk capital 危険資本 **kiken shihon** *(kee-kane she-hone)*

risk management 危機管理 **kiki kanri** *(kee-kee kahn-ree)*

rollback 物価引下げ **bukka hikisage** *(buu-kah he-kee-sah-gay)*

rolling stock 全車両 **zen sharyō** *(zen shah-rio)*

roll-over (money) 繰り越し **kurikoshi** *(kuu-ree-koe-she)*

ROM ROM **ROMU** *(roe-muu)*; 読み出し専用メモリ **yomidashi senyō memorii** *(yoe-me-dah-she sen-yoe may-moe-ree)*

rough draft 下書き **shita gaki** *(shtah gah-kee)*

rough estimate 概算見積書 **gaisan mitsumori sho** *(guy-sahn meet-sue-moe-ree show)*

round 会議 **kaigi** *(kye-gee)*; ラウンド **raundo** *(rah-uun-doe)*

routine work 決まりきった仕事 **kimarikitta shigoto** *(kee-mah-ree she-go-toe)*; 通常業務 **tsūjō gyōmu** *(t'sue-joe g'yoe-muu)*

royalty (income from literary work, etc.) 印税 **inzei** *(een-zay)*

royalty from patent 特許権使用料 **tokkyo ken shiyō ryō** *(toke-k'yoe ken she-yoe rio)*

rule (regulation) 規則 **kisoku** *(kee-so-kuu)*

rules of employment 就業規則 **shūgyō**

kisoku *(shuu-g'yoe kee-so-kuu)*
▪ All employees must abide by the rules of employment. 全社員は就業規則にサインしなければなりません。**Zen shain wa shūgyō kisoku ni sain shinakereba narimasen.** *(zen shah-een wah shuu-g'yoe kee-so-kuu nee sign she-nah-kay-ray-bah nah-ree-mah-sen.)*

run short (of supplies/goods) 不足する **fusoku suru** *(fuu-so-kuu sue-rue)*

rush 急ぐ **isogu** *(ee-so-guu)*; 殺到する **sattō suru** *(sat-toe sue-rue)*

rush order 急ぎの注文 **isogi no chūmon** *(ee-so-ghee no chew-moan)*
▪ This is a rush order. これは急ぎの注文です。**Kore wa isogi no chūmon désu.** *(koe-ray wah ee-so-ghee no chew-moan dess.)*

S

safe; safety 安全 **anzen** *(ahn-zen)*

safe-deposit box 貸し金庫 **kashi kinko** *(kah-she keen-koe)*
▪ Please put this in the safe-deposit box. これを貸し金庫に入れてください。**Kore wo kashi kinko ni irete kudasai.** *(koe-ray wah kah-she keen-koe nee ee-ray-tay kuu-dah-sigh.)*

safeguard (protection) 保護 **hogo** *(hoe-go)*

safely 無事に **buji ni** *(buu-jee nee)*

salaried worker サラリーマン **sarariiman** *(sah-rah-ree-mahn)*

salary (monthly) 月給 **gekkyū** *(gay-cue)*; 給料 **kyūryō** *(cue-rio)*; サラリー **sararii** *(sah-rah-ree)*; salary increase 昇給する **shōkyū suru** *(show-cue sue-rue)*

salary based on efficiency, merit 能力給 **nōryoku-kyū** *(no-rio-kuu-cue)*

salary income 給与所得 **kyūyo shotoku** *(k'yuu-yoe show-toe-kuu)*

sale 売り出し **uridashi** *(uu-ree-dah-she)*; セール **sēru** *(say-rue)*

sales 販売 **hanbai** *(hahn-by)*; sales (by volume) 売上げ **uriage** *(uu-ree-ah-gay)*

sales analysis 販売分析 **hanbai bunseki** *(hahn-by boon-say-kee)*

sales budget 販売予算 **hanbai yosan** *(hahn-by yoe-sahn)*
▪ The sales budget will be finished by Friday. 販売予算は金曜日までに出来上がります。**Hanbai yosan wa kin'yōbi made ni dekiarimasu.** *(hahn-by yoe-sahn wah keen-yoe-bee mah-day nee day-kee-ah-gah-ree-mahss.)*

sales engineer セールスエンジニア **sērusu enjinia** *(say-rue-sue en-jee-nee-ah)*

sales estimate 予想売上高 **yosō uriage daka** *(yoe-so uu-ree-ah-gay dah-kah)*; 売上げ見積もり **uriage mitsumori** *(uu-ree-ah-gay me-t'sue-moe-ree)*

sales force 販売員 **hanbai in** *(hahn-by een)*

sales forecasts 販売予測 **hanbai yosoku** *(hahn-by yoe-so-kuu)*

sales incentives 販売促進策 **hanbai sokushin saku** *(hahn-by so-kuu-sheen sah-kuu)*

sales management 販売管理 **hanbai kanri** *(hahn-by kahn-ree)*

sales promotion 販売促進 **hanbai sokushin** *(hahn-by so-kuu-sheen)*

sales quota 販売割り当て **hanbai wariate** *(hahn-by wah-ree-ay-tay)*; 販売ノルマ **hanbai noruma** *(hahn-by noh-rue-mah)*

sales tax 売上税 **uriage zei** *(uu-ree-ah-gay zay)*; 消費税 **shōhi zei** *(show-he zay)*

sales territory 販売地域 **hanbai chiiki** *(hahn-by chee-ee-kee)*

sales turnover 総売上高 **sō uriage daka** *(so uu-ree-ah-gay dah-kah)*

sales volume 販売量 **hanbai ryō** *(hahn-by rio)*; 売上高 **uriage daka** *(uu-ree-ah-gay dah-kah)*

salvage 回収する **kaishū suru** *(kye-shuu sue-rue)*

salvage charges 海難救助費 **kainan kyūjo hi** *(kye-nahn cue-joe he)*

sample 見本 **mihon** *(mee-hone)*; take a sample 見本をとる **mihon wo toru** *(me-hone oh toe-rue)*

sample line 見本種目 **mihon shumoku** *(me-hone shuu-moe-kuu)*

sample size 標本のサイズ **hyōhon no saizu** *(h'yoe-hone no sigh-zuu)*

sanctions 制裁 **seisai** *(say-sigh)*

satellite 衛星 **eisei** *(eh-ee-say-e)*

satellite broadband ブロードバンド衛星通信 **burōdobando eisei tsūshin** *(buu-roh-doh-bahn-doh aye-say t'sue-sheen)*
▪ The use of satellite broadband is spreading rapidly. ブロードバンド衛星通信はどんどん普及しています。**Burōdobando eisei tsūshin wa dondon fukyū shiteimasu.** *(broad-bahn-doh eh-ee-say t'sue-sheen wah doan-doan fuu-k'yuu shtay-mahss.)*

sauna bath サウナ **sauna** *(sah-uu-nah)*; 蒸し風呂 **mushi buro** *(muu-she buu-roe)*

save (put money into a checking account) 貯金する **chokin suru** *(choe-keen sue-rue)*

saving 倹約 **ken-yaku** *(ken-yah-kuu)*; 節約 **setsuyaku** *(say-t'sue yah-kuu)*

savings 貯蓄 **chochiku** *(choe-chee-kuu)*

savings account 普通預金 **futsū yokin** *(fuu-t'sue yoe-kee-n)*

savings bank 貯蓄銀行 **chochiku ginkō** *(choe-chee-kuu gheen-koe)*

savings bonds 貯蓄債券 **chochiku saiken** *(choe-chee-kuu sigh-ken)*

scandal 醜聞 **shūbun** *(shoo-boon)*; スキャンダル **sukyandaru** *(sue-k'yan-dah-rue)*

schedule 予定 **yotei** *(yoe-tay)*
▪ What is your schedule tomorrow? 明日の予定はいかがですか。**Ashita no yotei wa ikaga désu ka?** *(ah-shtah no yoe-tay wah ee-kah-gah dess kah?)*

schedule for production 生産日程 **seisan nittei** *(say-sahn neat-tay)*

scholarship 奨学金 **shōgakukin** *(show-gah-kuu-keen)*

school clique 学閥 **gaku batsu** *(gah-kuu bah-t'sue)*

scientist 科学者 **kagakusha** *(kah-gah-kuu-shah)*

screen スクリーン **sukurin** *(suu-kreen)*

screening 選別検査 **senbetsu kensa** *(sen-bait-sue ken-sah)*

scroll down/up スクロールダウン/アップ **sukurōru daun/appu** *(suu-kuu-roh down/ahp-puu)*
▪ To see all of the photos you must scroll down. 写真全体を見るにはスクロールダウンしなければなりません。**Shashin zentai wo miru niwa sukurōru daun shinakereba narimasen.** *(shah-sheen zen-tie oh me-ruu nee wah suu-kuu-roh-ruu*

down she-nah-kay-ray-bah nah-ree-mah-sen.)

seal (official registered name-stamp) 印鑑 **inkan** *(een-kahn)*; registered name stamp 実印 **jitsu-in** *(jeet-sue-een)*; regular name stamp 判子 **hanko** *(hahn-koe)*; sealed bid 封かん入札 **fūkan nyūsatsu** *(fuu-kahn n'yuu-sah-t'sue)*

search (investigate) 捜査 **sōsa** *(so-sah)*; 捜索 **sōsaku** *(so-sah-kuu)*; 捜す **sagasu** *(sah-gah-sue)*

seasonal 季節の **kisetsu no** *(kee-say-t'sue no)*

seat (in vehicle) 座席 **zaseki** *(zah-say-kee)*; シート **shiito** *(she-toe)*

seatbelt シートベルト **shiito beruto** *(she-toe bay-rue-toe)*

seat of honor (for guests or ranking people) 上座 **kamiza** *(kah-me-zah)*

secondary market 流通市場 **ryūtsū shijō** *(r'yuu-t'sue she-joe)*

secondary offering for securities 再売出し証券 **sai-uridashi shoken** *(sigh-uu-ree-dah-she show-kay-n)*

second-hand; used 中古 **chūko** *(chuu-koh)*

second mortgage 二次抵当 **niji teitō** *(nee-jee tay-toe)*

secret 秘密の **himitsu no** *(he-meet-sue no)*

secretary 秘書 **hisho** *(he-show)*

section (part of company) 課 **ka** *(kah)*

section chief/manager 課長 **kachō** *(kah-choe)*
▪ I have an appointment with the section manager Tanaka. 田中課長と約束しています。**Tanaka kachō to yakusoku shiteimasu.** *(tah-nah-kah kah-choe toe yahk-so-kuu shtay-mahss.)*

sector 部門 **bumon** *(buu-moan)*

secure; safe; safety 安全な **anzen (na)** *(ahn-zen nah)*

secured accounts 担保つき勘定 **tanpo tsuki kanjō** *(tahn-poe t'ski kahn-joe)*

secured liability 担保つき負債 **tanpo tsuki fusai** *(tahn-poe t'ski fuu-sigh)*

securities (bonds) 有価証券 **yūka shōken** *(yuu-kah show-ken)*

security セキュリティ **sekyuritii** *(say-cue-ree-tee)*
▪ My security filter is very good. 私のセキュリティのフィルターはとてもいいです。**Watakushi no sekyuritii no firuta wa totemo ii désu**. *(wah-tahk-she-no say-cue-ree-tee no fee-ruu-tah wa toe-tay-moe ee dess.)*

security (financial) 安全 **anzen** *(ahn-zen)*

security (mortgage, guarantee) 担保 **tanpo** *(tahn-poe)*; 抵当 **teitō** *(tay-toe)*

security pact 安全保障条約 **anzen hoshō jōyaku** *(ahn-zen hoe-show joe-yah-kuu)*

self-confidence 自信 **jishin** *(jee-sheen)*

self-declared bankruptcy 自己破産 **jiko hasan** *(jee-koe hah-sahn)*
▪ The number of people restoring to self-declared bankruptcy is increasing. 自己破産した人が増えている。**Jiko hasan shita hito ga fueteiru.** *(jee-koe hah-sahn shtah ssh-toe gah fway-tay-ee-rue.)*

self-employed 自営の **jiei no** *(jee-eh no)*

self-help efforts 自助努力 **jijo doryoku** *(jee-joe doe-rio-kuu)*

self-service セルフサービス **serufu sābisu** *(say-rue-fuu sah-bee-sue)*

sell 売る **uru** *(uu-rue)*; make a sale 売り込む **urikomu** *(uu-ree-koe-muu)*

sell direct 直売する **chokubai suru** *(choke-by sue-rue)*

sell-off 売却 **baikyaku** *(by-k'yaku)*; 処分 **shobun** *(show-buun)*

semiconductor 半導体 **handōtai** *(hahn-doe-tie)*

send (dispatch) 派遣する **haken suru** *(hah-ken sue-rue)*

senior in position 先輩 **senpai** *(sem-pie)*
▪ Is Mr. Kanda your senior? 神田さんはあなたの先輩ですか。**Kanda-san wa anata no senpai désu ka?** *(kahn-dah-sahn wah ah-nah-tah no sem-pie dess kah?)*

seniority (authority) 先任権 **sennin ken** *(sen-neen ken)*

seniority (long service) 年功 **nenkō** *(nane-kohh)*

seniority system 年功序列制 **nenkō joretsu sei** *(nane-koe joe-rate-sue say)*

sensational センセーショナル

sensor センサー **sensā** *(sen-sah)*

sequential control シーケンス制御 **shiikensu seigyo** *(she-ken-sue say-g'yoe)*

service (as in waiting on someone in a store) 取り扱い **toriatsukai** *(toe-ree-ah-t'sue-kye)*; サービス **sābisu** *(sah-bee-sue)*; service charge サービス料 **sābisu ryō** *(sah-bee-sue rio)*

service area allowance 勤務地手当 **kinmuchi teate** *(keen-muu-chee tay-ah-tay)*

service contract 定期点検契約 **teiki tenken keiyaku** *(tay-kee tane-kane kay-yah-kuu)*

session 立会 **tachi ai** *(tah-chee-aye)*

setback 失敗 **shippai** *(ship-pie)*; つまずき **tsumazuki** *(t'sue-mah-zuu-kee)*

settle accounts 決算する **kessan suru** *(case-sahn sue-rue)*; 清算する **seisan suru** *(say-sahn sue-rue)*

settlement (of accounts) 決算 **kessan** *(case-sahn)*

settlement 解決 **kaiketsu** *(kye-kate-sue)*

settlement in full 総決算 **sō kessan** *(so case-sahn)*

several いくつかの **ikutsuka no** *(ee-coot-sue-kah no)*

severance pay (retirement pay) 退職金 **taishoku kin** *(tie-show-kuu keen)*

shake-up 大改革 **daikaikaku** *(dye kye-kah-kuu)*

shape 形 **katachi** *(kah-tah-chee)*

share (stock) 株 **kabu** *(kah-buu)*; 株式 **kabushiki** *(kah-buu-she-kee)*
▪ I want to buy some Sony stock. ソニーの株を買いたいです。**Sony no kabu wo kaitai désu.** *(sony no kah-buu oh kye-tie dess.)*

shareholder 株主 **kabu nushi** *(kah-buu nuu-she)*

shareholder's equity 株主持分 **kabu nushi mochibun** *(kah-buu nuu-she moe-chee-boon)*; 自己資本 **jiko shihon** *(jee-koe she-hon)*

shareholder's meeting 株主総会 **kabu nushi sōkai** *(kah-buu nuu-she so-kye)*

share price 株価 **kabuka** *(kah-buu-kah)*

shift (take turns) 交代 **kōtai** *(koe-tie)*

shift work 交代制の仕事 **kōtai sei no shigoto** *(koe-tie say no she-go-toe)*

ship 出荷する **shukka suru** *(shuke-kah sue-rue)*; 発送する **hassō suru** *(hot-so sue-rue)*
▪ When will you ship that baggage? その荷物はいつ出荷しますか。**Sono nimotsu wa itsu shukka shimasu ka?** *(so-no nee-mote-sue wah eet-sue shuuk-kah she-mahss kah?)*

shipbuilding 造船 **zōsen** *(zohh-sen)*

ship fare; shipping cost 運賃 **unchin** *(uun-cheen)*

shipment 出荷 **shukka** *(shuke-kah)*

shipper 荷主 **ni nushi** *(nee nuu-she)*

shipping (forwarding) 出荷する **shukka suru** *(shuke-kah sue-rue)*

shipping agent 船会社代理店 **funagaisha dairiten** *(fuu-nah-guy-shah dye-ree-teen)*; 海運業者 **kaiun gyōsha** *(kye-uun g'yoe-shah)*

shipping charges 船積み費 **funazumi hi** *(fuu-nah-zuu-me he)*; 送料 **sōryō** *(so-rio)*; 輸送費 **yusō hi** *(yuu-so hee)*

shipping instructions 船積み指図書 **funazumi sashizu sho** *(fuu-nah-zuu-me sah-she-zuu show)*

shipping strike 海運ストライキ **kaiun sutoraiki** *(kye-uun sue-toe-rye-kee)*

shop (store) 店 **mise** *(me-say)*; stand, stall 売店 **baiten** *(by-ten)*

shopping 買い物 **kaimono** *(kye-moe-no)*; ショッピング **shoppingu** *(shope-peen-guu)*

shopping center ショッピングセンター **shoppingu sentā** *(shope-peen-guu sen-tah)*

shortage (deficiency) 不足 **fusoku** *(fuu-so-kuu)*

short delivery 短期取引 **tankitorihiki** *(tahn-kee toe-ree he-kee)*

short of 不足している **fusoku shiteiru** *(fuu-so-kuu shtay-rue)*

short selling 空売り **karauri** *(kah-rah uu-re)*

short shipment 積み残し品 **tsumi nokoshi hin** *(t'sue-me no-koe-she heen)*

short-term capital account 短期資本収入 **tanki shihon shūnyū** *(tahn-kee she-hone shuu-n'yuu)*

short-term debt 短期借入金 **tanki kariirekin** *(tahn-kee kah-ree-ee-ray keen)*

short-term financing 短期融資 **tanki yūshi** *(tahn-kee yuu-she)*

showroom ショールーム **shōrūm** *(show-room)*
▪ What time does the showroom open? ショールームは何時に開きますか。**Shōrūm wa nanji ni akimasu ka?** *(show-room wah nahn-jee nee ah-kee-mahss kah?)*

shrink-wrapping シュリンク包装 **shurinku hōsō** *(shuu-rin-kuu hoe-so)*

sick leave 傷病休暇 **shōbyō kyūka** *(show b'yoe cue-kah)*

sight draft 一覧払い為替手形 **ichiran barai kawase tegata** *(ee-chee-rahn bah-rye kah-wah-say tay-got-tah)*

sign; signature 署名 **shomei** *(show-may)*
▪ Where do I sign? どこに署名しますか。**Doko ni shomei shimasu ka?** *(doe-koe nee show-may she-mahss kah?)*

sign; symbol 印 **shirushi** *(she-ruu-*

she); シンボル **shimboru** *(sheem-boh-rue)*

signboard; just-in-time かんばん方式 **kanban hōshiki** *(kahn-bahn hoe-she-kee)*

silent partner 業務を担当しない社員 **gyōmu wo tantō shinai shain** *(g'yoe-muu oh tahn-toe she-nigh shah-een)*

simulate まねる **maneru** *(mah-nay-rue)*; シュミレート **shumirēto** *(shuu-me-ray-toe)*; 模擬実験 **mogi jikken** *(moe-gee jeek-ken)*

sing 歌う **utau** *(uu-tah-uu)*
- I will sing. 歌います。**Utaimasu.** *(uu-tie-mahss.)*
- Even when I'm drunk I can't sing. 酔っていても歌えません。**Yotteite mo utaemasen.** *(yote-tay ee-tay moe uu-tah-ay-mah-sen.)*

sinking fund 減債基金 **gensai kikin** *(gane-sigh kee-keen)*

site, website (internet) サイト **saito** *(sigh-toe)*; ホームページ **hōmu pēji** *(home page)*
- Please show me an interesting website. 面白いサイトを教えてください。**Omoshiroi saito wo oshiete kudasai.** *(oh-moe-she-roy sigh-toe oh oh-she-eh-tay kuu-dah-sie.)*

size サイズ **saizu** *(sigh-zuu)*

skilled labor 熟練した従業員 **jukuren shita jūgyōin** *(juu-kuu-ren she-tah juu-g'yoe-in)*; ベテラン社員 **beteran shain** *(bay-tay-run shah-in)*

slash 削減する **sakugen suru** *(sah-kuu-gen sue-rue)*

slide (photo) スライド **suraido** *(sue-rye-doe)*

slide projector スライド映写機 **suraido eisha-ki** *(sue-rye-doe eh-ee-shah-kee)*

sliding scale スライド制 **suraido sei** *(sue-rye-doe say)*

slogan スローガン **surōgan** *(suu-rohh-gahn)*

slot machine スロットマシン **surotto mashin** *(suu-rot-toh mah-sheen)*

slump 景気沈滞 **keiki chintai** *(kay-kee cheen-tie)*; 不景気 **fukeiki** *(fuu-kay-kee)*; 不況 **fukyō** *(fuu-k'yoe)*

small business 小企業 **shō kigyō** *(show kee-g'yoe)*

smartphone スマートフォン **sumātofon** *(suu-mah-toh-fone)*
- Is that a smartphone? それはスマートフォンですか。**Sore wa sumātofon désu ka?** *(soh-ray wah suu-mah-toh-fone dess kah?)*
- Windows Mobile is installed in smartphones. スマートフォンにはウィンドウズ・モバイルがインストールされています。**Sumātofon ni Windows Mobile ga instōru sarete imasu.** *(suu-mah-toh fone nee windows mobile ga enn-stoh-rue sah-ray-tay ee-mahss.)*

smoke (tobacco) タバコを吸う **tabako wo sū** *(tah-bah-koe oh-sue)*; No Smoking 禁煙 **kin'en** *(kee-en)*
- May I smoke in here? タバコを吸ってもいいですか。**Tabako wo sutte mo ii désu ka?** *(tah-bah-koe wo suu-tay moe ee dess kah?)*
- Would you please not smoke. I have an allergy. アレルギーなので、タバコはご遠慮願えますか。**Arerugii na no de, tabako wa go-enryo negaemasu ka?** *(ah-ray-rue-ghee nah no day tah-bah-koe wah go-en-rio nay-guy-mahss kah?)*

social expenses 交際費 **kōsai-hi** *(koe-sigh he)*

social insurance premium 社会保険料 **shakai hokenryō** *(shah-kye hoe-ken-rio)*

socialize おつきあいする **otsukiai suru** *(oat-ski-eye sue-rue)*

social security 社会保障 **shakai hoshō** *(shah-kie hoh-shohh)*

social security benefit 社会保障給付 **shakai hoshō kyūfu kin** *(shah-kye hoe-show k'yuu-fuu keen)*

social security system 社会保障制度 **shakai hoshō seido** *(shah-kye hoe-show say-doe)*

social welfare system 社会福祉制度 **shakai fukushi seido** *(shah-kye fuu-kuu-she say-doe)*

society (people in general) 社会 **shakai** *(shah-kie)*

socket (electrical) ソケット **soketto** *(soh-ket-toh)*

softcover (book) ソフトカバー **sofuto kabā** *(so-fuu-toe kah-bahh)*; ペーパーバック **pēpabakku** *(pay-pah back-kuu)*

soft goods 織物類 **orimono rui** *(oh-ree-moe-no rue-ee)*; 繊維製品 **sen'i seihin** *(sen-ee say-heen)*

soft loan ソフトローン **sofuto rōn** *(so-fuu-toe roan)*

soft sell 穏やかな商法 **odayaka na shōhō** *(oh-dah-yah-kah no show-hoe)*

software ソフトウェア **sofutowea** *(so-fuu-toe-way-ah)*

sole agent 総代理店 **sō dairiten** *(so dye-ree-ten)*
▪ Mitsui Norin is our sole agent. 三井農林は当社の総代理店です。**Mitsui Norin wa tōsha no sō dairiten désu.** *(meet-sue-ee-no-reen wah toe-shah no soh dye-ree-ten dess.)*

sole rights 独占権 **dokusen ken** *(doke-sen ken)*

solution 問題解決 **mondai kaiketsu** *(moan-dye kye-kay-t'sue)*; 解決法 **kaiketsu hō** *(kye-kay-t'sue hoe)*

solvency (financially) 支払能力 **shiharai nōryuku** *(she-hah-rye no-rio-kuu)*

source(s) 情報源 **jōhō gen** *(joe-hoe gen)*
▪ Which information sources were useful to you? どの情報源が利用しやすいですか。**Dono jōhō gen ga riyō shiyasuidésu ka?** *(doe-no johh-hohh gane gah ree-yohh she-yah-sue-ee dess kah?)*

South Africa 南アフリカ **Minami Afurika** *(me-nah-me Ah-fuu-ree-kah)*

South America 南アメリカ **Minami Amerika** *(me-nah-me Ah-may-ree-kah)*

soybeans 大豆 **daizu** *(dye-zuu)*
▪ Are you importing soybeans from America? アメリカから大豆を輸入していますか。**Amerika kara daizu wo yunyū shite imasu ka?** *(ah-may-ree-kah kah-rah dye-zuu oh yune-yuu shtay-mahss kah?)*

space (area) 空間 **kūkan** *(kuu-kahn)*; space (as in outer) 宇宙 **uchū** *(uu-chew)*

Spain スペイン **Supein** *(suu-pane)*

spam スパム **supamu** *(sue-pah-muu)*; 迷惑メール **meiwaku mēru** *(may-ee-wah-kuu may-rue)*
▪ Recently I've been receiving a lot of spam email. この頃たくさんの迷惑メールを受信しています。**Konogoro takusan no meiwaku mēru wo jushin shiteimasu.** *(koe-no-go-roe*

tah-kuu-sah-n no may-ee-wah-kuu may-rue oh juu-sheen shtay-mahss.)
▪ I am looking for some anti-spam software. 迷惑メール駆除ソフトを探しています。**Meiwaku mēru kujo sofuto wo sagashite imasu.** *(may-ee-wah-ku may-rue kuu-joe saw-fuu-toe oh sah-gah-shtay-mahss.)*

Spanish (person) スペイン人 **Supeinjin** *(suu-pane-jeen)*

speaker (electronic) スピーカー **supiikā** *(spee-kah)*

special 特殊 **tokushu** *(toke-shuu)*; 特別 **tokubetsu** *(toe-kuu-bait-sue)*

special characteristics (special points) 特徴 **tokuchō** *(toke-choe)*

special delivery mail 速達郵便 **sokutatsu yūbin** *(so-kuu-tot-sue yuu-been)*
▪ Please send this (mail) by special delivery. これを速達で送って下さい。**Kore wo sokutatsu de okutte kudasai.** *(koe-ray oh so-kuu-tot-sue day oh-kuu-tay kuu-dah-sigh.)*

special feature article 特集 **tokushū** *(toke-shuu)*

special idiosyncrasy 特性 **tokusei** *(toke-say)*; 特異性 **tokuisei** *(toke-ee-say)*

specialist 専門家 **senmonka** *(sem-moan-kah)*; specialize 専門的な **senmonteki na** *(sem-moan-tay-kee nah)*

special (unique) products 特選品 **tokusan hin** *(toke-sahn heen)*; special regional/area products 名物 **meibutsu** *(may-boot-sue)*; 名産品 **meisan hin** *(may-sahn heen)*

specialty goods 専門品 **senmon hin** *(sem-moan heen)*; 特産品 **tokusan hin** *(toe-kuu-sahn heen)*

specifications 仕様 **shiyō** *(she-yoe-u)*

speculation 憶測 **okusoku** *(oh-kuu-so-kuu)*

speculation; business venture 投機 **tōki** *(tohh-kee)*

speech 演説 **enzetsu** *(en-zay-t'sue)*

speedometer 速度計 **sokudo-kei** *(so-kuu-doe-kay)*

spending 支出 **shishutsu** *(she-shuu-t'sue)*; 歳出 **saishutsu** *(sigh-shuu-t'sue)*; 投資 **tōshi** *(toe-she)*

spoilage 仕損品 **shison hin** *(she-soan heen)*

spokesperson 代弁者 **daibensha** *(die-bane-shah)*; 広報担当 **kōhō tantō** *(koe-hoe tan-toe)*; スポークスマン **supōkusuman** *(suu-poe-kuu-sue man)*
▪ What is the name of your spokesperson? 広報担当のお名前は。**Kōhō tantō no o-namae wa?** *(koe-hoe tan-toe no oh-nah-my wah?)*

sponsor スポンサー **sponsā** *(spon-sah)*

spot delivery 現場渡し **genba watashi** *(gane-bah wah-tah-she)*

spot market 現物取引市場 **genbutsu torihiki shijō** *(gen-boot-sue toe-ree-hee-kee she-joe)*

spreadsheet スプレッドシート **supureddo shiito** *(sue-prayed-doe she-toe)*; 集計表 **shūkei hyō** *(shuu-kay h'yoe)*

Spring Wage Offensive 春闘 **shuntō** *(shune-toe)*

spyware スパイウェア **supaiwea** *(suu-pie-way-ah)*
▪ Which brand of spyware do you recommend? スパイウェアのブランドはどれを推薦しますか。**Supaiwea no burando wa dore wo suisen shimasu ka?** *(suu-pie-way-ah no buu-rahn-*

doh wah doh-ray wah suu-ee-sen she-mahss kah?)

square deal 公平な取引 **kōhei na torihiki** *(koe-hay nah toe-ree-he-kee)*

stability 安定性 **antei sei** *(ahn-tay say)*

stable 安定 **antei** *(ahn-tay)*; stabilize 安定する **antei suru** *(ahn-tay sue-rue)*

staff (staff member) 職員 **shokuin** *(show-kuu-een)*

staff assistant アシスタント **ashisutanto** *(ah-sheece-tahn-toe)*

staff organization スタッフ組織 **sutaffu soshiki** *(staff-fuu so-she-kee)*

stage (step) 段階 **dankai** *(dahn-kye)*

stagnation 低迷 **teimei** *(tay-may)*; 停滞 **teitai** *(tay-tie)*

stalemate 硬直状態 **kōchaku jōtai** *(koe-chah-kuu joe-tie)*

standard 基準 **kijun** *(kee-june)*

standard (average) 標準 **hyōjun** *(h'yoe-june)*; average quality 標準品質 **hyōjun hinshitsu** *(h'yoe-june heen-shee-t'sue)*

standard costs 標準原価 **hyōjun genka** *(h'yoe-june gane-kah)*

standard equipment 標準装備品 **hyōjun sōbi-hin** *(h'yoe-june so-bee-heen)*

standardization 規格化 **kikaku-ka** *(kee-kah-kuu-kah)*; 標準化 **hyōjun ka** *(h'yoe-june kah)*

standardized products 規格品 **kikaku hin** *(kee-kah-kuu heen)*

standard of living 生活水準 **seikatsu suijun** *(say-cot-sue sue-ee-june)*

standard practice 標準的な習慣 **hyōjun teki na shūkan** *(h'yoe-june tay-kee nah shuu-kahn)*

standard product 標準品 **hyōjun hin** *(h'yoe-june heen)*; 規格品 **kikaku hin** *(kee-kah-kuu heen)*

standard time 標準時 **hyōjun ji** *(h'yoe-june jee)*

standing charges/cost 固定費 **kotei hi** *(koe-tay he)*

standing order 継続発注 **keizoku hatchū** *(kay-zoe-kuu hot-chew)*

stapler ホッチキス **hotchikisu** *(hoe-chee-kee-sue)*
▪ Lend me your stapler for a second. ホッチキスをちょとかしてください。**Hotchikisu wo chotto kashite kudasai.** *(hoe-chee-kee-sue oh choe-toe kahsh-tay kuu-dah-sigh.)*

starting salary 初任給 **shōninkyū** *(shohh-neen-k'yuu)*
▪ My starting salary was very low. 私の初任給はとても低かったです。**Watakushi no shōninkyū wa totemo hiku katta désu.** *(wah-tah-she no shohh-neen-k'yuu wah toe-tay-moe he-kuu kah-tah dess.)*

start-up costs 創業開始費用 **sōgyō kaishi hiyō** *(so-g'yoe kye-she hee-yoe)*

statement 計算書 **keisan sho** *(kay-sahn show)*; 報告書 **hōkoku sho** *(hoe-koe-kuu show)*
▪ Please send me a statement (itemized bill). 計算書を送ってください。**Keisan sho wo okutte kudasai.** *(kay-sahn shoh oh oh-koot-tay kuu-dah-sie.)*

statement of accounts 勘定書 **kanjō sho** *(kahn-joe show)*; 決算報告書 **kessan hokōku sho** *(case-sahn hoe-koe-kuu show)*

statistics 統計 **tōkei** *(toe-kay)*

status 身分 **mibun** *(me-boon)*

status quo 現状 **genjō** *(gane-johh)*

status symbol ステータスシンボル **sutētasu shinboru** *(stay-tah-suu sheen-boh-rue)*

statute 法令 **hōrei** *(hoe-ray)*

statute of limitations 時効 **jikō** *(jee-koe)*

steel 鉄鋼 **tekkō** *(take-koh)*

steel mill 製鉄所 **seitetsu jo** *(say-tay-t'sue joe)*

steering wheel ハンドル **handoru** *(hahn-doe-rue)*

step (stage; grade) 段階 **dankai** *(dahn-kye)*

stereo system ステレオセット **sutereo setto** *(suu-tay-ree-oh set-oh)*
- I want to buy a stereo system. ステレオセットを買いたいです。**Sutereo setto wo kaitai désu.** *(suu-tay-ree-oh set oh kie-tie dess.)*
- How much is that stereo system? そのステレオセットはいくらですか。**Sono sutereo setto wa ikura désu ka?** *(soe-no suu-tay-ree-oh set wah ee-kuu-rah dess kah?)*

stereo TV ステレオテレビ **sutereo terebi** *(sue-tay-ray-oh tay-ray-bee)*

stock (shares) 株 **kabu** *(kah-buu)*; 株式 **kabushiki** *(kah-buu-she-kee)*

stockbroker 株式仲買人 **kabushiki nakagai nin** *(kah-buu-she-kee nah-kah-guy neen)*; 証券会社 **shōken gaisha** *(show-ken guy-shah)*

stock certificate 株券 **kabu ken** *(kah-buu ken)*

stock company 株式会社 **kabushiki gaisha** *(kah-buu-she-kee guy-shah)*

stock control 在庫管理 **zaiko hin kanri** *(zye-koe heen kahn-ree)*

stock exchange 株式取引所 **kabushiki torihiki sho** *(kah-buu-she-kee toe-ree-he-kee show)*; 証券取引所 **shōken torihiki sho** *(show-ken toe-ree-he-kee show)*

stockholder 株主 **kabu nushi** *(kah-buu nuu-she)*

stockholder's equity 株主持分 **kabu nushi mochibun** *(kah-buu nuu-she moe-chee-boon)*; 自己資本 **jiko shihon** *(jee-koe she-hon)*

stock index 株価指数 **kabuka shisū** *(kah-buu-kah she-sue)*

stock market 株式市場 **kabushiki shijō** *(kah-buu-she-kee she-joe)*

stock option ストックオプション **sutokku opushon** *(stoke-kuu oh-puu-shone)*

stock portfolio 持ち株明細 **mochi kabu meisai** *(moe-chee-kah-buu may-sigh)*

stock split 株式分割 **kabushiki bunkatsu** *(kah-buu-she-kee boon-cot-sue)*

stock turnover (securities) 株式回転率 **kabushiki kaiten-ritsu** *(kah-buu-she-kee kye-ten-ree-t'sue)*

stop-loss order 逆指し値注文 **gyaku sashine chūmon** *(g'yah-kuu sah-she-nay chew-moan)*

storage 倉庫 **sōko** *(so-koe)*; 保管 **hokan** *(hoe-kahn)*

storehouse (warehouse) 倉庫 **sōko** *(so-koe)*

strategy 戦略 **senryaku** *(sen-r'yah-kuu)*
- We are having a conference about a new marketing strategy. 新しい販売戦略について会議があります。**Atarashii hanbai senryaku ni tsuite kaigi ga arimasu.** *(ah-tah-rah-shee hahn-by sen-re-yah-kuu nee t'suee-tay kie-gee gah ah-ree-mahss.)*

streamline 合理化する **gōri-ka suru** *(go-ree-kah sue-rue)*; スリム化する **surimu-ka suru** *(sue-ree-muu-kah sue-rue)*
▪ The president streamlined the new management. 社長が変わって経営は合理化されました。**Shachō ga kawatte keiei wa gōri ka saremashita.** *(shah-chohh gah kah-wot-tay kay-eh-ee wah gohh-ree kah sah-ray-mah-she-tah.)*

stress ストレス **sutoresu** *(stow-ray-sue)*

stress management ストレス対策 **sutoresu taisaku** *(stow-ray-sue tie-sah-kuu)*

strike ストライキ **sutoraiki** *(stow-rye-kee)*; スト **suto** *(stow)*

strikebreaker スト破り **suto yaburi** *(stow yah-buu-ree)*

strong 強い **tsuyoi** *(t'sue-yoe-ee)*; intense 強烈な **kyōretsu na** *(k'yoe-ray-t'sue nah)*; durable 丈夫な **jōbu na** *(joe-buu nah)*

structure 組織 **soshiki** *(so-she-kee)*

subcontract 下請けにだす **shitauke ni dasu** *(shtah-uu-kay nee dah-sue)*; 外注する **gai-chū suru** *(guy-chew sue-rue)*

subcontractor 下請け業者 **shitahuke gyōsha** *(shtah-uu-kay g'yoe-shah)*

subject (topic) 話題 **wadai** *(wah-dye)*; 問題 **mondai** *(moan-dye)*

sublet 又貸し **matagashi** *(mah-tah gah-she)*

submit a bid 入札する **nyūsatsu suru** *(nuu-sah-t'sue sue-rue)*

subscribe 予約する **yoyaku suru** *(yoe-yah-kuu sue-rue)*; 定期購読する **teiki kōdoku suru** *(tay-kee koh-doh-ku sue-rue)*

subscriber 購読者 **kōdokusha** *(koe-doke-shah)*

subscription (定期)購読 (**teiki**) **kōdoku** *((tay-kee) koe-doe-kuu)*

subscription price 予約金 **yoyaku kin** *(yoe-yah-kuu keen)*

subsidiary 子会社 **ko gaisha** *(koe guy-shah)*

subsidy 補助金 **hojo kin** *(hoe-joe keen)*; 助成金 **josei kin** *(joe-say keen)*

substandard 標準以下の **hyōjun ika no** *(h'yoe-june ee-kah no)*

subtle 微妙な **bimyō na** *(beam-yoe nah)*

suburb 郊外 **kōgai** *(koe-guy)*
▪ Do you live in a suburb? 郊外にお住いですか。**Kōgai ni o-sumai désu ka?** *(koe-guy nee oh-sue-my dess kah?)*

subway 地下鉄 **chikatetsu** *(chee-kah-tay-t'sue)*
▪ Is there a subway station? 地下鉄の駅はありますか。**Chikatetsu no eki wa arimasu ka?** *(chee-kah-tay-t'sue no ay-kee wah ah-ree-mahss kah?)*
▪ Let's go by subway. 地下鉄で行きましょう。**Chikatetsu de ikimashō.** *(chee-kah-tay-t'sue day ee-kee-mah-show.)*
▪ Are the subways crowded at this time of the day? この時間帯地下鉄は込んでいますか。**Kono jikan tie chikatetsu wa konde imasu ka?** *(koe-no jee-kahn tie chee-kah-tay-t'sue wah kone-day ee-mahss kah?)*

subway line 地下鉄の路線 **chikatetsu no rosen** *(chee-kah-tay-t'sue no roe-sen)*
▪ Does this subway line go to the Ginza? この路線は銀座行きですか。**Kono rosen wa Ginza yuki désu ka?** *(koe-no roe-sen wa geen-zah yuu-kee dess kah?)*

▪ Which subway line goes to Roppongi? 六本木行きの路線はどれでしょうか。**Roppongi yuki no rosen wa dore desho ka?** *(rope-pone-ghee yuu-kee no chee-kah-tay-t'sue sen wah doe-ray day-show kah?)*

succeed 成功する **seikō suru** *(say-koe sue-rue)*

suit 訴訟 **soshō** *(so-show)*

summarize 要約する **yōyaku suru** *(yoe-yah-kuu sue-rue)*

summary (outline) 大要 **taiyō** *(tie-yoe)*; 要点 **yōten** *(yoe-ten)*; 要旨 **yōshi** *(yoe-shi)*

sum of money 金額 **kingaku** *(keen-gah-kuu)*; sum total 全額 **zen gaku** *(zen gah-kuu)*

sundry (miscellaneous goods) 雑貨 **zakka** *(zahk-kah)*

superior (boss) 上司 **jōshi** *(joe-she)*

supermarket スーパー **supā** *(suu-pahh)*

superpower 超大国 **chōtaikoku** *(chohh-tie-koh-kuu)*
▪ China has become a superpower. 中国は超大国になりました。**Chūgoku wa chōtaikoku ni narimashita.** *(chuu-go-kuu wah chohh-tie-koh-kuu nee nah-ree-mah-ssh-tah.)*

supervisor 監督 **kantoku** *(kahn-toe-kuu)*

supplement (publication) 別冊 **bessatsu** *(base-sah-t'sue)*

supplier 供給者 **kyōkyū sha** *(k'yoe-cue shah)*

supplies 資材 **shizai** *(she-zye)*; 必需品 **hitsuju hin** *(hee-t'sue-juu heen)*

supply and demand 需要と供給 **juyō to kyōkyū** *(juu-yoe toe k'yoe-cue)*

supply department 資材部 **shizai bu** *(she-zye buu)*; 用度課 **yōdo ka** *(yoe-doe kah)*

support activities 支援活動 **shien katsudō** *(she-en cot-sue-doe)*

surcharge 追加料金 **tsuika ryōkin** *(t'sue-kah rio-keen)*
▪ Will there be a surcharge? 追加料金はかかりますか。**Tsuika ryō kin wa kakarimasu ka?** *(t'sue-kah rio-keen wah kah-kah-ree-mahss kah?)*

surplus 黒字 **kuroji** *(kuu-roe-jee)*

surplus capital 資本剰余金 **shihon jōyo kin** *(she-hone joe-yoe keen)*

surplus goods 余剰品 **yojō hin** *(yoe-joe heen)*

surtax 付加税 **fuka zei** *(fuu-kah zay)*

suspend payment 支払いを停止する **shiharai wo teishi suru** *(she-hah-rye wo tay-she sue-rue)*

suspension; prohibition 差し止め **sashitome** *(sah-she-toh-may)*

switch スイッチ **suitchi** *(sue-ee-chee)*

sworn statement 宣誓陳述書 **sensei chinjutsu sho** *(sen-say cheen-jute-sue show)*

symposium 座談会 **zadankai** *(zah-dahn-kye)*; 討論会 **tōron kai** *(toe-ron kye)*; シンポジウム **shinpojiumu** *(sheen-poe-jee-uu-muu)*

syndicate シンジケート **shinjikēto** *(sheen-jee-kay-toe)*

syndicate a project シンジケートをつくる **shinjikēto wo tsukuru** *(sheen-jee-kay-toe oh t'sue-kuu-rue)*

synopsis 要旨 **yōshi** *(yohh-she)*; 概要 **gaiyō** *(gah-ee-yoe)*; あらすじ **arasuji** *(ah-rah-sue-jee)*
▪ I would like to read a synopsis of your book. 本のあらすじを読みたいで

す。**Hon no arasuji wo yomitai désu.** *(hoan no ah-rah-sue-jee oh yoe-me-tie dess.)*

synthetic (material) 合成の **gōsei no** *(go-say no)*

system 制度 **seido** *(say-doe)*; システム **shisutemu** *(she-stay-muu)*
▪ What system do you think is best? どのシステムが一番いいと思いますか。**Dono shisutemu ga ichiban ii to omoimasu ka?** *(doe-no she-stay-muu gah ee-chee-bahn ee toe oh-moe-ee-mahss kah?)*

systematic (methodical) 組織的な **soshiki-teki na** *(so-shee-kee-tay-kee nah)*

systems analysis システム分析 **shisutemu bunseki** *(she-tay-muu boon-say-kee)*

systems design システム設計 **shisutemu sekkei** *(she-stay-muu sake-kay)*

systems engineering システム工学 **shisutemu kōgaku** *(she-stay-muu koe-gah-kuu)*

systems management システム管理 **shisutemu kanri** *(she-stay-muu kahn-ree)*

T

table of contents 目次 **mokuji** *(moe-kuu-jee)*

tactics 戦術 **senjutsu** *(sen-jute-sue)*

tag (product label) ラベル **raberu** *(rah-bay-rue)*

take-home pay 手取り(給料) **te-dori (kyūryō)** *(tay-doe-ree cue-rio)*
▪ My take-home pay is not enough to go around. 私の手取りは十分ではありません。**Watakushi no te-dori wa jūbun dewa arimasen.** *(wah-tah-she no tay-doe-ree wah juu-boon day-wah ah-ree-mah-sen.)*

take over 乗っ取り **nottori** *(note-toe-ree)*; 企業買収 **kigyō baishū** *(kee-g'yoe by-shuu)*

tangible assets 有形資産 **yūkei shisan** *(yuu-kay she-sahn)*

tanker タンカー **tankā** *(tahn-kah)*

tape テープ **tēpu** *(tay-puu)*

tape recorder テープレコーダー **tēpu rekōdā** *(tay-puu ray-koe-dah)*

target (for sales, etc.) 目標 **mokuhyō** *(moe-kuu-h'yoe)*

target price 目標価格 **mokuhyō kakaku** *(moe-kuu-h'yoe kah-kah-kuu)*

tariff 関税 **kanzei** *(kahn-zay)*

tariff barriers 関税障壁 **kanzei shōheki** *(kahn-zay show-hay-kee)*

tariff classification 関税分類 **kanzei bunrui** *(kahn-zay boon-rue-ee)*

tariff differential 関税率格差 **kanzei ritsu kakusa** *(kahn-zay ree-t'sue kah-kuu-sah)*

tariff rate (tax) 関税率 **kanzei ritsu** *(kahn-zay ree-t'sue)*

tariff war 関税戦争 **kanzei sensō** *(kahn-zay sen-so)*

task force タスクフォース **tasuku fōsu** *(tahss-kuu foe-sue)*

tax 税金 **zeikin** *(zay-keen)*

taxable income 課税所得 **kazei shotoku** *(kah-zay show-toe-kuu)*

tax accountant, licensed (licensed tax accountant) 税理士 **zeirishi** *(zay-ree-she)*

tax accounting 税務会計 **zeimu kaikei** *(zay-muu kye-kay)*

tax allowance 課税控除 **kazei kōjo** *(kah-zay koe-joe)*

taxation 課税 **kazei** *(kah-zay)*

tax base 課税基準 **kazei kijun** *(kah-zay kee-june)*

tax burden 租税負担 **sozei futan** *(so-zay fuu-tahn)*

tax business 税務 **zeimu** *(zay-muu)*

tax collector 収税管 **shūzei kan** *(shuu-zay kahn)*

tax deduction 税額控除 **zei kōjo** *(zay koe-joe)*

tax evasion 脱税 **datsu zei** *(dot-sue zay)*

tax-free income 非課税所得 **hi kazei shotoku** *(he kah-zay show-toe-kuu)*

tax haven 非課税国 **hi kazei koku** *(he kah-zay koe-kuu)*; タックスヘブン **tax haven**; 租税回避国 **sozei kaihi koku** *(so-zay kye-he koe-kuu)*

taxi タクシー **takushii** *(tahk-she)*
▪ Please call a taxi (for me). タクシーをよんでください。**Takushii wo yonde kudasai.** *(tahk-she oh yoan-day kuu-dah-sigh.)*

tax investigation 税務調査 **zeimu chōsa** *(zay-muu choe-sah)*

tax office 税務署 **zeimusho** *(zay-muu-show)*

tax payment 納税額 **nōzei gaku** *(no-zay gah-kuu)*

tax relief 租税軽減 **sozei keigen** *(so-zay kay-gen)*

tax return 納税申告 **nōzei shinkoku** *(no-zay sheen-koe-kuu)*

tax shelter 税金避難手段 **zeikin hinan shudan** *(zay-keen he-nahn shuu-dahn)*; 租税回避国 **sozei kaihi koku** *(so-zay kye-he koe-kuu)*

tax treaty 租税条約 **sozei jōyaku** *(so-zay joe-yah-kuu)*

technical knowhow 技術上のノウハウ **gijutsu jō no nou hau** *(ghee-jute-sue joe no knowhow)*

technical tie-up 技術提携 **gijutsu teikei** *(ghee-jute-sue tay-kay)*

telecommunications 電気通信 **denki tsūshin** *(dane-kee t'sue-sheen)*; テレコミュニケーション **terekomyunikēshon** *(tay-ray-koe-muu-nee-kay-shone)*

telegram 電信 **denshin** *(dane-sheen)*; 電報 **denpō** *(dane-poe)*

telephone 電話 **denwa** *(dane-wah)*

telephone card テレホンカード **terehon kādo** *(tay-ray-hone kah-doh)*
▪ You should buy a telephone card. テレホンカードを買ったほうがいいです。**Terehon kādo wo katta hoh ga ii désu.** *(tay-ray-hone kah-doh oh kaht-tah hohh gah ee dess.)*
▪ You can also buy international telephone cards. 国際テレホンカードも買うことができます。**Kokusai terehon kādo mo kau koto ga dekimasu.** *(koke-sie tay-ray-hone kah-doh moh kow koh-toh gah day-kee-mahss.)*

television テレビ **terebi** *(tay-ray-bee)*

telex テレックス **terekkusu** *(tay-rake-kuu-sue)*

teller (bank) 出納係 **suitō gakari** *(sweet-oh gah-kah-ree)*

temporary 仮の **kari no** *(kah-ree no)*; 一時的な **ichiji-teki na** *(ee-chee-jee-tay-kee nah)*

temporary employment 臨時雇い **rinji yatoi** *(reen-jee yah-toe-ee)*; 期間従

業員 **kikan jūgyōin** *(kee-kahn juu-g'yoe-in)*

temporary transfer (to related company) 出向 **shūkkō** *(shuuk-kohh)*

tender 入札する **nyūsatsu suru** *(n'yuu-sah-t'sue sue-rue)*

tender offer 株式公開買付け **kabushiki kōkai kaitsuke** *(kah-buu-she-kee koe-kye kye-t'sue-kee)*

ten-thousand-yen note 一万円札 **ichi-man-en satsu** *(ee-chee-mahn-en sah-t'sue)*

term 期間 **kikan** *(kee-kahn)*; 契約期間 **keiyaku kikan** *(kay-yah-kuu kee-kahn)*

terminal (computer) ターミナル **tāminaru** *(tah-me-nah-rue)*

terminal (destination) 終点 **shūten** *(shuu-tane)*

terminate 廃止する **haishi suru** *(high-she sue-rue)*; 終了する **shūryō suru** *(shuu-rio sue-rue)*

term insurance 定期保険 **teiki hoken** *(tay-kee hoe-ken)*

term loan タームローン **tāmu rōn** *(tah-muu roan)*

terms of sale 販売条件 **hanbai jōken** *(hahn-by joe-ken)*

terms of trade 交易条件 **kōeki jōken** *(koe-ay-kee joe-ken)*

terrible 酷い **hidoi** *(he-doy)*

territorial waters 領海 **ryōkai** *(rio-kye)*

territory 地域 **chiiki** *(chee-ee-kee)*

thanks for your efforts おつかれさま **otsukare-sama** *(oh-t'sue-kah-ray-sah-mah)*

that (thing, topic) 例の **rei no** *(ray no)*

theme 主題 **shudai** *(shuu-dye)*; テーマ **tēma** *(tay-mah)*

thermostat サーモスタット **sāmosuttato** *(sah-moe-staht-toe)*

through bill of lading 通し船荷証券 **tōshi funani shōken** *(toe-she-fuu-nah-nee show-ken)*

ticker tape (for stocks) 株式相場表示テープ **kabushiki sōba hyōji tēpu** *(kah-buu-she-kee so-bah h'yoe-jee tay-puu)*

tie-up 提携する **teikei suru** *(tay-kay sue-rue)*
▪ I would like to tie-up with a medium-sized Japanese company. 中規模の日本の会社と提携したいです。**Chū-kibo no Nihon no kaisha to teikei shittai désu.** *(chew-kee-boe no nee-hone no kye-shah toe tay-kay she-tie dess.)*

tight market 逼迫した市況 **hippaku shita shikyō** *(hip-pah-kuu she-tah she-k'yoe)*

tight with money (stingy) けち **kechi** *(kay-chee)*

time and motion study 時間動作研究 **jikan dōsa kenkyū** *(jee-kahn doe-sah ken-cue)*

time deposit 定期預金 **teiki yokin** *(tay-kee yoe-keen)*

time difference 時差 **jisa** *(jee-sah)*

time-share タイムシェア **taimu shea** *(tie-muu shay-ah)*
▪ I will be staying in a time-share hotel. タイムシェアのホテルに泊まります。**Taimu shea no hoteru ni tomarimasu.** *(tie-muu-shay-ah no hoe-tay-rue nee toe-mah-ree-mahss.)*
▪ Are there many time-share hotels in Japan? 日本には、タイムシェアのホテルがたくさんありますか。**Nihon ni wa taimu shea no hoteru ga takusan**

arimasu ka? *(nee-hone nee-wah tie-muu shay-ah no hoe-tay-rue gah tahk-sahn ah-ree-mahss kah?)*
▪ Is the time-share hotel in a good location? タイムシェアのホテルはいい場所にありますか。**Taimu-shea no hoteru wa ii basho ni ari masu ka?** *(tie-muu-shay-ah hoe-tay-rue wah ee bah-show nee ah-ree-mahss kah?)*

time-sharing タイムシェアリング **taimu shearingu** *(tie-muu shay-ah-een-guu)*

timetable 時刻表 **jikoku hyō** *(jee-koe-kuu h'yoe)*; 時間割 **jikan wari** *(jee-kahn wah-ree)*

time zone 時間帯 **jikan tai** *(jee-kahn tie)*

tip (gratuity) チップ **chippu** *(cheap-puu)*

tip (inside information) 機密情報 **kimitsu jōhō** *(kee-me-t'sue joe-hoe)*

tire タイヤ **taiya** *(tie-yah)*

title (of book, article) 表題 **hyōdai** *(h'yoe-dye)*; 題名 **daimei** *(dye-may)*

title (of company manager/executive) 肩書き **katagaki** *(kah-tah-gah-kee)*

title タイトル **taitoru** *(tie-toh-ruu)*; 名称 **meishō** *(may-show)*
▪ What is the title of the program you are using? 使っているプログラムのタイトルはなんですか。**Tsukatte iru puroguramu no taitoru wa nan désu ka?** *(t'su-kaht-tay-ee-ruu puu-roh-guu-rah-muu no tie-toh-ruu wah nahn dess kah?)*
▪ What is the title of that song? その歌のタイトルは何ですか。**Sono uta no taitoru wa nan désu ka?** *(soh-no uu-tah no tie-toh-ruu wah nahn dess kah?)*

title to (power over) 権限 **kengen** *(kane-gane)*

toast (in celebration) 祝杯 **shukuhai** *(shuu-kuu-high)*; to give a toast 祝杯をあげる **shukuhai wo ageru** *(shuu-kuu-high oh ah-gay-rue)*

Tokyo Chamber of Commerce & Industry 東京商工会議所 **Tōkyō Shōkō Kaigisho** *(toe-k'yoe show-koe kye-ghee-show)*

Tokyo Stock Exchange 東京証券取引所 **Tokyo Shōken Torihiki sho** *(toe-k'yoe show-ken toe-ree-he-kee show)*

Tokyo Stock Price Index 東証株価指数 **Tōshō kabuka shisū** *(toe-show kah-buu-kah she-suu)*

tonnage 容積トン数 **yōseki ton sū** *(yoe-say-kee tone sue)*

tools 道具 **dōgu** *(doe-guu)*; ツール **tūru** *(t'sue-uu-ruu)*
▪ We (I) do not have the necessary tools. 必要な道具を持っていません。**Hitsuyō na dōgu wo motteimasen.** *(heat-sue-yoe nah doe-guu oh moat-tay-mah-sen.)*

too soon 早すぎる **hayasugiru** *(hah-yah-sue-ghee-ree)*

topic 話題 **wadai** *(wah-dye)*

top management 経営陣 **keiei jin** *(kay-ee jeen)*

top price 最高価格 **saikō kakaku** *(sigh-koe kah-kah-kuu)*

top quality 最高品質 **saikō hinshitsu** *(sigh-koe heen-sheet-sue)*

total 総計 **sōkei** *(so-kay)*

total quality control (TQC) TQC **Tii Kyū Shii** *(tea-cue-she)*; 全社的品質管理 **zensha-teki hinshitsu kanri** *(zen-shah-tay-kee heen-she-t'sue kahn-ree)*

total sum 総額 **sō gaku** *(so gah-kuu)*

trade (business) 取引 **torihiki** *(toe-ree-he-kee)*; 貿易 **bōeki** *(boe-eh-kee)*

trade agreement 貿易協定 **bōeki kyōtei** *(boe-eh-kee k'yoe-tay)*

trade and commerce 通商貿易 **tsūshō bōeki** *(t'sue-show boe-eh-kee)*

trade association 業界 **gyōkai** *(gyoe-kye)*; 商業組合 **shōgyō kumiai** *(show-g'yoe kuu-me-eye)*

trade barrier 貿易障害 **bōeki shōgai** *(boe-eh-kee show-guy)*; 関税障壁 **kanzei shōheki** *(kahn-zay show-hay-kee)*

trade commission 貿易委員会 **bōeki i'in-kai** *(boe-eh-kee ee-een-kye)*

trade credit 取引先信用 **torihiki saki shin'yō** *(toe-ree-he-kee sah-kee sheen-yoe)*; 企業間信用 **kigyō kan shin'yō** *(kee-g'yoe kahn sheen-yoe)*

trade discount 業者間割引 **gyōsha kan waribiki** *(g'yoe-sah kahn wah-ree-bee-kee)*

trade friction 貿易摩擦 **bōeki masatsu** *(boe-eh-kee mah-sah-t'sue)*

trademark 登録商標 **tōroku shōhyō** *(toe-roe-kuu show-h'yoe)*; トレードマーク **torēdo māku** *(toe-ray-doe mah-kuu)*

trade mission 通商使節 **tsūshō shisetsu** *(t'sue-show she-say-t'sue)*

trader 貿易業者 **bōeki gyōsha** *(boe-ee-kee g'yoe-sha)*; ディーラー **diirā** *(dee-rahh)*

trade secret 企業秘密 **kigyō himitsu** *(kee-g'yoe he-me-t'sue)*

trade union 労働組合 **rōdō kumiai** *(roe-doe kuu-me-eye)*

trading; dealing 商い **akinai** *(ah-kee-nie)*; 取引 **torihiki** *(tohh-ree-hee-kee)*
▪ I don't want to deal with that company. その会社とは取引したくありません。**Sono kaisha to wa torihiki shitaku arimasen.** *(soe-no kie-shah toe wah tohh-ree-hee-kee she-tah-kuu ah-ree-mah-sen.)*

trading company 商事会社 **shōji gaisha** *(show-jee guy-shah)*; 貿易会社 **bōeki gaisha** *(boe-eh-kee guy-hah)*; 商社 **shōsha** *(show-shah)*

trading floor (exchange) 立会場 **tachiai jō** *(tah-chee-eye joe)*

train (educate) 訓練する **kunren suru** *(coon-ren sue-rue)*

trainee 実習生 **jisshū sei** *(jeesh-shuu-say)*

transaction 取引 **torihiki** *(toe-ree-he-kee)*

transfer (money) 振替え **furikae** *(fuu-ree-kye)*; 送金 **sōkin** *(so-keen)*

transfer by computer 転送する **tensō suru** *(ten-so sue-rue)*

translate 翻訳する **hon'yaku suru** *(hone-yah-kuu sue-rue)*
▪ Please translate this. これを翻訳してください。**Kore wo hon'yaku shite kudasai.** *(koe-ray oh hone-yah-kuu shtay kuu-dah-sigh.)*

translation 訳文 **yakubun** *(yah-kuu-boon)*

translator 翻訳者 **hon'yaku sha** *(hone-yah-kuu shah)*

transmission (vehicle) トランスミッション **toransumisshon** *(toe-rahns-meesh-shone)*; 変速機 **hensoku ki** *(hen-so-kuu kee)*

transport; conveyance 輸送 **yusō** *(yuu-sohh)*
▪ The goods have already been transported to the warehouse. 品物はもう倉庫に運ばれました。**Shinamono**

wa mō sōko ni hakobaremashita. *(she-nah-moh-no wah mohh sohh-koh nee hah-koh-bah-ray-mah-sshtah.)*

transportation 運輸 **un'yu** *(uun-yuu)*; 輸送 **yusō** *(yuu-so)*

transportation charge 運賃 **unchin** *(uun-cheen)*; 運送料 **unsō-ryō** *(uun-so-rio)*

transportation expenses 輸送費 **yusō hi** *(yuu-so he)*; 交通費 **kōtsū hi** *(koe-t'sue-he)*

transportation terminal 輸送ターミナル **yusō tāminaru** *(yuu-so tah-me-nah-rue)*

travel (trip) 旅行 **ryokō** *(rio-koe)*; 旅 **tabi** *(tah-bee)*

travel expenses 旅費 **ryo hi** *(rio he)*

traveler's check 旅行者用小切手 **ryokōsha yō kogitte** *(rio-koe-shah yoe koe-gheet-tay)*; トラベラーズチェック **toraberāzu chekku** *(toe-rah-bay-rah-zuu check)*
▪ Are traveler's checks acceptable? トラベラーズチェックでいいですか。**Toraberāzu chekku de ii désu ka?** *(toe-rah-bay-rah-zuu check day ee dess kah?)*

treasurer 会計 **kaikei** *(kie-kay)*

treatment 処理 **shori** *(show-ree)*; 措置 **sochi** *(so-chee)*

treaty 条約 **jōyaku** *(joe-yah kuu)*

trend 傾向 **keikō** *(kay-koe)*; 動向 **dōkō** *(doe-koe)*; トレンド **torendo** *(toe-ren-doe)*

trial period 試用期間 **shiyō kikan** *(she-yoe kee-kahn)*; お試し期間 **o-tameshi kikan** *(oh-tah-may-she kee-kahn)*

trial use 試用 **shiyō** *(she-yoe)*

trouble-shoot 問題解決 **mondai kaiketsu** *(moan-dye kye-kate-sue)*

truck トラック **torakku** *(toe-rahk-kuu)*

truckload 貸切貨物 **kashikiri kamotsu** *(kah-she-kee-ree kah-moat-sue)*

trust 信用 **shin'yō** *(sheen-yoe)*; problem of trust 信用問題 **shin'yō mondai** *(sheen-yoe moan-dye)*

trust (financial institution) 信託 **shintaku** *(sheen-tah-kuu)*

trust bank 信託銀行 **shintaku ginkō** *(sheen-tah-kuu gheen-koe)*

trustee 受託者 **jutaku sha** *(juu-tah-kuu shah)*

trust fund 信託資金 **shintaku shikin** *(sheen-tah-kuu she-keen)*

tuner チューナー **chūnā** *(chew-nah)*

turnover 回転(率) **kaiten (ritsu)** *(kye-ten (ree-t'sue))*

two-shift system 二交代制 **ni-kōtai sei** *(nee-koe-tie say)*

type; kind 種類 **shurui** *(shuu-rue-ee)*
▪ How many types do you have? いくつの種類がありますか。**Ikutsu no shurui ga arimasu ka?** *(ee-coot-sue no shuu-rue-ee gah ah-ree-mahss kah?)*

U

ultimatum 最後通告 **saigo tsūkoku** *(sigh-go t'sue-koe-kuu)*

unaccompanied goods 別送品 **bessō hin** *(bay-so heen)*

unanimously 満場一致 **manjōitchi** *(mahn-joe-eech-chee)*

uncollectible (accounts) 焦げ付いた **kogetsuki** *(koe-gate-sue-kee)*

undercapitalized 投資不足の **tōshi busoku no** *(toe-she buu-so-kuu no)*; 資金不足の **shikin busoku no** *(she-keen buu-so-kuu no)*

under consideration 検討中 **kentō chū** *(ken-toe chew)*
▪ Your application is under consideration. あなたの申請は、ただいま検討中です。**Anata no shinsei wa tadaima kentō chū désu.** *(ah-nah-toe no sheen-say wah tah-dah ee-mah ken-toe chew dess.)*

undercut (price) 値段を切り下げる **nedan wo kirisageru** *(nay-dahn oh kee-ree-sah-guy-rue)*

underdeveloped nations 後進国 **kōshin koku** *(koe-sheen koe-kuu)*

understanding 合意 **gōi** *(go-ee)*

underestimate; undervalue 過小評価する **kashō hyōka suru** *(kah-show h'yoe-kah sue-rue)*

underpaid 支払い不足の **shiharai busoku no** *(she-hah-rye buu-so-kuu no)*

undersigned 署名者 **shomei sha** *(show-may shah)*

understaffed 人手不足(の) **hitode busoku (no)** *(ssh-toh-day-buu-so-kuu no)*

understanding (agreement) 協定 **kyōtei** *(k'yoe-tay)*

understanding (comprehension) 理解 **rikai** *(ree-kye)*; 了解 **ryōkai** *(rio-kye)*

underwriter of insurance 保険業者 **hoken gyōsha** *(hoe-ken g'yoe-shah)*

underwriter of securities 引受業者 **hikiuke gyōsha** *(he-kee-uu-kay g'yoe-shah)*

unearned revenue 不労所得 **furō shotoku** *(fuu-roe show-toe-kuu)*

unemployed 無職(の) **mushoku (no)** *(muu-sho-kuu no)*
▪ He has been unemployed for more than a year. あの人は一年以上無職です。**Anohito wa ichi-nen ijō mushoku désu.** *(ah-no-ssh-toe wah ee-chee-nane ee-johh muu-show-kuu dess.)*

unemployment 失業 **shitsugyō** *(sheet-sue-g'yoe)*

unemployment benefits 失業手当給付金 **shitsugyō teate kyūfukin** *(sheet-sue-g'yohh tay-ah-tay cue-fuu kee-n)*

unemployment compensation 失業手当 **shitsugyō teate** *(sheet-sue-g'yoe tay-ah-tay)*

unemployment insurance 失業保険 **shitsugyō hoken** *(sheet-sue-g'yohh hoh-kane)*

unexpected 意外 **igai** *(ee-guy)*; 予想外 **yosōgai** *(yoe-so-guy)*

unfair (unreasonable) 不公平な **fu-kōhei na** *(fuu-koe-hay nah)*
▪ I believe those are unfair conditions. それは不公平な条件だと思います。**Sore wa fu-kōhei na jōken da to omoimasu.** *(so-ray wah fuu-koe-hay nah joe-ken dah toe oh-moe-ee-mahss.)*

unfair competition 不当競争 **futō kyōsō** *(fuu-toe k'yoe-so)*

unfavorable 不利な **furi na** *(fuu-ree nah)*

unfeasible 実行不可能な **jikkō fukanō na** *(jee-koe fuu-kah-no nah)*

uniform 制服 **seifuku** *(say-fuu-kuu)*; ユニフォーム **unifōmu** *(uu-nee-fohh-muu)*

union (labor) 労働組合 **rōdō kumiai** *(roe-doe kuu-me-eye)*; union member 組合員 **kumiai-in** *(kuu-mee-eye-een)*

union contract 労働契約 **rōdō keiyaku** *(roe-doe kay-yah-kuu)*

union label 組合ラベル **kumiai raberu** *(kuu-me-eye raa-bee-ruu)*

unique ユニーク **yuniiku** *(yuu-nee-kuu)*; 唯一の **yui'itsu no** *(yuu-eet-tsue no)*

unit 部門 **bumon** *(buu-moan)*; 単位 **tan'i** *(tahn-ee)*

unit cost 単位原価 **tan-i genka** *(tahn-ee gane-kah)*

unit price 単価 **tanka** *(tahn-kah)*

universal (the whole world) 全世界の **zen-sekai no** *(zen-say-kye no)*; 世界共通の **sekai kyōtsū no** *(say-kye k'yoe-t'sue no)*

university 大学 **daigaku** *(dye-gah-kuu)*

unlisted number 非公開電話番号 **hikōkai denwa bangō** *(he-koe-kah-ee dane-wah bahn-go)*

unprofitable 利益にならない **rieki ni naranai** *(ree-eh-kee nee nah-rah-nie)*; 儲からない **mōkaranai** *(moe-kah-rah-nigh)*
▪ The suspension of the unprofitable business unit was announced. 儲からない事業の中止が発表された。**Mōkaranai jigyō no chūshi ga happyō sareta.** *(moh-kah-rah-nie jeeg-yoe no chuu-she gah hop-p'yoh sah-ray-tah.)*

unsecured liability 無担保負債 **mu-tanpo fusai** *(muu-tahm-poe fuu-sigh)*

unsecured loan 信用貸し **shin'yō gashi** *(sheen-yoe gah-she)*

unskilled labor 非熟練労働者 **hi-jukuren rōdō sha** *(he juu-kuu-ren roe-doe shah)*

unstable 不安定 **fuantei** *(fuu-ahn-tay)*

upgrade (computer) アップグレードする **appu gurēdo suru** *(ahp-guu-ree-doe sue-rue)*; バージョンを上げる **bājon wo ageru** *(bah-joen wo ah-gay-rue)*

upload アップロード **appurōdo** *(ahpu-roh-doh)*
▪ I want to upload this file to the Internet. インターネットにこのファイルをアップロードしたいです。**Intānetto ni kono fairu wo appurōdo shitai désu.** *(in-tah-net-toh nee koh-no fie-ruu oh ahpu-rod-doh she-tie dess.)*

upscale 高級な **kōkyū na** *(koe-cue nah)*

up-to-date (newest) 最新の **saishin no** *(sie-sheen no)*
▪ Is this the up-to-date software? これは一番新しいソフトウェアですか。**Kore wa ichiban atarashii sofutowea désu ka?** *(koe-ray wah ee-chee-bahn ah-tah-rah-shee soe-fuu-toe-way-ah dess kah?)*

up to expectations 期待通りに **kitai dōri ni** *(kee-tie doe-ree nee)*

upturn 好転 **kōten** *(koe-tane)*

urgent business 急ぎの用 **isogi no yō** *(ee-so-ghee no yoe)*; 急用 **kyūyō** *(cue-yoe)*
▪ I have urgent business with Mr. Kato. 加藤さんに急ぎの用があります。**Kato-san ni isogi no yō ga arimasu.** *(kah-toe-sahn nee ee-so-ghee no yoe gah ah-ree-mahss.)*

use 使用 **shiyō** *(she-yoe)*; to use 使う **tsukau** *(t'sue-kah-uu)*

user 顧客 **kokyaku** *(koe-k'yah-kuu)*; 利用者 **riyō sha** *(ree-yoe-shah)*; ユーザー **yūzā** *(yuu-zah)*

user-friendly ユーザーフレンドリー **yūzā furendorii** *(yuu-zah fuu-ren-doe-ree)*; 使いやすい **tsukai yasui**

(t'sue-kye yah-suu-ee); 分かりやすい **wakari yasui** *(wah-kah-ree yah-suu-ee)*

user name ユーザーネーム **yūzā nēmu** *(yuu-zah nay-muu)*
▪ What is your user name? ユーザーネームはなんですか。**Yūzā nēmu wa nan désu ka?** *(yuu-zah nay-muu wah nahn dess kah?)*

use tax 使用税 **shiyō zei** *(she-yoe zay)*

utilities 公共料金 **kōkyō ryōkin** *(koe-k'yoe rio-keen)*; utility expenses 水道光熱費 **suidō kōnetsu hi** *(koe-nate-sue he)*

V

vacation バケーション **bakēshon** *(bay-kay-shone)*; 休暇 **kyūka** *(cue-kah)*

valid 有効な **yūkō na** *(yuu-koe nah)*

validate 有効と認める **yūkō to mitomeru** *(yuu-koe to me-toe-may-rue)*

valid for one year 一年間有効 **ichi-nen kan yūkō** *(ee-chee-nen kahn yuu-koe)*
▪ This document is valid for one year. この書類は一年間有効です。**Kono shorui wa ichi-nen kan yūkō désu.** *(koe-no show-rue-ee wah ee-chee-nen kahn yuu-koe dess.)*

valuable 値打ちがある **neuchi ga aru** *(nay-uu-chee gah ah-rue)*

valuables 貴重品 **kichōhin** *(kee-choe-heen)*
▪ Do you have a safe for valuables? 貴重品の金庫はありますか。**Kichōhin no kinko wa arimasu ka?** *(kee-choe-heen no keen-koe wah ah-ree-mahss kah?)*

valuation (financial) 評価 **hyōka** *(h'yoe-kah)*

valuation (real estate) 査定 **satei** *(sah-tay)*

value 価値 **kachi** *(kah-chee)*

value-added tax 付加価値税 **fuka-kachi zei** *(fuu-kah-kah-chee zay)*

value, book (book value) 帳簿価額 **chōbo kagaku** *(choe-boe kah-gah-kuu)*

value, face (face value) 額面価格 **gakumen kakaku** *(gah-kuu-men kah-kah-kuu)*

value for duty 税額査定価格 **zeigaku satei kakaku** *(zay-gah-kuu sah-tay kah-kah-kuu)*

variable annuity 変額年金 **hengaku nenkin** *(hane-gah-kuu nen-keen)*

variable costs 変動費 **hendō hi** *(hane-doe he)*

variable import duty 変動輸入付加税 **hendō yunyū fuka zei** *(hane-doe yuun-yuu fuu-kah-zay)*

variable rate 変動金利 **hendō kinri** *(hane-doe keen-ree)*

variety 変化 **henka** *(hane-kah)*; 色々 **iro-iro** *(ee-roe-ee-roe)*

vendor 売主 **uri nushi** *(uu-ree nuu-shee)*; 販売業者 **hanbai gyōsha** *(hahn-by g'yoe-shah)*

vendor's lien 売主保留権 **uri nushi horyū ken** *(uu-ree nuu-she hoe-r'yuu ken)*

venture business ベンチャー企業 **benchā kigyō** *(ben-chah kee-g'yoe)*

venture capital ベンチャーキャピタル **benchā kyapitaru** *(ben-chah k'yah-pi-tah-rue)*

verification 検証 **kenshō** *(kane-show)*

verify 証明する **shōmei suru** *(show-may sue-rue)*
▪ Can anyone verify that? 誰かそれを証明できますか。**Dareka sore wo shōmei dekimasu ka?** *(dah-ray gah soh-ray oh shoh-may day-kee-mahss kah?)*

vertical integration 垂直統合 **suichoku tōgō** *(sue-ee-choe-kuu toe-go)*

vessel 本船 **honsen** *(hoan-sen)*

vested interest 既得利権 **kitoku riken** *(kee-toe-kuu ree-ken)*

vested rights 既得権 **kitoku ken** *(kee-toe-kuu ken)*

veto 拒否権 **kyohi ken** *(k'yoe-he ken)*

via (as in via Los Angeles) 経由 **keiyu** *(kay-yuu)*

vice chief (vice director) 次長 **jichō** *(jee-choe)*

vice-president 副社長 **fuku shachō** *(fuu-kuu shah-choe)*

video ビデオ **bideo** *(bee-day-oh kah-set-toe)*
▪ May I look at this video cassette? このビデオをみてもいいですか。**Kono bideo wo mitemo ii désu ka?** *(kone-no bee-day-oh oh me-tay-moe ee dess kah?)*
▪ Which video? どのビデオ。**Dono bideo?** *(doe-no bee-day-oh?)*
▪ The video in that box. その箱に入っているビデオ。**Sono hako ni haitte-iru bideo.** *(soe-no hah-koh nee hite-tay-ee-rue no bee-day-oh.)*

video arcade ゲームセンター **gēmu sentā** *(gay-muu sen-tah)*
▪ I want to see a video arcade. ゲームセンターを見てみたいです。**Gēmu sentā wo mitemitai désu.** *(gay-muu sen-tah oh me-tay-me-tie dess.)*
▪ Is there a video arcade near the hotel? ホテルの近くにゲームセンターがありますか。**Hoteru no chikaku ni gēmu sentā ga arimasu ka?** *(hoh-tay-ruu no chee-kah-kuu nee gay-muu sen-tah gah ah-ree-mahss kah?)*

video camera ビデオカメラ **bideo kamera** *(bee-day-oh kah-may-rah)*
▪ I want to take a video camera to the stadium. スタジアムにビデオカメラをもっていきたいです。**Sutajiamu ni bideo kamera wo motte ikitai désu.** *(suu-tah-jee-ah-muu nee bee-day-oh kah-may-rah oh mote-tay ee-kee-tie dess.)*
▪ Where can I buy a video camera? ビデオカメラはどこで買えますか。**Bideo kamera wa doko de kae mahss ka?** *(bee-day-oh kah-may-rah wah doe-koe day kah-ay mahss kah?)*

video casette player ビデオデッキ **bideo dekki** *(bee-day-oh day-kee)*

video disc ビデオディスク **bideo disuku** *(bee-day-oh disk-uu)*; laser disc レーザーディスク **rēzā disuku** *(ray-zah disk-uu)*

video games ビデオゲーム **bideo gēmu** *(bee-day-oh gay-muu-zuu)*
▪ I want to buy several video games. いくつかビデオゲームを買いたいです。**Ekutsu ka bideo gēmu wo kaitai désu.** *(ee-kuu t'sue-kah bee-day-oh gay-muu oh kie-tie dess.)*

video recorder ビデオレコーダー **bideo rekōdā** *(bee-day-oh ray-koe-dah)*

vinyl ビニール **biniiru** *(bee-nee-rue)*; made of vinyl ビニール製の **biniiru-sei no** *(bee-nee-rue-say no)*

violation 違反 **ihan** *(ee-hahn)*

VIP Room VIPルーム **Bip-Pu rūmu** *(beep-puu rue-muu)*; 特別待合室 **tokubetsu machiai shitsu** *(toe-kuu-*

bait-sue mah-chee-eye sheet-sue); 貴賓室 **kihin shitsu** *(kee-hee-she-t'sue)*

virus ウイルス **uirusu** *(wie-ruu-suu)*

visa ビザ **biza** *(bee-zah)*
- Do you have a visa? ビザはありますか。**Biza wa arimasu ka?** *(bee-zah wah ah-ree-mahss kah?)*

visible balance of trade 商品貿易収支 **shōhin bōeki shūshi** *(show-heen boe-eh-kee shu-she)*

visitor 訪問者 **hōmon-sha** *(hoe-moan-shah)*; お客さん **okyaku-san** *(oh-k'yahck-sahn)*

volatile market 気まぐれ市況 **kimagure shikyō** *(kee-mah-guu-ray she-k'yoe)*

volatility 変動 **hendō** *(hen-doe)*

volume 量 **ryō** *(rio)*; 出来高 **deki daka** *(day-kee dah-kah)*; 取引高 **torihiki daka** *(toe-ree-hee-kee dah-kah)*

volume discount 数量割引 **sūryō waribiki** *(sue-rio wah-ree-bee-kee)*

volume, sales (sales volume) 販売量 **hanbai ryō** *(hahn-by rio)*; 売上高 **uriage daka** *(uu-ree-ah-gay dah-kah)*

vote 投票する **tōhyō suru** *(toe-h'yoe sue-rue)*

voting rights 投票権 **tōhyō ken** *(toe-h'yoe ken)*; 選挙権 **senkyo ken** *(say-n k'yoe-kay-n)*

voucher 伝票 **denpyō** *(den-p'yoe)*; 証明書 **shōmei sho** *(show-may show)*; 引換券 **hikikae ken** *(hee-kee-kah-ay ken)*

W

wage (income) 賃金 **chingin** *(cheen-gheen)*; 給料 **kyūryō** *(cue-rio)*

wage based on job position 職能給 **shokunō kyū** *(show-kuu-noh cue)*

wage based on seniority 年功序列賃金 **nenkō joretsu chingin** *(nen-koe joe-rate-sue cheen-gheen)*

wage differential 賃金格差 **chingin kakusa** *(cheen-gheen kah-kuu-sah)*

wage dispute 賃上げ闘争 **chin-age tōsō** *(cheen-ah-gay toe-so)*

wage earner 賃金労働者 **chingin rōdō sha** *(cheen-gheen roe-doe shah)*

wage freeze 賃金凍結 **chingin tōketsu** *(cheen-gheen toe-kate-sue)*

wage level 賃金水準 **chingin suijun** *(cheen-gheen suu-ee-june)*

wage-price spiral 賃金と物価の悪循環 **chingin to bukka no aku-junkan** *(buke-kah to cheen-gheen no ah-kuu-june-kahn)*

wager 賭け事 **kakegoto** *(kah-kay-go-toe)*; 賭け **kake** *(kah-kay)*

wage regulations 賃金調整 **chingin chōsei** *(cheen-gheen choe-say)*

wage scale 賃金水準 **chingin suijun** *(cheen-gheen sue-ee-june)*

wage structure 給与体系 **kyūyo taikei** *(cue-yoe tie-kay)*

waiver clause 免責条項 **menseki jōkō** *(men-say-kee joe-koe)*

waiver clause for insurance 棄権約款 **kiken yakkan** *(kee-ken yahk-kahn)*

wake-up telephone call モーニングコール **moningu kōru** *(morning call)*
- I would like a 6 o'clock wake-up

call. 六時にモーニングコールをお願いします。**Roku-ji ni moningu kōru wo onegai shimasu.** *(roe-kuu-jee nee morning call oh oh-nay-guy she-mahss.)*

walkout (strike) ストライキ **sutoraiki** *(stow-rye-kee)*

want ad 募集広告 **boshū kōkoku** *(boe-shuu koe-koe-kuu)*; 求人広告 **kyūjin kōkoku** *(cue-jeen koe-coke)*

warehouse 倉庫 **sōko** *(so-koe)*

warehouseman 倉庫業者 **sōko gyōsha** *(so-koe g'yoe-shah)*

warn 注意する **chūi suru** *(chew-ee sue-rue)*

warrant (legal document) 令状 **rei jō** *(ray joe)*

warrant (security) 保証書 **hoshō sho** *(hoe-show show)*

warranty 保証 **hoshō** *(hoe-show)*

warranty period 保証期間 **hoshō kikan** *(hoe-show kee-kahn)*

wasted asset 減耗資産 **genmō shisan** *(gane-moe she-sahn)*

waybill 貨物運送状 **kamotsu unsō jō** *(kah-moat-sue uun-so joe)*

weak point 苦手な **nigate na** *(nee-gah-tay nah)*

wealth 財産 **zaisan** *(zye-sahn)*

wear and tear 消耗 **shōmō** *(show-moe)*; 損傷 **sonshō** *(soan-show)*

weblog ウェブログ **webbu rogu** *(weh-buu roh-guu)*
▪ I like "weblog" better than "blog". 私はブログよりウェブログが好きです。**Watakushi wa burogu yori webbu rogu ga suki désu.** *(wah-tahk-she wa buu-roh-guu yoh-ree weh-buu roh-guu gah skee dess.)*
▪ I write on my weblog every day. 私は、毎日ウェブログに書き込みをしています。**Watashi wa mainichi weburogu ni kakikomi wo shite imasu.** *(wah-tah-she wah my-nee-chee weh-buu-roh-guu nee kah-kee-koh-me oh shtay-mahss.)*

website ウェブサイト **webbu saito** *(web-buu sie-toh)*
▪ Do you have a website? ウェブサイトを持っていますか。**Webbu saito wo motte imasu ka?** *(web-buu sie-toh oh mote-tay ee-mahss kah?)*
▪ What is your website's URL? ウェブサイトのURLはなんですか。**Webbu saito no URL wa nan désu ka?** *(web-sie-toh no yuu-ah-rue-eh-rue wah nahn dess kah?)*
▪ I don't have a website. ウェブサイトを持ってません。**Webbu saito wo mottemasen.** *(web-buu sie-toh oh mote-tay-mah-sen.)*

weekly pay 週給 **shū kyū** *(shuu cue)*

weekly returns 週報 **shū hō** *(shuu-hoe)*

weight 重量 **jūryō** *(juu-rio)*; 目方 **mekata** *(may-kah-tah)*; gross weight 総重量 **sōjūryō** *(so-juu-rio)*; net weight 正味量 **shōmiryō** *(show-me-rio)*

weighted average 加重平均 **kajū heikin** *(kah-juu hay-keen)*

welcome (as on sign) 歓迎します **kangei shimasu** *(kahn-gay she-mahss)*; welcome speech 歓迎のことば **kangei no kotoba** *(kahn-gay no koe-toe-bah)*

welfare 生活保護 **seikatsuhogo** *(say-kaht-suu-hoh-go)*; 福祉 **fukushi** *(fuu-kuu-she)*

Western food 洋食 **yōshoku** *(yoe-show-kuu)*
▪ Let's eat Western food today. 今

日は洋食を食べましょう。**Kyō wa yōshoku wo tabemashō.** *(k'yoe wah yoe-show-kuu oh tah-bay-mah-show.)*

wheel (vehicle) 車輪 **sharin** *(shah-reen)*

white collar worker ホワイトカラー **howaito karā** *(hoe-why-toe kah-rah)*; 事務職 **jimushoku** *(jee-muu-show-kuu)*

White Paper (issued by the government) 白書 **Haku Sho** *(hah-kuu show)*

whole country 全国 **zenkoku** *(zen-koe-kuu)*

wholesale 卸売り **oroshi-uri** *(oh-roe-she-uu-ree)*

wholesale market 卸売市場 **oroshi-uri shijō** *(oh-roe-she-uu-ree she-joe)*

wholesale price 卸売価格 **oroshi-uri kakaku** *(oh-roe-she-uu-ree kah-kah-kuu)*

wholesaler 卸売業者 **oroshi-uri gyōsha** *(oh-roe-she-uu-ree g'yoe-sah)*; 問屋 **ton'ya** *(tone-yah)*; primary wholesaler 一次問屋 **chi-ji don'ya** *(ee-chee-jee done-yah)*

wholesale trade 卸売り業 **oroshi-uri gyō** *(oh-roe-she-uu-ree g'yoe)*

Wi-Fi ワイファイ **Wai-Fai** *(wie-fie)* ▪ Wi-Fi is the brand name of the wire-less system (LAN). Wi-Fi は、無線LANのブランド名です。**Wai-Fai wa musen LAN no betsumei désu.** *(wie-fie wah muu-sen LAN no bay-t'sue-may dess.)* ▪ Is Wi-Fi available in Tokyo? 東京ではワイファイは有効ですか? **Tokyo dewa Wai-Fai wa yukō désu ka?** *(toe-k'yoe day-wah Wie-Fie wah yuu-koh dess kah?)*

windfall profits 偶発利益 **gūhatsu rieki** *(guu-hot-sue ree-eh-kee)*

window dressing 粉飾する **funshoku suru** *(fuun-show-kuu sue-rue)*

windshield フロントガラス **furonto garasu** *(fuu-roan-toe gah-rah-sue)*

wire (metal) 針金 **harigane** *(hah-ree-gah-nay)*

wireless ワイヤレス **waiyaresu** *(wie-yah-ray-suu)*; 無線 **musen** *(muu-sen)* ▪ Are you connected to a wireless (LAN) system? インターネットを無線LANで接続していますか。**Intānetto wo musen LAN de setsuzoku shite imasu ka?** *(een-tah-net-toh oh muu-sen LAN day say-t'sue-zoo-kuu shtay-mahss kah?)* ▪ In my case, I prefer a wireless system. 私としては、ワイヤレスシステムの方がいいです。**Watakushi to shite wa, waiyaresu shisutemu no hō ga ii désu.** *(wah-tahk-she toh she-tay wah, wie-yah-ray-suu she-suu-tay-muu no hoh gah ee dess.)*

wire transfer 電信為替 **denshin kawase** *(dane-sheen kah-wah-say)*

withdraw (take out, pull out) 引き出す **hikidasu** *(hee-kee-dah-sue)*; 引き落とし **hiki otoshi** *(kee-kee oh-toe-she)*

withhold (at source) 源泉徴収 **gensen chōshū** *(gane-sen choe-shuu)*

withholding tax 源泉課税 **gensen kazei** *(gane-sen kah-zay)*

witness 証人 **shōnin** *(show-neen)*

word-processor ワープロ **wāpuro** *(wah-puu-roe)*

work (job) 仕事 **shigoto** *(she-go-toe)*; to work 働く **hataraku** *(hah-tah-rah-kuu)*

work (operation) 操業する **sogyō suru** *(so-g'yoe sue-rue)*

workaholic 商売熱心な **shōbai nesshin na** *(show-by nay-sheen nah)*; 仕事中毒の **shigoto chūdoku no** *(she-go-toe chuu-doe-kuu no)*

work conditions 労働条件 **rōdō jōken** *(roe-doe joe-ken)*

work council 労使協議会 **rōshi kyōgi kai** *(roe-she k'yoe-ghee kye)*

work cycle 作業サイクル **sagyō saikuru** *(sah-g'yoe sigh-kuu-rue)*

workday 就業日 **shūgyo-bi** *(shuu-g'yoe-bee)*

worker 労働者 **rōdōsha** *(roe-doe-shah)*; 従業員 **jūgyō-in** *(juu-g'yoe-een)*; 社員 **shain** *(shah-een)*

workers compensation insurance 労災保険 **rōsai hoken** *(roe-sigh hoe-ken)*

work force 労働力 **rodō ryoku** *(roe-doe rio-kuu)*

working capital 運転資金 **unten shikin** *(uun-ten she-keen)*

working class 労働者階級 **rōdō sha kaikyū** *(roe-doe shah kye-cue)*

working committee 運営委員会 **unei i'in-kai** *(uu-n-eh-ee ee-een-kye)*

working contract 工事契約 **kōji keiyaku** *(koe-jee kay-yah-kuu)*

working funds 運転資金 **unten shikin** *(uun-tane she-keen)*

working hours 労働時間 **rōdō jikan** *(roe-doe jee-kahn)*; 勤務時間 **kinmu jikan** *(keen-muu jee-kahn)*

working papers 監査調書 **kansa chōsho** *(kahn-sah choe-show)*

work in progress 仕掛品 **shikakari hin** *(she-kah-kah-ree heen)*

workload 仕事量 **shigoto ryō** *(she-go-toe rio)*

work on contract 契約による仕事 **keiyaku ni yoru shigoto** *(kay-yah-kuu nee yoe-rue she-go-toe)*

work order 作業命令 **sagyō meirei** *(sah-g'yoe may-ray)*

workplace 仕事場 **shigoto-ba** *(she-go-toe-bah)*; 職場 **shokuba** *(show-kuu-bah)*

workshop 作業場 **sagyō-ba** *(sah-g'yoe-bah)*

workstation ワークステーション **wāku sutēshon** *(wah-kuu stay-shone)*

World Bank 世界銀行 **Sekai Ginkō** *(say-kye gheen-koe)*

worm; virus ウイルス **uirusu** *(uu-ee-rue-suu)*
▪ Can you remove a virus from my computer? 私のコンピュータからウイルスを駆除することができますか。**Watakushi no konpyūta kara uirusu wo kujyo surukoto ga dekimasu ka?** *(wah-tahk-she no kome-p'yuu-tah kah-rah uu-ee rue-suu oh kuu-joe sue-rue koh-toe gah day-kee-mahss kah?)*

worth, net (net worth) 正味資産 **shōmi shisan** *(show-me she-sahn)*

worthless 価値のない **kachi no nai** *(kah-chee no nigh)*

writ 令状 **rei jō** *(ray joe)*

write-down 評価損 **hyōka-son** *(h'yoe-kah-soan)*

write off 帳消しにする **chōkeshi ni suru** *(choe-kay-she nee sue-rue)*

written agreement 契約書 **keiyaku sho** *(kay-yah-kuu show)*

written bid 記入入札 **kin'yū nyūsatsu** *(keen-yuu n'yuu-sah-t'sue)*

X

x-ray examination エックス線検査 **ekkusu sen kensa** *(ek-kuu-suu-sen ken-sah)*; レントゲン検査 **rentogen kensa** *(ren-toe-gen ken-sah)*
▪ I had an x-ray taken this year. 今年レントゲン検査を受けました。**Kotoshi rentogen kensa wo ukemashita.** *(koe-toe-she ren-toe-gane ken-sah wo uu-kay-mahsh-tah.)*

x-rays エックス線 **ekkusu sen** *(ek-kuu-suu-sen)*

Y

yacht ヨット **yotto** *(yote-toe)*

yard (measure) ヤード **yādo** *(yah-doe)*

yardstick (figurative usage) 判断の基準 **handan no kijun** *(hahn-dahn no kee-june)*

year 年 **toshi** *(toe-she)*; 年度 **nendo** *(nen-doe)*

year, fiscal (fiscal year) 会計年度 **kaikei nendo** *(kye-kay nen-doe)*

year-end 年末の **nenmatsu no** *(nen-mah-t'sue no)*

yen 円 **en** *(en)*

yen terms 円で **en de** *(en day)*

yield 利回り **rimawari** *(ree-mah-wah-ree)*

yield-to-maturity 満期利回り **manki rimawari** *(mahn-kee ree-mah-wah-ree)*

Z

zero ゼロ **zero** *(zay-roe)*

zero-coupon ゼロクーポン債 **zero kūpon sai** *(zay-roe kuu-poan sigh)*

zero interest rate ゼロ金利 **zero kinri** *(zay-roe keen-ree)*

ZIP Code 郵便番号 **yūbin bangō** *(yuu-bean bahn-go)*

zone (region) 地域 **chiiki** *(chee-ee-kee)*

zoom lens ズームレンズ **zūmu renzu** *(zuu-muu ren-zuu)*